DATE DUE			

The Catholic Tradition:
The Savior, Vol. 1

The Catholic Tradition

REV. CHARLES J. DOLLEN
DR. JAMES K. McGOWAN
DR. JAMES J. MEGIVERN
EDITORS

The Catholic Tradition

The Saviour

Volume 1

A Consortium Book

Library of Congress Card Catalog Number: 79-1977
ISBN: 0-8434-0732-8
ISBN: 0-8434-0725-5 series

The publisher gratefully acknowledges permission to quote from the
following copyrighted sources. In cases where those properties contain
scholarly apparatus such as footnotes, such footnotes have been omitted
in the interest of the general reader.

THE CATHOLIC UNIVERSITY OF AMERICA PRESS, INC.
  Book Seven from *The Fathers of the Church*, Volume 25, *St. Hilary of
  Poitiers: The Trinity*, translated by Stephen McKenna, C.SS.R., copy-
  right 1954; "Tome to Flavian" from *The Fathers of the Church*,
  Volume 34, *St. Leo the Great: Letters* translated by Brother Edmund
  Hunt, C.S.C., copyright © 1957; "Orthodox Faith: Book III" from
  The Fathers of the Church, Volume 37, *St. John of Damascus: Writings*,
  translated by Frederic H. Chase, Jr., copyright © 1958.

CHRISTIAN LITERATURE COMPANY
  "Theological Oration" by Gregory of Nazianzen from *A Select Library
  of Nicene and Post-Nicene Fathers*, Volume VII, 1894.

DOUBLEDAY & COMPANY, INC.
  Chapters 39–49 reprinted from *On the Truth of the Catholic Faith,
  Book IV: Salvation* by St. Thomas Aquinas, translated by Charles J.
  O'Neil. Copyright © 1957 by Doubleday & Company, Inc. Used by
  permission of Doubleday & Company, Inc.

WM. B. EERDMANS PUBLISHING CO.
  "Against Heresies" by Irenaeus from *The Ante-Nicene Fathers*, Volume I,
  edited by Rev. Alexander Roberts, D.D. and James Donaldson, LL.D.
  1969 American reprint of the Edinburgh Edition; "Treatise on Christ
  and Antichrist" by Hippolytus from *The Ante-Nicene Fathers*, Volume V,
  edited by Rev. Alexander Roberts, D.D. and James Donaldson, LL.D.
  1965 American reprint of the Edinburgh Edition.

Table of Contents

Introduction

The Catholic Tradition is a 14 volume anthology of excerpts from the great Catholic writers from antiquity to the present day. *The Catholic Tradition* is intended for the armchair reader who has not studied theology or church history and has not time to struggle unassisted through 198 books. The publisher's intention is to provide such a reader with a compact home library that will permit him to familiarize himself with the great Catholic writers and their works. The works included in *The Catholic Tradition* are all religious in subject. The publisher did not include fiction or nonfiction books on secular subjects written by Catholic authors.

The Catholic Tradition arranges the writings according to religious subjects. There are seven religious subjects, each of which is covered in two volumes: The Church; Mass and the Sacraments; Sacred Scripture; The Saviour; Personal Ethics; Social Thought; and Spirituality. Within each subject, the writings are arranged in chronological order, which permits the reader to follow the development of Catholic thought across 2000 years.

Each excerpt in *The Catholic Tradition* is preceded by a brief biographical and explanatory introduction to help the reader understand the world in which the writer lived and wrote, and the problems with which he was dealing.

The selection of the excerpts and the writing of the introductions has been a long and difficult process. The task of making the final selections was particularly arduous (as such choices always are); the most modern authors, about whose writing there is yet no final judgment provoking the most debate. The selection of authors was made originally in the publisher's offices and then submitted to the three editors of the series who refined the selection. The editors submitted their selection to an unofficial board of scholars who very kindly made constructive comments.

The process of assembling the many hundreds of books from which to make the final selection was in itself a vast task. Many of the books under consideration were very scarce and not available in bookstores or libraries. The work of collecting the books and then making selections among them stretched over a three year period, and many books were selected for inclusion and later rejected after careful scrutiny and reflection.

The editing of *The Catholic Tradition* was a long and difficult job because the literature of Roman Catholicism is a vast and complex body. Of all the Christian denominations, the Roman Catholic Church is by far the oldest and largest. Its ranks include a tremendous number of saints and scholars, writers and thinkers, mystics and preachers: many of whom felt so strongly about their faith that they were willing to die for it. They have left an incomparably rich legacy of art and writing. Selecting from it is not simple.

The selections that we made are representative of the best of mainstream Catholic writing. Generally, they should be intelligible to a thoughtful layman. Some however, may prove more technical than others, and some of the very recent writers may seem controversial. The reader should bear in mind that some theological questions simply do not admit of facile answers, and that some of the earlier writers were considered controversial in their own days. It is also well to remember that the writings gathered here, brilliant and revered as their authors may be, are not necessarily official statements of Church policy. But they are, all of them, solidly part of the Catholic tradition.

The writers are all Catholics, many of them clergymen, some of them converts to Catholicism. They all wrote as loyal servants of the Church and from a Catholic point of view. When they wrote on personal ethics they proceeded from the assumption that man's goal was to imitate Christ, not simply to follow a secular set of ethical rules. When they wrote on social problems they expressed the need to solve social problems because they loved their neighbors, not for the material enrichment of society. Their writings on Christ reflect an intense struggle to bend human language to divine definition. Taken together, their writings form a literary tradition that is Roman Catholic at heart. That tradition has certain ingredients that are not present in the literary traditions of the other Christian denominations. Particularly, the heritage of liturgical ceremony and mystical contemplation have left an incomparable treasure of literature that is here presented in the volumes entitled *Mass and the Sacraments,* and *Spirituality.*

The whole corpus of Catholic thinking and writing, distilled here in *The Catholic Tradition,* is generally considered by scholars to have three important periods: the ancient, or patristic, period; the high middle-ages, which is the era of St. Thomas Aquinas and sometimes called the scholastic period; finally the time in which we live today, the last 100 years. These three epochs are golden ages of Catholic writing. They are separated from each other by the generally unproductive eras of the dark ages and the Reformation.

Through all these epochs the great Catholic writers have preserved and developed the Christian message: love God; love your fellow man. Each writer wrote conscious of the tradition behind him, conscious that he was building on the work of men before him, adapting their work to changed conditions or continuing their work on the outer edges of human speculation.

The present day writers, those of the third great era of Catholic writing, are the most important part of *The Catholic Tradition.* Here for the first time their thinking is presented along with the work of their predecessors; here can be seen the stunning achievement of today's Catholic writing, and how it follows logically from the writing of the patristic and scholastic thinkers.

The present day writers presented in *The Catholic Tradition* number 114, over half of the total number of writers chosen.

Their writing will probably prove more intelligible to the average reader because they write in today's idiom and they address contemporary problems.

Oddly enough, many if not most of the modern writers are not familiar to the average Catholic. St. Augustine, and St. Thomas Aquinas are household names, but only serious Catholic readers today are familiar with the masterful writings of Karl Rahner, Edward Schillebeeckx, Raymond Brown, and Gustavo Gutiérrez. None the less, these men are representative of a great historical flowering of Catholic writing today and their names may well echo down the ages.

THE PUBLISHER

St. Irenaeus
140-202

The first historical mention of Irenaeus occurs when in the year 177 a.d., during the persecution of Marcus Aurelius, the clergy of Lyon and Vienne sent him to the pope with a letter about the Montanist troubles. He was probably a native of Smyrna in Asia Minor, for he says himself that as a child he listened to Polycarp. When he returned from his mission to Rome, he was chosen bishop of Lyon, and he worked strenuously to oppose Gnosticism and to carry the Gospel to many parts of eastern Gaul.

During the century that separates Irenaeus from the New Testament writings, Christian leaders had to deal with a number of developments that challenged the Church's understanding of Jesus and His significance. Gnosticism was the chief challenge, and all the early writers had to confront it, but it is generally acknowledged that Irenaeus was the most effective anti-Gnostic apologist of the second century. It is true that he used material from Justin Martyr, Hegesippus, and others, but he did so in such a way that he has been called the "founder of Christian theology . . . the first to formulate in dogmatic terms the entire Christian doctrine" (Quasten).

Irenaeus was the first to try to express in speculative terms the relationship between the Father and the Son: the Son "is in the Father and has the Father in himself." But the most mem-

orable and characteristic feature of his theology is his theory of recapitulation (anakephalaiosis): Jesus is the second Adam, the new Head by whom the whole human race is renovated and restored. The Son of God became what we are in order to make us what He is. In the face of Gnostic dualism his great emphasis was on the unity of Christ, so that some of his expressions became classical for the later tradition, including "one and the same" and "true man and true God."

Irenaeus' main work, Against Heresies, *strangely enough, has not survived in the original Greek, except for a few quotations by later authors. A very literal Latin translation, which some think was made during his lifetime (c. 200) is all that has come down to us. It is composed of five books. Book I is an extremely interesting sketch of the bewildering variety of types of Gnosticism. The next three books contain his refutation of these teachings: book II with arguments from reason, book III from the traditions of the Church, and book IV from the sayings of the Lord. Book V deals almost exclusively with the resurrection of the flesh, which all the Gnostics denied.*

The following selection consists of the final ten chapters (16-25) of Book III. It is not easy reading, for it comes from a world that is strikingly different both from that of the New Testament and that of later Christendom. Irenaeus is the first Christian writer to have something like our New Testament (at least 22 of its 27 books), and to begin to call these "Scriptures" the way that the Old Testament books had been from the start. And the way that he appeals to these writings and interprets them is not always fully persuasive, but he sets the tone for much of what will follow.

AGAINST HERESIES

BOOK III

CHAPTER XVI

PROOFS FROM THE APOSTOLIC WRITINGS, THAT JESUS CHRIST
WAS ONE AND THE SAME, THE ONLY BEGOTTEN SON OF GOD,
PERFECT GOD AND PERFECT MAN.

But there are some who say that Jesus was merely a receptacle of Christ, upon whom the Christ, as a dove, descended from above, and that when He had declared the unnameable Father He entered into the Pleroma in an incomprehensible and invisible manner: for that He was not comprehended, not only by men, but not even by those powers and virtues which are in heaven, and that Jesus was the Son, but that Christ was the Father, and the Father of Christ, God; while others say that He merely suffered in outward appearance, being naturally impassible. The Valentinians, again, maintain that the dispensational Jesus was the same who passed through Mary, upon whom that Saviour from the more exalted [region] descended, who was also termed *Pan*, because He possessed the names (*vocabula*) of all those who had produced Him; but that [this latter] shared with Him, the dispensational one, His power and His name; so that by His means death was abolished, but the Father was made known by that Saviour who had descended from above, whom they do also allege to be Himself the receptacle of Christ and of the entire Pleroma; confessing, indeed, in tongue one Christ Jesus, but being divided in [actual] opinion: for, as I have already observed, it is the practice of these men to say that there was one Christ, who was produced by Monogenes, for the confirmation of the Pleroma; but that another, the Saviour, was sent [forth] for the glorification of the Father; and yet another, the dispensational one, and whom they represent as having suffered, who also bore [in himself] Christ, that Saviour who returned into the Pleroma. I judge it necessary therefore to take into account the entire mind of the apostles regarding our Lord Jesus Christ, and to show that not only did they never hold any such opinions regarding Him; but, still further, that they announced through the Holy Spirit, that those who should teach such doctrines were agents of Satan, sent forth for the purpose of overturning the faith of some, and drawing them away from life.

That John knew the one and the same Word of God, and that He was the only begotten, and that He became incarnate for our salvation, Jesus Christ our Lord, I have sufficiently proved from the word of John himself. And Matthew, too, recognising one and the same Jesus Christ, exhibiting his generation as a man from the Virgin, even as God did promise David that He would raise up from the fruit of his body an eternal King, having made the same promise to Abraham a long time previously, says: "The book of the generation of Jesus Christ, the son of David, the son of Abraham." Then, that he might free our mind from suspicion regarding Joseph, he says: "But the birth of Christ was on this wise. When His mother was espoused to Joseph, before they came together, she was found with child of the Holy Ghost." Then, when Joseph had it in contemplation to put Mary away, since she proved with child, [Matthew tells us of] the angel of God standing by him, and saying: "Fear not to take unto thee Mary thy wife: for that which is conceived in her is of the Holy Ghost. And she shall bring forth a son, and thou shalt call His name Jesus; for He shall save His people from their sins. Now this was done, that it might be fulfilled which was spoken of the Lord by the prophet: Behold, a virgin shall conceive, and bring forth a son, and they shall call His name Emmanuel, which is, God with us;" clearly signifying that both the promise made to the fathers had been accomplished, that the Son of God was born of a virgin, and that He Himself was Christ the Saviour whom the prophets had foretold; not, as these men assert, that Jesus was He who was born of Mary, but that Christ was He who descended from above. Matthew might certainly have said, "Now the birth of *Jesus* was on this wise;" but the Holy Ghost, foreseeing the corrupters [of the truth], and guarding by anticipation against their deceit, says by Matthew, "But the birth of *Christ* was on this wise;" and that He is Emmanuel, lest perchance we might consider Him as a mere man: for "not by the will of the flesh, nor by the will of man, but by the will of God, was the Word made flesh;" and that we should not imagine that Jesus was one, and Christ another, but should know them to be one and the same.

Paul, when writing to the Romans, has explained this very point: "Paul, an apostle of Jesus Christ, predestinated unto the Gospel of God, which He had promised by His prophets in the holy Scriptures, concerning His Son, who was made to Him of the seed of David according to the flesh, who was predestinated the Son of God with power through the Spirit of holiness, by the resurrection from the dead of our Lord Jesus Christ." And again, writing to the Romans about Israel, he says: "Whose are the fathers, and from whom is Christ according to the flesh, who is God over all, blessed for ever." And again, in his Epistle to the Galatians, he says: "But when the fulness of time had come, God sent forth His Son, made of a woman, made under the law, to redeem them that were under the law, that we might receive the adoption;" plainly indicating one God, who did by the prophets make promise of the Son, and one Jesus Christ our Lord, who was of the seed of David according to His birth from Mary; and that Jesus Christ was appointed the Son of God with power, according to the Spirit of holiness, by the resurrection from the dead, as being the first begotten in all the creation; the Son of God being made the Son of man, that through Him we may receive the adoption,—humanity sustaining, and receiving, and embracing the Son of God. Wherefore Mark also says: "The beginning of the Gospel of Jesus Christ, the Son of God; as it is written in the prophets." Knowing one and the same Son of God, Jesus Christ, who was announced by the prophets, who from the fruit of David's body was Emmanuel, "the messenger of great counsel of the Father;" through whom God caused the day-spring and the Just One to arise to the house of David, and raised up for him an horn of salvation, "and established a testimony in Jacob;" as David says when discoursing on the causes of His birth: "And He appointed a law in Israel, that another generation might know [Him,] the children which should be born from these, and they arising shall themselves declare to their children, so that they might set their hope in God, and seek after His commandments." And again, the angel said, when bringing good tidings to Mary: "He shall be great, and shall be called the Son of the Highest; and the Lord shall give unto Him the throne of His father David;" acknowledging that He who is the Son of the Highest, the same is Himself also the Son of David. And David, knowing by the Spirit the dispensation of the advent of this Person, by which He is supreme over all the living and dead, confessed Him as Lord, sitting on the right hand of the Most High Father.

But Simeon also—he who had received an intimation from the Holy Ghost that he should not see death, until first he had beheld Christ Jesus—taking Him, the first-begotten of the Virgin, into his hands, blessed God, and said, "Lord, now lettest Thou Thy servant depart in peace, according to Thy word: because mine eyes have seen Thy salvation, which Thou hast prepared before the face of all people; a light to lighten the Gentiles, and the glory of Thy people Israel;" confessing thus, that the infant whom he was holding in his hands, Jesus, born of Mary, was Christ Himself, the Son of God, the light of all, the glory of Israel itself, and the peace and refreshing of those who had fallen asleep. For He was already despoiling men, by removing their ignorance, conferring upon them His own knowledge, and scattering abroad those who recognised Him, as Esaias says: "Call His name, Quickly spoil, Rapidly divide." Now these are the works of Christ. He therefore was Himself Christ, whom Simeon carrying [in his arms] blessed the Most High; on beholding whom the shepherds glorified God; whom John, while yet in his mother's womb, and He (Christ) in that of Mary, recognising as the Lord, saluted with leaping; whom the Magi, when they had seen, adored, and offered their gifts [to Him], as I have already stated, and prostrated themselves to the eternal King, departed by another way, not now returning by the way of the Assyrians. "For before the child shall have knowledge to cry, Father or mother, He shall receive the power of Damascus, and the spoils of Samaria, against the king of the Assyrians;" declaring, in a mysterious manner indeed, but emphatically, that the Lord did fight with a hidden hand against Amalek. For this cause, too, He suddenly removed those

6

children belonging to the house of David, whose happy lot it was to have been born at that time, that He might send them on before into His kingdom; He, since He was Himself an infant, so arranging it that human infants should be martyrs, slain, according to the Scriptures, for the sake of Christ, who was born in Bethlehem of Judah, in the city of David.

Therefore did the Lord also say to His disciples after the resurrection, "O thoughtless ones, and slow of heart to believe all that the prophets have spoken! Ought not Christ to have suffered these things, and to enter into His glory?" And again does He say to them: "These are the words which I spake unto you while I was yet with you, that all things must be fulfilled which were written in the law of Moses, and in the prophets, and in the Psalms, concerning Me. Then opened He their understanding, that they should understand the Scriptures, and said unto them, Thus it is written, and thus it behoved Christ to suffer, and to rise again from the dead, and that repentance for the remission of sins be preached in His name among all nations." Now this is He who was born of Mary; for He says: "The Son of man must suffer many things, and be rejected, and crucified, and on the third day rise again." The Gospel, therefore, knew no other son of man but Him who was of Mary, who also suffered; and no Christ who flew away from Jesus before the passion; but Him who was born it knew as Jesus Christ the Son of God, and that this same suffered and rose again, as John, the disciple of the Lord, verifies, saying: "But these are written, that ye might believe that Jesus is the Christ, the Son of God, and that believing ye might have eternal life in His name,"— foreseeing these blasphemous systems which divide the Lord, as far as lies in their power, saying that He was formed of two different substances. For this reason also he has thus testified to us in his Epistle: "Little children, it is the last time; and as ye have heard that Antichrist doth come, now have many antichrists appeared; whereby we know that it is the last time. They went out from us, but they were not of us; for if they had been of us, they would have continued with us: but [they departed], that they might be made manifest that they are not of us. Know ye therefore, that every lie is from without, and is

7

not of the truth. Who is a liar, but he that denieth that Jesus is the Christ? This is Antichrist."

But inasmuch as all those before mentioned, although they certainly do with their tongue confess one Jesus Christ, make fools of themselves, thinking one thing and saying another; for their hypotheses vary, as I have already shown, alleging, [as they do,] that one Being suffered and was born, and that this was Jesus; but that there was another who descended upon Him, and that this was Christ, who also ascended again; and they argue, that he who proceeded from the Demiurge, or he who was dispensational, or he who sprang from Joseph, was the Being subject to suffering; but upon the latter there descended from the invisible and ineffable [places] the former, whom they assert to be incomprehensible, invisible, and impassible: they thus wander from the truth, because their doctrine departs from Him who is truly God, being ignorant that His only-begotten Word, who is always present with the human race, united to and mingled with His own creation, according to the Father's pleasure, and who became flesh, is Himself Jesus Christ our Lord, who did also suffer for us, and rose again on our behalf, and who will come again in the glory of His Father, to raise up all flesh, and for the manifestation of salvation, and to apply the rule of just judgment to all who were made by Him. There is therefore, as I have pointed out, one God the Father, and one Christ Jesus, who came by means of the whole dispensational arrangements [connected with Him], and gathered together all things in Himself. But in every respect, too, He is man, the formation of God; and thus He took up man into Himself, the invisible becoming visible, the incomprehensible being made comprehensible, the impassible becoming capable of suffering, and the Word being made man, thus summing up all things in Himself: so that as in super-celestial, spiritual, and invisible things, the Word of God is supreme, so also in things visible and corporeal He might possess the supremacy, and, taking to Himself the pre-eminence, as well as constituting Himself Head of the Church, He might draw all things to Himself at the proper time.

With Him is nothing incomplete or out of due season, just as with the Father there is nothing incongruous. For all

8

these things were foreknown by the Father; but the Son works them out at the proper time in perfect order and sequence. This was the reason why, when Mary was urging [Him] on to [perform] the wonderful miracle of the wine, and was desirious before the time to partake of the cup of emblematic significance, the Lord, checking her untimely haste, said, "Woman, what have I to do with thee? mine hour is not yet come"— waiting for that hour which was foreknown by the Father. This is also the reason why, when men were often desirous to take Him, it is said, "No man laid hands upon Him, for the hour of His being taken was not yet come;" nor the time of His passion, which had been foreknown by the Father; as also says the prophet Habakkuk, "By this Thou shalt be known when the years have drawn nigh; Thou shalt be set forth when the time comes; because my soul is disturbed by anger, Thou shalt remember Thy mercy." Paul also says: "But when the fulness of time came, God sent forth His Son." By which is made manifest, that all things which had been foreknown of the Father, our Lord did accomplish in their order, season, and hour, foreknown and fitting, being indeed one and the same, but rich and great. For He fulfils the bountiful and comprehensive will of His Father, inasmuch as He is Himself the Saviour of those who are saved, and the Lord of those who are under authority, and the God of all those things which have been formed, the only-begotten of the Father, Christ who was announced, and the Word of God, who became incarnate when the fulness of time had come, at which the Son of God had to become the Son of man.

All, therefore, are outside of the [Christian] dispensation, who, under pretext of knowledge, understand that Jesus was one, and Christ another, and the Only-begotten another, from whom again is the Word, and that the Saviour is another, whom these disciples of error allege to be a production of those who were made Æons in a state of degeneracy. Such men are to outward appearance sheep; for they appear to be like us, by what they say in public, repeating the same words as we do; but inwardly they are wolves. Their doctrine is homicidal, conjuring up, as it does, a number of gods, and simulating many Fathers, but lowering and dividing the Son of God in

9

many ways. These are they against whom the Lord has cautioned us beforehand; and His disciple, in his Epistle already mentioned, commands us to avoid them, when he says: "For many deceivers are entered into the world, who confess not that Jesus Christ is come in the flesh. This is a deceiver and an antichrist. Take heed to them, that ye lose not what ye have wrought." And again does he say in the Epistle: "Many false prophets are gone out into the world. Hereby know ye the Spirit of God: Every spirit that confesseth that Jesus Christ is come in the flesh is of God; and every spirit which separates Jesus Christ is not of God, but is of antichrist." These words agree with what was said in the Gospel, that "the Word was made flesh, and dwelt among us." Wherefore he again exclaims in his Epistle, "Every one that believeth that Jesus is the Christ, has been born of God;" knowing Jesus Christ to be one and the same, to whom the gates of heaven were opened, because of His taking upon Him flesh: who shall also come in the same flesh in which He suffered, revealing the glory of the Father.

Concurring with these statements, Paul, speaking to the Romans, declares: "Much more they who receive abundance of grace and righteousness for [eternal] life, shall reign by one, Christ Jesus." It follows from this, that he knew nothing of that Christ who flew away from Jesus; nor did he of the Saviour above, whom they hold to be impassible. For if, in truth, the one suffered, and the other remained incapable of suffering, and the one was born, but the other descended upon him who was born, and left him again, it is not one, but two, that are shown forth. But that the apostle did know Him as one, both who was born and who suffered, namely Christ Jesus, he again says in the same Epistle: "Know ye not, that so many of us as were baptized in Christ Jesus were baptized in His death? that like as Christ rose from the dead, so should we also walk in newness of life." But again, showing that Christ did suffer, and was Himself the Son of God, who died for us, and redeemed us with His blood at the time appointed beforehand, he says: "For how is it, that Christ, when we were yet without strength, in due time died for the ungodly? But God commendeth His love towards us, in that, while we were yet sinners, Christ died for us. Much more, then, being now justified by His blood, we shall be saved from wrath through Him. For if, when we were enemies, we were reconciled to God by the death of His Son; much more, being reconciled, we shall be saved by His life." He declares in the plainest manner, that the same Being who was laid hold of, and underwent suffering, and shed His blood for us, was both Christ and the Son of God, who did also rise again, and was taken up into heaven, as he himself [Paul] says: "But at the same time, [it is] Christ [that] died, yea rather, that is risen again, who is even at the right hand of God." And again, "Knowing that Christ, rising from the dead, dieth no more:" for, as himself foreseeing, through the Spirit, the subdivisions of evil teachers [with regard to the Lord's person], and being desirous of cutting away from them all occasion of cavil, he says what has been already stated, [and also declares:] "But if the Spirit of Him that raised up Jesus from the dead dwell in you, He that raised up Christ from the dead shall also quicken your mortal bodies." This he does not utter to those alone who wish to hear: Do not err, [he says to all:] Jesus Christ, the Son of God, is one and the same, who did by suffering reconcile us to God, and rose from the dead; who is at the right hand of the Father, and perfect in all things; "who, when He was buffeted, struck not in return; who, when He suffered, threatened not;" and when He underwent tyranny, He prayed His Father that He would forgive those who had crucified Him. For He did Himself truly bring in salvation: since He is Himself the Word of God, Himself the Only-begotten of the Father, Christ Jesus our Lord.

CHAPTER XVII

THE APOSTLES TEACH THAT IT WAS NEITHER CHRIST NOR THE SAVIOUR, BUT THE HOLY SPIRIT, WHO DID DESCEND UPON JESUS. THE REASON FOR THIS DESCENT.

It certainly was in the power of the apostles to declare that Christ descended upon Jesus, or that the so-called superior Saviour [came down] upon the dispensational one, or he who is from the invisible places upon him from the Demiurge; but they neither knew nor said anything of the kind: for, had they known it, they would have also certainly stated it. But what really was the case, that did they record, [namely,] that the Spirit of God as a dove descended upon Him; this Spirit, of whom it was declared by Isaiah, "And the Spirit of God shall rest upon Him," as I have already said. And again: "The Spirit of the Lord is upon Me, because He hath anointed Me." That is the Spirit of whom the Lord declares, "For it is not ye that speak, but the Spirit of your Father which speaketh in you." And again, giving to the disciples the power of regeneration into God, He said to them, "Go and teach all nations, baptizing them in the name of the Father, and of the Son, and of the Holy Ghost." For [God] promised, that in the last times He would pour Him [the Spirit] upon [His] servants and handmaids, that they might prophesy; wherefore He did also descend upon the Son of God, made the Son of man, becoming accustomed in fellowship with Him to dwell in the human race, to rest with human beings, and to dwell in the workmanship of God, working the will of the Father in them, and renewing them from their old habits into the newness of Christ.

This Spirit did David ask for the human race, saying, "And stablish me with Thine all-governing Spirit;" who also, as Luke says, descended at the day of Pentecost upon the disciples after the Lord's ascension, having power to admit all nations to the entrance of life, and to the opening of the new covenant; from whence also, with one accord in all languages, they uttered praise to God, the Spirit bringing distant tribes to unity, and offering to the Father the first-fruits of all nations. Wherefore also the Lord promised to send the Comforter, who should join us to God. For as a compacted lump of dough cannot be formed of dry wheat without fluid matter, nor can a loaf possess unity, so, in like manner, neither could we, being many, be made one in Christ Jesus without the water from heaven. And as dry earth does not bring forth unless it receive moisture, in like manner we also, being originally a dry tree, could never have brought forth fruit unto life without the voluntary rain from above. For our bodies have received unity among themselves by means of that layer which leads to incorruption; but our souls, by means of the Spirit. Wherefore both are necessary, since both contribute towards the life of God, our Lord compassionating that erring Samaritan woman—

who did not remain with one husband, but committed fornication by [contracting] many marriages—by pointing out, and
promising to her living water, so that she should thirst no more,
nor occupy herself in acquiring the refreshing water obtained by
labour, having in herself water springing up to eternal life. The
Lord, receiving this as a gift from His Father, does Himself also
confer it upon those who are partakers of Himself, sending the
Holy Spirit upon all the earth.

Gideon, that Israelite whom God chose, that he might
save the people of Israel from the power of foreigners, foreseeing this gracious gift, changed his request, and prophesied
that there would be dryness upon the fleece of wool (a type of
the people), on which alone at first there had been dew; thus
indicating that they should no longer have the Holy Spirit from
God, as saith Esaias, "I will also command the clouds, that they
rain no rain upon it," but that the dew, which is the Spirit of
God, who descended upon the Lord, should be diffused throughout all the earth, "the spirit of wisdom and understanding, the
spirit of counsel and might, the spirit of knowledge and piety,
the spirit of the fear of God." This Spirit, again, He did confer
upon the Church, sending throughout all the world the Comforter from heaven, from whence also the Lord tells us that the
devil, like lightning, was cast down. Wherefore we have need of
the dew of God, that we be not consumed by fire, nor be
rendered unfruitful, and that where we have an accuser there
we may have also an Advocate, the Lord commending to the
Holy Spirit His own man, who had fallen among thieves, whom
He Himself compassionated, and bound up his wounds, giving
two royal *denaria;* so that we, receiving by the Spirit the image
and superscription of the Father and the Son, might cause the
denarium entrusted to us to be fruitful, counting out the
increase [thereof] to the Lord.

The Spirit, therefore, descending under the predestined
dispensation, and the Son of God, the Only-begotten, who is
also the Word of the Father, coming in the fulness of time,
having become incarnate in man for the sake of man, and fulfilling all the conditions of human nature, our Lord Jesus Christ
being one and the same, as He Himself the Lord doth testify,
as the apostles confess, and as the prophets announce,—all the

doctrines of these men who have invented putative Ogdoads and Tetrads, and imagined subdivisions [of the Lord's person], have been proved falsehoods. These men do, in fact, set the Spirit aside altogether; they understand that Christ was one and Jesus another; and they teach that there was not one Christ, but many. And if they speak of them as united, they do again separate them: for they show that one did indeed undergo sufferings, but that the other remained impassible; that the one truly did ascend to the Pleroma, but the other remained in the intermediate place; that the one does truly feast and revel in places invisible and above all name, but that the other is seated with the Demiurge, emptying him of power. It will therefore be incumbent upon thee, and all others who give their attention to this writing, and are anxious about their own salvation, not readily to express acquiescence when they hear abroad the speeches of these men: for, speaking things resembling the [doctrine of the] faithful, as I have already observed, not only do they hold opinions which are different, but absolutely contrary, and in all points full of blasphemies, by which they destroy those persons who, by reason of the resemblance of the words, imbibe a poison which disagrees with their constitution, just as if one, giving lime mixed with water for milk, should mislead by the similitude of the colour; as a man superior to me has said, concerning all that in any way corrupt the things of God and adulterate the truth, "Lime is wickedly mixed with the milk of God."

CHAPTER XVIII

CONTINUATION OF THE FOREGOING ARGUMENT. PROOFS FROM THE WRITINGS OF ST. PAUL, AND FROM THE WORDS OF OUR LORD, THAT CHRIST AND JESUS CANNOT BE CONSIDERED AS DISTINCT BEINGS; NEITHER CAN IT BE ALLEGED THAT THE SON OF GOD BECAME MAN MERELY IN APPEARANCE, BUT THAT HE DID SO TRULY AND ACTUALLY.

As it has been clearly demonstrated that the Word, who existed in the beginning with God, by whom all things were made, who was also always present with mankind, was in these last days, according to the time appointed by the Father, united to His own workmanship, inasmuch as He became a man liable to suffering, [it follows] that every objection is set aside of those who say, "If our Lord was born at that time, Christ had therefore no previous existence." For I have shown that the Son of God did not then begin to exist, being with the Father from the beginning; but when He became incarnate, and was made man, He commenced afresh the long line of human beings, and furnished us, in a brief, comprehensive manner, with salvation; so that what we had lost in Adam—namely, to be according to the image and likeness of God—that we might recover in Christ Jesus.

For as it was not possible that the man who had once for all been conquered, and who had been destroyed through disobedience, could reform himself, and obtain the prize of victory; and as it was also impossible that he could attain to salvation who had fallen under the power of sin,—the Son effected both these things, being the Word of God, descending from the Father, becoming incarnate, stooping low, even to death, and consummating the arranged plan of our salvation, upon whom [Paul], exhorting us unhesitatingly to believe, again says, "Who shall ascend into heaven? that is, to bring down Christ; or who shall descend into the deep? that is, to liberate Christ again from the dead." Then he continues, "If thou shalt confess with thy mouth the Lord Jesus, and shalt believe in thine heart that God hath raised Him from the dead, thou shalt be saved." And he renders the reason why the Son of God did these things, saying, "For to this end Christ both lived, and died, and revived, that He might rule over the living and the dead." And again, writing to the Corinthians, he declares, "But we preach Christ Jesus crucified;" and adds, "The cup of blessing which we bless, is it not the communion of the blood of Christ?"

But who is it that has had fellowship with us in the matter of food? Whether is it he who is conceived of by them as the Christ above, who extended himself through Horos, and imparted a form to their mother; or is it He who is from the Virgin, Emmanuel, who did eat butter and honey, of whom the prophet declared, "He is also a man, and who shall know him?" He was likewise preached by Paul: "For I delivered," he says, "unto you first of all, that Christ died for our sins, according to the Scriptures; and that He was buried, and rose again the third day, according to the Scriptures." It is plain, then, that Paul knew no other Christ besides Him alone, who both suffered, and was buried, and rose again, who was also born, and whom he speaks of as man. For after remarking, "But if Christ be preached, that He rose from the dead," he continues, rendering the reason of His incarnation, "For since by man came death, by man [came] also the resurrection of the dead." And everywhere, when [referring to] the passion of our Lord, and to His human nature, and His subjection to death, he employs the name of Christ, as in that passage: "Destroy not him with thy meat for whom Christ died." And again: "But now, in Christ, ye who sometimes were far off are made nigh by the blood of Christ." And again: "Christ has redeemed us from the curse of the law, being made a curse for us: for it is written, Cursed is every one that hangeth upon a tree." And again: "And through thy knowledge shall the weak brother perish, for whom Christ died;" indicating that the impassible Christ did not descend upon Jesus, but that He Himself, because He was Jesus Christ, suffered for us; He, who lay in the tomb, and rose again, who descended and ascended,—the Son of God having been made the Son of man, as the very name itself doth declare. For in the name of Christ is implied, He that anoints, He that is anointed, and the unction itself with which He is anointed. And it is the Father who anoints, but the Son who is anointed by the Spirit, who is the unction, as the Word declares by Isaiah, "The Spirit of the Lord is upon me, because He hath anointed me,"— pointing out both the anointing Father, the anointed Son, and the unction, which is the Spirit.

The Lord Himself, too, makes it evident who it was that suffered; for when He asked the disciples, "Who do men say that I, the Son of man, am?" and when Peter had replied, "Thou art the Christ, the Son of the living God;" and when he had been commended by Him [in these words], "That flesh and blood had not revealed it to him, but the Father who is in heaven," He made it clear that He, the Son of man, is Christ the Son of the living God. "For from that time forth," it is said, "He began to show to His disciples, how that He must go unto Jerusalem, and suffer many things of the priests, and be rejected, and crucified, and rise again the third day." He who was acknowledged by Peter as Christ, who pronounced him blessed

16

because the Father had revealed the Son of the living God to him, said that He must Himself suffer many things, and be crucified; and then He rebuked Peter, who imagined that He was the Christ as the generality of men supposed [that the Christ should be], and was averse to the idea of His suffering, [and] said to the disciples, "If any man will come after Me, let him deny himself, and take up his cross, and follow Me. For whosoever will save his life, shall lose it; and whosoever will lose it for My sake shall save it." For these things Christ spoke openly, He being Himself the Saviour of those who should be delivered over to death for their confession of Him, and lose their lives.

If, however, He was Himself not to suffer, but should fly away from Jesus, why did He exhort His disciples to take up the cross and follow Him,—that cross which these men represent Him as not having taken up, but [speak of Him] as having relinquished the dispensation of suffering? For that He did not say this with reference to the acknowledging of the *Stauros* (cross) above, as some among them venture to expound, but with respect to the suffering which He should Himself undergo, and that His disciples should endure, He implies when He says, "For whosoever will save his life, shall lose it; and whosoever will lose, shall find it. And that His disciples must suffer for His sake, He [implied when He] said to the Jews, "Behold, I send you prophets, and wise men, and scribes: and some of them ye shall kill and crucify." And to the disciples He was wont to say, "And ye shall stand before governors and kings for My sake; and they shall scourge some of you, and slay you, and persecute you from city to city." He knew, therefore, both those who should suffer persecution, and He knew those who should have to be scourged and slain because of Him; and He did not speak of any other cross, but of the suffering which He should Himself undergo first, and His disciples afterwards. For this purpose did He give them this exhortation: "Fear not them which kill the body, but are not able to kill the soul; but rather fear Him who is able to send both soul and body into hell;" [thus exhorting them] to hold fast those professions of faith which they had made in reference to Him. For He promised to confess before His Father those who should

17

confess His name before men; but declared that He would deny those who should deny Him, and would be ashamed of those who should be ashamed to confess Him. And although these things are so, some of these men have proceeded to such a degree of temerity, that they even pour contempt upon the martyrs, and vituperate those who are slain on account of the confession of the Lord, and who suffer all things predicted by the Lord, and who in this respect strive to follow the footprints of the Lord's passion, having become martyrs of the suffering One; these we do also enrol with the martyrs themselves. For, when inquisition shall be made for their blood, and they shall attain to glory, then all shall be confounded by Christ, who have cast a slur upon their martyrdom. And from this fact, that He exclaimed upon the cross, "Father, forgive them, for they know not what they do," the long-suffering, patience, compassion, and goodness of Christ are exhibited, since He both suffered, and did Himself exculpate those who had maltreated Him. For the Word of God, who said to us, "Love your enemies, and pray for those that hate you," Himself did this very thing upon the cross; loving the human race to such a degree, that He even prayed for those putting Him to death. If, however, any one, going upon the supposition that there are two [Christs], forms a judgment in regard to them, that [Christ] shall be found much the better one, and more patient, and the truly good one, who, in the midst of His own wounds and stripes, and the other [cruelties] inflicted upon Him, was beneficent, and unmindful of the wrongs perpetrated upon Him, than he who flew away, and sustained neither injury nor insult.

This also does likewise meet [the case] of those who maintain that He suffered only in appearance. For if He did not truly suffer, no thanks to Him, since there was no suffering at all; and when we shall actually begin to suffer, He will seem as leading us astray, exhorting us to endure buffeting, and to turn the other cheek, if He did not Himself before us in reality suffer the same; and as He misled them by seeming to them what He was not, so does He also mislead us, by exhorting us to endure what He did not endure Himself. [In that case] we shall be even above the Master, because we suffer and sustain what our Master never bore or endured. But as our Lord is alone truly Master, so the Son of God is truly good and patient, the Word of God the Father having been made the Son of man. For He fought and conquered; for He was man contending for the fathers, and through obedience doing away with disobedience completely: for He bound the strong man, and set free the weak, and endowed His own handiwork with salvation, by destroying sin. For He is a most holy and merciful Lord, and loves the human race.

Therefore, as I have already said, He caused man (human nature) to cleave to and to become one with God. For unless man had overcome the enemy of man, the enemy would not have been legitimately vanquished. And again: unless it had been God who had freely given salvation, we could never have possessed it securely. And unless man had been joined to God, he could never have become a partaker of incorruptibility. For it was incumbent upon the Mediator between God and men, by His relationship to both, to bring both to friendship and concord, and present man to God, while He revealed God to man. For, in what way could we be partakers of the adoption of sons, unless we had received from Him through the Son that fellowship which refers to Himself, unless His Word, having been made flesh, had entered into communion with us? Wherefore also He passed through every stage of life, restoring to all communion with God. Those, therefore, who assert that He appeared putatively, and was neither born in the flesh nor truly made man, are as yet under the old condemnation, holding out patronage to sin; for, by their showing, death has not been vanquished, which "reigned from Adam to Moses, even over them that had not sinned after the similitude of Adam's transgression." But the law coming, which was given by Moses, and testifying of sin that it is a sinner, did truly take away his (death's) kingdom, showing that he was no king, but a robber; and it revealed him as a murderer. It laid, however, a weighty burden upon man, who had sin in himself, showing that he was liable to death. For as the law was spiritual, it merely made sin to stand out in relief, but did not destroy it. For sin had no dominion over the spirit, but over man. For it behoved Him who was to destroy sin, and redeem man under the power of death, that He should Himself be made that very same thing which he was, that is, man; who had been drawn by sin into bondage, but was held by death, so that sin should be destroyed by man, and man should go forth from death. For as by the disobedience of the one man who was originally moulded from virgin soil, the many were made sinners, and forfeited life; so was it necessary that, by the obedience of one man, who was originally born from a virgin, many should be justified and receive salvation. Thus, then, was the Word of God made man, as also Moses says: "God, true are His works." But if, not having been made flesh, He did appear as if flesh, His work was not a true one. But what He did appear, that He also was: God recapitulated in Himself the ancient formation of man, that He might kill sin, deprive death of its power, and vivify man; and therefore His works are true.

CHAPTER XIX

JESUS CHRIST WAS NOT A MERE MAN, BEGOTTEN FROM JOSEPH IN THE ORDINARY COURSE OF NATURE, BUT WAS VERY GOD, BEGOTTEN OF THE FATHER MOST HIGH, AND VERY MAN, BORN OF THE VIRGIN.

But again, those who assert that He was simply a mere man, begotten by Joseph, remaining in the bondage of the old disobedience, are in a state of death; having been not as yet joined to the Word of God the Father, nor receiving liberty through the Son, as He does Himself declare: "If the Son shall make you free, ye shall be free indeed." But, being ignorant of Him who from the Virgin is Emmanuel, they are deprived of His gift, which is eternal life; and not receiving the incorruptible Word, they remain in mortal flesh, and are debtors to death, not obtaining the antidote of life. To whom the Word says, mentioning His own gift of grace: "I said, Ye are all the sons of the Highest, and gods; but ye shall die like men." He speaks undoubtedly these words to those who have not received the gift of adoption, but who despise the incarnation of the pure generation of the Word of God, defraud human nature of promotion into God, and prove themselves ungrateful to the Word of God, who became flesh for them. For it was for this end that the Word of God was made man, and He who was the Son of God became the Son of man, that man, having been taken into the Word, and receiving the adoption, might become the son of God. For by no other means could we have attained to incorruptibility and immortality, unless we had been united to incorruptibility and immortality. But how could we be joined to incorruptibility and immortality, unless, first, incorruptibility and immortality had become that which we also are, so that the corruptible might be swallowed up by incorruptibility, and the mortal by immortality, that we might receive the adoption of sons?

For this reason [it is said], "Who shall declare His generation?" since "He is a man, and who shall recognise Him?" But he to whom the Father which is in heaven has revealed Him, knows Him, so that he understands that He who "was not born either by the will of the flesh, or by the will of man," is the Son of man, this is Christ, the Son of the living God. For I have shown from the Scriptures, that no one of the sons of Adam is as to everything, and absolutely, called God, or named Lord. But that He is Himself in His own right, beyond all men who ever lived, God, and Lord, and King Eternal, and the Incarnate Word, proclaimed by all the prophets, the apostles, and by the Spirit Himself, may be seen by all who have attained to even a small portion of the truth. Now, the Scriptures would not have testified these things of Him, if, like others, He had been a mere man. But that He had, beyond all others, in Himself that pre-eminent birth which is from the Most High Father, and also experienced that pre-eminent generation which is from the Virgin, the divine Scriptures do in both respects testify of Him: also, that He was a man without comeliness, and liable to suffering; that He sat upon the foal of an ass; that He received for drink, vinegar and gall; that He was despised among the people, and humbled Himself even to death; and that He is the holy Lord, the Wonderful, the Counsellor, the Beautiful in appearance, and the Mighty God, coming on the clouds as the judge of all men;—all these things did the Scriptures prophesy of Him.

For as He became man in order to undergo temptation, so also was He the Word that He might be glorified; the Word remaining quiescent, that He might be capable of being tempted, dishonoured, crucified, and of suffering death, but the human nature being swallowed up in it (the divine), when it conquered, and endured [without yielding], and performed acts of kindness, and rose again, and was received up [into heaven]. He therefore, the Son of God, our Lord, being the Word of the Father, and the Son of man, since He had a generation as to His human nature from Mary—who was descended from mankind, and who was herself a human being—was made the Son of man. Wherefore also the Lord Himself gave us a sign, in the depth below, and in the height above, which man did not ask for, because he never expected that a virgin could conceive, or that it was possible that one remaining a virgin could bring forth a son, and that what was thus born should be *"God with us,"* and descend to those things which are of the earth beneath, seeking the sheep which had perished, which was indeed His own peculiar handiwork, and ascend to the height above, offering and commending to His Father that human nature (*hominem*) which had been found, making in His own person the firstfruits of the resurrection of man; that, as the Head rose from the dead, so also the remaining part of the body—[namely, the body] of every man who is found in life—when the time is fulfilled of that condemnation which existed by reason of disobedience, may arise, blended together and strengthened through means of joints and bands by the increase of God, each of the members having its own proper and fit position in the body. For there are many mansions in the Father's house, inasmuch as there are also many members in the body.

CHAPTER XX

GOD SHOWED HIMSELF, BY THE FALL OF MAN, AS PATIENT, BENIGN, MERCIFUL, MIGHTY TO SAVE. MAN IS THEREFORE MOST UNGRATEFUL IF, UNMINDFUL OF HIS OWN LOT, AND OF THE BENEFITS HELD OUT TO HIM, HE DO NOT ACKNOWLEDGE DIVINE GRACE.

Long-suffering therefore was God, when man became a defaulter, as foreseeing that victory which should be granted to him through the Word. For, when strength was made perfect in weakness, it showed the kindness and transcendent power of God. For as He patiently suffered Jonah to be swallowed by the whale, not that he should be swallowed up and perish altogether, but that, having been cast out again, he might be the more subject to God, and might glorify Him the more who had conferred upon him such an unhoped-for deliverance, and might bring the Ninevites to a lasting repentance, so that they should be converted to the Lord, who would deliver them from death, having been struck with awe by that portent which had been wrought in Jonah's case, as the Scripture says of them, "And they returned each from his evil way, and the unrighteousness which was in their hands, saying, Who knoweth if God will repent, and turn away His anger from us, and we shall not perish?"—so also, from the beginning, did God permit man to be swallowed up by the great whale, who was the author of transgression, not that he should perish altogether when so engulphed; but, arranging and preparing the plan of salvation, which was accomplished by the Word, through the sign of Jonah, for those who held the same opinion as Jonah regarding the Lord, and who confessed, and said, "I am a servant of the Lord, and I worship the Lord God of heaven, who hath made the sea and the dry land." [This was done] that man, receiving an unhoped-for salvation from God, might rise from the dead, and glorify God, and repeat that word which was uttered in prophecy by Jonah: "I cried by reason of mine affliction to the Lord my God, and He heard me out of the belly of hell;" and that he might always continue glorifying God, and giving thanks without ceasing, for that salvation which he has derived from Him, "that no flesh should glory in the Lord's presence;" and that man should never adopt an opposite opinion with regard to God, supposing that the incorruptibility which belongs to him is his own naturally, and by thus not holding the truth, should boast with empty superciliousness, as if he were naturally like to God. For he (Satan) thus rendered him (man) more ungrateful towards his Creator, obscured the love which God had towards man, and blinded his mind not to perceive what is worthy of God, comparing himself, with, and judging himself equal to, God.

This, therefore, was the [object of the] long-suffering of God, that man, passing through all things, and acquiring the knowledge of moral discipline, then attaining to the resurrection from the dead, and learning by experience what is the source of his deliverance, may always live in a state of gratitude to the Lord, having obtained from Him the gift of incorruptibility, that he might love Him the more; for "he to whom more is forgiven, loveth more:" and that he may know himself, how mortal and weak he is; while he also understands respecting God, that He is immortal and powerful to such a degree as to confer immortality upon what is mortal, and eternity upon what is temporal; and may understand also the other attributes of God displayed towards himself, by means of which being instructed he may think of God in accordance with the divine greatness. For the glory of man [is] God, but [His] works [are the glory] of God; and the receptacle of all His wisdom and power [is] man. Just as the physician is proved by his patients, so is God also revealed through men. And therefore Paul declares, "For God hath concluded all in unbelief, that He may have mercy upon all;" not saying this in reference to spiritual Æons, but to man, who had been disobedient to God, and being cast off from immortality, then obtained mercy, receiving through the Son of God that adoption which is [accomplished] by Himself. For he who holds, without pride and boasting, the true glory (opinion) regarding created things and the Creator, who is the Almighty God of all, and who has granted existence to all; [such an one,] continuing in His love and subjection, and giving of thanks, shall also receive from Him the greater glory of promotion, looking forward to the time when he shall become like Him who died for him, for He, too, "was made in the likeness of sinful flesh," to condemn sin, and to cast it, as now a condemned thing, away beyond the flesh, but that He might call man forth into His own likeness, assigning him as [His own] imitator to God, and imposing on him His Father's law, in order that he may see God, and granting him power to receive the Father; [being] the Word of God who dwelt in man, and became the Son of man, that He might accustom man to receive God, and God to dwell in man, according to the good pleasure of the Father.

On this account, therefore, the Lord Himself, who is Emmanuel from the Virgin, is the sign of our salvation, since it was the Lord Himself who saved them, because they could not be saved by their own instrumentality; and, therefore, when Paul sets forth human infirmity, he says: "For I know that there dwelleth in my flesh no good thing," showing that the "good thing" of our salvation is not from us, but from God. And again: "Wretched man that I am, who shall deliver me from the body of this death?" Then he introduces the Deliverer, [saying,] "The grace of Jesus Christ our Lord." And Isaiah declares this also, [when he says:] "Be ye strengthened, ye hands that hang down, and ye feeble knees; be ye encouraged, ye feeble-minded; be comforted, fear not: behold, our God has given judgment with retribution, and shall recompense: He will come Himself, and will save us." Here we see, that not by ourselves, but by the help of God, we must be saved.

Again, that it should not be a mere man who should save us, nor [one] without flesh—for the angels are without flesh—[the same prophet] announced, saying: "Neither an elder, nor angel, but the Lord Himself will save them, because He loves them, and will spare them: He will Himself set them free." And that He should Himself become very man, visible, when He should be the Word giving salvation, Isaiah again says: "Behold, city of Zion: thine eyes shall see our salvation." And that it was not a mere man who died for us, Isaiah says: "And the holy Lord remembered His dead Israel, who had slept in the land of sepulture; and He came down to preach His salvation to them, that He might save them." And Amos (Micah) the prophet declares the same: "He will turn again, and will have compassion upon us: He will destroy our iniquities, and will cast our sins into the depths of the sea." And again, specifying the place of His advent, he says: "The Lord hath spoken from Zion, and He has uttered His voice from Jerusalem." And that it is from that region which is towards the south of the inheritance of Judah that the Son of God shall come, who is God, and who was from Bethlehem, where the Lord was born, [and] will send out His praise through all the earth, thus says the prophet Habakkuk: "God shall come from the south, and the Holy One from Mount Effrem. His power covered the heavens over, and the earth is full of His praise. Before His face shall go forth the Word, and His feet shall advance in the plains." Thus he indicates in clear terms that He is God, and that His advent was [to take place] in Bethlehem, and from Mount Effrem, which is towards the south of the inheritance, and that [He is] man. For he says, "His feet shall advance in the plains:" and this is an indication proper to man.

CHAPTER XXI

A VINDICATION OF THE PROPHECY IN ISAIAH (VII. 14) AGAINST THE MISINTERPRETATIONS OF THEODOTION, AQUILA, THE EBIONITES, AND THE JEWS. AUTHORITY OF THE SEPTUAGINT VERSION. ARGUMENTS IN PROOF THAT CHRIST WAS BORN OF A VIRGIN.

God, then was made man, and the Lord did Himself save us, giving us the token of the Virgin. But not as some allege, among those now presuming to expound the Scripture, [thus:] "Behold, a young woman shall conceive, and bring forth a son," as Theodotion the Ephesian has interpreted, and Aquila of Pontus, both Jewish proselytes. The Ebionites, following these, assert that He was begotten by Joseph; thus destroying, as far as in them lies, such a marvellous dispensation of God, and setting aside the testimony of the prophets which proceeded from God. For truly this prediction was uttered before the removal of the people to Babylon; that is, anterior to the supremacy acquired by the Medes and Persians. But it was interpreted into Greek by the Jews themselves, much before the period of our Lord's advent, that there might remain no suspicion that perchance the Jews, complying with our humour, did put this interpretation upon these words. They indeed, had they been cognizant of our future existence, and that we should use these proofs from the Scriptures, would themselves never have hesitated to burn their own Scriptures, which do declare that all other nations partake of [eternal] life, and show that they who boast themselves as being the house of Jacob and the people of Israel, are disinherited from the grace of God.

For before the Romans possessed their kingdom, while as yet the Macedonians held Asia, Ptolemy the son of Lagus, being anxious to adorn the library which he had founded in Alexandria, with a collection of the writings of all men, which were [works] of merit, made request to the people of Jerusalem, that they should have their Scriptures translated into the Greek language. And they—for at that time they were still subject to the Macedonians—sent to Ptolemy seventy of their elders, who were thoroughly skilled in the Scriptures and in both the languages, to carry out what he had desired. But he, wishing to test them individually, and fearing lest they might perchance, by taking counsel together, conceal the truth in the Scriptures, by their interpretation, separated them from each other, and commanded them all to write the same translation. He did this with respect to all the books. But when they came together in the same place before Ptolemy, and each of them compared his own interpretation with that of every other, God was indeed glorified, and the Scriptures were acknowledged as truly divine. For all of them read out the common translation [which they had prepared] in the very same words and the very same names, from beginning to end, so that even the Gentiles present perceived that the Scriptures had been interpreted by the inspiration of God. And there was nothing astonishing in God having done this,—He who, when, during the captivity of the people under Nebuchadnezzar, the Scriptures had been corrupted, and when after seventy years, the Jews had returned to their own land, then, in the times of Artaxerxes king of the Persians, inspired Esdras the priest, of the tribe of Levi, to recast all the words of the former prophets, and to re-establish with the people the Mosaic legislation.

Since, therefore, the Scriptures have been interpreted with such fidelity, and by the grace of God, and since from these God has prepared and formed again our faith towards His Son, and has preserved to us the unadulterated Scriptures in Egypt, where the house of Jacob flourished, fleeing from the famine in Canaan; where also our Lord was preserved when He fled from the persecution set on foot by Herod; and [since] this interpretation of these Scriptures was made prior to our Lord's descent [to earth], and came into being before the Christians appeared—for our Lord was born about the forty-first year of the reign of Augustus; but Ptolemy was much earlier, under whom the Scriptures were interpreted;—[since these things are so, I say,] truly these men are proved to be impudent and presumptuous, who would now show a desire to make different translations, when we refute them out of these Scriptures, and shut them up to a belief in the advent of the Son of God. But *our* faith is stedfast, unfeigned, and the only true one, having clear proof from these Scriptures, which were interpreted in the way I have related; and the preaching of the Church is without interpolation. For the apostles, since they are of more ancient date than all these [heretics], agree with this aforesaid translation; and the translation harmonizes with the tradition of the apostles. For Peter, and John, and Matthew, and Paul, and the rest successively, as well as their followers, did set forth all prophetical [announcements], just as the interpretation of the elders contains them.

For the one and the same Spirit of God, who proclaimed by the prophets what and of what sort the advent of the Lord should be, did by these elders give a just interpretation of what had been truly prophesied; and He did Himself, by the apostles, announce that the fulness of the times of the adoption had arrived, that the kingdom of heaven had drawn nigh, and that *He* was dwelling within those that believe on Him who was born Emmanuel of the Virgin. To this effect they testify, [saying,] that before Joseph had come together with Mary, while she therefore remained in virginity, "she was found with child of the Holy Ghost;" and that the angel Gabriel said unto her, "The Holy Ghost shall come upon thee, and the power of the Highest shall overshadow thee; therefore also that holy thing which shall be born of thee shall be called the Son of God;" and that the angel said to Joseph in a dream, "Now this was done, that it might be fulfilled which was spoken by Isaiah the Prophet, Behold, a virgin shall be with child." But the elders have thus interpreted what Esaias said: "And the Lord, moreover, said unto Ahaz, Ask for thyself a sign from the Lord thy God out of the depth below, or from the height above. And Ahaz said, I will not ask, and I will not tempt the Lord. And he said, It is not a small thing for you to weary men; and how does the Lord weary them? Therefore the Lord himself shall give you a sign; Behold, a virgin shall conceive, and bear a son; and ye shall call His name Emmanuel. Butter and honey shall He eat: before He knows or chooses out things that are evil, He shall exchange them for what is good; for before the child knows good or evil, He shall not consent to evil, that He may choose that which is good." Carefully, then, has the Holy Ghost pointed out, by what has been said, His birth from a virgin, and His essence, that He is God (for the name Emmanuel indicates this). And He shows that He is a man, when He says, "Butter and honey shall He eat;" and in that He terms Him a child also, [in saying,] "before He knows good and evil;" for these are all the tokens of a human infant. But that He "will not consent to evil, that He may choose that which is good,"— this is proper to God; that by the fact, that He shall eat butter and honey, we should not understand that He is a mere man only, nor, on the other hand, from the name Emmanuel, should suspect Him to be God without flesh.

And when He says, "Hear, O house of David," He performed the part of one indicating that He whom God promised David that He would raise up from the fruit of his belly (*ventris*) an eternal King, is the same who was born of the Virgin, herself of the lineage of David. For on this account also, He promised that the King should be "of the fruit of his *belly*," which was the appropriate [term to use with respect] to a virgin conceiving, and not "of the fruit of his *loins*," nor "of the fruit of his *reins*," which expression is appropriate to a generating man, and a woman conceiving by a man. In this promise, therefore, the Scripture excluded all virile influence; yet it certainly is not mentioned that He who was born was not from the will of man. But it has fixed and established "the fruit of the *belly*," that it might declare the generation of Him who should be [born] from the Virgin, as Elisabeth testified when filled with the Holy Ghost, saying to Mary, "Blessed art thou among women, and blessed is the fruit of thy belly;" the Holy Ghost pointing out to those willing to hear, that the promise which God had made, of raising up a King from the fruit of [David's] belly, was fulfilled in the birth from the Virgin, that is, from Mary. Let those, therefore, who alter the passage of Isaiah thus, "Behold, a young woman shall conceive," and who will have Him to be Joseph's son, also alter the form of the promise which was given to David, when God promised him to raise up, from the fruit of his belly, the horn of Christ the King. But they did not understand, otherwise they would have presumed to alter even this passage also.

But what Isaiah said, "From the height above, or from the depth beneath," was meant to indicate, that "He who descended was the same also who ascended." But in this that he said, "The Lord Himself shall give you a sign," he declared an unlooked-for thing with regard to His generation, which could have been accomplished in no other way than by God the Lord of all, God Himself giving a sign in the house of David. For what great thing or what sign should have been in this, that a young woman conceiving by a man should bring forth,—a thing which happens to all women that produce offspring? But since an unlooked-for salvation was to be provided for men through the help of God, so also was the unlooked-for birth from a virgin accomplished; God giving this sign, but man not working it out.

On this account also, Daniel, foreseeing His advent, said that a stone, cut out without hands, came into this world. For this is what "without hands" means, that His coming into this world was not by the operation of human hands, that is, of those men who are accustomed to stone-cutting; that is, Joseph taking no part with regard to it, but Mary alone co-operating with the pre-arranged plan. For this stone from the earth derives existence from both the power and the wisdom of God. Wherefore also Isaiah says: "Thus saith the Lord, Behold, I deposit in the foundations of Zion a stone, precious, elect, the chief, the corner-one, to be had in honour." So, then, we understand that His advent in human nature was not by the will of a man, but by the will of God.

Wherefore also Moses giving a type, cast his rod upon the earth, in order that it, by becoming flesh, might expose and swallow up all the opposition of the Egyptians, which was lifting itself up against the pre-arranged plan of God; that the Egyptians themselves might testify that it is the finger of God which works salvation for the people, and not the son of Joseph. For if He were the son of Joseph, how could He be greater than Solomon, or greater than Jonah, or greater than David, when He was generated from the same seed, and was a descendant of these men? And how was it that He also pronounced Peter blessed, because he acknowledged Him to be the Son of the living God?

But besides, if indeed He had been the son of Joseph, He could not, according to Jeremiah, be either king or heir. For Joseph is shown to be the son of Joachim and Jechoniah, as also Matthew sets forth in his pedigree. But Jechoniah, and all his posterity, were disinherited from the kingdom; Jeremiah thus declaring, "As I live, saith the Lord, if Jechoniah the son of Joachim king of Judah had been made the signet of my right hand, I would pluck him thence, and deliver him into the hand of those seeking thy life." And again: "Jechoniah is dishonoured as a useless vessel, for he has been cast into a land which he knew not. Earth, hear the word of the Lord: Write this man a disinherited person; for none of his seed, sitting on the throne of David, shall prosper, or be a prince in Judah." And again, God speaks of Joachim his father: "Therefore thus saith the Lord concerning Joachim his father, king of Judea, There shall be from him none sitting upon the throne of David: and his dead body shall be cast out in the heat of day, and in the frost of night. And I will look upon him, and upon his sons, and will bring upon them, and upon the inhabitants of Jerusalem, upon the land of Judah, all the evils that I have pronounced against them." Those, therefore, who say that He was begotten of Joseph, and that they have hope in Him, do cause themselves to be disinherited from the kingdom, falling under the curse and rebuke directed against Jechoniah and his seed. Because for this reason have these things been spoken concerning Jechoniah, the [Holy] Spirit foreknowing the doctrines of the evil teachers; that they may learn that from his seed—that is, from Joseph—He was not to be born, but that, according to the promise of God, from David's belly the King eternal is raised up, who sums up all things in Himself, and has gathered into Himself the ancient formation [of man].

For as by one man's disobedience sin entered, and death obtained [a place] through sin; so also by the obedience of one man, righteousness having been introduced, shall cause life to fructify in those persons who in times past were dead. And as the protoplast himself, Adam, had his substance from untilled and as yet virgin soil ("for God had not yet sent rain, and man had not tilled the ground"), and was formed by the hand of God, that is, by the Word of God, for "all things were made by

Him," and the Lord took dust from the earth and formed man; so did He who is the Word, recapitulating Adam in Himself, rightly receive a birth, enabling Him to gather up Adam [into Himself], from Mary, who was as yet a virgin. If, then, the first Adam had a man for his father, and was born of human seed, it were reasonable to say that the second Adam was begotten of Joseph. But if the former was taken from the dust, and God was his Maker, it was incumbent that the latter also, making a recapitulation in Himself, should be formed as man by God, to have an analogy with the former as respects His origin. Why, then, did not God again take dust, but wrought so that the formation should be made of Mary? It was that there might not be another formation called into being, nor any other which should [require to] be saved, but that the very same formation should be summed up [in Christ as had existed in Adam], the analogy having been preserved.

CHAPTER XXII

CHRIST ASSUMED ACTUAL FLESH, CONCEIVED AND BORN OF THE VIRGIN.

Those, therefore, who allege that He took nothing from the Virgin do greatly err, [since,] in order that they may cast away the inheritance of the flesh, they also reject the analogy [between Him and Adam]. For if the one [who sprang] from the earth had indeed formation and substance from both the hand and workmanship of God, but the other not from the hand and workmanship of God, then He who was made after the image and likeness of the former did not, in that case, preserve the analogy of man, and He must seem an inconsistent piece of work, not having wherewith He may show His wisdom. But this is to say, that He also appeared putatively as man when He was not man, and that He was made man while taking nothing from man. For if He did not receive the substance of flesh from a human being, He neither was made man nor the Son of man; and if He was not made what we were, He did no great thing in what He suffered and endured. But every one will allow that we are [composed of] a body taken from the earth, and a soul receiving spirit from God. This, therefore, the Word of God was made, recapitulating in Himself His own handiwork; and on this account does He confess Himself the Son of man, and blesses "the meek, because they shall inherit the earth." The Apostle Paul, moreover, in the Epistle to the Galatians, declares plainly, "God sent His Son, made of a woman." And again, in that to the Romans, he says, "Concerning His Son, who was made of the seed of David according to the flesh, who was predestinated as the Son of God with power, according to the spirit of holiness, by the resurrection from the dead, Jesus Christ our Lord."

Superfluous, too, in that case is His descent into Mary; for why did He come down into her if He were to take nothing of her? Still further, if He had taken nothing of Mary, He would never have availed Himself of those kinds of food which are derived from the earth, by which that body which has been taken from the earth is nourished; nor would He have hungered, fasting those forty days, like Moses and Elias, unless His body was craving after its own proper nourishment; nor, again, would John His disciple have said, when writing of Him, "But Jesus, being wearied with the journey, was sitting [to rest];" nor would David have proclaimed of Him beforehand, "They have added to the grief of my wounds;" nor would He have wept over Lazarus, nor have sweated great drops of blood; nor have declared, "My soul is exceeding sorrowful;" nor, when His side was pierced, would there have come forth blood and water. For all these are tokens of the flesh which had been derived from the earth, which He had recapitulated in Himself, bearing salvation to His own handiwork.

Wherefore Luke points out that the pedigree which traces the generation of our Lord back to Adam contains seventy-two generations, connecting the end with the beginning, and implying that it is He who has summed up in Himself all nations dispersed from Adam downwards, and all languages and generations of men, together with Adam himself. Hence also was Adam himself termed by Paul "the figure of Him that was to come," because the Word, the Maker of all things, had formed beforehand for Himself the future dispensation of the human race, connected with the Son of God; God having predestined that the first man should be of an animal nature, with this view, that he might be saved by the spiritual One. For inasmuch as He had a pre-existence as a saving Being, it was necessary that what might be saved should also be called into existence, in order that the Being who saves should not exist in vain.

In accordance with this design, Mary the Virgin is found obedient, saying, "Behold the handmaid of the Lord; be it unto me according to thy word." But Eve was disobedient; for she did not obey when as yet she was a virgin. And even as she, having indeed a husband, Adam, but being nevertheless as yet a virgin (for in Paradise "they were both naked, and were not ashamed," inasmuch as they, having been created a short time previously, had no understanding of the procreation of children: for it was necessary that they should first come to adult age, and then multiply from that time onward), having become disobedient, was made the cause of death, both to herself and to the entire human race; so also did Mary, having a man betrothed [to her], and being nevertheless a virgin, by yielding obedience, become the cause of salvation, both to herself and the whole human race. And on this account does the law term a woman betrothed to a man, the wife of him who had betrothed her, although she was as yet a virgin; thus indicating the back-reference from Mary to Eve, because what is joined together could not otherwise be put asunder than by inversion of the process by which these bonds of union had arisen; so that the former ties be cancelled by the latter, that the latter may set the former again at liberty. And it has, in fact, happened that the first compact looses from the second tie, but that the second tie takes the position of the first which has been cancelled. For this reason did the Lord declare that the first should in truth be last, and the last first. And the prophet, too, indicates the same, saying, "Instead of fathers, children have been born unto thee." For the Lord, having been born "the First-begotten of the dead," and receiving into His bosom the ancient fathers, has regenerated them into the life of God, He having been made Himself the beginning of those that live, as Adam became the beginning of those who die. Wherefore also Luke, commencing the genealogy with the Lord, carried it back to Adam, indicating that it was He who regenerated them into the Gospel of life, and not they Him. And thus also it was that the knot of Eve's disobedience was loosed by the obedience of Mary. For what the virgin Eve had bound fast through unbelief, this did the virgin Mary set free through faith.

CHAPTER XXIII

ARGUMENTS IN OPPOSITION TO TATIAN, SHOWING THAT IT WAS CONSONANT TO DIVINE JUSTICE AND MERCY THAT THE FIRST ADAM SHOULD FIRST PARTAKE IN THAT SALVATION OFFERED TO ALL BY CHRIST.

It was necessary, therefore, that the Lord, coming to the lost sheep, and making recapitulation of so comprehensive a dispensation, and seeking after His own handiwork, should save that very man who had been created after His image and likeness, that is, Adam, filling up the times of His condemnation, which had been incurred through disobedience,— [times] "which the Father had placed in His own power." [This was necessary,] too, inasmuch as the whole economy of salvation regarding man came to pass according to the good pleasure of the Father, in order that God might not be conquered, nor His wisdom lessened, [in the estimation of His creatures.] For if man, who had been created by God that he might live, after losing life, through being injured by the serpent that had corrupted him, should not any more return to life, but should be utterly [and for ever] abandoned to death, God would [in that case] have been conquered, and the wickedness of the serpent would have prevailed over the will of God. But inasmuch as God is invincible and long-suffering, He did indeed show Himself to be long-suffering in the matter of the correction of man and the probation of all, as I have already observed; and by means of the second man did He bind the strong man, and spoiled his goods, and abolished death, vivifying that man who had been in a state of death. For at the first Adam became a vessel in his (Satan's) possession, whom he did also hold under his power, that is, by bringing sin on him iniquitously, and under colour of immortality entailing death upon him. For, while promising that they should be as gods, which was in no way possible for him to be, he wrought death in them: wherefore he who had led man captive, was justly captured in his turn by God; but man, who had been led captive, was loosed from the bonds of condemnation.

But this is Adam, if the truth should be told, the first formed man, of whom the Scripture says that the Lord spake, "Let Us make man after Our own image and likeness;" and we are all from him: and as we are from him, therefore have we all inherited his title. But inasmuch as man is saved, it is fitting that he who was created the original man should be saved. For it is too absurd to maintain, that he who was so deeply injured by the enemy, and was the first to suffer captivity, was not rescued by Him who conquered the enemy, but that his children were,—those whom he had begotten in the same captivity. Neither would the enemy appear to be as yet conquered, if the old spoils remained with him. To give an illustration: If a hostile force had overcome certain [enemies], had bound them, and led them away captive, and held them for a long time in servitude, so that they begat children among them; and somebody, compassionating those who had been made slaves, should overcome this same hostile force; he certainly would not act equitably, were he to liberate the children of those who had been led captive, from the sway of those who had enslaved their fathers, but should leave these latter, who had suffered the act of capture, subject to their enemies,—those, too, on whose very account he had proceeded to this retaliation,—the children succeeding to liberty through the avenging of their fathers' cause, but not so that their fathers, who suffered the act of capture itself, should be left [in bondage]. For God is neither devoid of power nor of justice, who has afforded help to man, and restored him to His own liberty.

It was for this reason, too, that immediately after Adam had transgressed, as the Scripture relates, He pronounced no curse against Adam personally, but against the ground, in reference to his works, as a certain person among the ancients has observed: "God did indeed transfer the curse to the earth, that it might not remain in man." But man received, as the punishment of his transgression, the toilsome task of tilling the earth, and to eat bread in the sweat of his face, and to return to the dust from whence he was taken. Similarly also did the woman [receive] toil, and labour, and groans, and the pangs of parturition, and a state of subjection, that is, that she should serve her husband; so that they should neither perish altogether when cursed by God, nor, by remaining unreprimanded, should be led to despise God. But the curse in all its fulness fell upon the serpent, which had beguiled them. "And God," it is declared, "said to the serpent: Because thou hast done this, cursed art thou above all cattle, and above all the beasts of the earth." And this same thing does the Lord also say in the Gospel, to those who are found upon the left hand: "Depart from me, ye cursed, into everlasting fire, which my Father hath prepared for the devil and his angels;" indicating that eternal fire was not originally prepared for man, but for him who beguiled man, and caused him to offend—for him, I say, who is chief of the apostasy, and for those angels who became apostates along with him; which [fire], indeed, they too shall justly feel, who, like him, persevere in works of wickedness, without repentance, and without retracing their steps.

[These act] as Cain [did, who], when he was counselled by God to keep quiet, because he had not made an equitable division of that share to which his brother was entitled, but with envy and malice thought that he could domineer over him, not only did not acquiesce, but even added sin to sin, indicating his state of mind by his action. For what he had planned, that did he also put in practice: he tyrannized over and slew him; God subjecting the just to the unjust, that the former might be proved as the just one by the things which he suffered, and the latter detected as the unjust by those which he perpetrated. And he was not softened even by this, nor did he stop short with that evil deed; but being asked where his brother was, he said, "I know not; am I my brother's keeper?" extending and aggravating [his] wickedness by his answer. For if it is wicked to slay a brother, much worse is it thus insolently and irreverently to reply to the omniscient God as if he could baffle Him. And for this he did himself bear a curse about with him, because he gratuitously brought an offering of sin, having had no reverence for God, nor being put to confusion by the act of fratricide.

The case of Adam, however, had no analogy with this, but was altogether different. For, having been beguiled by another under the pretext of immortality, he is immediately seized with terror, and hides himself; not as if he were able to escape from God; but, in a state of confusion at having transgressed His command, he feels unworthy to appear before and to hold converse with God. Now, "the fear of the Lord is the beginning of wisdom;" the sense of sin leads to repentance, and God bestows His compassion upon those who are penitent. For [Adam] showed his repentance by his conduct, through means of the girdle [which he used], covering himself with fig-leaves, while there were many other leaves, which would have irritated his body in a less degree. He, however, adopted a dress conformable to his disobedience, being awed by the fear of God; and resisting the erring, the lustful propensity of his flesh (since he had lost his natural disposition and child-like mind, and had come to the knowledge of evil things), he girded a bridle of continence upon himself and his wife, fearing God, and waiting for His coming, and indicating, as it were, some such thing [as follows]: Inasmuch as, he says, I have by disobedience lost that robe of sanctity which I had from the Spirit, I do now also acknowledge that I am deserving of a covering of this nature, which affords no gratification, but which gnaws and frets the body. And he would no doubt have retained this clothing for ever, thus humbling himself, if God, who is merciful, had not clothed them with tunics of skins instead of fig-leaves. For this purpose, too, He interrogates them, that the blame might light upon the woman; and again, He interrogates her, that she might convey the blame to the serpent. For she related what had occurred. "The serpent," says she, "beguiled me, and I did eat." But He put no question to the serpent; for He knew that he had been the prime mover in the guilty deed; but He pronounced the curse upon him in the first instance, that it might fall upon man with a mitigated rebuke. For God detested him who had led man astray, but by degrees, and little by little, He showed compassion to him who had been beguiled.

Wherefore also He drove him out of Paradise, and removed him far from the tree of life, not because He envied him the tree of life, as some venture to assert, but because He pitied him, [and did not desire] that he should continue a sinner for ever, nor that the sin which surrounded him should be immortal, and evil interminable and irremediable. But He set a bound to his [state of] sin, by interposing death, and thus causing sin to cease, putting an end to it by the dissolution of the flesh, which should take place in the earth, so that man, ceasing at length to live to sin, and dying to it, might begin to live to God.

For this end did He put enmity between the serpent and the woman and her seed, they keeping it up mutually: He, the sole of whose foot should be bitten, having power also to tread upon the enemy's head; but the other biting, killing, and impeding the steps of man, until the seed did come appointed to tread down his head,—which was born of Mary, of whom the prophet speaks: "Thou shalt tread upon the asp and the basilisk; thou shalt trample down the lion and the dragon;"—indicating that sin, which was set up and spread out against man, and which rendered him subject to death, should be deprived of its power, along with death, which rules [over men]; and that the lion, that is, antichrist, rampant against mankind in the latter days, should be trampled down by Him; and that He should bind "the dragon, that old serpent." and subject him to the power of man, who had been conquered, so that all his might should be trodden down. Now Adam had been conquered, all life having been taken away from him: wherefore, when the foe was conquered in his turn, Adam received new life; and the last enemy, death, is destroyed, which at the first had taken possession of man. Therefore, when man has been liberated, "what is written shall come to pass. Death is swallowed up in victory. O death, where is thy victory? O death, where is thy sting?" This could not be said with justice, if that man, over whom death did first obtain dominion, were not set free. For his salvation is death's destruction. When therefore the Lord vivifies man, that is, Adam, death is at the same time destroyed.

All therefore speak falsely who disallow his (Adam's) salvation, shutting themselves out from life for ever, in that they do not believe that the sheep which had perished has been found. For if it has not been found, the whole human race is still held in a state of perdition. False, therefore, is that man who first started this idea, or rather, this ignorance and blindness—Tatian. As I have already indicated, this man entangled himself with all the heretics. This dogma, however, has been invented by himself, in order that, by introducing something new, independently of the rest, and by speaking vanity, he might acquire for himself hearers void of faith, affecting to be esteemed a teacher, and endeavouring from time to time to employ sayings of this kind often [made use of] by Paul: "In Adam we all die;" ignorant, however, that "where sin abounded, grace did much more abound." Since this, then, has been clearly shown, let all his disciples be put to shame, and let them wrangle about Adam, as if some great gain were to accrue to them if he be not saved; when they profit nothing more [by that], even as the serpent also did not profit when persuading man [to sin], except to this effect, that he proved him a transgressor, obtaining man as the first-fruits of his own apostasy. But he did not know God's power. Thus also do those who disallow Adam's salvation gain nothing, except this, that they render themselves heretics and apostates from the truth, and show themselves patrons of the serpent and of death.

CHAPTER XXIV

RECAPITULATION OF THE VARIOUS ARGUMENTS ADDUCED AGAINST GNOSTIC IMPIETY UNDER ALL ITS ASPECTS. THE HERETICS, TOSSED ABOUT BY EVERY BLAST OF DOCTRINE, ARE OPPOSED BY THE UNIFORM TEACHING OF THE CHURCH, WHICH REMAINS SO ALWAYS, AND IS CONSISTENT WITH ITSELF.

Thus, then, have all these men been exposed, who bring in impious doctrines regarding our Maker and Framer, who also formed this world, and above whom there is no other God; and those have been overthrown by their own arguments who teach falsehoods regarding the substance of our Lord, and the dispensation which He fulfilled for the sake of His own creature man. But [it has, on the other hand, been shown], that the preaching of the Church is everywhere consistent, and continues in an even course, and receives testimony from the prophets, the apostles, and all the disciples—as I have proved—through [those in] the beginning, the middle, and the end, and through the entire dispensation of God, and that well-grounded system which tends to man's salvation, namely, our faith; which, having been received from the Church, we do preserve, and which always, by the Spirit of God, renewing its youth, as if it were some precious deposit in an excellent vessel, causes the vessel itself containing it to renew its youth also. For this gift of God has been entrusted to the Church, as breath was to the first created man, for this purpose, that all the members receiving it may be vivified; and the [means of] communion with Christ has been distributed throughout it, that is, the Holy Spirit, the earnest of incorruption, the means of confirming our faith, and the ladder of ascent to God. "For in the Church," it is said, "God hath set apostles, prophets, teachers," and all the other means through which the Spirit works; of which all those are not partakers who do not join themselves to the Church, but defraud themselves of life through their perverse opinions and infamous behaviour. For where the Church is, there is the Spirit of God; and where the Spirit of God is, there is the Church, and every kind of grace; but the Spirit is truth. Those, therefore, who do not partake of Him, are neither nourished into life from the mother's breasts, nor do they enjoy that most limpid fountain which issues from the body of Christ; but they dig for themselves broken cisterns out of earthly trenches, and drink putrid water out of the mire, fleeing from the faith of the Church lest they be convicted; and rejecting the Spirit, that they may not be instructed.

Alienated thus from the truth, they do deservedly wallow in all error, tossed to and fro by it, thinking differently in regard to the same things at different times, and never attaining to a well-grounded knowledge, being more anxious to be sophists of words than disciples of the truth. For they have not been founded upon the one rock, but upon the sand, which has in itself a multitude of stones. Wherefore they also imagine many gods, and they always have the excuse of searching [after truth] (for they are blind), but never succeed in finding it. For they blaspheme the Creator, Him who is truly God, who also furnishes power to find [the truth]; imagining that they have discovered another god beyond God, or another Pleroma, or another dispensation. Wherefore also the light which is from

God does not illumine them, because they have dishonoured and despised God, holding Him of small account, because, through His love and infinite benignity, He has come within reach of human knowledge (knowledge, however, not with regard to His greatness, or with regard to His essence—for that has no man measured or handled—but after this sort: that we should know that He who made, and formed, and breathed in them the breath of life, and nourishes us by means of the creation, establishing all things by His Word, and binding them together by His Wisdom—this is He who is the only true God); but they dream of a non-existent being above Him, that they may be regarded as having found out the great God, whom nobody, [they hold,] can recognise as holding communication with the human race, or as directing mundane matters: that is to say, they find out the god of Epicurus, who does nothing either for himself or others; that is, he exercises no providence at all.

CHAPTER XXV

THIS WORLD IS RULED BY THE PROVIDENCE OF ONE GOD, WHO IS BOTH ENDOWED WITH INFINITE JUSTICE TO PUNISH THE WICKED, AND WITH INFINITE GOODNESS TO BLESS THE PIOUS, AND IMPART TO THEM SALVATION.

God does, however, exercise a providence over all things, and therefore He also gives counsel; and when giving counsel, He is present with those who attend to moral discipline. It follows then of course, that the things which are watched over and governed should be acquainted with their ruler; which things are not irrational or vain, but they have understanding derived from the providence of God. And, for this reason, certain of the Gentiles, who were less addicted to [sensual] allurements and voluptuousness, and were not led away to such a degree of superstition with regard to idols, being moved, though but slightly, by His providence, were nevertheless convinced that they should call the Maker of this universe the Father, who exercises a providence over all things, and arranges the affairs of our world.

42

Again, that they might remove the rebuking and judicial power from the Father, reckoning that as unworthy of God, and thinking that they had found out a God both without anger and [merely] good, they have alleged that one [God] judges, but that another saves, unconsciously taking away the intelligence and justice of both deities. For if the judicial one is not also good, to bestow favours upon the deserving, and to direct reproofs against those requiring them, he will appear neither a just nor a wise judge. On the other hand, the good God, if he is merely good, and not one who tests those upon whom he shall send his goodness, will be out of the range of justice and goodness; and his goodness will seem imperfect, as not saving all; [for it should do so,] if it be not accompanied with judgment.

Marcion, therefore, himself, by dividing God into two, maintaining one to be good and the other judicial, does in fact, on both sides, put an end to deity. For he that is the judicial one, if he be not good, is not God, because he from whom goodness is absent is no God at all; and again, he who is good, if he has no judicial power, suffers the same [loss] as the former, by being deprived of his character of deity. And how can they call the Father of all wise, if they do not assign to Him a judicial faculty? For if He is wise, He is also one who tests [others]; but the judicial power belongs to him who tests, and justice follows the judicial faculty, that it may reach a just conclusion; justice calls forth judgment, and judgment, when it is executed with justice, will pass on to wisdom. Therefore the Father will excel in wisdom all human and angelic wisdom, because He is Lord, and Judge, and the Just One, and Ruler over all. For He is good, and merciful, and patient, and saves whom He ought: nor does goodness desert Him in the exercise of justice, nor is His wisdom lessened; for He saves those whom He should save, and judges those worthy of judgment. Neither does He show Himself unmercifully just: for His goodness, no doubt, goes on before, and takes precedency.

The God, therefore, who does benevolently cause His sun to rise upon all, and sends rain upon the just and unjust, shall judge those who, enjoying His equally distributed kindness, have led lives not corresponding to the dignity of His bounty; but who have spent their days in wantonness and luxury, in opposition to His benevolence, and have, moreover, even blasphemed Him who has conferred so great benefits upon them.

Plato is proved to be more religious than these men, for he allowed that the same God was both just and good, having power over all things, and Himself executing judgment, expressing himself thus, "And God indeed, as He is also the ancient Word, possessing the beginning, the end, and the mean of all existing things, does everything rightly, moving round about them according to their nature; but retributive justice always follows Him against those who depart from the divine law." Then, again, he points out that the Maker and Framer of the universe is good. "And to the good," he says, "no envy ever springs up with regard to anything;" thus establishing the goodness of God, as the beginning and the cause of the creation of the world, but not ignorance, nor an erring Æon, nor the consequence of a defect, nor the Mother weeping and lamenting, nor another God or Father.

Well may their Mother bewail them, as capable of conceiving and inventing such things; for they have worthily uttered this falsehood against themselves, that their Mother is beyond the Pleroma, that is, beyond the knowledge of God, and that their entire multitude became a shapeless and crude abortion: for it apprehends nothing of the truth; it falls into void and darkness: for their wisdom (*Sophia*) was void, and wrapped up in darkness; and Horos did not permit her to enter the Pleroma: for the Spirit (Achamoth) did not receive them into the place of refreshment. For their father, by begetting ignorance, wrought in them the sufferings of death. We do not misrepresent [their opinions on] these points; but they do themselves confirm, they do themselves teach, they do glory in them, they imagine a lofty [mystery] about their Mother, whom they represent as having been begotten without a father, that is, without God, a female from a female, that is, corruption from error.

We do indeed pray that these men may not remain in the pit which they themselves have dug, but separate themselves from a Mother of this nature, and depart from Bythus, and stand away from the void, and relinquish the shadow; and that they, being converted to the Church of God, may be lawfully begotten, and that Christ may be formed in them, and that they may know the Framer and Maker of this universe, the only true God and Lord of all. We pray for these things on their behalf, loving them better than they seem to love themselves. For our love, inasmuch as it is true, is salutary to them, if they will but receive it. It may be compared to a severe remedy, extirpating the proud and sloughing flesh of a wound; for it puts an end to their pride and haughtiness. Wherefore it shall not weary us, to endeavour with all our might to stretch out the hand unto them. Over and above what has been already stated, I have deferred to the following book to adduce the words of the Lord; if, by convincing some among them, through means of the very instruction of Christ. I may succeed in persuading them to abandon such error, and to cease from blaspheming their Creator, who is both God alone, and the Father of our Lord Jesus Christ. Amen.

St. Hippolytus of Rome
170-235

Hippolytus claimed St. Irenaeus as his teacher and does as a matter of fact repeat the recapitulation theology of the bishop of Lyon. As the last Christian writer in Rome to use the Greek language, Hippolytus was unusually prolific. After his rigorism led him into schism in 217, he spent nearly twenty years as antipope, only being reconciled in the last year or two of his life. Of his dogmatic works, the one reprinted here is the only one that has survived.

Ever immersed in controversy, Hippolytus is not one from whom the best of balance is to be expected. In his polemic Against Noetus *he refutes modalism only to fall into subordinationism in his effort to explain the relation of Father and Son. In the process, however, he seems to have introduced into theology the term* hypostania *(subsist) which subsequently was to play a central role in the development of the tradition, as is evident in the prominent use of "hypostatic union."*

It is easily overlooked that a long struggle for precise language had to be endured before inadequate terms were eliminated and preferred concepts were elaborated. Thus, in the above mentioned work, Hippolytus has two statements back to back, one of which would be heretical and the other of which would express classical orthodoxy a few generations later: "For neither was the Lord, prior to the Incarnation and when by himself, yet perfect Son . . . Nor could the flesh subsist (hypostanai) by itself apart from the Word, because it has its subsistence in the Word." Later authors repudiated the former and gratefully adopted the latter.

Christ and Antichrist was written about the year 200 and its Greek text has come down to us complete, preserved in three manuscripts. It is not a great work but is of some special interest because "it is the most comprehensive discussion of the problem of Antichrist in patristic literature" (Quasten). The question it addresses was one of the most puzzling in early Christianity, and this work attests to the seriousness with which (at least some) Roman Christians viewed Revelation and the book of Daniel. Hippolytus sets out to identify who the Antichrist was to be, what his coming was to achieve, when it was to take place, how he would deceive people and stir up persecution of the saints, how he would glorify himself as God, and what his end would be when the Lord suddenly appeared to reward the good and punish the wicked by fire.

Against this apocalyptic framework, of course, the entire understanding of Jesus and his role in history takes on a special hue. The worldview is clearly that of a persecuted minority that looks to the day when the scales will be balanced and God's justice will prevail. Hippolytus had the stages of these developments rather neatly worked out so that the climax was still a good distance in the future and the scenario up to his time was totally credible. And in later centuries there would be all manner of attempts to parallel his historical guesswork. But for mainstream Christian tradition this mode of interpretation was of limited duration and validity. Symbols turned into allegories proved simply unmanageable, and most retreated to the safer position of emphasizing that part of Christian faith concerning these end-events is that we know neither the day nor the hour— nor the other details that imagination would love to fill in. Hippolytus has thus served us well in demonstrating a type of theologizing that simply could not survive as Christianity became a world faith.

TREATISE ON CHRIST
AND ANTICHRIST

PART II

DOGMATICAL AND HISTORICAL

As it was your desire, my beloved brother Theophilus, to be thoroughly informed on those topics which I put summarily before you, I have thought it right to set these matters of inquiry clearly forth to your view, drawing largely from the Holy Scriptures themselves as from a holy fountain, in order that you may not only have the pleasure of hearing them on the testimony of men, but may also be able, by surveying them in the light of (divine) authority, to glorify God in all. For this will be as a sure supply furnished you by us for your journey in this present life, so that by ready argument applying things ill understood and apprehended by most, you may sow them in the ground of your heart, as in a rich and clean soil. By these, too, you will be able to silence those who oppose and gainsay the word of salvation. Only see that you do not give these things over to unbelieving and blasphemous tongues, for that is no common danger. But impart them to pious and faithful men, who desire to live holily and righteously with fear. For it is not to no purpose that the blessed apostle exhorts Timothy, and says, "O Timothy, keep that which is committed to thy trust, avoiding profane and vain babblings, and oppositions of science falsely so called; which some professing have erred concerning the faith." And again, "Thou therefore, my son, be strong in the grace that is in Christ Jesus. And the things that thou has heard of me in many exhortations, the same commit thou to faithful men, who shall be able to teach others also." If, then, the blessed (apostle) delivered these things with a pious caution, which could be easily known by all, as he perceived in the spirit that "all men have not faith," how much greater will be our danger, if, rashly and without thought, we commit the revelations of God to profane and unworthy men?

For as the blessed prophets were made, so to speak, eyes for us, they foresaw through faith the mysteries of the word, and became ministers of these things also to succeeding generations, not only reporting the past, but also announcing the present and the future, so that the prophet might not appear to be one only for the time being, but might also predict the future for all generations, and so be reckoned a (true) prophet. For these fathers were furnished with the Spirit, and largely honoured by the Word Himself; and just as it is with instruments of music, so had they the Word always, like the plectrum, in union with them, and when moved by Him the prophets announced what God willed. For they spake not of their own power (let there be no mistake as to that), neither did they declare what pleased themselves. But first of all they were endowed with wisdom by the Word, and then again were rightly instructed in the future by means of visions. And then, when thus themselves fully convinced, they spake those things which were revealed by God to them alone, and concealed from all others. For with what reason should the prophet be called a prophet, unless he in spirit foresaw the future? For if the prophet spake of any chance event, he would not be a prophet then in speaking of things which were under the eye of all. But one who sets forth in detail things yet to be, was rightly judged a prophet. Wherefore prophets were with good reason called from the very first "seers." And hence we, too, who are rightly instructed in what was declared aforetime by them, speak not of our own capacity. For we do not attempt to make any change one way or another among ourselves in the words that were spoken of old by them, but we make the Scriptures in which these are written public, and read them to those who can believe rightly; for that is a common benefit for both parties: for him who speaks, in holding in memory and setting forth correctly things uttered of old; and for him who hears, in giving attention to the things spoken. Since, then, in this there is a work assigned to both parties together, viz., to him who speaks, that he speak forth faithfully without regard to risk, and to him who hears, that he hear and receive in faith that which is spoken, I beseech you to strive together with me in prayer to God.

Do you wish then to know in what manner the Word of God, who was again the Son of God, as He was of old the Word, communicated His revelations to the blessed prophets in former times? Well, as the Word shows His compassion and His denial of all respect of persons by all the saints, He enlightens them and adapts them to that which is advantageous for us, like a skilful physician, understanding the weakness of men. And the ignorant He loves to teach, and the erring He turns again to His own true way. And by those who live by faith He is easily found; and to those of pure eye and holy heart, who desire to knock at the door, He opens immediately. For He casts away none of His servants as unworthy of the divine mysteries. He does not esteem the rich man more highly than the poor, nor does He despise the poor man for his poverty. He does not disdain the barbarian, nor does He set the eunuch aside as no man. He does not hate the female on account of the woman's act of disobedience in the beginning, nor does He reject the male on account of the man's transgression. But He seeks all, and desires to save all, wishing to make all the children of God, and calling all the saints unto one perfect man. For there is also one Son (or Servant) of God, by whom we too, receiving the regeneration through the Holy Spirit, desire to come all unto one perfect and heavenly man.

For whereas the Word of God was without flesh, He took upon Himself the holy flesh by the holy Virgin, and prepared a robe which He wove for Himself, like a bridegroom, in the sufferings of the cross, in order that by uniting His own power with our mortal body, and by mixing the incorruptible with the corruptible, and the strong with the weak, He might save perishing man. The web-beam, therefore, is the passion of the Lord upon the cross, and the warp on it is the power of the Holy Spirit, and the woof is the holy flesh wrought (woven) by the Spirit, and the thread is the grace which by the love of Christ binds and unites the two in one, and the combs or (rods) are the Word; and the workers are the patriarchs and prophets who weave the fair, long, perfect tunic for Christ; and the

Word passing through these, like the combs or (rods), completes through them that which His Father willeth.

But as time now presses for the consideration of the question immediately in hand, and as what has been already said in the introduction with regard to the glory of God, may suffice, it is proper that we take the Holy Scriptures themselves in hand, and find out from them what, and of what manner, the coming of Antichrist is; on what occasion and at what time that impious one shall be revealed; and whence and from what tribe (he shall come); and what his name is, which is indicated by the number in the Scripture; and how he shall work error among the people, gathering them from the ends of the earth; and (how) he shall stir up tribulation and persecution against the saints; and how he shall glorify himself as God; and what his end shall be; and how the sudden appearing of the Lord shall be revealed from heaven; and what the conflagration of the whole world shall be; and what the glorious and heavenly kingdom of the saints is to be, when they reign together with Christ; and what the punishment of the wicked by fire.

Now, as our Lord Jesus Christ, who is also God, was prophesied of under the figure of a lion, on account of His royalty and glory, in the same way have the Scriptures also aforetime spoken of Antichrist as a lion, on account of his tyranny and violence. For the deceiver seeks to liken himself in all things to the Son of God. Christ is a lion, so Antichrist is also a lion; Christ is a king, so Antichrist is also a king. The Saviour was manifested as a lamb; so he too, in like manner, will appear as a lamb, though within he is a wolf. The Saviour came into the world in the circumcision, and he will come in the same manner. The Lord sent apostles among all the nations, and he in like manner will send false apostles. The Saviour gathered together the sheep that were scattered abroad, and he in like manner will bring together a people that is scattered abroad. The Lord gave a seal to those who believed on Him, and he will give one in like manner. The Saviour appeared in the form of man, and he too will come in the form of a man. The Saviour raised up and showed His holy flesh like a temple, and he will raise a temple of stone in Jerusalem. And his seductive arts we shall exhibit in what follows. But for the present let us turn to the question in hand.

Now the blessed Jacob speaks to the following effect in his benedictions, testifying prophetically of our Lord and Saviour: "Judah, let thy brethren praise thee; thy hand shall be on the neck of thine enemies; thy father's children shall bow down before thee. Judah is a lion's whelp: from the shoot, my son, thou art gone up: he stooped down, he couched as a lion, and as a lion's whelp; who shall rouse him up? A ruler shall not depart from Judah, nor a leader from his thighs, until he come for whom it is reserved; and he shall be the expectation of the nations. Binding his ass to a vine, and his ass's colt to the vine tendril; he shall wash his garment in wine, and his clothes in the blood of the grapes. His eyes shall be gladsome as with wine, and his teeth shall be whiter than milk."

Knowing, then, as I do, how to explain these things in detail, I deem it right at present to quote the words themselves. But since the expressions themselves urge us to speak of them, I shall not omit to do so. For these are truly divine and glorious things, and things well calculated to benefit the soul. The prophet, in using the expression, *a lion's whelp,* means him who sprang from Judah and David according to the flesh, who was not made indeed of the seed of David, but was conceived by the (power of the) Holy Ghost, and came forth from the holy shoot of earth. For Isaiah says, "There shall come forth a rod out of the root of Jesse, and a flower shall grow up out of it." That which is called by Isaiah a *flower,* Jacob calls a shoot. For first he shot forth, and then he flourished in the world. And the expression, "he stooped down, he couched as a lion, and as a lion's whelp," refers to the three days' sleep (death, couching) of Christ; as also Isaiah says, "How is faithful Sion become an harlot! it was full of judgment; in which righteousness lodged (couched); but now murderers." And David says to the same effect, "I laid me down (couched) and slept; I awaked: for the Lord will sustain me;" in which words he points to the fact of his sleep and rising again. And Jacob says, "Who shall rouse him up?" And that is just what David and Paul both refer to, as when Paul says, "and God the Father, who raised Him from the dead."

And in saying, "A ruler shall not depart from Judah, nor a leader from his thighs, until he come for whom it is reserved; and he shall be the expectation of the nations," he referred the fulfilment (of that prophecy) to Christ. For He is our expectation. For we expect Him, (and) by faith we behold Him as He comes from heaven with power.

"Binding his ass to a vine:" that means that He unites His people of the circumcision with His own calling (vocation). For He was the vine. "And his ass's colt to the vine-tendril:" that denotes the people of the Gentiles, as He calls the circumcision and the uncircumcision unto one faith.

"He shall wash his garment in wine," that is, according to that voice of His Father which came down by the Holy Ghost at the Jordan. "And his clothes in the blood of the grape." In the blood of what grape, then, but just His own flesh, which hung upon the tree like a cluster of grapes?—from whose side also flowed two streams, of blood and water, in which the nations are washed and purified, which (nations) He may be supposed to have as a robe about Him.

"His eyes gladsome with wine." And what are the eyes of Christ but the blessed prophets, who foresaw in the Spirit, and announced beforehand, the sufferings that were to befall Him, and rejoiced in seeing Him in power with spiritual eyes, being furnished (for their vocation) by the word Himself and His grace?

And in saying, "And his teeth (shall be) whiter than milk," he referred to the commandments that proceed from the holy mouth of Christ, and which are pure (purify) as milk.

Thus did the Scriptures preach beforetime of this lion and lion's whelp. And in like manner also we find it written regarding Antichrist. For Moses speaks thus: "Dan is a lion's whelp, and he shall leap from Bashan." But that no one may err by supposing that this is said of the Saviour, let him attend carefully to the matter. "Dan," he says, "is a lion's whelp;" and which Antichrist is destined to spring. For as Christ springs from the tribe of Judah, so Antichrist is to spring from the tribe of Dan. And that the case stands thus, we see also from the words of Jacob: "Let Dan be a serpent, lying upon the ground, biting the horse's heel." What, then, is meant by the serpent but Antichrist, that deceiver who is mentioned in Genesis, who deceived Eve and supplanted Adam (πτερνίσας, bruised Adam's heel)? But since it is necessary to prove this assertion by sufficient testimony, we shall not shrink from the task.

That it is in reality out of the tribe of Dan, then, that that tyrant and king, that dread judge, that son of the devil, is destined to spring and arise, the prophet testifies when he says, "Dan shall judge his people, as (he is) also one tribe in Israel." But some one may say that this refers to Samson, who sprang from the tribe of Dan, and judged the people twenty years. Well, the prophecy had its partial fulfilment in Sampson, but its complete fulfilment is reserved for Antichrist. For Jeremiah also speaks to this effect: "From Dan we are to hear the sound of the swiftness of his horses: the whole land trembled *at the sound of the neighing, of the driving of his horses.*" And another prophet says: "He shall gather together all his strength, from the east even to the west. They whom he calls, and they whom he calls not, shall go with him. He shall make the sea white with the sails of his ships, and the plain black with the shields of his armaments. And whosoever shall oppose him in war shall fall by the sword." That these things, then, are said of no one else but that tyrant, and shameless one, and adversary of God, we shall show in what follows.

But Isaiah also speaks thus: "And it shall come to pass, that when the Lord hath performed His whole work upon Mount Zion and on Jerusalem, He will punish (visit) the stout mind, the king of Assyria, and the greatness (height) of the glory of his eyes. For he said, By my strength will I do it, and by the wisdom of my understanding I will remove the bounds of the peoples, and will rob them of their strength: and I will make the inhabited cities tremble, and will gather the whole world in my hand like a nest, and I will lift it up like eggs that are left. And there is no one that shall escape or gainsay me, *and open the mouth and chatter. Shall the axe boast itself without him that heweth therewith? or shall the saw magnify itself without him that shaketh (draweth) it? As if one should raise a rod or a staff, and the staff should lift itself up:* and not thus. But the Lord shall send dishonour unto thy honour; and into thy glory a burning fire shall burn. And the light of Israel shall be a fire, and shall sanctify him in flame, and shall consume the forest like grass."

And again he says in another place: "How hath the exactor ceased, and how hath the oppressor ceased! God hath broken the yoke of the rulers of sinners, He who smote the people in wrath, and with an incurable stroke: He that strikes the people with an incurable stroke, which He did not spare. He ceased (rested) confidently: the whole earth shouts with rejoicing. The trees of Lebanon rejoiced at thee, and the cedar of Lebanon, (saying), Since thou art laid down, no feller is come up against us. Hell from beneath is moved at meeting thee: all the mighty ones, the rulers of the earth, are gathered together— the lords from their thrones. All the kings of the nations, all they shall answer together, and shall say, And thou, too, art taken as we; and thou art reckoned among us. Thy pomp is brought down to earth, thy great rejoicing: they will spread decay under thee; and the worm shall be thy covering. How art thou fallen from heaven, O Lucifer, son of the morning! He is cast down to the ground who sends off to all the nations. And thou didst say in thy mind, I will ascend into heaven, I will set my throne above the stars of heaven: I will sit down upon the lofty mountains towards the north: I will ascend above the clouds: I will be like the Most High. Yet now thou shalt be brought down to hell, and to the foundations of the earth! They that see thee shall wonder at thee, and shall say, This is the man that excited the earth, that did shake kings, that made the whole world a wilderness, and destroyed the cities, that released not those in prison. All the kings of the earth did lie in honour, every one in his own house; but thou shalt be cast out on the mountains like a loathsome carcase, with many who fall, pierced through with the sword, and going down to hell. As a garment stained with blood is not pure, so neither shall thou be comely (or clean); because thou hast destroyed my land, and slain my people. Thou shalt not abide, enduring for ever, a wicked seed. Prepare thy children for slaughter, for the sins of thy father, that they rise not, neither possess my land."

St. Hippolytus of Rome

Ezekiel also speaks of him to the same effect, thus: "Thus saith the Lord God, Because thine heart is lifted up, and thou hast said, I am God, I sit in the seat of God, in the midst of the sea; yet art thou a man, and not God, (though) thou hast set thine heart as the heart of God. Art thou wiser than Daniel? Have the wise not instructed thee in their wisdom? With thy wisdom or with thine understanding hast thou gotten thee power, and gold and silver in thy treasures? By thy great wisdom and by thy traffic hast thou increased thy power? Thy heart is lifted up in thy power. Therefore thus saith the Lord God: Because thou hast set thine heart as the heart of God: behold, therefore I will bring strangers upon thee, plagues from the nations: and they shall draw their swords against thee, and against the beauty of thy wisdom; and they shall level thy beauty to destruction; and they shall bring thee down; and thou shalt die by the death of the wounded in the midst of the sea. Wilt thou yet say *before them that slay thee, I am God? But thou art a man, and no God, in the hand of them that wound thee. Thou shalt die the deaths of the uncircumcised by the hand of* strangers: for I have spoken it, saith the Lord."

These words then being thus presented, let us observe somewhat in detail what Daniel says in his visions. For in distinguishing the kingdoms that are to rise after these things, he showed also the coming of Antichrist in the last times, and the consummation of the whole world. In expounding the vision of Nebuchadnezzar, then, he speaks thus: "Thou, O king, sawest, and behold a great image standing before thy face: the head of which was of fine gold, its arms and shoulders of silver, its belly and its thighs of brass, and its legs of iron, (and) its feet part of iron and part of clay. Thou sawest, then, till that a stone was cut out without hands, and smote the image upon the feet that were of iron and clay, and brake them to an end. Then were the clay, the iron, the brass, the silver, (and) the gold broken, and became like the chaff from the summer threshing-floor; and the strength (fulness) of the wind carried them away, and there was no place found for them. And the stone that smote the image became a great mountain, and filled the whole earth."

Now if we set Daniel's own visions also side by side with this, we shall have one exposition to give of the two together, and shall (be able to) show how concordant with each other they are, and how true. For he speaks thus: "I Daniel saw, and behold the four winds of the heaven strove upon the great sea. And four great beasts came up from the sea, diverse one from another. The first (was) like a lioness, and had wings as of an eagle. I beheld till the wings thereof were plucked, and it was lifted up from the earth, and made stand upon the feet as a man, and a man's heart was given to it. And behold a second beast like to a bear, and it was made stand on one part, and it had three ribs in the mouth of it. I beheld, and lo a beast like a leopard, and it had upon the back of it four wings of a fowl, and the beast had four heads. After this I saw, and behold a fourth beast, dreadful and terrible, and strong exceedingly: it had iron teeth *and claws of brass,* which devoured and brake in pieces, and it stamped the residue with the feet of it; and it was diverse from all the beasts that were before it, and it had ten horns. I considered its horns, and behold there came up among them another little horn, and before it there were three of the first horns plucked up by the roots; and behold in this horn were eyes like the eyes of man, and a mouth speaking great things."

"I beheld till the thrones were set, and the Ancient of days did sit: and His garment was white as snow, and the hair of His head like pure wool: His throne was a flame of fire, His wheels were a burning fire. A stream of fire flowed before Him. Thousand thousands ministered unto Him, and ten thousand times ten thousand stood around Him: the judgment was set, and the books were opened. I beheld then, because of the voice of the great words which the horn spake, till the beast was slain and perished, and his body given to the burning of fire. And the dominion of the other beasts was taken away."

"I saw in the night vision, and, behold, one like the Son of man was coming with the clouds of heaven, and came to the Ancient of days, and was brought near before Him. And there was given Him dominion, and honour, and the kingdom; and all peoples, tribes, and tongues shall serve Him: His dominion is an everlasting dominion, which shall not pass away, and His kingdom shall not be destroyed."

Now since these things, spoken as they are with a mystical meaning, may seem to some hard to understand, we shall keep back nothing fitted to impart an intelligent apprehension of them to those who are possessed of a sound mind. He said, then, that a "lioness came up from the sea," and by that he meant the kingdom of the Babylonians in the world, which also was the head of gold on the image. In saying that "it had wings as of an eagle," he meant that Nebuchadnezzar the king was lifted up and was exalted against God. Then he says, "the wings thereof were plucked," that is to say, his glory was destroyed; for he was driven out of his kingdom. And the words, "a man's heart was given to it, and it was made stand upon the feet as a man," refer to the fact that he repented and recognised himself to be only a man, and gave the glory to God.

Then, after the lioness, he sees a "second beast like a bear," and that denoted the Persians. For after the Babylonians, the Persians held the sovereign power. And in saying that there were "three ribs in the mouth of it," he pointed to three nations, viz., the Persians, and the Medes, and the Babylonians; which were also represented on the image by the silver after the gold. Then (there was) "the third beast, a leopard," which meant the Greeks. For after the Persians, Alexander of Macedon obtained the sovereign power on subverting Darius, as is also shown by the brass on the image. And in saying that it had "four wings of a fowl," he taught us most clearly how the kingdom of Alexander was partitioned. For in speaking of "four heads," he made mention of four kings, viz., those who arose out of that (kingdom). For Alexander, when dying, partitioned out his kingdom into four divisions.

Then he says: "A fourth beast, dreadful and terrible; it had iron teeth and claws of brass." And who are these but the Romans? which (kingdom) is meant by the iron—the kingdom which is now established; for the legs of that (image) were of iron. And after this, what remains, beloved, but the toes of the feet of the image, in which part is iron and part clay, mixed together? And mystically by the toes of the feet he meant the kings who are to arise from among them; as Daniel also says (in the words), "I considered the beast, and lo there were ten horns behind it, among which shall rise another (horn), an offshoot, and shall pluck up by the roots the three (that were) before it." And under this was signified none other than Antichrist, who is also himself to raise the kingdom of the Jews. He says that three horns are plucked up by the root by him, viz., the three kings of Egypt, and Libya, and Ethiopia, whom he cuts off in the array of battle. And he, after gaining terrible power over all, being nevertheless a tyrant, shall stir up tribulation and persecution against men, exalting himself against them. For Daniel says: "I considered the horn, and behold that horn made war with the saints, and prevailed against them, till the beast was slain and perished, and its body was given to the burning of fire."

After a little space the stone will come from heaven which smites the image and breaks it in pieces, and subverts all the kingdoms, and gives the kingdom to the saints of the Most High. This is the stone which becomes a great mountain, and fills the whole earth, of which Daniel says: "I saw in the night visions, and behold one like the Son of man came with the clouds of heaven, and came to the Ancient of days, and was brought near before Him. And there was given Him dominion, and glory, and a kingdom; and all peoples, tribes, and languages shall serve Him: and His dominion is an everlasting dominion, which shall not pass away, and His kingdom shall not be destroyed." He showed all power given by the Father to the Son, who is ordained Lord of things in heaven, and things on earth, and things under the earth, and Judge of all: of things in heaven, because He was born, the Word of God, before all (ages); and of things on earth, because He became man in the midst of men, to recreate our Adam through Himself; and of things under the earth, because He was also reckoned among the dead, preaching the Gospel to the souls of the saints, (and) by death overcoming death.

As these things, then, are in the future, and as the ten toes of the image are equivalent to (so many) democracies, and the ten horns of the fourth beast are distributed over ten kingdoms, let us look at the subject a little more closely, and consider these matters as in the clear light of a personal survey.

The golden head of the image and the lioness denoted the Babylonians; the shoulders and arms of silver, and the bear, represented the Persians and Medes; the belly and thighs of brass, and the leopard, meant the Greeks, who held the sovereignty from Alexander's time; the legs of iron, and the beast dreadful and terrible, expressed the Romans, who hold the sovereignty at present; the toes of the feet which were part clay and part iron, and the ten horns, were emblems of the kingdoms that are yet to rise; the other little horn that grows up among them meant the Antichrist in their midst; the stone that smites the earth and brings judgment upon the world was Christ.

These things, beloved, we impart to you with fear, and yet readily, on account of the love of Christ, which surpasseth all. For if the blessed prophets who preceded us did not choose to proclaim these things, though they knew them, openly and boldly, lest they should disquiet the souls of men, but recounted them mystically in parables and dark sayings, speaking thus, "Here is the mind which hath wisdom," how much greater risk shall we run in venturing to declare openly things spoken by them in obscure terms! Let us look, therefore, at the things which are to befall this unclean harlot in the last days; and (let us consider what and what manner of tribulation is destined to visit her in the wrath of God before the judgment as an earnest of her doom.

Come, then, O blessed Isaiah; arise, tell us clearly what thou didst prophesy with respect to the mighty Babylon. For thou didst speak also of Jerusalem, and thy word is accomplished. For thou didst speak boldly and openly: "Your country is desolate, your cities are burned with fire; your land, strangers devour it in your presence, and it is desolate as overthrown by man strangers. The daughter of Sion shall be left as a cottage in a vineyard, and as a lodge in a garden of cucumbers, as a besieged city." What then? Are not these things come to pass? Are not the things announced by thee fulfilled? Is not their country, Judea, desolate? Is not the holy place burned with fire? Are not their walls cast down? Are not their cities destroyed? Their land, do not strangers devour it? Do not the Romans rule the country? And indeed these impious people hated thee, and did saw thee asunder, and they crucified Christ. Thou art dead in the world, but thou livest in Christ.

Which of you, then, shall I esteem more than thee? Yet Jeremiah, too, is stoned. But if I should esteem Jeremiah most, yet Daniel too has his testimony. Daniel, I commend thee above all; yet John too gives no false witness. With how many mouths and tongues would I praise you; or rather the Word who spake in you! Ye died with Christ; and ye will live with Christ. Hear ye, and rejoice; behold the things announced by you have been fulfilled in their time. For ye saw these things yourselves first, and then ye proclaimed them to all generations. Ye ministered the oracles of God to all generations. Ye prophets were called, that ye might be able to save all. For then is one a prophet indeed, when, having announced beforetime things about to be, he can afterwards show that they have actually happened. Ye were the disciples of a good Master. These words I address to you as if alive, and with propriety. For ye hold already the crown of life and immortality which is laid up for you in heaven.

Speak with me, O blessed Daniel. Give me full assurance, I beseech thee. Thou dost prophesy concerning the lioness in Babylon; for thou wast a captive there. Thou hast unfolded the future regarding the bear; for thou wast still in the world, and didst see the things come to pass. Then thou speakest to me of the leopard; and whence canst thou know this, for thou art already gone to thy rest? Who instructed thee to announce these things, but He who formed thee in (from) thy mother's womb? That is God, thou sayest. Thou hast spoken indeed, and that not falsely. The leopard has arisen; the he-goat is come; he hath smitten the ram; he hath broken his horns in pieces; he hath stamped upon him with his feet. He has been exalted by his fall; (the) four horns have come up from under that one. Rejoice, blessed Daniel! thou hast not been in error: all these things have come to pass.

After this again thou hast told me of the beast dreadful and terrible. "It had iron teeth and claws of brass: it devoured and brake in pieces, and stamped the residue with the feet of it." Already the iron rules; already it subdues and breaks all in pieces; already it brings all the unwilling into subjection;

already we see these things ourselves. Now we glorify God, being instructed by thee.

But as the task before us was to speak of the harlot, be thou with us, O blessed Isaiah. Let us mark what thou sayest about Babylon. "Come down, sit upon the ground, O virgin daughter of Babylon; sit, O daughter of the Chaldeans; thou shalt no longer be called tender and delicate. Take the millstone, grind meal, draw aside thy veil, shave the grey hairs, make bare the legs, pass over the rivers. Thy shame shall be uncovered, thy reproach shall be seen: I will take justice of thee, I will no more give thee over to men. As for thy Redeemer, (He is) the Lord of hosts, the Holy One of Israel is his name. Sit thou in compunction, get thee into darkness, O daughter of the Chaldeans: thou shalt no longer be called the strength of the kingdom.

"I was wroth with my people; I have polluted mine inheritance, I have given them into thine hand: and thou didst show them no mercy; but upon the ancient (the elders) thou hast very heavily laid thy yoke. And thou saidst, I shall be a princess for ever: thou didst not lay these things to thy hearts, neither didst remember thy latter end. Therefore hear now this, thou that art delicate; that sittest, that art confident, that sayest in thine heart, I am, and there is none else; I shall not sit as a widow, neither shall I know the loss of children. But now these two things shall come upon thee in one day, widowhood and the loss of children: they shall come upon thee suddenly in thy sorcery, in the strength of thine enchantments mightily, in the hope of thy fornication. For thou hast said, I am, and there is none else. And thy fornication shall be thy shame, because thou hast said in thy heart, I am. And destruction shall come upon thee, and thou shalt not know it. *(And there shall be) a pit, and thou shalt fall into it; and misery shall fall upon thee, and thou shalt not be able to be made clean; and destruction shall come upon thee, and thou shalt not know it.* Stand now with thy enchantments, and with the multitude of thy sorceries, which thou hast learned from thy youth; if so be thou shalt be able to be profited. Thou art wearied in thy counsels. Let the astrologers of the heavens stand and save thee; let the star-gazers announce to thee what shall come upon thee. Behold, they shall all be as sticks for the fire; so shall they be burned, and they shall not deliver their soul from the flame. Because thou hast coals of fire, sit upon them; so shall it be for thy help. Thou art wearied with change from thy youth. Man has gone astray (each one) by himself; and there shall be no salvation for thee." These things does Isaiah prophesy for thee. Let us see now whether John has spoken to the same effect.

For he sees, when in the isle Patmos, a revelation of awful mysteries, which he recounts freely, and makes known to others. Tell me, blessed John, apostle and disciple of the Lord, what didst thou see and hear concerning Babylon? Arise, and speak; for it sent thee also into banishment. "And there came one of the seven angels which had the seven vials, and talked with me, saying unto me, Come hither; I will show unto thee the judg-ment of the great whore that sitteth upon many waters; with whom the kings of the earth have committed fornication, and the inhabitants of the earth have been made drunk with the wine of her fornication. And he carried me away in the spirit into the wilderness: and I saw a woman sit upon a scarlet-coloured beast, full of names of blasphemy, having seven heads and ten horns. And the woman was arrayed in purple and scarlet colour, and decked with gold, and precious stone, and pearls, having a golden cup in her hand, full of abominations and filthiness of the fornication of the earth. Upon her forehead was a name written, Mystery, Babylon the Great, the Mother of Harlots and Abominations of the Earth.

"And I saw the woman drunken with the blood of the saints, and with the blood of the martyrs of Jesus: and when I saw her, I wondered with great admiration. And the angel said unto me, Wherefore didst thou marvel? I will tell thee the mystery of the woman, and of the beast that carrieth her, which hath the seven heads and the ten horns. The beast that thou sawest was, and is not; and shall ascend out of the bottomless pit, and go into perdition: and they that dwell on the earth shall wonder (whose name was not written in the book of life from the foundation of the world) when they behold the beast that was, and is not, and yet shall be.

"And here is the mind that has wisdom. The seven heads are seven mountains, on which the woman sitteth. And there are seven kings: five are fallen, and one is, and the other is not yet come; and when he cometh, he must continue a short space. And the beast that was *and* is not, (even he is the eighth,) and is of the seven, and goeth into perdition. And the ten horns which thou sawest are ten kings, which have received no kingdom as yet; but receive power as kings one hour with the beast. These have one mind, and shall give their power and strength unto the beast. These shall make war with the Lamb, and the Lamb shall overcome them: for he is Lord of lords, and King of kings; and they that are with Him are called, and chosen, and faithful.

"And he saith to me, The waters which thou sawest, where the whore sitteth, are peoples, and multitudes, and nations, and tongues. And the ten horns which thou sawest, and the beast, these shall hate the whore, and shall make her desolate and naked, and shall eat her flesh, and burn her with fire. For God hath put in their hearts to fulfil His will, and to agree, and give their kingdom unto the beast, until the words of God shall be fulfilled. And the woman which thou sawest is that great city, which reigneth over the kings of the earth.

"After these things I saw another angel come down from heaven, having great power; and the earth was lightened with his glory. And he cried mightily with a strong voice, saying, Babylon the great is fallen, is fallen, and is become the habitation of devils, and the hold of every foul spirit, *and a cage of every unclean* and hateful bird. For all nations have drunk of the wine of the wrath of her fornication, and the kings of the earth have committed fornication with her, and the merchants of the earth are waxed rich through the abundance of her delicacies. And I heard another voice from heaven, saying, Come out of her, my people, that ye be not partakers of her sins, and that ye receive not of her plagues: for her sins did cleave even unto heaven, and God hath remembered her iniquities.

"Reward her even as she rewarded (you), and double unto her double, according to her works: in the cup which she hath filled, fill to her double. How much she hath glorified herself, and lived deliciously, so much torment and sorrow give her: for she saith in her heart, I sit a queen, and am no widow, and shall see no sorrow. Therefore shall her plagues come in one day, death, and mourning, and famine; and she shall be utterly burned with fire: for strong is the Lord God who judgeth her. And the kings of the earth, who have committed fornication, and lived deliciously with her, shall bewail her, and lament for her, when they shall see the smoke of her burning, standing afar off for the fear of her torment, saying, Alas, alas! that great city Babylon, that mighty city! for in one hour is thy judgment come. And the merchants of the earth shall weep and mourn over her; for no man shall buy their merchandise any more. The merchandise of gold, and silver, and precious stones, and of pearls, and fine linen, and purple, and silk, and scarlet, and all thyine wood, and all manner vessels of ivory, and all manner vessels of most precious wood, and of brass, and iron, and marble, and cinnamon, and spices, and odours, and ointments, and frankincense, and wine, and oil, and fine flour, and wheat, and beasts, and sheep, and goats, and horses, and chariots, and slaves (bodies), and souls of men. And the fruits that thy soul lusted after are departed from thee, and all things which were dainty and goodly have perished from thee, and thou shalt find them no more at all. The merchants of these things, which were made rich by her, shall stand afar off for the fear of her torment, weeping and wailing, and saying, Alas, alas! that great city, that was clothed in fine linen, and purple, and scarlet, and decked with gold, and precious stones, and pearls! for in one hour so great riches is come to nought. And every shipmaster, and all the company in ships, and sailors, and as many as trade by sea, stood afar off, and cried, when they saw the smoke of her burning, saying, What city is like unto this great city? And they cast dust on their heads, and cried, weeping and wailing, saying, Alas, alas! that great city, wherein were made rich all that had ships in the sea by reason of her fatness! for in one hour is she made desolate.

"Rejoice over her, thou heaven, and ye angels, and apostles, and prophets; for God hath avenged you on her. And a mighty angel took up a stone like a great millstone, and cast it into the sea, saying, Thus with violence shall that great city Babylon be thrown down, and shall be found no more at all. And the voice of harpers and musicians, and of pipers and trumpeters, shall be heard no more at all in thee; and no craftsman, of whatsoever

66

craft he be, shall be found any more in thee; and the sound of a millstone shall be heard no more at all in thee; and the light of a candle shall shine no more at all in thee; and the voice of the bridegroom and of the bride shall be heard no more at all in thee: for thy merchants were the great men of the earth; for by thy sorceries were all nations deceived. And in her was found the blood of prophets and of saints, and of all that were slain upon the earth."

With respect, then, to the particular judgment in the torments that are to come upon it in the last times by the hand of the tyrants who shall arise then, the clearest statement has been given in these passages. But it becomes us further diligently to examine and set forth the period at which these things shall come to pass, and how the little horn shall spring up in their midst. For when the legs of iron have issued in the feet and toes, according to the similitude of the image and that of the terrible beast, as has been shown in the above, (then shall be the time) when the iron and the clay shall be mingled together. Now Daniel will set forth this subject to us. For he says, "And one week will make a covenant with many, and it shall be that in the midst (half) of the week my sacrifice and oblation shall cease." By one week, therefore, he meant the last week which is to be at the end of the whole world; of which week the two prophets Enoch and Elias will take up the half. For they will preach 1,260 days clothed in sackcloth, proclaiming repentance to the people and to all the nations.

For as two advents of our Lord and Saviour are indicated in the Scriptures, the one being His first advent in the flesh, which took place without honour by reason of His being set at nought, as Isaiah spake of Him aforetime, saying, "We saw Him, and He had no form nor comeliness, but His form was despised (and) rejected (lit. = deficient) above all men; a man smitten and familiar with bearing infirmity, (for His face was turned away); He was despised, and esteemed not." But His second advent is announced as glorious, when He shall come from heaven with the host of angels, and the glory of His Father, as the prophet saith, "Ye shall see the King in glory;" and, "I saw one like the Son of man coming with the clouds of heaven; and he came to the Ancient of days, and he was brought to Him. And there were given Him dominion, and honour, and glory, and the kingdom; all tribes and languages shall serve Him: His dominion is an everlasting dominion, which shall not pass away." Thus also two forerunners were indicated. The first was John the son of Zacharias, who appeared in all things a forerunner and herald of our Saviour, preaching of the heavenly light that had appeared in the world. He first fulfilled the course of forerunner, and that from his mother's womb, being conceived by Elisabeth, in order that to those, too, who are children from their mother's womb he might declare the new birth that was to take place for their sakes by the Holy Ghost and the Virgin.

He, on hearing the salutation addressed to Elisabeth, leaped with joy in his mother's womb, recognising God the Word conceived in the womb of the Virgin. Thereafter he came forward preaching in the wilderness, proclaiming the baptism of repentance to the people, (and thus) announcing prophetically salvation to the nations living in the wilderness of the world. After this, at the Jordan, seeing the Saviour with his own eye, he points Him out, and says, "Behold the Lamb of God, that taketh away the sin of the world!" He also first preached to those in Hades, becoming a forerunner there when he was put to death by Herod, that there too he might intimate that the Saviour would descend to ransom the souls of the saints from the hand of death.

But since the Saviour was the beginning of the resurrection of all men, it was meet that the Lord alone should rise from the dead, by whom too the judgment is to enter for the whole world, that they who have wrestled worthily may be also crowned worthily by Him, by the illustrious Arbiter, to wit, who Himself first accomplished the course, and was received into the heavens, and was set down on the right hand of God the Father, and is to be manifested again at the end of the world as Judge. It is a matter of course that His forerunners must appear first, as He says by Malachi and the angel, "I will send to you Elias the Tishbite before the day of the Lord, the great and notable day, comes; and he shall turn the hearts of the fathers to the children, and the disobedient to the wisdom of the just, lest I come and smite the earth utterly." These, then, shall come and proclaim the manifestation of Christ that is to be from heaven; and they shall also perform signs and wonders, in order that men may be put to shame and turned to repentance for their surpassing wickedness and impiety.

For John says, "And I will give power unto my two witnesses, and they shall prophesy a thousand two hundred and threescore days, clothed in sackcloth." That is the half of the week whereof Daniel spake. "These are the two olive trees and the two candlesticks standing before the Lord of the earth. And if any man will hurt them, fire will proceed out of their mouth, and devour their enemies; and if any man will hurt them, he must in this manner be killed. These have power to shut heaven, that it rain not in the days of their prophecy; and have power over waters, to turn them to blood, and to smite the earth with all plagues as often as *they will. And when* they shall have finished their course and their testimony," what saith the prophet? "the beast that ascendeth out of the bottomless pit shall make war against them, and shall overcome them, and kill them," because they will not give glory to Antichrist. For this is meant by the little horn that grows up. He, being now elated in heart, begins to exalt himself, and to glorify himself as God, persecuting the saints and blaspheming Christ, even as Daniel says, "I considered the horn, and, behold, in the horn were eyes like the eyes of man, and a mouth speaking great things; and he opened his mouth to blaspheme God. And that horn made war against the saints, and prevailed against them until the beast was slain, and perished, and his body was given to be burned."

But as it is incumbent on us to discuss this matter of the beast more exactly, and in particular the question how the Holy Spirit has also mystically indicated his name by means of a number, we shall proceed to state more clearly what bears upon him. John then speaks thus: "And I beheld another beast coming up out of the earth; and he had two horns, like a lamb, and he spake as a dragon. And he exercised all the power of the first beast before him; and he made the earth and them which dwell therein to worship the first beast, whose deadly wound was healed. And he did great wonders, so that he maketh fire come down from heaven on the earth in the sight of men, and deceiveth them that dwell on the earth by means of those miracles which he had power to do in the sight of the beast, saying to them that dwell on the earth, that they should make an image to the beast which had the wound by a sword and did live. And he had power to give life unto the image of the beast, *that the image of the beast should both speak,* and cause that as many as would not worship the image of the beast should be killed. And he caused all, both small and great, rich and poor, free and bond, to receive a mark in their right hand or in their forehead; and that no man might buy or sell, save he that had the mark, the name of the beast, or the number of his name. Here is wisdom. Let him that hath understanding count the number of the beast; for it is the number of a man, and his number is six hundred threescore and six."

By the beast, then, coming up out of the earth, he means the kingdom of Antichrist; and by the two horns he means him and the false prophet after him. And in speaking of "the horns being like a lamb," he means that he will make himself like the Son of God, and set himself forward as king. And the terms, "he spake like a dragon," mean that he is a deceiver, and not truthful. And the words, "he exercised all the power of the first beast before him, and caused the earth and them which dwell therein to worship the first beast, whose deadly wound was healed," signify that, after the manner of the law of Augustus, by whom the empire of Rome was established, he too will rule and govern, sanctioning everything by it, and taking greater glory to himself. For this is the fourth beast, whose head was wounded and healed again, in its being broken up or even dishonoured, and partitioned into four crowns; and he then (Antichrist) shall with knavish skill heal it, as it were, and restore it. For this is what is meant by the prophet when he says, "He will give life unto the image, and the image of the beast will speak." For he will act with vigour again, and prove strong by reason of the laws established by him; and he will cause all those who will not worship the image of the beast to be put to death. Here the faith and the patience of the saints will appear, for he says: "And he will cause all, both small and great, rich and poor, free and bond, to receive a mark in their right hand or in their forehead; that no man might buy or sell, save he that had the mark, the name of the beast, or the number of his name." For, being full of guile, and exalting himself against the servants of God, with the wish to afflict them and persecute them out of the world, because they give not glory to him, he will order incense-pans to be set up by all everywhere, that no man among the saints may be able to buy or sell without first sacrificing; for this is what is meant by the mark received upon the right hand. And the word—"in their forehead"—indicates that all are crowned, and put on a crown of fire, and not of life, but of death. For in this wise, too, did Antiochus Epiphanes the king of Syria, the descendant of Alexander of Macedon, devise measures against the Jews. He, too, in the exaltation of his heart, issued a decree in those times, that "all should set up shrines before their doors, and sacrifice, and that they should march in procession to the honour of Dionysus, waving chaplets of ivy;" and that those who refused obedience should be put to death by strangulation and torture. But he also met his due recompense at the hand of the Lord, the righteous Judge and all-searching God; for he died eaten up of worms. And if one desires to inquire into that more accurately, he will find it recorded in the book of the Maccabees.

But now we shall speak of what is before us. For such measures will he, too, devise, seeking to afflict the saints in every way. For the prophet and apostle says: "Here is wisdom, Let him that hath understanding count the number of the beast; for it is the number of a man, and his number is six hundred threescore and six." With respect to his name, it is not in our power to explain it exactly, as the blessed John understood it and was instructed about it, but only to give a conjectural account of it; for when he appears, the blessed one will show us what we seek to know. Yet as far as our doubtful apprehension of the matter goes, we may speak. Many names indeed we find, the letters of which are the equivalent of this number: such as, for instance, the word Titan, an ancient and notable name; or Evanthas, for it too makes up the same number; and many others which might be found. But, as we have already said, the wound of the first beast was healed, and he (the second beast) was to make the image speak, that is to say, he should be powerful; and it is manifest to all that those who at present still hold the power are Latins. If, then, we take the name as the name of a single man, it becomes *Latinus*. Wherefore we ought neither to give it out as if this were certainly his name, nor again ignore the fact that he may not be otherwise designated. But having the mystery of God in our heart, we ought in fear to keep faithfully what has been told us by the blessed prophets, in order that when those things come to pass, we may be prepared for them, and not deceived. For when the times advance, he too, of whom these things are said, will be manifested.

But not to confine ourselves to these words and arguments alone, for the purpose of convincing those who love to study the oracles of God, we shall demonstrate the matter by many other proofs. For Daniel says, "And these shall escape out of his hand, even Edom, and Moab, and the chief of the children of Ammon." Ammon and Moab are the children born to Lot by his daughters, and their race survives even now. And Isaiah says: "And they shall fly in the boats of strangers, plundering the sea together, and (they shall spoil) them of the east: and they shall lay hands upon Moab first; and the children of Ammon shall first obey them."

In those times, then, he shall arise and meet them. And when he has overmastered three horns out of the ten in the array of war, and has rooted these out, viz., Egypt, and Libya, and Ethiopia, and has got their spoils and trappings, and has brought the remaining horns which suffer into subjection, he will begin to be lifted up in heart, and to exalt himself against God as master of the whole world. And his first expedition will be against Tyre and Berytus, and the circumjacent territory. For by storming these cities first he will strike terror into the others, as Isaiah says, "Be thou ashamed, O Sidon; the sea hath spoken, even the strength of the sea hath spoken, saying, I travailed not, nor brought forth children; neither did I nurse up young men, nor bring up virgins. But when the report comes to Egypt, pain shall seize them for Tyre."

These things, then, shall be in the future, beloved; and when the three horns are cut off, he will begin to show himself as God, as Ezekiel has said aforetime: "Because thy heart has been lifted up, and thou hast said, I am God." And to the like effect Isaiah says: "For thou hast said in thine heart, I will ascend into heaven, I will exalt my throne above the stars of heaven: I will be like the Most High. Yet now thou shall be brought down to hell (Hades), to the foundations of the earth." In like manner also Ezekiel: "Wilt thou yet say to those who slay thee, I am God? But thou (shalt be) a man, and no God."

As his tribe, then, and his manifestation, and his destruction, have been set forth in these words, and as his name has also been indicated mystically, let us look also at his action. For he will call together all the people to himself, out of every country of the dispersion, making them his own, as though they were his own children and promising to restore their country, and establish again their kingdom and nation, in order that he may be worshipped by them as God, as the prophet says: "He will collect his whole kingdom, from the rising of the sun even to its setting: they whom he summons and they whom he does not summon shall march with him." And Jeremiah speaks of him thus in a parable: "The partridge cried, (and) gathered what he did not hatch, making himself riches without judgment: in the midst of his days they shall leave him, and at his end he shall be a fool."

It will not be detrimental, therefore, to the course of our present argument, if we explain the art of that creature, and show that the prophet has not spoken without a purpose in using the parable (or similitude) of the creature. For as the partridge is a vainglorious creature, when it sees near at hand the nest of another partridge with young in it, and with the parent-bird away on the wing in quest of food, it imitates the cry of the other bird, and calls the young to itself; and they, taking it to be their own parent, run to it. And it delights itself proudly in the alien pullets as in its own. But when the real parent-bird returns, and calls them with its own familiar cry, the young recognise it, and forsake the deceiver, and betake themselves to the real parent. This thing, then, the prophet has adopted as a simile, applying it in a similar manner to Antichrist. For he will allure mankind to himself, wishing to gain possession of those who are not his own, and promising deliverance to all, while he is unable to save himself.

73

He then, having gathered to himself the unbelieving everywhere throughout the world, comes at their call to persecute the saints, their enemies and antagonists, as the apostle and evangelist says: "There was in a city a judge, which feared not God, neither regarded man: and there was a widow in that city, who came unto him, saying, Avenge me of mine adversary. And he would not for a while: but afterward he said within himself, Though I fear not God, nor regard man; yet because this widow troubleth me, I will avenge her."

By the unrighteous judge, who fears not God, neither regards man, he means without doubt Antichrist, as he is a son of the devil and a vessel of Satan. For when he has the power, he will begin to exalt himself against God, neither in truth fearing God, nor regarding the Son of God, who is the Judge of all. And in saying that there was a widow in the city, he refers to Jerusalem itself, which is a widow indeed, forsaken of her perfect, heavenly spouse, God. She calls Him her adversary, and not her Saviour; for she does not understand that which was said by the prophet Jeremiah: "Because they obeyed not the truth, a spirit of error shall speak then to this people and to Jerusalem." And Isaiah also to the like effect: "Forasmuch as the people refuseth to drink the water of Siloam that goeth softly, but chooseth to have Rasin and Romeliah's son as king over you: therefore, lo, the Lord bringeth up upon you the water of the river, strong and full, even the king of Assyria." By the king he means metaphorically Antichrist, as also another prophet saith: "And this man shall be the peace from me, when the Assyrian shall come up into your land, and when he shall tread in your mountains."

And in like manner Moses, knowing beforehand that the people would reject and disown the true Saviour of the world, and take part with error, and choose an earthly king, and set the heavenly King at nought, says: "Is not this laid up in store with me, and sealed up among my treasures? In the day of vengeance I will recompense (them), and in the time when their foot shall slide." They did slide, therefore, in all things, as they were found to be in harmony with the truth in nothing: neither as concerns the law, because they became transgressors; nor as concerns the prophets, because they cut off even the prophets themselves; nor as concerns the voice of the Gospels, because they crucified the Saviour Himself; nor in believing the apostles, because they persecuted them. At all times they showed themselves enemies and betrayers of the truth, and were found to be haters of God, and not lovers of Him; and such they shall be then when they find opportunity: for, rousing themselves against the servants of God, they will seek to obtain vengeance by the hand of a mortal man. And he, being puffed up with pride by their subserviency, will begin to despatch missives against the saints, commanding to cut them all off everywhere, on the ground of their refusal to reverence and worship him as God, according to the word of Esaias: "Woe to the wings of the vessels of the land, beyond the rivers of Ethiopia: (woe to him) who sendeth sureties by the sea, and letters of papyrus (upon the water; for nimble messengers will go) to a nation anxious and expectant, and a people strange and bitter against them; a nation hopeless and trodden down."

But we who hope for the Son of God are persecuted and trodden down by those unbelievers. For the *wings of the vessels* are the churches; and the sea is the world, in which the Church is set, like a ship tossed in the deep, but not destroyed; for she has with her the skilled Pilot, Christ. And she bears in her midst also the trophy (which is erected) over death; for she carries with her the cross of the Lord. For her prow is the east, and her stern is the west, and her hold is the south, and her tillers are the two Testaments; and the ropes that stretch around her are the love of Christ, which binds the Church; and the net which she bears with her is the laver of the regeneration which renews the believing, whence too are these glories. As the wind the Spirit from heaven is present, by whom those who believe are sealed: she has also anchors of iron accompanying her, viz., the holy commandments of Christ Himself, which are strong as iron. She has also mariners on the right and on the left, assessors like the holy angels, by whom the Church is always governed and defended. The ladder in her leading up to the sailyard is an emblem of the passion of Christ, which brings the faithful to the ascent of heaven. And the top-sails aloft upon the yard are the company of prophets, martyrs, and apostles, who have entered into their rest in the kingdom of Christ.

Now, concerning the tribulation of the persecution which is to fall upon the Church from the adversary, John also speaks thus: "And I saw a great and wondrous sign in heaven; a woman clothed with the sun, and the moon under her feet, and upon her head a crown of twelve stars. And she, being with child, cries, travailing in birth, and pained to be delivered. And the dragon stood before the woman which was ready to be delivered, for to devour her child as soon as it was born. And she brought forth a man-child, who is to rule all the nations: and the child was caught up unto God and to His throne. And the woman fled into the wilderness, where she hath the place prepared of God, that they should feed her there a thousand two hundred and threescore days. And then when the dragon saw *it*, he persecuted the woman which brought forth the man-*child*. And to the woman were given two wings of the great eagle, that she might fly into the wilderness, where she is nourished for a time, and times, and half a time, from the face of the serpent. And the serpent cast (out of his mouth water as a flood after the woman, that he might cause her to be carried away of the flood. And the earth helped the woman, and opened her mouth, and swallowed up the flood which the dragon cast) out of his mouth. And the dragon was wroth with the woman, and went to make war with the saints of her seed, which keep the commandments of God, and have the testimony of Jesus."

By the "woman then clothed with the sun," he meant most manifestly the Church, endued with the Father's word, whose brightness is above the sun. And by "the moon under her feet" he referred to her being adorned, like the moon, with heavenly glory. And the words, "upon her head a crown of twelve stars," refer to the twelve apostles by whom the Church was founded. And those, "she, being with child, cries, travailing in birth, and pained to be delivered," mean that the Church will not cease to bear from her heart the Word that is persecuted by the unbelieving in the world. "And she brought forth," he says, "a man-child, who is to rule all the nations;" by which is meant that the Church, always bringing forth Christ, the perfect man-child of God, who is declared to be God and man, becomes the instructor of all the nations. And the words, "her child was caught up unto God and to His throne," signify that he who is always born of her is a heavenly king, and not an earthly; even as David also declared of old when he said, "The Lord said unto my Lord, Sit Thou at my right hand, until I make Thine enemies Thy footstool." "And the dragon," he says, "saw and persecuted the woman which brought forth the man-*child*. And to the woman were given two wings of the great eagle, that she might fly into the wilderness, where she is nourished for a time, and times, and half a time, from the face of the serpent." That refers to the one thousand two hundred and threescore days (the half of the week) during which the tyrant is to reign and persecute the Church, which flees from city to city, and seeks concealment in the wilderness among the mountains, possessed of no other defence than the two wings of the great eagle, that is to say, the faith of Jesus Christ, who, in stretching forth His holy hand on the holy tree, unfolded two wings, the right and the left, and called to Him all who believed upon Him, and covered them as a hen her chickens. For by the mouth of Malachi also He speaks thus: "And unto you that fear my name shall the Sun of righteousness arise with healing in His wings."

The Lord also says, "When ye shall see the abomination of desolation stand in the holy place (whoso readeth, let him understand), then let them which be in Judea flee into the mountains, and let him which is on the housetop not come down to take his clothes; neither let him which is in the field return back to take anything out of his house. And woe unto them that are with child, and to them that give suck, in those days! for then shall be great tribulation, such as was not since the beginning of the world. And except those days should be shortened, there should no flesh be saved." And Daniel says, "And they shall place the abomination of desolation a thousand two hundred and ninety days. Blessed is he that waiteth, and cometh to the thousand two hundred and ninety-five days."

And the blessed Apostle Paul, writing to the Thessalonians, says: "Now we beseech you, brethren, concerning the coming of our Lord Jesus Christ, and our gathering together at it, that ye be not soon shaken in mind, or be troubled, neither by spirit, nor by word, nor by letters as from us, as that the day of the

Lord is at hand. Let no man deceive you by any means; for (that day shall not come) except there come the falling away first, and that man of sin be revealed, the son of perdition, who opposeth and exalteth himself above all that is called God, or that is worshipped: so that he sitteth in the temple of God, showing himself that he is God. Remember ye not, that when I was yet with you, I told you these things? And now ye know what withholdeth, that he might be revealed in his time. For the mystery of iniquity doth already work; only he who now letteth (will let), until he be taken out of the way. And then shall that wicked be revealed, whom the Lord Jesus shall consume with the Spirit of His mouth, and shall destroy with the brightness of His coming: (even him) whose coming is after the working of Satan, with all power, and signs, and lying wonders, and with all deceivableness of unrighteousness in them that perish; because they received not the love of the truth. And for this cause God shall send them strong delusion, that they should believe a lie: that they all might be damned who believed not the truth, but had pleasure in unrighteousness." And Esaias says, "Let the wicked be cut off, that he behold not the glory of the Lord."

These things, then, being to come to pass, beloved, and the one week being divided into two parts, and the abomination of desolation being manifested then, and the two prophets and forerunners of the Lord having finished their course, and the whole world finally approaching the consummation, what remains but the coming of our Lord and Saviour Jesus Christ from heaven, for whom we have looked in hope? who shall bring the conflagration and just judgment upon all who have refused to believe on Him. For the Lord says, "And when these things begin to come to pass, then look up, and lift up your heads; for your redemption draweth nigh." "And there shall not a hair of your head perish." "For as the lightning cometh out of the east, and shineth even unto the west, so shall also the coming of the Son of man be. For wheresoever the carcase is, there will the eagles be gathered together." Now the fall took place in paradise; for Adam fell there. And He says again, "Then shall the Son of man send His angels, and they shall gather together His elect from the four winds of heaven." And David also, in announcing prophetically the judgment and coming of the Lord, says, "His going forth is from the end of the heaven, and His circuit unto the end of the heaven: and there is no one hid from the heat thereof." By the heat he means the conflagration. And Esaias speaks thus: "Come, my people, enter thou into thy chamber, (and) shut thy door: hide thyself as it were for a little moment, until the indignation of the Lord be overpast." And Paul in like manner: "For the wrath of God is revealed from heaven against all ungodliness and unrighteousness of men, who hold the truth of God in unrighteousness."

Moreover, concerning the resurrection and the kingdom of the saints, Daniel says, "And many of them that sleep in the dust of the earth shall arise, some to everlasting life, (and some to shame and everlasting contempt)." Esaias says, "The dead men shall arise, and they that are in their tombs shall awake; for the dew from thee is healing to them." The Lord says, "Many in that day shall hear the voice of the Son of God, and they that hear shall live." And the prophet says, "Awake, thou that sleepest, and arise from the dead, and Christ shall give thee light." And John says, "Blessed and holy is he that hath part in the first resurrection: on such the second death hath no power." For the second death is the lake of fire that burneth. And again the Lord says, "Then shall the righteous shine forth as the sun shineth in his glory." And to the saints He will say, "Come, ye blessed of my Father, inherit the kingdom prepared for you from the foundation of the world." But what saith He to the wicked? "Depart from me, ye cursed, into everlasting fire, prepared for the devil and his angels, which my Father prepared." And John says, "Without are dogs, and sorcerers, and whoremongers, and murderers, and idolaters, and whosover maketh and loveth a lie; for your part is in the hell of fire." And in like manner also Esaias: "And they shall go forth and look upon the carcases of the men that have transgressed against me. And their worm shall not die, neither shall their fire be quenched; and they shall be for a spectacle to all flesh."

Concerning the resurrection of the righteous, Paul also speaks thus in writing to the Thessalonians: "We would not have you to be ignorant concerning them which are asleep, that ye sorrow not even as others which have no hope. For if we believe that Jesus died and rose again, even so them also which sleep in Jesus will God bring with Him. For this we say unto you by the word of the Lord, that we which are alive (and) remain unto the coming of the Lord, shall not prevent them which are asleep. For the Lord Himself shall descend from heaven with a shout, with the voice and trump of God, and the dead in Christ shall rise first. Then we which are alive (and) remain shall be caught up together with them in the clouds to meet the Lord in the air; and so shall we ever be with the Lord."

These things, then, I have set shortly before thee, O Theophilus, drawing them *from Scripture itself,* in order that, maintaining in faith what is written, and anticipating the things that are to be, thou mayest keep thyself void of offence both toward God and toward men, "looking for that blessed hope and appearing of our God and Saviour," when, having raised the saints among us, He will rejoice with them, glorifying the Father. To Him be the glory unto the endless ages of the ages. Amen.

Origen
185-253

Origen has been called the father of Christian theology and the founder of biblical science. He was "the outstanding teacher and scholar of the early Church, a man of spotless character, encyclopedic learning, and one of the most original thinkers the world has ever seen." But it was also "Origen's destiny to be a sign of contradiction during his lifetime as well as after his death. There is hardly anyone who made so many friends or so many enemies." (Quasten). His benefactor, a man named Ambrose whom he had converted from Valentinianism, put unlimited means at his disposal to assist his prodigious literary activity. He is thought to have produced over six thousand works, although later conversions caused many of them to be destroyed.

Origen was born of Christian parents and his father died a martyr in 202. Bishop Demetrius soon after placed the teen-aged Origen in charge of the famous school for catechumens in Alexandria. He labored with great success until complications with the bishop caused him to move to Caesarea in 231 and open another school, over which he presided for almost twenty years.

The Dialogue with Heraclides is actually the minutes of a discussion held at a meeting of bishops summoned to examine the opinions of a certain Bishop Heraclides whose orthodoxy *had been called into question. It was an informal, not a judicial, gathering; Origen had apparently been called in to straighten out the situation by clarifying the meaning of certain theological formulations. The work was unknown until 1941 when British soldiers discovered it in a cave south of Cairo, along with several other papyri, all of which probably date from the late 6th century.*

Origen leads the discussion so that Heraclides has to answer and express himself according to Origen's terms. The Logos theology of the Fourth Gospel was apparently at issue, since Origen's cross-examination was aimed at getting Heraclides to admit the pre-existence and independent existence of the Son. Heraclides was thus probably suspected of some kind of modalism.

The awkwardness of some of the expressions in light of later refinements will be obvious. The strong emphasis on the independent existence of the Son in relation to the Father resulted in the acceptability (for a time) of speaking of them as "two Gods" with "one power." This misleading formulation would ultimately have to be abandoned, but it is important to see from the context that what was being defended was what will later be expressed as "two persons" in "one nature." As Owen Chadwick has put it: "Origen's theology is intended to steer a middle course . . . Only the doctrine that the Logos is both separate from and one with the Father avoids heresy . . . He (Origen) begins by thinking of two Gods and then tries to explain how they are one, never vice versa."

The latter part of the discussion wanders far afield. The main business had been attended to and Origen invited questions on any other points of theology. An awkward one based on Leviticus 17:11 was thrown at him: "Is the soul the blood?" Theologians of all ages can take comfort from watching a master like Origen squirm as he tries to avoid offending the unlearned yet make it clear that much in Scripture is to be understood figuratively, not literally, spiritually, not physically.

The Dialogue with Heraclides *is unique in giving us so vivid a picture of the early Church's greatest theologian in operation, sharing his insights publicly in a way that commends itself to all generations.*

DIALOGUE WITH HERACLIDES

A fter the bishops present had raised questions concerning the faith of the bishop Heraclides, that he might confess before all the faith which he held, and after each one had said what he thought and asked questions, Heraclides said:

I also believe what the sacred Scriptures say: "In the beginning was the Word, and the Word was with God, and the Word was God. He was in the beginning with God. All things were made by him, and without him nothing was made." Accordingly, we hold the same faith that is taught in these words, and we believe that Christ took flesh, that he was born, that he went up to heaven in the flesh in which he rose again, that he is sitting at the right hand of the Father, and that thence he shall come and judge the living and the dead, being God and man.

Origen said: Since once an inquiry has begun it is proper to say something upon the subject of the inquiry, I will speak. The whole church is present and listening. It is not right that there should be any difference in knowledge between one church and another, for you are not the false church.

I charge you, father Heraclides: God is the almighty, the uncreated, the supreme God who made all things. Do you hold this doctrine?

Heracl.: I do. That is what I also believe.

Orig.: Christ Jesus who was in the form of God, being other than the God in whose form he existed, was he God before he came into the body or not?

Heracl.: He was God before.

Orig.: Was he God before he came into the body or not?

Heracl.: Yes, he was.

Orig.: Was he God distinct from this God in whose form he existed?

Heracl.: Obviously he was distinct from another being and, since he was in the form of him who created all things, he was distinct from him.

Orig.: Is it true then that there was a God, the Son of God, the only begotten of God, the firstborn of all creation, and that we need have no fear of saying that in one sense there are two Gods, while in another there is one God?

Heracl.: What you say is evident. But we affirm that God is the almighty, God without beginning, without end, containing all things and not contained by anything; and that his Word is the Son of the living God, God and man, through whom all things were made, God according to the spirit, man inasmuch as he was born of Mary.

Orig.: You do not appear to have answered my question. Explain what you mean. For perhaps I failed to follow you. Is the Father God?

Heracl.: Assuredly.

Orig.: Is the Son distinct from the Father?

Heracl.: Of course, How can he be Son if he is also Father?

Orig.: While being distinct from the Father is the Son himself also God?

Heracl.: He himself is also God.

Orig.: And do two Gods become a unity?

Heracl.: Yes.

Orig.: Do we confess two Gods?

Heracl.: Yes. The power is one.

Orig.: But as our brethren take offence at the statement that there are two Gods, we must formulate the doctrine carefully, and show in what sense they are two and in what sense the two are one God. Also the holy Scriptures have taught that several things which are two are one. And not only things which are two, for they have also taught that in some instances more than two, or even a very much larger number of things, are one. Our present task is not to broach a problematic subject only to pass it by and deal cursorily with the matter, but for the sake of the simple folk to chew up, so to speak, the meat, and little by little to instil the doctrine in the ears of our hearers . . . . Accordingly, there are many things which are two that are said in the Scriptures to be one. What passages of Scripture? Adam is one person, his wife another. Adam is distinct from his wife, and his wife is distinct from her husband. Yet it is said in the story of the creation of the world that they two are one: "For the two shall be one flesh." Therefore, sometimes two beings can become one flesh. Notice, however, that in the case of Adam and Eve it is not said that the two shall become one spirit, nor that the two shall become one soul, but that they shall become one flesh. Again, the righteous man is distinct from Christ; but he is said by the apostle to be one with Christ: "For he that is joined to the Lord is one spirit." Is it not true that the one is of a subordinate nature or of a low and inferior nature, while Christ's nature is divine and glorious and blessed? Are they therefore no longer two? Yes, for the man and the woman are "no longer two but one flesh," and the righteous man and Christ are "one spirit." So in relation to the Father and God of the universe, our Saviour and Lord is not one flesh, nor one spirit, but something higher than flesh and spirit, namely, one God. The appropriate word when human beings are joined to one another is flesh. The appropriate word when a righteous man is joined to Christ is spirit. But the word when Christ is united to the Father is not flesh, nor spirit, but more honourable than these—God. That is why we understand in this sense "I and the Father are one." When we pray, because of the one party let us preserve the duality, because of the other party let us hold to the unity. In this way we avoid falling into the opinion of those who have been separated from the Church and turned to the illusory notion of monarchy, who abolish the Son as distinct from the Father and virtually abolish the Father also. Nor do we fall into the other blasphemous doctrine which denies the deity of Christ. What then do the divine Scriptures mean when they say: "Beside me there is no other God, and there shall be none after me," and "I am and there is no God but me"? In these utterances we are not to think that the unity applies to the God of the universe . . . in separation from Christ, and certainly not to Christ in separation from God. Let us rather say that the sense is the same as that of Jesus' saying, "I and my Father are one."

It is necessary to study these doctrines because there has been much disturbance in this church. Often people write and demand a signature of the bishop and of those they suspect, asking that they should give their signatures in the presence of all the people, that there may be no further disturbance or dispute about this question. Accordingly, with the permission of God and secondly of the bishops, thirdly of the presbyters, and also of the people, I will again say what I think on this subject. Offering is universally made to Almighty God through Jesus Christ inasmuch as, in respect of his deity, he is akin to the Father. Let there be no double offering, but an offering to God through God. I shall seem to be speaking in a daring manner. When we pray let us abide by the agreements. If the word: "Thou shalt not respect the person of man, nor allow thyself to be impressed by the person of the mighty" is not realized . . . If this is not realized . . . these agreements, it will give rise to fresh disputes . . . . If a man is a bishop or a presbyter, he is not a bishop, he is not a presbyter. If he is a deacon, he is not a deacon, nor even a layman. If he is a layman, he is not a layman, nor is there a meeting of the congregation. If you assent, let these agreed usages prevail.

Some people raise the objection that, with reference to the problem of deity, while I have thus attributed deity to Jesus Christ substantially, I have professed before the church my faith that at the resurrection the body which rose had been a corpse. But since our Saviour and Lord took a body, let us examine what the body was. The church alone in distinction from all the heresies that deny the resurrection confesses the resurrection of the dead body. For from the fact that the firstfruits were raised from the dead, it follows that the dead are raised. "Christ the firstfruits"; on that account his body became a corpse. For if his body had not become a corpse, capable of being wrapped in a grave-cloth, of receiving the ointment and all the other things applied to dead bodies, and of being laid in a tomb—these are things that cannot be done to a spiritual body. For it is entirely impossible for that which is spiritual to become a corpse, neither can that which is spiritual become insensible. For if it were possible for that which is spiritual to become a corpse, we would have reason to fear lest after the resurrection of the dead, when our body is raised, according to the apostle's saying, "It is sown animate, it is raised spiritual," we shall all die . . . . In fact "Christ being raised from the dead dies no more." And not only Christ, but those who are Christ's, when they are raised from the dead, die no more. If you agree to these statements, they also with the solemn testimony of the people shall be made legally binding and established.

What else is there to be said concerning the faith? Do you agree to this, Maximus? Say.

Maximus: May everyone hold the same doctrines as I do. Before God and the Church I both give my signature and make my oath. But the reason why I raised a certain question was in order that I might be in no doubt or uncertainty at all. For the brethren know that this is what I said: "I need the help of my brother and instruction on this point." If the spirit was truly given back to the Father, in accordance with the saying, "Father, into thy hands I commend my spirit," and if without the spirit the flesh died and lay in the tomb, how was the tomb opened and how are the dead to rise again?

Orig.: That man is a composite being we have learnt from the sacred Scriptures. For the apostle says, "May God sanctify your spirit and your soul and your body," and "May he sanctify you wholly, and may your entire spirit and soul and body be preserved unblameable at the coming of our Lord Jesus Christ." This spirit is not the Holy Spirit, but part of the constitution of man, as the same apostle teaches when he says: "The spirit bears witness with our spirit." For if it were the Holy Spirit he would not have said: "The spirit bears witness with our spirit." So then our Saviour and Lord, wishing to save man in the way in which he wished to save him, for this reason desired in this way to save the body, just as it was likewise his will to save also the soul; he also wished to save the remaining part of man, the spirit. The whole man would not have been saved unless he had taken upon him the whole man. They do away with the salvation of the human body when they say that the body of the Saviour is spiritual. They do away with the salvation of the human spirit, concerning which the apostle says: "No man knows the things of man except the spirit of man that is in him." . . . Because it was his will to save the spirit of man, about which the apostle said this, he also assumed the spirit of man. At the time of the passion these three were separated. At the time of the resurrection these three were united. At the time of the passion they were separated—how? The body in the tomb, the soul in Hades, the spirit was put in the hands of the Father. The soul in Hades: "Thou shalt not leave my soul in Hades." If the spirit was put into the hands of the Father, he gave the spirit as a deposit. It is one thing to make a gift, another thing to hand over, and another to leave in deposit. He who makes a deposit does so with the intention of receiving back that which he has deposited. Why then had he to give the spirit to the Father as a deposit? The question is beyond me and my powers and my understanding. For I am not endowed with knowledge to enable me to say that, just as the body was not able to go down to Hades, even if this is alleged by those who affirm that the body of Jesus was spiritual, so also neither could the spirit go down to Hades, and therefore he gave the spirit to the Father as a deposit until he should have risen from the dead . . . . After he had entrusted this deposit to the Father, he took it back again. When? Not at the actual moment of the resurrection, but immediately after the resurrection. My witness is the text of the gospel. The Lord Jesus Christ rose again from the dead. Mary met him and he said to her: "Touch me not." For he wished anyone that touched him to touch him in his entirety, that having touched him in his entirety he might be benefited in body from his body, in soul from his soul, in spirit from his spirit. "For I am not yet ascended to the Father." He ascends to the Father and comes to the disciples. Accordingly he ascends to the Father. Why? To receive back the deposit.

All the questions about the faith which disturbed us have been examined. But we must realize that at the divine tribunal we are not judged for faith alone, as if our life were left unexamined, nor for our life alone, as if our faith were not subject to scrutiny. We are justified on the ground that both are correct. We are punished for both if both are incorrect. There are some, however, who will not be punished for both, but for one of the two: some for their faith because it is defective, but not because their life is lacking in right conduct; others, again, will not be punished for their faith, but will be for their life, on the ground that they have lived a life contrary to right reason. My opinion is that in the Proverbs of Solomon these two kinds (I mean that which concerns our belief and knowledge and that which concerns our manner of life) are mentioned by Solomon in the following words: "Who shall boast that he has a pure heart? Or who shall present himself saying that he is free from sins?" The difference between these we take to be this: the "heart" means the thought, the "sins" refer to actions. "Who shall boast that he has a pure heart" which is undefiled by the knowledge falsely so-called, undefiled by falsehood? Or "who shall present himself saying that he is free from sins," having done nothing amiss in his practical conduct? If then we wish to be saved, let us not be concerned about faith to the neglect of practical conduct of life, nor again let us place our confidence in our life. Let us realize, let us comprehend, let us believe that it is on the ground of both that we either receive our acquittal or blessedness, nor receive the opposite of these. The things that are liable to punishment, therefore, are not merely the terrible and fearful sins which should not even be named, whether sins of life or of thought, but also sins commonly thought to be of less importance. That is why, it seems, the apostle puts side by side with acts which are abominable, infamous, and revolting (if I may so say) things which are regarded by most people as of little significance. What does he say? "Be not deceived; neither fornicators, nor adulterers, nor effeminate men, nor homosexuals, nor thieves, nor drunkards, nor revilers, shall inherit the kingdom of God." You see that together with such gross sinners as the homosexual person, the effeminate man, the adulterer, the fornicator, he enumerates the drunkard, the reviler—sins thought by all of us to be of small account, so that we may be taught that it is not for the great sins alone that we are excluded from the kingdom of God, but also for these which are commonly supposed to be of minor significance. Therefore, let us not revile, nor be drunkards, nor extort, nor steal, nor do anything wrong, even if we are "deceived."

If there is any further point to raise concerning the Rule of faith, mention it. We will speak still further upon the Scripture.

Dionysius said: Is the soul the blood?

THE CATHOLIC TRADITION: The Saviour

Orig.: It has come to my notice, and I say this with full knowledge of the facts, that some of the folk here and in the neighbourhood suppose that after the soul has departed this life it is incapable of feeling, but is in the tomb, in the body. And I know that on this question I was impelled to deal very severely with the other Heraclides and Celer his predecessor, so severely in fact that I would have preferred to leave the subject and to go away. But for the sake of honour and for the subject under debate he summoned us to deal with it. We agreed to discuss the matter; he made a statement . . . how the former cleared himself before us, as though before God, by his orthodox statements.

Accordingly, the question posed by the beloved Dionysius forces our hand. I shall first set out the passages which trouble them, lest any one of them be omitted, and by God's permission we will answer each one of them in accordance with your request. The disturbing passage is as follows: "The soul of all flesh is blood." This text has terribly distressed those who have not understood it. Also, "Ye shall not eat the soul with the flesh; pay strict heed to see that you eat no blood; ye shall not eat the soul with the flesh." The disturbing text is this one. For the other distressing texts are far less emphatic in expressing the idea suggested here. For my part, according to my measure of understanding, and praying for assistance in reading the divine words (for we are in need of help lest our minds should conceive ideas diverging from the truth), I have found that incorporeal things are given the same names as all the corporeal things, so that just as corporeal things apply to the outer man, those which are given the same names as corporeal things apply to the inner man. The Bible says that man is two men: "For if our outward man perish, yet our inward man is renewed day by day," and "I rejoice in the law of God after the inward man." These two men the apostle everywhere shows to be distinct. In my judgment he would not have ventured to invent this notion out of his own head, but rather said this because he had clearly understood statements in the Scriptures which are obscurely expressed. Some people imagine that there is a mere repetition when in the story of the creation of the world after the creation of man we read "God took dust of the earth and formed man." The corollary of this interpretation is that it is the body which is the part "after the image," and that God is given a human form, or that the form of God is shaped like the human body. But we are not so crazy as to say either that God is composed of a superior and an inferior element so that that which is in his image is like him in both elements, which constitute God in his completeness, or that that which is in his image consisted rather in the inferior part and not in the superior.

The questions are highly delicate. We need hearers who have an acute understanding. I therefore charge those who listen to pay heed to themselves lest they should make me liable to the accusation of casting holy things to the dogs, to shameless souls. For the barkers, like dogs, those who think only of fornication and abuse, do nothing but yelp like dogs, and it is not right for me to cast holy things before such folk. So also I charge my hearers that they do not make me liable to the accusation of laying splendid pearls, which we try to collect like good merchants, before people steeped in the impurities of their bodies, and who are therefore called swine. For I would say that a person who continually steeps himself and wallows in the filth of life and makes no attempt to live a pure life, a holy life, is simply a swine. If then, because the kingdom of heaven is like a merchant seeking goodly pearls, I find the goodly pearls, and having bought them at the price of weariness and sleeplessness I fling them before pleasure-loving souls, and those who are steeped in the filth of the body and in impurity, then I also will be a transgressor because I am casting pearls before swine. But when the swine have got the pearls, because they do not perceive their beauty nor see their excellence, they tread them under foot by speaking evil of what was rightly said, and not only do they trample the pearls under foot, but they also turn and rend those who supplied them with the pearls.

I beseech you, therefore, be transformed. Resolve to learn that in you there is the capacity to be transformed, and to put off the form of a swine, which is in an impure soul, and the shape of a dog, which is that of a man who barks and reviles and pours out abuse. It is also possible to be transformed from the shape of snakes; for a wicked man is described as a serpent and "the offspring of vipers." If, then, we are willing to understand

91

that in us there is the power to be transformed from being serpents, swine, and dogs, let us learn from the apostle that the transformation depends upon us. For he says this: "We all, when with unveiled face we reflect the glory of the Lord, are transformed into the same image." If you are like a barking dog, and if the Word has moulded and transformed you, you have been transformed from being a dog to being a man. If you were impure and the Word came to your soul and you submitted yourself to the moulding of the Word, you changed from being a swine to being a man. If you were a savage beast, and heard the Word that tames and softens, that changes you into a man, by the will of the Word you will no longer be called a serpent, the offspring of vipers. For if it were impossible for these serpents, serpents in their soul because of wickedness, to be changed, the Saviour (or John) would not have said: "Do therefore fruits worthy of repentance." After repentance you are no longer a serpent, the offspring of vipers.

Since it is our task to speak about man, and to inquire whether the soul of man is not blood, and since this subject required us to discuss in detail the doctrine of the two men, and as we have come to a mysterious subject, I beseech you that you do not cause me to be accused of casting pearls before swine, of throwing holy things to the dogs, of flinging divine things to serpents, of giving the serpent a share in the tree of life. That I may avoid this accusation, be transformed, put off evil, quarrelling, wrath, strife, anger, division of opinion, that there may not be any further schisms among you but that "you may be firmly established in the same mind and the same judgment."

To speak makes me embarrassed, and not to speak makes me embarrassed. Because of those who are worthy I would speak, lest I be accused of depriving of the word those able to understand it. Because of the unworthy I shrink from speaking for the reasons I have given, lest I should be flinging holy things to dogs and casting pearls before swine. It was the work of Jesus only to know how to distinguish among his hearers between those without and those within, so that he spoke to those without in parables, but explained the parables to those who entered into his house. To remain without and to enter into the house have a mystical meaning. "Why should I judge those that are without?" Every sinner is without. That is why those without are addressed in parables in case they should be able to leave the things without and enter within. To enter the house has a mystical meaning: He who enters Jesus' house is his true disciple. He enters by holding the doctrine of the church, by living a life according to the teaching of the church. "Within" and "without" are spiritual terms.

You see how long an introduction I have given in order to prepare my hearers. I shrink from speaking. When I am on the point of speaking I put it off. What is my purpose in doing this? To shape my discourse so as to heal the souls of my hearers.

At the creation of man, then, there was first created the man that is "after the image," in whom there was nothing material. He who is in the image is not made out of matter. "And God said, Let us make man in our image and likeness, and let them have dominion" and so on. And when God made man he did not take dust of the earth, as he did the second time, but he made him in the image of God. That that which is in the image of God is understood as immaterial and superior to all corporeal existence not only by Moses but also by the apostle is shown by his words, as follows: "Putting off the old man with his deeds and putting on the new which is renewed in the knowledge of him who created him."

Therefore in each one of us there are two men. Why does Scripture say that the soul of all flesh is blood? It is a great problem. Just as the outward man has the same name as the inward man, so also this is true of his members, so that one may say that every member of the outward man has a name corresponding to what is true of the inward man.

The outward man has eyes, and the inward man also is said to have eyes: "Lighten my eyes lest I sleep in death." This does not refer to these eyes, nor to physical sleep, nor to ordinary death. "The commandment of the Lord, luminous, enlightens the eyes." By keeping the commandments of the Lord we do not become more sharp-sighted physically but by keeping the divine commands we become more sharp-sighted in mind. The eyes of our inward man see with greater perception: "Open my eyes and I shall comprehend the wonders of thy Law." It is not that his eyes were veiled; but our eyes are our mind. It is for Jesus alone to unveil them, that we may be able to understand the Scriptures and comprehend what is obscurely expressed.

The outward man has ears, and the inward man also is said to have ears. "He that has ears to hear, let him hear." They all had ears as organs of physical sense; but they had not all succeeded in having the inward ears which are purified. To possess the latter sort of ears is not part of our natural constitution; the former are part of our nature. And because the former sort of ears are part of our nature the prophet says, "Hear ye deaf, and ye blind, look and see. Who is deaf but my servants, and who is blind but those who are their lords? Even the servants of God are blinded." That to become deaf is what we bring upon ourselves—let us pay attention: what I am saying will affect all of us; it is necessary to describe the inward man to discover what the blood is—that to become deaf in respect of the inward ears is something we bring upon ourselves, hear the declaration of the prophet: "Sinners are alienated from the womb; they have erred from the womb. They have spoken lies. Wrath is upon them after the likeness of the serpent, like a deaf adder which stops her ears, which does not hear the voice of those who enchant her and the incantation pronounced by a wise man." And all of you also who are aware that you are responsible, if you hear the word and the incantation pronounced by a wise man and listen to the enchanting words, so that he may check your wrath and iniquity, and if, then, you shut your ears, and do not throw them wide open to accept what is said, then to you apply the words: "Wrath is on them after the likeness of the serpent like a deaf adder which stops her ears, which does not hear the voice of those who enchant her and the incantation pronounced by a wise man."

The outward man has nostrils with which to smell, and so perceives good and bad smells; and the inner man with different nostrils perceives the good smell of righteousness and the bad smell of sins. Of the good smell the apostle teaches us when he says, "We are a sweet savour of Christ unto God in every place, among them that are saved and them that are perishing; to the one a savour of death unto death, to the others a savour of life

94

unto life." And Solomon also says in the Song of Songs, putting the words into the mouth of the daughter of Jerusalem: "After thee we will run to the odour of thy perfumes." As, then, we perceive with our nostrils good and bad smells in the world of sense, so also for the inward man there is a perception of the good smell of righteousness such as the apostle had, and an evil smell of sins, which is possessed by the person whose divine senses are in good health. What is the evil smell of sins? That of which the prophet says this: "My sores have become foul and rotten in face of my foolishness."

The outward man has the sense of taste; and the inner man also has a spiritual taste, of which it is said: "Taste and see that the Lord is kindly."

The outward man has physical touch. The inner man also has touch, that touch by which the woman with the issue of blood touched the hem of Jesus' garment. She touched it. For he witnessed to the fact saying, "Who touched me?" Yet just before Peter said to him, "The crowds throng you and you say, Who touched me?" He imagined that those who touched him, touched by physical, not spiritual contact. Those, therefore, who thronged Jesus did not touch him. For they did not touch him by faith. Only the woman, who had a sort of divine touch, touched Jesus and by this was healed. And because she touched him with a divine touch, power went out from Jesus at her divine touch. He says therefore: "Who touched me? For I have felt power to go forth from me." Concerning this more divine touch John says: "And our hands have handled concerning the word of life."

In this way we possess other hands, concerning which it is said: "Let the lifting up of my hands be an evening sacrifice." For it is not when I lift up these hands, while the hands of my soul hang down instead of being lifted up by holy and good works, that the lifting up of my hands becomes an evening sacrifice. I also have feet of a different kind, concerning which Solomon commands me saying, "Let not thy foot stumble."

There is a curious saying in Ecclesiastes. To anyone that does not understand it it will seem meaningless, but it is for the wise man that Ecclesiastes says: "The wise man has his eyes in his head." In what head? Every man, even the blockhead and the fool, has his bodily eyes in his bodily head. But "the wise man has his eyes" (those of which I have already spoken, which are enlightened by the Lord's commandment) "in his head," in Christ, since "Christ is the head of a man," the apostle says. The thinking faculty is in Christ.

"My belly, my belly is in pain," says Jeremiah. In what belly is he in pain? That in which we too feel pain, that by which, when it is in travail bringing the people to birth; "I suffer pain in my belly and my sense"—not these senses, but those of my heart.

Even if I pass on to the fine parts of the body, I see them in the soul under an unfleshly form. "Lord, reprove me not in thine anger; chastise me not in thy anger. Have pity on me, Lord, for I am feeble. Heal me Lord, for my bones are troubled." What bones of the prophet were troubled? The constitution of his soul and the firmness of his mind was troubled, and he implored the Lord for the restoration of those bones. "Our bones are scattered in Hades." What bones of the speaker were scattered in Hades? Consider, I pray you, the sinner, consider his frame in the domain of sin, in the domain of the dead, in the domain of evil, and you will say of such a man that his bones are scattered. "All my bones will say, Lord who is like unto thee?" They are the bones which speak, converse with, and perceive God, whereas these bones are incapable of perception, as is shown by the sons of physicians; when they saw off a man's bones, he does not feel the saw. "All my bones will say, Lord who is like unto thee?" All the bones are those which belong to the inner man.

The inner man has a heart. "Hear me, ye who have lost your heart." They possessed a heart, that of the body; it was not that heart which they lost. But when a man neglects to cultivate his intellectual life, and in consequence of much idleness his thinking capacity has atrophied, he has lost his heart, and it is to such a person that the words are added: "Hear me, ye who have lost your heart."

"The hairs of your head are all numbered." What hairs? Those by virtue of which they were Nazirites in a spiritual sense.

Thus you have all the parts of the visible body in the inner man. Do not doubt, then, concerning the blood also because it has the same name as physical blood, like the other members of the body. It is that which belongs to the inner man. It is that blood which is poured forth from a sinful soul. For "The blood of your souls shall be required." It does not say "your blood" but "the blood of your souls." And "I will require the blood at the hand of the watchman." What kind of blood does God require at the hand of the watchman, but that which is poured forth from the sinner? Thus the heart of the fool perishes, and it is said, "Hear me, ye who have lost your heart," because there is poured forth the blood and the vital power of the soul.

If one comprehends what the soul is, and that it belongs to the inner man, and that it is in that part there is the element which is "in the image," it is clear that Paul was right when he said: "For it were better to depart and to be with Christ." Before the resurrection the righteous man is with Christ and in his soul he lives with Christ. That is why it is better to depart and to be with Christ. But according to you who say that the soul remains in the tomb with the body, it has not left the body, it does not rest, it does not dwell in the paradise of God, it does not repose in the bosom of Abraham. According to you who maintain such absurd doctrines it would not be better to depart and to be with Christ. For one is not with Christ as soon as one departs if the soul is the blood. If the soul remains in the tombs, how can it be with Christ? But according to my view and that of the word of God, the soul which has departed from the troubles, the sweat, and the body, that which can say, "Lord now lettest thou thy servant depart in peace," is that which departs in peace and rests with Christ. It is thus that the soul of Abraham understood the words: "As for thee, thou shalt go in peace to thy fathers, having lived to a good old age." He departed to his fathers. What fathers? Those of whom Paul says: "For this cause I bow my knees to the Father of whom all fatherhood is derived." In our view it was in this sense that Aaron was set free. Also it is written in Ecclesiastes concerning the just man who has fought a good fight, who is departing from the fetter of the body, that "From the house of the prisoners he will go forth to be a king." Thus I am persuaded to die for the truth, thus I readily despise what is called death. Bring wild beasts, bring crosses, bring fire, bring tortures. I know that as soon as I die, I come forth from the body, I rest with Christ. Therefore let us struggle, therefore let us wrestle, let us groan being in the body, not as if we shall again be in the tombs in the body, because we shall be set free from it, and shall change our body to one which is more spiritual. Destined as we are to be with Christ, how we groan while we are in the body!

Bishop Philip came in, and Demetrius, another bishop, said: Brother Origen teaches that the soul is immortal.

Orig.: The remark of father Demetrius has given us the starting point for another problem. He asserted that we have said the soul is immortal. To this remark I will say that the soul is immortal and the soul is not immortal. Let us first define the meaning of the word "death," and determine all its possible senses. I will try to show all its meanings not by appealing to the Greeks,.but all its meanings as found in the divine Scripture. Perhaps one more learned than I will point out other senses also. But for the present I am aware of three kinds of death. What are these three kinds of death? According to the apostle, a man may live unto God and die unto sin. This death is a blessed thing. A man dies to sin. This death my Lord died. "For in that he died, he died unto sin." I know also another sort of death, according to which a man dies to God; concerning this it was said: "The soul that sins, it shall die." And I know of a third kind of death, according to which we commonly suppose that those who are separated from the body die. For "Adam lived nine hundred and thirty years and died."

There being, then, three kinds of death, let us see whether the human soul is immortal in respect of the three kinds of death, or if not in respect of the three, yet in respect of some of them. The death that is a matter of moral indifference all men die. It is that which we consider dissolution. No soul of man dies this death. For if it did so, it would not be punished after death. It is said: "Men shall seek for death and shall not find it." In this sense every human soul is immortal. But in the other meanings, the soul in one sense is mortal, and blessed if it dies to sin. It is of this death that Balaam spoke when he prophesied, praying by divine inspiration: "May my soul die among the souls of the just." Concerning this death Balaam made his astonishing prophecy, and by the word of God he made for himself a splendid prayer. For he prayed that he might die to sin that he might live unto God. And this account he said: "May my soul die among the souls of the just and my posterity be like their posterity." There is another death in respect of which we are not immortal, although we have the power by exercising vigilance to avoid death. And perhaps that which is mortal in the soul is not for ever mortal. For in so far as it gives way to sin, so that the word is realized which says, "the soul that sins, it shall die," the soul is mortal and dies a real death. But if it is found firmly established in blessedness so that it is inaccessible to death, because it has eternal life, it is no longer mortal but in this sense has even become immortal. How is it that the apostle says of God: "He who alone has immortality"? On investigation I find that Christ Jesus "died for all apart from God." There you have the explanation how God alone has immortality.

Let us therefore take up eternal life. Let us take up that which depends upon our decision. God does not give it to us. He sets it before us. "Behold, I have set life before they face." It is in our power to stretch out our hand, to do good works, and to lay hold on life and deposit it in our soul. This life is the Christ who said: "I am the life." This life is that which now is present in shadow, but then will be face to face. "For the spirit before our face is Christ of whom we may say, In his shadow we shall live among the nations." If the mere shadow of life that is yours offers you so many good things, that shadow which Moses had when he prophesied, that shadow which Isaiah possessed when he saw the Lord Sabaoth sitting upon a throne high and lifted up, which Jeremiah had when he heard the words: "Before I formed thee in the womb, I knew thee, and before thou didst come forth from the womb I sanctified thee," which Ezekiel had when he saw the Cherubim, when he saw the wheels, the ineffable mysteries: what sort of life shall we live when we are no longer living under the shadow of life but are in life itself. For now "our life is hid with Christ; but when Christ, who is our life, shall appear, then shall we also appear with him in glory." Let us haste towards this life, groaning and grieving that we are in this tent, that we dwell in the body. So long as we are present in the body, we are absent from the Lord. Let us long to be absent from the body and to be present with the Lord, that being present with him we may become one with the God of the universe and his only begotten Son, being saved in all things and becoming blessed, in Jesus Christ, to whom be the glory and the power for ever and ever. Amen.

St. Athanasius
295-373

It was in the fourth century that Christianity became the state religion of the Roman Empire and that the doctrine about Christ (Christology) emerged in conflicting forms that called for some resolution. Here we see that doctrinal development is not always in a straight line. "How did it happen that the Christological legacy of Origen, imcomplete though it may have been, could partly have been lost?" (Grillmeier). Whatever the explanation, a titanic struggle had to take place before the formulae to be adopted by the fifth century Councils were secure. The man whose life was virtually identical with that struggle was Athanasius of Alexandria.

Athanasius received a good classical education and entered the ranks of the clergy in 312 and was ordained a deacon in 318. He accompanied Bishop Alexander to the Council of Nicaea in 325, and upon Alexander's death in 328 Athanasius was chosen his successor. For the next forty-five years his battle with Arianism resulted in his being forced to spend no less than seventeen of those years in banishment outside his see on five different occasions. Seldom is an individual's life characterized by so single-minded a drive. He was the chief instrument by which the threat of Arianism was eliminated.

His work On the Incarnation of the Word, *however, predates all this, and is thus of special interest, since it shows us*

Athanasius in his early days with the particular outlook on the meaning of Christ that was to inspire his polemic for a lifetime. The work is intended to set forth simply the positive content of the Christian faith, drawing chiefly from the Scriptures rather than from philosophical speculations. It is thus a statement of the traditional faith as he had met and embraced it.

Athanasius never separated Christology from Soteriology. Who Jesus was took on crucial importance in light of what He was supposed to have done. If He was not divine, there simply was no redemption. The Incarnation of the Word was the only remedy capable of healing the corruption of mankind. The reasons for this and the answers to objections against it make up the substance of the work.

Athanasius was not a speculative or creative theologian. He did not in early or later works contribute new concepts or terms to meet various challenges. That part was left for others. But he knew with unerring instinct that Arius' refusal to grant the Word fully divine status undermined the entire Christian faith. The formulations of Athanasius might leave other aspects open (e.g., the questions concerning Christ's human soul), but he was certain that they expressed what the New Testament Logos doctrine required. A faithful "minister of the Word" dared do no less.

The following selection contains the first five chapters of the work, sketching God's plan of creation, then the fall, the resulting "divine dilemma" solved by the Incarnation, then the role of the Death and the Resurrection of Christ. It omits chapters 6 through 8 which are Athanasius' refutations of objections by Jews and Pagans.

ON THE INCARNATION

CHAPTER I

CREATION AND THE FALL

I n our former book we dealt fully enough with a few of the chief points about the heathen worship of idols, and how those false fears originally arose. We also, by God's grace, briefly indicated that the Word of the Father is Himself divine, that all things that are owe their being to His will and power, and that it is through Him that the good Father gives order to creation, by Him that all things are moved, and through Him that they receive their being. Now, Macarius, true lover of Christ, we must take a step further in the faith of our holy religion, and consider also the Word's becoming Man and His divine Appearing in our midst. That mystery the Jews traduce, the Greeks deride, but we adore; and your own love and devotion to the Word also will be the greater, because in His Manhood He seems so little worth. For it is a fact that the more unbelievers pour scorn on Him, so much the more does He make His Godhead evident. The things which they, as men, rule out as impossible, He plainly shows to be possible; that which they deride as unfitting, His goodness makes most fit; and things which these wiseacres laugh at as "human" He by His inherent might declares divine. Thus by what seems His utter poverty and weakness on the cross He overturns the pomp and parade of idols, and quietly and hiddenly wins over the mockers and unbelievers to recognise Him as God.

Now in dealing with these matters it is necessary first to recall what has already been said. You must understand why it is that the Word of the Father, so great and so high, has been made manifest in bodily form. He has not assumed a body as proper to His own nature, far from it, for as the Word He is without body. He has been manifested in a human body for this reason only, out of the love and goodness of His Father, for the salvation of us men. We will begin, then, with the creation of the world and with God its Maker, for the first fact that you must grasp is this: *the renewal of creation has been wrought by the Self-same Word Who made it in the beginning.* There is thus no inconsistency between creation and salvation; for the One Father has employed the same Agent for both works, effecting the salvation of the world through the same Word Who made it at the first.

In regard to the making of the universe and the creation of all things there have been various opinions, and each person has propounded the theory that suited his own taste. For instance, some say that all things are self-originated and, so to speak, haphazard. The Epicureans are among these; they deny that there is any Mind behind the universe at all. This view is contrary to all the facts of experience, their own existence included. For if all things had come into being in this automatic fashion, instead of being the outcome of Mind, though they existed, they would all be uniform and without distinction. In the universe everything would be sun or moon or whatever it was, and in the human body the whole would be hand or eye or foot. But in point of fact the sun and the moon and the earth are all different things, and even within the human body there are different members, such as foot and hand and head. This distinctness of things argues not a spontaneous generation but a prevenient Cause; and from that Cause we can apprehend God, the Designer and Maker of all.

Others take the view expressed by Plato, that giant among the Greeks. He said that God had made all things out of pre-existent and uncreated matter, just as the carpenter makes things only out of wood that already exists. But those who hold this view do not realise that to deny that God is Himself the Cause of matter is to impute limitation to Him, just as it is undoubtedly a limitation on the part of the carpenter that he can make nothing unless he has the wood. How could God be called Maker and Artificer if His ability to make depended on some other cause, namely on matter itself? If He only worked up existing matter and did not Himself bring matter into being, He would be not the Creator but only a craftsman.

Then, again, there is the theory of the Gnostics, who have invented for themselves an Artificer of all things other than the Father of our Lord Jesus Christ. These simply shut their eyes to the obvious meaning of Scripture. For instance, the Lord, having reminded the Jews of the statement in Genesis, "He Who created them in the beginning made them male and female . . . ," and having shown that for that reason a man should leave his parents and cleave to his wife, goes on to say with reference to the Creator, "What therefore *God* has joined together, let no man put asunder." How can they get a creation independent of the Father out of that? And, again, St. John, speaking all inclusively, says, "All things became by Him and without Him came nothing into being." How then could the Artificer be someone different, other than the Father of Christ?

Such are the notions which men put forward. But the impiety of their foolish talk is plainly declared by the divine teaching of the Christian faith. From it we know that, because there is Mind behind the universe, it did not originate itself; because God is infinite, not finite, it was not made from pre-existent matter, but out of nothing and out of non-existence absolute and utter God brought it into being through the Word. He says as much in Genesis: "In the beginning God created the heavens and the earth;" and again through that most helpful book *The Shepherd*, "Believe thou first and foremost that there is One God Who created and arranged all things and brought them out of non-existence into being." Paul also indicates the same thing when he says, "By faith we understand that the worlds were framed by the Word of God, so that the things which we see now did not come into being out of things which had previously appeared." For God is good—or rather, of all goodness He is Fountainhead, and it is impossible for one who is good to be mean or grudging about anything. Grudging existence to none, therefore, He made all things out of nothing through His own Word, our Lord Jesus Christ; and of all these His earthly creatures He reserved especial mercy for the race of men. Upon them, therefore, upon men who, as animals, were essentially impermanent, He bestowed a grace which other creatures lacked—namely, the impress of His own Image, a share in the reasonable being of the very Word Himself, so that, reflecting Him and themselves becoming reasonable and expressing the Mind of God even as He does, though in limited degree, they might continue for ever in the blessed and only true life of the saints in paradise. But since the will of man could turn either way, God secured this grace that He had given by making it conditional from the first upon two things—namely, a law and a place. He set them in His own paradise, and laid upon them a single prohibition. If they guarded the grace and retained the loveliness of their original innocence, then the life of paradise should be theirs, without sorrow, pain or care, and after it the assurance of immortality in heaven. But if they went astray and became vile, throwing away their birthright of beauty, then they would come under the natural law of death and live no longer in paradise, but, dying outside of it, continue in death and in corruption. This is what Holy Scripture tells us, proclaiming the command of God, "Of every tree that is in the garden thou shalt surely eat, but of the tree of the knowledge of good and evil ye shall not eat, but in the day that ye do eat, ye shall surely die." *"Ye shall surely die"*—not just die only, but remain in the state of death and of corruption.

You may be wondering why we are discussing the origin of men when we set out to talk about the Word's becoming Man. The former subject is relevant to the latter for this reason: it was our sorry case that caused the Word to come down, our transgression that called out His love for us, so that He made haste to help us and to appear among us. It is we who were the cause of His taking human form, and for our salvation that in His great love He was both born and manifested in a human body. For God had made man thus (that is, as an embodied spirit), and had willed that he should remain in incorruption. But men, having turned from the contemplation of God to evil of their own devising, had come inevitably under the law of death. Instead of remaining in the state in which God had created them, they were in process of becoming corrupted entirely, and death had them completely under its dominion. For the transgression of the commandment was making them turn back again according to their nature; and as they had at the beginning come into being out of non-existence, so were

106

they now on the way to returning, through corruption, to non-existence again. The presence and love of the Word had called them into being; inevitably, therefore, when they lost the knowledge of God, they lost existence with it; for it is God alone Who exists, evil is non-being, the negation and antithesis of good. By nature, of course, man is mortal, since he was made from nothing; but he bears also the Likeness of Him Who is, and if he preserves that Likeness through constant contemplation, then his nature is deprived of its power and he remains incorrupt. So it is affirmed in Wisdom: "The keeping of His laws is the assurance of incorruption." And being incorrupt, he would be henceforth as God, as Holy Scripture says, "I have said, Ye are gods and sons of the Highest all of you: but ye die as men and fall as one of the princes."

This, then, was the plight of men. God had not only made them out of nothing, but had also graciously bestowed on them His own life by the grace of the Word. Then, turning from eternal things to things corruptible, by counsel of the devil, they had become the cause of their own corruption in death; for, as I said before, though they were by nature subject to corruption, the grace of their union with the Word made them capable of escaping from the natural law, provided that they retained the beauty of innocence with which they were created. That is to say, the presence of the Word with them shielded them even from natural corruption, as also Wisdom says: "God created man for incorruption and as an image of His own eternity; but by envy of the devil death entered into the world." When this happened, men began to die, and corruption ran riot among them and held sway over them to an even more than natural degree, because it was the penalty of which God had forewarned them for transgressing the commandment. Indeed, they had in their sinning surpassed all limits; for, having invented wickedness in the beginning and so involved themselves in death and corruption, they had gone on gradually from bad to worse, not stopping at any one kind of evil, but continually, as with insatiable appetite, devising new kinds of sins. Adulteries and thefts were everywhere, murder and rapine filled the earth, law was disregarded in corruption and injustice, all kinds of iniquities were perpetrated by all, both singly and in common.

Cities were warring with cities, nations were rising against nations, and the whole earth was rent with factions and battles, while each strove to outdo the other in wickedness. Even crimes contrary to nature were not unknown, but as the martyr-apostle of Christ says: "Their women changed the natural use into that which is against nature; and the men also, leaving the natural use of the woman, flamed out in lust towards each other, perpetrating shameless acts with their own sex, and receiving in their own persons the due recompense of their pervertedness."

CHAPTER II

THE DIVINE DILEMMA AND ITS SOLUTION IN THE INCARNATION

We saw in the last chapter that, because death and corruption were gaining ever firmer hold on them, the human race was in process of destruction. Man, who was created in God's image and in his possession of reason reflected the very Word Himself, was disappearing, and the work of God was being undone. The law of death, which followed from the Transgression, prevailed upon us, and from it there was no escape. The thing that was happening was in truth both monstrous and unfitting. It would, of course, have been unthinkable that God should go back upon His word and that man, having transgressed, should not die; but it was equally monstrous that beings which once had shared the nature of the Word should perish and turn back again into non-existence through corruption. It was unworthy of the goodness of God that creatures made by Him should be brought to nothing through the deceit wrought upon man by the devil; and it was supremely unfitting that the work of God in mankind should disappear, either through their own negligence or through the deceit of evil spirits. As, then, the creatures whom He had created reasonable, like the Word, were in fact perishing, and such noble works were on the road to ruin, what then was God, being Good, to do? Was He to let corruption and death have their way with them? In that case, what was the use of having made them in the beginning? Surely it would have been better never to have been created at all than, having been created, to be neglected and perish; and, besides that, such indifference to the ruin of His own work before His very eyes would argue not goodness in God but limitation, and that far more than if He had never created men at all. It was impossible, therefore, that God should leave man to be carried off by corruption, because it would be unfitting and unworthy of Himself.

Yet, true though this is, it is not the whole matter. As we have already noted, it was unthinkable that God, the Father of Truth, should go back upon His word regarding death in order to ensure our continued existence. He could not falsify Himself; what, then, was God to do? Was He to demand repentance from men for their transgression? You might say that that was worthy of God, and argue further that, as through the Transgression they became subject to corruption, so through repentance they might return to incorruption again. But repentance would not guard the Divine consistency, for, if death did not hold dominion over men, God would still remain untrue. Nor does repentance recall men from what is according to their nature; all that it does is to make them cease from sinning. Had it been a case of a trespass only, and not of a subsequent corruption, repentance would have been well enough; but when once transgression had begun men came under the power of the corruption proper to their nature and were bereft of the grace which belonged to them as creatures in the Image of God. No, repentance could not meet the case. What—or, rather *Who* was it that needed for such grace and such recall as we required? Who, save the Word of God Himself, Who also in the beginning had made all things out of nothing? His part it was, and His alone, both to bring again the corruptible to incorruption and to maintain for the Father His consistency of character with all. For He alone, being Word of the Father and above all, was in consequence both able to recreate all, and worthy to suffer on behalf of all and to be an ambassador for all with the Father.

For this purpose, then, the incorporeal and incorruptible and immaterial Word of God entered our world. In one sense, indeed, He was not far from it before, for no part of creation had ever been without Him Who, while ever abiding in union with the Father, yet fills all things that are. But now He entered the world in a new way, stooping to our level in His love and Self-revealing to us. He saw the reasonable race, the race of men that, like Himself, expressed the Father's Mind, wasting out of existence, and death reigning over all in corruption. He saw that corruption held us all the closer, because it was the penalty for the Transgression; He saw, too, how unthinkable it would be for the law to be repealed before it was fulfilled. He saw how unseemly it was that the very things of which He Himself was the Artificer should be disappearing. He saw how the surpassing wickedness of men was mounting up against them; He saw also their universal liability to death. All this He saw and, pitying our race, moved with compassion for our limitation, unable to endure that death should have the mastery, rather than that His creatures should perish and the work of His Father for us men come to nought, He took to Himself a body, a human body even as our own. Nor did He will merely to become embodied or merely to appear; had that been so, He could have revealed His divine majesty in some other and better way. No, He took *our* body, and not only so, but He took it directly from a spotless, stainless virgin, without the agency of human father—a pure body, untainted by intercourse with man. He, the Mighty One, the Artificer of all, Himself prepared this body in the virgin as a temple for Himself, and took it for His very own, as the instrument through which He was known and in which He dwelt. Thus, taking a body like our own, because all our bodies were liable to the corruption of death, He surrendered His body to death in place of all, and offered it to the Father. This He did out of sheer love for us, so that in His death all might die, and the law of death thereby be abolished because, when He had fulfilled in His body that for which it was appointed, it was thereafter voided of its power for men. This He did that He might turn again to incorruption men who had turned back to corruption, and make them alive through death by the appropriation of His body and by the grace of His resurrection. Thus He would make death to disappear from them as utterly as straw from fire.

The Word perceived that corruption could not be got rid of otherwise than through death; yet He Himself, as the Word, being immortal and the Father's Son, was such as could not die. For this reason, therefore, He assumed a body capable of death, in order that it, through belonging to the Word Who is above all, might become in dying a sufficient exchange for all, and, itself remaining incorruptible through His indwelling, might thereafter put an end to corruption for all others as well, by the grace of the resurrection. It was by surrendering to death the body which He had taken, as an offering and sacrifice free from every stain, that He forthwith abolished death for His human brethren by the offering of the equivalent. For naturally, since the Word of God was above all, when He offered His own temple and bodily instrument as a substitute for the life of all, He fulfilled in death all that was required. Naturally also, through this union of the immortal Son of God with our human nature, all men were clothed with incorruption in the promise of the resurrection. For the solidarity of mankind is such that, by virtue of the Word's indwelling in a single human body, the corruption which goes with death has lost its power over all. You know how it is when some great king enters a large city and dwells in one of its houses; because of his dwelling in that single house, the whole city is honoured, and enemies and robbers cease to molest it. Even so is it with the King of all; He has come into our country and dwelt in one body amidst the many, and in consequence the designs of the enemy against mankind have been foiled, and the corruption of death, which formerly held them in its power, has simply ceased to be. For the human race would have perished utterly had not the Lord and Saviour of all, the Son of God, come among us to put an end to death.

This great work was, indeed, supremely worthy of the goodness of God. A king who has founded a city, so far from neglecting it when through the carelessness of the inhabitants it is attacked by robbers, avenges it and saves it from destruction, having regard rather to his own honour than to the people's neglect. Much more, then, the Word of the All-good Father was not unmindful of the human race that He had called to be; but rather, by the offering of His own body He abolished the death which they had incurred, and corrected their neglect by His own teaching. Thus by His own power He restored the whole nature of man. The Saviour's own inspired disciples assure us of this. We read in one place: "For the love of Christ constraineth us, because we thus judge that, if One died on behalf of all, then all died, and He died for all that we should no longer live unto ourselves, but unto Him who died and rose again from the dead, even our Lord Jesus Christ." And again another says: "But we behold Him Who hath been made a little lower than the angels, even Jesus, because of the suffering of death crowned with glory and honour, that by the grace of God He should taste of death on behalf of every man." The same writer goes on to point out why it was necessary for God the Word and none other to become Man: "For it became Him, for Whom are all things and through Whom are all things, in bringing many sons unto glory, to make the Author of their salvation perfect through suffering." He means that the rescue of mankind from corruption was the proper part only of Him Who made them in the beginning. He points out also that the Word assumed a human body, expressly in order that He might offer it in sacrifice for other like bodies: "Since then the children are sharers in flesh and blood, He also Himself assumed the same, in order that through death He might bring to nought him that hath the power of death, that is to say, the Devil, and might rescue those who all their lives were enslaved by the fear of death." For by the sacrifice of His own body He did two things: He put an end to the law of death which barred our way; and He made a new beginning of life for us, by giving us the hope of resurrection. By man death has gained its power over men; by the Word made Man death has been destroyed and life raised up anew. That is what Paul says, that true servant of Christ: "For since by man came death, by man came also the resurrection of the dead. Just as in Adam all die, even so in Christ shall all be made alive," and so forth. Now, therefore, when we die we no longer do so as men condemned to death, but as those who are even now in process of rising we await the general resurrection of all, "which in its own times He shall show," even God Who wrought it and bestowed it on us.

This, then, is the first cause of the Saviour's becoming Man. There are, however, other things which show how wholly fitting is His blessed presence in our midst; and these we must now go on to consider.

CHAPTER III

THE DIVINE DILEMMA AND ITS SOLUTION IN
THE INCARNATION—continued

When God the Almighty was making mankind through His own Word, He perceived that they, owing to the limitation of their nature, could not of themselves have any knowledge of their Artificer, the Incorporeal and Uncreate. He took pity on them, therefore, and did not leave them destitute of the knowledge of Himself, lest their very existence should prove purposeless. For of what use is existence to the creature if it cannot know its Maker? How could men be reasonable beings if they had no knowledge of the Word and Reason of the Father, through Whom they had received their being? They would be no better than the beasts, had they no knowledge save of earthly things; and why should God have made them at all, if He had not intended them to know Him? But, in fact, the good God has given them a share in His own Image, that is, in our Lord Jesus Christ, and has made even themselves after the same Image and Likeness. Why? Simply in order that through this gift of Godlikeness in themselves they may be able to perceive the Image Absolute, that is the Word Himself, and through Him to apprehend the Father; which knowledge of their Maker is for men the only really happy and blessed life.

But, as we have already seen, men, foolish as they are, thought little of the grace they had received, and turned away from God. They defiled their own soul so completely that they not only lost their apprehension of God, but invented for themselves other gods of various kinds. They fashioned idols for themselves in place of the truth and reverenced things that are not, rather than God Who is, as St. Paul says, "worshipping the creature rather than the Creator." Moreover, and much worse, they transferred the honour which is due to God to material objects such as wood and stone, and also to man; and further even than that they went, as we said in our former book. Indeed, so impious were they that they worshipped evil spirits as gods in satisfaction of their lusts. They sacrificed brute beasts and immolated men, as the just due of these deities,

113

thereby bringing themselves more and more under their insane control. Magic arts also were taught among them, oracles in sundry places led men astray, and the cause of everything in human life was traced to the stars, as though nothing existed but that which could be seen. In a word, impiety and lawlessness were everywhere, and neither God nor His Word was known. Yet He had not hidden Himself from the sight of men nor given the knowledge of Himself in one way only; but rather He had unfolded it in many forms and by many ways.

God knew the limitation of mankind, you see; and though the grace of being made in His Image was sufficient to give them knowledge of the Word and through Him of the Father, as a safeguard against their neglect of this grace, He provided the works of creation also as means by which the Maker might be known. Nor was this all. Man's neglect of the indwelling grace tends ever to increase; and against this further frailty also God made provision by giving them a law, and by sending prophets, men whom they knew. Thus, if they were tardy in looking up to heaven, they might still gain knowledge of their Maker from those close at hand; for men can learn directly about higher things from other men. Three ways thus lay open to them, by which they might obtain the knowledge of God. They could look up into the immensity of heaven, and by pondering the harmony of creation come to know its Ruler, the Word of the Father, Whose all-ruling providence makes known the Father to all. Or, if this was beyond them, they could converse with holy men, and through them learn to know God, the Artificer of all things, the Father of Christ, and to recognise the worship of idols as the negation of the truth and full of all impiety. Or else, in the third place, they could cease from lukewarmness and lead a good life merely by knowing the law. For the law was not given only for the Jews, nor was it solely for their sake that God sent the prophets, though it was to the Jews that they were sent and by the Jews that they were persecuted. The law and the prophets were a sacred school of the knowledge of God and the conduct of the spiritual life for the whole world.

So great, indeed, were the goodness and the love of God. Yet men, bowed down by the pleasures of the moment and by the frauds and illusions of the evil spirits, did not lift up their heads towards the truth. So burdened were they with their wickednesses that they seemed rather to be brute beasts than reasonable men, reflecting the very Likeness of the Word.

What was God to do in face of this dehumanising of mankind, this universal hiding of the knowledge of Himself by the wiles of evil spirits? Was He to keep silence before so great a wrong and let men go on being thus deceived and kept in ignorance of Himself? If so, what was the use of having made them in His own Image originally? It would surely have been better for them always to have been brutes, rather than to revert to that condition when once they had shared the nature of the Word. Again, things being as they were, what was the use of their ever having had the knowledge of God? Surely it would have been better for God never to have bestowed it, than that men should subsequently be found unworthy to receive it. Similarly, what possible profit could it be to God Himself, Who made men, if when made they did not worship Him, but regarded others as their makers? This would be tantamount to His having made them for others and not for Himself. Even an earthly king, though he is only a man, does not allow lands that he has colonised to pass into other hands or to desert to other rulers, but sends letters and friends and even visits them himself to recall them to their allegiance, rather than allow His work to be undone. How much more, then, will God be patient and painstaking with His creatures, that they be not led astray from Him to the service of those that are not, and that all the more because such error means for them sheer ruin, and because it is not right that those who had once shared His Image should be destroyed.

What, then, was God to do? What else could He possibly do, being God, but renew His Image in mankind, so that through it men might once more come to know Him? And how could this be done save by the coming of the very Image Himself, our Saviour Jesus Christ? Men could not have done it, for they are only made after the Image; nor could angels have done it, for they are not the images of God. The Word of God came in His own Person, because it was He alone, the Image of the Father, Who could recreate man made after the Image.

In order to effect this re-creation, however, He had first to do away with death and corruption. Therefore He assumed a human body, in order that in it death might once for all be destroyed, and that men might be renewed according to the Image. The Image of the Father only was sufficient for this need. Here is an illustration to prove it.

You know what happens when a portrait that has been painted on a panel becomes obliterated through external strains. The artist does not throw away the panel, but the subject of the portrait has to come and sit for it again, and then the likeness is re-drawn on the same material. Even so was it with the All-holy Son of God. He, the Image of the Father, came and dwelt in our midst, in order that He might renew mankind made after Himself, and seek out His lost sheep, even as He says in the gospel: "I came to seek and to save that which was lost." This also explains His saying to the Jews: "Except a man be born anew . . . ." He was not referring to a man's natural birth from his mother, as they thought, but to the re-birth and re-creation of the soul in the Image of God.

Nor was this the only thing which only the Word could do. When the madness of idolatry and irreligion filled the world and the knowledge of God was hidden, whose part was it to teach the world about the Father? Man's, would you say? But men cannot run everywhere over the world, nor would their words carry sufficient weight if they did, nor would they be, unaided, a match for the evil spirits. Moreover, since even the best of men were confused and blinded by evil, how could they convert the souls and minds of others? You cannot put straight in others what is warped in yourself. Perhaps you will say, then, that creation was enough to teach men about the Father. But if that had been so, such great evils would never have occurred. Creation was there all the time, but it did not prevent men from wallowing in error. Once more, then, it was the Word of God, Who sees all that is in man and moves all things in creation, Who alone could meet the needs of the situation. It was His part and His alone, Whose ordering of the universe reveals the Father, to renew the same teaching. But how was He to do it? By the same means as before, perhaps you will say, that is, through the works of creation. But this was proven insufficient. Men had

116

neglected to consider the heavens before, and now they were looking in the opposite direction. Wherefore, in all naturalness and fitness, desiring to do good to men, as Man He comes, taking to Himself a body like the rest; and through His actions done in that body, as it were on their own level, He teaches those who would not learn by other means to know Himself, the Word of God, and through Him the Father.

He deals with them as a good teacher with his pupils, coming down to their level and using simple means. St. Paul says as much: "Because in the wisdom of God the world in its wisdom knew not God, God thought fit through the simplicity of the News proclaimed to save those who believe." Men had turned from the contemplation of God above, and were looking for Him in the opposite direction, down among created things and things of sense. The Saviour of us all, the Word of God, in His great love took to Himself a body and moved as Man among men, meeting their senses, so to speak, half way. He became Himself an object for the senses, so that those who were seeking God in sensible things might apprehend the Father through the works which He, the Word of God, did in the body. Human and human-minded as men were, therefore, to whichever side they looked in the sensible world they found themselves taught the truth. Were they awe-stricken by creation? They beheld it confessing Christ as Lord. Did their minds tend to regard men as Gods? The uniqueness of the Saviour's works marked Him, alone of men, as Son of God. Were they drawn to evil spirits? They saw them driven out by the Lord and learned that the Word of God alone was God and that the evil spirits were not gods at all. Were they inclined to hero-worship and the cult of the dead? Then the fact that the Saviour had risen from the dead showed them how false these other deities were, and that the Word of the Father is the one true Lord, the Lord even of death. For this reason was He both born and manifested as Man, for this He died and rose, in order that, eclipsing by His works all other human deeds, He might recall men from all the paths of error to know the Father. As He says Himself, "I came to seek and to save that which was lost."

When, then, the minds of men had fallen finally to the level of sensible things, the Word submitted to appear in a body, in order that He, as Man, might centre their senses on Himself, and convince them through His human acts that He Himself is not man only but also God, the Word and Wisdom of the true God. This is what Paul wants to tell us when he says: "That ye, being rooted and grounded in love, may be strong to apprehend with all the saints what is the length and breadth and height and depth, and to know the love of God that surpasses knowledge, so that ye may be filled unto all the fulness of God." The Self-revealing of the Word is in every dimension—above, in creation; below, in the Incarnation; in the depth, in Hades; in the breadth, throughout the world. All things have been filled with the knowledge of God.

For this reason He did not offer the sacrifice on behalf of all immediately He came, for if He had surrendered His body to death and then raised it again at once He would have ceased to be an object of our senses. Instead of that, He stayed in His body and let Himself be seen in it, doing acts and giving signs which showed Him to be not only man, but also God the Word. There were thus two things which the Saviour did for us by becoming Man. He banished death from us and made us anew; and, invisible and imperceptible as in Himself He is, He became visible through His works and revealed Himself as the Word of the Father, the Ruler and King of the whole creation.

There is a paradox in this last statement which we must now examine. The Word was not hedged in by His body, nor did His presence in the body prevent His being present elsewhere as well. When He moved His body He did not cease also to direct the universe by His Mind and might. No. The marvellous truth is, that being the Word, so far from being Himself contained by anything, He actually contained all things Himself. In creation He is present everywhere, yet is distinct in being from it; ordering, directing, giving life to all, containing all, yet is He Himself the Uncontained, existing solely in His Father. As with the whole, so also is it with the part. Existing in a human body, to which He Himself gives life, He is still Source of life to all the universe, present in every part of it, yet outside the whole; and He is revealed both through the works of His body and through His activity in the world. It is, indeed, the function of soul to *behold* things that are outside the body,

118

but it cannot energise or move them. A man cannot transport things from one place to another, for instance, merely by thinking about them; nor can you or I move the sun and the stars just by sitting at home and looking at them. With the Word of God in His human nature, however, it was otherwise. His body was for Him not a limitation, but an instrument, so that He was both in it and in all things, and outside all things, resting in the Father alone. At one and the same time—this is the wonder—as Man He was living a human life, and as Word He was sustaining the life of the universe, and as Son He was in constant union with the Father. Not even His birth from a virgin, therefore, changed Him in any way, nor was He defiled by being in the body. Rather, He sanctified the body by being in it. For His being in everything does not mean that He shares the nature of everything, only that He gives all things their being and sustains them in it. Just as the sun is not defiled by the contact of its rays with earthly objects, but rather enlightens and purifies them, so He Who made the sun is not defiled by being made known in a body, but rather the body is cleansed and quickened by His indwelling, "Who did no sin, neither was guile found in His mouth."

You must understand, therefore, that when writers on this sacred theme speak of Him as eating and drinking and being born, they mean that the body, as a body, was born and sustained with the food proper to its nature; while God the Word, Who was united with it, was at the same time ordering the universe and revealing Himself through His bodily acts as not man only but God. Those acts are rightly said to be His acts, because the body which did them did indeed belong to Him and none other; moreover, it was right that they should be thus attributed to Him as Man, in order to show that His body was a real one and not merely an appearance. From such ordinary acts as being born and taking food, He was recognised as being actually present in the body; but by the extraordinary acts which He did through the body He proved Himself to be the Son of God. That is the meaning of His words to the unbelieving Jews: "If I do not the works of My Father, believe Me not; but if I do, even if ye believe not Me, believe My works, that ye may know that the Father is in Me and I in the Father."

Invisible in Himself, He is known from the works of creation; so also, when His Godhead is veiled in human nature, His bodily acts still declare Him to be not man only, but the Power and Word of God. To speak authoritatively to evil spirits, for instance, and to drive them out, is not human but divine; and who could see Him curing all the diseases to which mankind is prone, and still deem Him mere man and not also God? He cleansed lepers, He made the lame to walk, He opened the ears of the deaf and the eyes of the blind, there was no sickness or weakness that He did not drive away. Even the most casual observer can see that these were acts of God. The healing of the man born blind, for instance, who but the Father and Artificer of man, the Controller of his whole being, could thus have restored the faculty denied at birth? He Who did thus must surely be Himself the Lord of birth. This is proved also at the outset of His becoming Man. He formed His own body from the virgin; and that is no small proof of His Godhead, since He Who made that was the Maker of all else. And would not anyone infer from the fact of that body being begotten of a virgin only, without human father, that He Who appeared in it was also the Maker and Lord of all beside?

Again, consider the miracle at Cana. Would not anyone who saw the substance of water transmuted into wine understand that He Who did it was the Lord and Maker of the water that He changed? It was for the same reason that He walked on the seas as on dry land—to prove to the onlookers that He had mastery over all. And the feeding of the multitude, when He made little into much, so that from five loaves five thousand mouths were filled—did not that prove Him none other than the very Lord Whose Mind is over all?

CHAPTER IV

THE DEATH OF CHRIST

All these things the Saviour thought fit to do, so that, recognising His bodily acts as works of God, men who were blind to His presence in creation might regain knowledge of the Father. For, as I said before, who that saw His authority over evil spirits and their response to it could doubt that He was, indeed, the Son, the Wisdom and the Power of God? Even the very creation broke silence at His behest and, marvellous to relate, confessed with one voice before the cross, that monument of victory, that He Who suffered thereon in the body was not man only, but Son of God and Saviour of all. The sun veiled his face, the earth quaked, the mountains were rent asunder, all men were stricken with awe. These things showed that Christ on the cross was God, and that all creation was His slave and was bearing witness by its fear to the presence of its Master.

Thus, then, God the Word revealed Himself to men through His works. We must next consider the end of His earthly life and the nature of His bodily death. This is, indeed, the very centre of our faith, and everywhere you hear men speak of it; by it, too, no less than by His other acts, Christ is revealed as God and Son of God.

We have dealt as far as circumstances and our own understanding permit with the reason for His bodily manifestation. We have seen that to change the corruptible to incorruption was proper to none other than the Saviour Himself, Who in the beginning made all things out of nothing; that only the Image of the Father could re-create the likeness of the Image in men, that none save our Lord Jesus Christ could give to mortals immortality, and that only the Word Who orders all things and is alone the Father's true and sole-begotten Son could teach men about Him and abolish the worship of idols. But beyond all this, there was a debt owing which must needs be paid; for, as I said before, all men were due to die. Here, then, is the second reason why the Word dwelt among us, namely that having proved His Godhead by His works, He might offer the sacrifice on behalf of all, surrendering His own temple to death in place of all, to settle man's account with death and free him from the primal transgression. In the same act also He showed Himself mightier than death, displaying His own body incorruptible as the first-fruits of the resurrection.

You must not be surprised if we repeat ourselves in dealing with this subject. We are speaking of the good pleasure of God and of the things which He in His loving wisdom thought fit to do, and it is better to put the same thing in several ways than to run the risk of leaving something out. The body of the Word, then, being a real human body, in spite of its having been uniquely formed from a virgin, was of itself mortal and, like other bodies, liable to death. But the indwelling of the Word loosed it from this natural liability, so that corrpution could not touch it. Thus it happened that two opposite marvels took place at once: the death of all was consummated in the Lord's body; yet, because the Word was in it, death and corruption were in the same act utterly abolished. Death there had to be, and death for all, so that the due of all might be paid. Wherefore, the Word, as I said, being Himself incapable of death, assumed a mortal body, that He might offer it as His own in place of all, and suffering for the sake of all through His union with it, "might bring to nought Him that had the power of death, that is, the devil, and might deliver them who all their lifetime were enslaved by the fear of death."

Have no fear, then. Now that the common Saviour of all has died on our behalf, we who believe in Christ no longer die, as men died aforetime, in fulfilment of the threat of the law. That condemnation has come to an end; and now that, by the grace of the resurrection, corruption has been banished and done away, we are loosed from our mortal bodies in God's good time for each, so that we may obtain thereby a better resurrection. Like seeds cast into the earth, we do not perish in our dissolution, but like them shall rise again, death having been brought to nought by the grace of the Saviour. That is why blessed Paul, through whom we all have surety of the resurrection, says: "This corruptible must put on incorruption and this mortal must put on immortality; but when this corruptible shall have put on incorruption and this mortal shall have put on immortality, then shall be brought to pass the saying that is written, 'Death is swallowed up in victory. O Death, where is thy sting? O Grave, where is thy victory?' "

"Well then," some people may say, "if the essential thing was that He should surrender His body to death in place of all, why did He not do so as Man privately, without going to the length of public crucifixion? Surely it would have been more suitable for Him to have laid aside His body with honour than to endure so shameful a death." But look at this argument closely, and see how merely human it is, whereas what the Saviour did was truly divine and worthy of His Godhead for several reasons. The first is this. The death of men under ordinary circumstances is the result of their natural weakness. They are essentially impermanent, so after a time they fall ill and when worn out they die. But the Lord is not like that. He is not weak, He is the Power of God and Word of God and Very Life Itself. If He had died quietly in His bed like other men it would have looked as if He did so in accordance with His nature, and as though He was indeed no more than other men. But because He was Himself Word and Life and Power His body was made strong, and because the death had to be accomplished, He took the occasion of perfecting His sacrifice not from Himself, but from others. How could He fall sick, Who had healed others? Or how could that body weaken and fail by means of which others are made strong? Here, again, you may say, "Why did He not prevent death, as He did sickness?" Because it was precisely in order to be able to die that He had taken a body, and to prevent the death would have been to impede the resurrection. And as to the unsuitability of sickness for His body, as arguing weakness, you may say, "Did He then not hunger?" Yes, He hungered, because that was the property of His body, but He did not die of hunger, because He Whose body hungered was the Lord. Similarly, though He died to ransom all, He did not see corruption. His body rose in perfect soundness, for it was the body of none other than the Life Himself.

Someone else might say, perhaps, that it would have been better for the Lord to have avoided the designs of the Jews against Him, and so to have guarded His body from death altogether. But see how unfitting this also would have been for Him. Just as it would not have been fitting for Him to give His body to death by His own hand, being Word and being Life, so also it was not consonant with Himself that He should avoid the death inflicted by others. Rather, He pursued it to the uttermost, and in pursuance of His nature neither laid aside His body of His own accord nor escaped the plotting Jews. And this action showed no limitation or weakness in the Word; for He both waited for death in order to make an end of it, and hastened to accomplish it as an offering on behalf of all. Moreover, as it was the death of all mankind that the Saviour came to accomplish, not His own, He did not lay aside His body by an individual act of dying, for to Him, as Life, this simply did not belong; but He accepted death at the hands of men, thereby completely to destroy it in His own body.

There are some further considerations which enable one to understand why the Lord's body had such an end. The supreme object of His coming was to bring about the resurrection of the body. This was to be the monument to His victory over death, the assurance to all that He had Himself conquered corruption and that their own bodies also would eventually be incorrupt; and it was in token of that and as a pledge of the future resurrection that He kept His body incorrupt. But there again, if His body had fallen sick and the Word had left it in that condition, how unfitting it would have been! Should He Who healed the bodies of others neglect to keep His own in health? How would His miracles of healing be believed, if this were so? Surely people would either laugh at Him as unable to dispel disease or else consider Him lacking in proper human feeling because He could do so, but did not.

Then, again, suppose without any illness He had just concealed His body somewhere, and then suddenly reappeared and said that He had risen from the dead. He would have been regarded merely as a teller of tales, and because there was no witness of His death, nobody would believe His resurrection. Death had to precede resurrection, for there could be no resurrection without it. A action, in order that the Saviour might utterly abolish death in whatever form they offered it to Him. A generous wrestler, virile and strong, does not himself choose his antagonists, lest it should be thought that of some of them he is afraid. Rather, he lets the spectators choose them, and that all the more if these are hostile, so that he may overthrow whomsoever they match against him and thus vindicate his superior strength. Even so was it with Christ. He, the Life of all, our Lord and Saviour, did not arrange the manner of his own death lest He should seem to be afraid of some other kind. No. He accepted and bore upon the cross a death inflicted by others, and those others His special enemies, a death which to them was supremely terrible and by no means to be faced; and

He did this in order that, by destroying even this death, He might Himself be believed to be the Life, and the power of death be recognised as finally annulled. A marvellous and mighty paradox has thus occurred, for the death which they thought to inflict on Him as dishonour and disgrace has become the glorious monument to death's defeat. Therefore it is also, that He neither endured the death of John, who was beheaded, nor was He sawn asunder, like Isaiah: even in death He preserved His body whole and undivided, so that there should be no excuse hereafter for those who would divide the Church.

So much for the objections of those outside the Church. But if any honest Christian wants to know why He suffered death on the cross and not in some other way, we answer thus: in no other way was it expedient for us, indeed the Lord offered for our sakes the one death that was supremely good. He had come to bear the curse that lay on us; and how could He "become a curse" otherwise than by accepting the accursed death? And that death is the cross, for it is written "Cursed is every one that hangeth on a tree." Again, the death of the Lord is the ransom of all, and by it "the middle wall of partition" is broken down and the call of the Gentiles comes about. How could He have called us if He had not been crucified, for it is only on the cross that a man dies with arms outstretched? Here, again, we see the fitness of His death and of those outstretched arms: it was that He might draw His ancient people with the one and the Gentiles with the other, and join both together in Himself. Even so, He foretold the manner of His redeeming death, "I, if I be lifted up, will draw all men unto Myself." Again, the air is the sphere of the devil, the enemy of our race who, having fallen from heaven, endeavours with the other evil spirits who shared in his disobedience both to keep souls from the truth and to hinder the progress of those who are trying to follow it. The apostle refers to this when he says, "According to the prince of the power of the air, of the spirit that now worketh in the sons of disobedience." But the Lord came to overthrow the devil and to purify the air and to make "a way" for us up to heaven, as the apostle says, "through the veil, that is to say, His flesh." This had to be done through death, and by what other kind of death could it be done, save by a death in the air, that is, on the cross? Here, again, you see how right and natural it was that the Lord should suffer thus; for being thus "lifted up," He cleansed the air from all the evil influences of the enemy. "I beheld Satan as lightning falling," He says; and thus He re-opened the road to heaven, saying again, "Lift up your gates, O ye princes, and be ye lift up, ye everlasting doors." For it was not the Word Himself Who needed an opening of the gates, He being Lord of all, nor was any of His works closed to their Maker. No, it was we who needed it, we whom He Himself upbore in His own body—that body which He first offered to death on behalf of all, and then made through it a path to heaven.

CHAPTER V

THE RESURRECTION

Fitting indeed, then, and wholly consonant was the death on the cross for us; and we can see how reasonable it was, and why it is that the salvation of the world could be accomplished in no other way. Even on the cross He did not hide Himself from sight; rather, He made all creation witness to the presence of its Maker. Then, having once let it be seen that it was truly dead, He did not allow that temple of His body to linger long, but forthwith on the third day raised it up, impassible and incorruptible, the pledge and token of His victory.

It was, of course, within His power thus to have raised His body and displayed it as alive directly after death. But the all-wise Saviour did not do this, lest some should deny that it had really or completely died. Besides this, had the interval between His death and resurrection been but two days, the glory of His incorruption might not have appeared. He waited one whole day to show that His body was really dead, and then on the third day showed it incorruptible to all. The interval was no longer, lest people should have forgotten about it and grown doubtful whether it were in truth the same body. No, while the affair was still ringing in their ears and their eyes were still straining and their minds in turmoil, and while those who had put Him to death were still on the spot and themselves witnessing to the fact of it, the Son of God after three days showed His once dead body immortal and incorruptible; and it was evident to all that it was from no natural weakness that the body which the Word indwelt had died, but in order that in it by the Saviour's power death might be done away.

A very strong proof of this destruction of death and its conquest by the cross is supplied by a present fact, namely this. All the disciples of Christ despise death; they take the offensive against it and, instead of fearing it, by the sign of the cross and by faith in Christ trample on it as on something dead. Before the divine advent of the Saviour even the holiest of men were afraid of death, and mourned the dead as those who perish. But now that the Saviour has raised His body, death is no longer terrible, but all those who believe in Christ tread it underfoot as nothing, and prefer to die rather than to deny their faith in Christ, knowing full well that when they die they do not perish, but live indeed, and become incorruptible through the resurrection. But that devil who of old wickedly exulted in death, now that the pains of death are loosed, he alone it is who remains truly dead. There is proof of this too; for men who, before they believe in Christ, think death horrible and are afraid of it, once they are converted despise it so completely that they go eagerly to meet it, and themselves become witnesses of the Saviour's resurrection from it. Even children hasten thus to die, and not men only, but women train themselves by bodily discipline to meet it. So weak has death become that even women, who used to be taken in by it, mock at it now as a dead thing robbed of all its strength. Death has become like a tyrant who has been completely conquered by the legitimate monarch; bound hand and foot as he now is, the passers-by jeer at him, hitting him and abusing him, no longer afraid of his cruelty and rage, because of the king who has conquered him. So has death been conquered and branded for what it is by the Saviour on the cross. It is bound hand and foot, all who are in Christ trample it as they pass and as witnesses to Him deride it, scoffing and saying, "O Death, where is thy victory? O Grave, where is thy sting?"

Is this a slender proof of the impotence of death, do you think? Or is it a slight indication of the Saviour's victory over it, when boys and young girls who are in Christ look beyond this present life and train themselves to die? Every one is by nature afraid of death and of bodily dissolution; the marvel of marvels is that he who is enfolded in the faith of the cross despises this natural fear and for the sake of the cross is no longer cowardly in face of it. The natural property of fire is to burn. Suppose, then, that there was a substance such as the Indian asbestos is said to be, which had no fear of being burnt, but rather displayed the impotence of the fire by proving itself unburnable. If anyone doubted the truth of this, all he need do would be to wrap himself up in the substance in question and then touch the fire. Or, again, to revert to our former figure, if anyone wanted to see the tyrant bound and helpless, who used to be such a terror to others, he could do so simply by going into the country of the tyrant's conqueror. Even so, if anyone still doubts the conquest of death, after so many proofs and so many martyrdoms in Christ and such daily scorn of death by His truest servants, he certainly does well to marvel at so great a thing, but he must not be obstinate in unbelief and disregard of plain facts. No, he must be like the man who wants to prove the property of the asbestos, and like him who enters the conqueror's dominions to see the tyrant bound. He must embrace the faith of Christ, this disbeliever in the conquest of death, and come to His teaching. Then he will see how impotent death is and how completely conquered. Indeed, there have been many former unbelievers and deriders who, after they became believers, so scorned death as even themselves to become martyrs for Christ's sake.

If, then, it is by the sign of the cross and by faith in Christ that death is trampled underfoot, it is clear that it is Christ Himself and none other Who is the Archvictor over death and has robbed it of its power. Death used to be strong and terrible, but now, since the advent of the Saviour and the death and resurrection of His body, it is despised; and obviously it is by the very Christ Who mounted on the cross that it has been destroyed and vanquished finally. When the sun rises after the night and the whole world is lit up by it, nobody doubts that it is the sun which has thus shed its light everywhere and driven away the dark. Equally clear is it, since this utter scorning and trampling down of death has ensued upon the Saviour's manifestation in the body and His death on the cross, that it is He Himself Who brought death to nought and daily raises monuments to His victory in His own disciples. How can you think otherwise, when you see men naturally weak hastening to death, unafraid at the prospect of corruption, fearless of the descent into Hades, even indeed with eager soul provoking it, not shrinking from tortures, but preferring thus to rush on death for Christ's sake, rather than to remain in this present life? If you see with your own eyes men and women and children, even, thus welcoming death for the sake of Christ's religion, how can you be so utterly silly and incredulous and maimed in your mind as not to realise that Christ, to Whom these all bear witness Himself gives the victory to each, making death completely powerless for those who hold His faith and bear the sign of the cross? No one in his senses doubts that a snake is dead when he sees it trampled underfoot, especially when he knows how savage it used to be; nor, if he sees boys making fun of a lion, does he doubt that the brute is either dead or completely bereft of strength. These things can be seen with our own eyes, and it is the same with the conquest of death. Doubt no longer, then, when you see death mocked and scorned by those who believe in Christ, that by Christ death was destroyed, and the corruption that goes with it resolved and brought to end.

What we have said is, indeed, no small proof of the destruction of death and of the fact that the cross of the Lord is the monument to His victory. But the resurrection of the body to immortality, which results henceforward from the work of Christ, the common Saviour and true Life of all, is more effectively proved by facts than by words to those whose mental vision is sound. For, if, as we have shown, death was destroyed and everybody tramples on it because of Christ, how much more did He Himself first trample and destroy it in His own body! Death having been slain by Him, then, what other issue could there be than the resurrection of His body and its open demonstration as the monument of His victory? How could the destruction of death have been manifested at all, had not the Lord's body been raised? But if anyone finds even this insufficient, let him find proof of what has been said in present facts. Dead men cannot take effective action; their power of influence on others lasts only till the grave. Deeds and actions that energise others belong only to the living. Well, then, look at the facts in this case. The Saviour is working mightily among men, every day He is invisibly persuading numbers of people all over the world, both within and beyond the Greek-speaking world, to accept His faith and be obedient to His teaching. Can anyone, in face of this, still doubt that He has risen and lives, or rather that He is Himself the Life? Does a dead man prick the consciences of men, so that they throw all the traditions of their fathers to the winds and bow down before the teaching of Christ? If He is no longer active in the world, as He must needs be if He is dead, how is it that He makes the living to cease from their activities, the adulterer from his adultery, the murderer from murdering, the unjust from avarice, while the profane and godless man becomes religious? If He did not rise, but is still dead, how is it that He routs and persecutes and overthrows the false gods, whom unbelievers think to be alive, and the evil spirits whom they worship? For where Christ is named, idolatry is destroyed and the fraud of evil spirits is exposed; indeed, no such spirit can endure that Name, but takes no flight on sound of it. This is the work of One Who lives, not of one dead; and, more than that, it is the work of God. It would be absurd to say that the evil spirits whom He drives out and the idols which He destroys are alive, but that He Who drives out and destroys, He Whom they themselves acknowledge to be Son of God, is dead.

In a word, then, those who disbelieve in the resurrection have no support in facts, if their gods and evil spirits do not drive away the supposedly dead Christ. Rather, it is He Who convicts them of being dead. We are agreed that a dead person can do nothing: yet the Saviour works mightily every day, drawing men to religion, persuading them to virtue, teaching them about immortality, quickening their thirst for heavenly things, revealing the knowledge of the Father, inspiring strength in face of death, manifesting Himself to each, and displacing the irreligion of idols; while the gods and evil spirits of the unbelievers can do none of these things, but rather become dead at Christ's presence, all their ostentation barren and void. By the sign of the cross, on the contrary, all magic is stayed, all sorcery confounded, all the idols are abandoned and deserted, and all senseless pleasure ceases, as the eye of faith looks up from earth to heaven. Whom, then, are we to call dead? Shall we call Christ dead, Who effects all this? But the dead have not the faculty to effect anything. Or shall we call death dead, which effects nothing whatever, but lies as lifeless and ineffective as are the evil spirits and the idols? The Son of God, "living and effective," is active every day and effects the salvation of all; but death is daily proved to be stripped of all its strength, and it is the idols and the evil spirits who are dead, not He. No room for doubt remains, therefore, concerning the resurrection of His body.

Indeed, it would seem that he who disbelieves this bodily rising of the Lord is ignorant of the power of the Word and Wisdom of God. If He took a body to Himself at all, and made it His own in pursuance of His purpose, as we have shown that He did, what was the Lord to do with it, and what was ultimately to become of that body upon which the Word had descended? Mortal and offered to death on behalf of all as it was, it could not but die; indeed, it was for that very purpose that the Saviour had prepared it for Himself. But on the other hand it could not remain dead, because it had become the very temple of Life. It therefore died, as mortal, but lived again because of the Life within it; and its resurrection is made known through its works.

It is, indeed, in accordance with the nature of the invisible God that He should be thus known through His works; and those who doubt the Lord's resurrection because they do not now behold Him with their eyes, might as well deny the very laws of nature. They have ground for disbelief when works are lacking; but when the works cry out and prove the fact so clearly, why do they deliberately deny the risen life so manifestly shown? Even if their mental faculties are defective, surely their eyes can give them irrefragable proof of the power and Godhead of Christ. A blind man cannot see the sun, but he knows that it is above the earth from the warmth which it affords; similarly, let those who are still in the blindness of unbelief recognise the Godhead of Christ and the resurrection which He has brought about through His manifested power in others. Obviously He would not be expelling evil spirits and despoiling idols, if He were dead, for the evil spirits would not obey one who was dead. If, on the other hand, the very naming of Him drives them forth, He clearly is not dead; and the more so that the spirits, who perceive things unseen by men, would know if He were so and would refuse to obey Him. But, as a matter of fact, what profane persons doubt, the evil spirits *know*—namely that He is God; and for that reason they flee from Him and fall at His feet, crying out even as they cried when He was in the body, "We know Thee Who Thou art, the Holy One of God," and, "Ah, what have I in common with Thee, Thou Son of God? I implore Thee, torment me not."

Both from the confession of the evil spirits and from the daily witness of His works, it is manifest, then, and let none presume to doubt it, that the Saviour has raised His own body, and that He is very Son of God, having His being from God as from a Father, Whose Word and Wisdom and Whose Power He is. He it is Who in these latter days assumed a body for the salvation of us all, and taught the world concerning the Father. He it is Who has destroyed death and freely graced us all with incorruption through the promise of the resurrection, having raised His own body as its first-fruits, and displayed it by the sign of the cross as the monument to His victory over death and its corruption.

St. Gregory Nazianzen
330-390

In all of early Christianity there is nothing quite like the trio of great theologians who put Cappadocia on the Christian map. The three of them—Basil and his younger brother Gregory of Nyssa, and their lifelong friend Gregory Nazianzen—were responsible for the final triumph of Nicene orthodoxy over both Arianism and Apollinarianism. Each had his own special talents but in combination their brilliance illuminated the entire Church, stabilizing it after a long period of turmoil and controversy.

Gregory Nazianzen, although his father was a bishop, was still unbaptized when he went to Caesarea to begin higher studies. He met Basil there and the two of them went on to Athens for further study around 350. After he had returned home his father almost forcibly ordained him a presbyter and he preached his first sermon at Easter in 362. In a few short years his brother, sister, father, and mother all died, and Gregory went into seclusion. But when Basil died in 379 and political events made the time ripe for reviving orthodoxy in Constantinople, Gregory was called to become its bishop.

Arianism had predominated in Constantinople for nearly forty years. Gregory, by his extraordinary preaching, turned that city around in two years. Called "the theologian" of the Eastern Church, and remembered as one of the greatest orators in Christian antiquity, his fame rests almost entirely on these *two years (379 and 380). Jerome was among the many who came from a distance to hear his remarkable teaching.*

Of the forty-five of his Orations that have come down to us, five of them (numbers 27 to 31) are singled out as the Theological Orations *on which his title as Theologian depends. We have selected two of them (29 and 30) for inclusion here. They are the two containing his chief attack upon Arianism. He sets out to show that the orthodox doctrine of the coequality of Father and Son is both more Christian and more logical than any Arian concept of a subordinate deity. His ample use of the Bible in his expositions is evident throughout and explains why Jerome found him "mighty in the Scriptures."*

When the Emperor Theodosius opened the Second Ecumenical Council in Constantinople in 381 to complete the work of Nicaea, he recognized Gregory as bishop of the capital. But when some late-comers from Egypt and Macedonia objected to his position, he became so disgusted that he resigned and went back to Nazianzus and spent his last years in semi-monastic retirement.

Together with Basil Gregory Nazianzen thus played a vital, if brief, role in the final defeat of Arianism. In doing so he made lasting contributions, such as the word "procession" to describe the relationship of the Holy Spirit to the Father and the Son. He added other precisions in Christology as well. He seems to have had more than his share of bad health and personal grief, and to have gravitated toward a more monastic lifestyle whenever he could manage it. But for those two crucial years in Constantinople his was the voice of the Christian Church reaffirming the Word of God.

THEOLOGICAL ORATIONS

XXIX. THE THIRD THEOLOGICAL ORATION

ON THE SON

This then is what might be said to cut short our opponents' readiness to argue and their hastiness with its consequent insecurity in all matters, but above all in those discussions which relate to God. But since to rebuke others is a matter of no difficulty whatever, but a very easy thing, which any one who likes can do; whereas to substitute one's own belief for theirs is the part of a pious and intelligent man; let us, relying on the Holy Ghost, Who among them is dishonoured, but among us is adored, bring forth to the light our own conceptions about the Godhead, whatever these may be, like some noble and timely birth. Not that I have at other times been silent; for on this subject alone I am full of youthful strength and daring; but the fact is that under present circumstances I am even more bold to declare the truth, that I may not (to use the words of Scripture) by drawing back fall into the condemnation of being displeasing to God. And since every discourse is of a twofold nature, the one part establishing one's own, and the other overthrowing one's opponents' position; let us first of all state our own position, and then try to controvert that of our opponents;—and both as briefly as possible, so that our arguments may be taken in at a glance (like those of the elementary treatises which they have devised to deceive simple or foolish persons), and that our thought may not be scattered by reason of the length of the discourse, like water which is not contained in a channel, but flows to waste over the open land.

II. The three most ancient opinions concerning God are Anarchia, Polyarchia, and Monarchia. The first two are the sport of the children of Hellas, and may they continue to be so factious, and thus anarchical, and thus disorderly. For both these tend to the same thing, namely disorder; and this to dissolution, for disorder is the first step to dissolution.

But Monarchy is that which we hold in honour. It is, however, a Monarchy that is not limited to one Person, for it is possible for Unity if at variance with itself to come into a condition of plurality; but one which is made of an equality of Nature and a Union of mind, and identity of motion, and a convergence of its elements to unity—a thing which is impossible to the created nature—so that though numerically distinct there is no severance of Essence. Therefore' Unity having from all eternity arrived by motion at Duality, found its rest in Trinity. This is what we mean by Father and Son and Holy Ghost. The Father is the Begetter and the Emitter; without passion, of course, and without reference to time, and not in a corporeal manner. The Son is the Begotten, and the Holy Ghost the Emission; for I know not how this could be expressed in terms altogether excluding visible things. For we shall not venture to speak of "an overflow of goodness," as one of the Greek Philosophers dared to say, as if it were a bowl overflowing, and this in plain words in his Discourse on the First and Second Causes. Let us not ever look on this Generation as involuntary, like some natural overflow, hard to be retained, and by no means befitting our conception of Deity. Therefore let us confine ourselves within our limits, and speak of the Unbegotten and the Begotten and That which proceeds from the Father, as somewhere God the Word Himself saith.

III. When did these come into being? They are above all "When." But, if I am to speak with something more of boldness,—when the Father did. And when did the Father come into being. There never was a time when He was not. And the same thing is true of the Son and the Holy Ghost. Ask me again, and again I will answer you, When was the Son begotten? When the Father was not begotten. And when did the Holy Ghost proceed? When the Son was, not proceeding but, begotten—beyond the sphere of time, and above the grasp of reason; although we cannot set forth that which is above time, if we avoid as we desire any expression which conveys the idea of time. For such expressions as "when" and "before" and "after" and "from the beginning" are not timeless, however much we may force them; unless indeed we were to take the Aeon, that interval which is coextensive with the eternal things, and is not divided or measured by any motion, or by the revolution of the sun, as time is measured.

How then are They not alike unoriginate, if They are coeternal? Because They are from Him, though not after Him. For that which is unoriginate is eternal, but that which is eternal is not necessarily unoriginate, so long as it may be referred to the Father as its origin. Therefore in respect of Cause They are not unoriginate; but it is evident that the Cause is not necessarily prior to its effects, for the sun is not prior to its light. And yet They are in some sense unoriginate, in respect of time, even though you would scare simple minds with your quibbles, for the Sources of Time are not subject to time.

IV. But how can this generation be passionless? In that it is incorporeal. For if corporeal generation involves passion, incorporeal generation excludes it. And I will ask of you in turn, How is He God if He is created? For that which is created is not God. I refrain from reminding you that here too is passion if we take the creation in a bodily sense, as time, desire, imagination, thought, hope, pain, risk, failure, success, all of which and more than all find a place in the creature, as is evident to every one. Nay, I marvel that you do not venture so far as to conceive of marriages and times of pregnancy, and dangers of miscarriage, as if the Father could not have begotten at all if He had not begotten thus; or again, that you did not count up the modes of generation of birds and beasts and fishes, and bring under some one of them the Divine and Ineffable Generation, or even eliminate the Son out of your new hypothesis. And you cannot even see this, that as His Generation according to the flesh differs from all others (for where among men do you know of a Virgin Mother?), so does He differ also in His spiritual Generation; or rather He, Whose Existence is not the same as ours, differs from us also in His Generation.

V. Who then is that Father Who had no beginnine? One Whose very Existence had no beginning; for one whose existence had a beginning must also have begun to be a Father. He did not then become a Father after He began to be, for His being had no beginning. And He is Father in the Absolute sense, for He is not also Son; just as the Son is Son in the absolute sense, because He is not also Father. These names do not belong to us in the absolute sense, because we are both, and not one more than the other; and we are of both, and not of one only; and so we are divided, and by degrees become men, and perhaps not even men, and such as we did not desire, leaving and being left, so that only the relations remain, without the underlying facts.

But the objector says, the very form of the expression "He begat" and "He was begotten," brings in the idea of a beginning of generation. But what if you do not use this expression, but say, "He had been begotten from the beginning" so as readily to evade your far-fetched and time-loving objections? Will you bring Scripture against us, as if we were forging something contrary to Scripture and to the truth? Why, every one knows that in practice we very often find tenses interchanged when time is spoken of; and especially is this the custom of Holy Scripture, not only in respect of the past tense, and of the present; but even of the future, as for instance "Why did the heathen rage?" when they had not yet raged; and "they shall cross over the river on foot," where the meaning is they did cross over. It would be a long task to reckon up all the expressions of this kind which students have noticed.

VI. So much for this point. What is their next objection, how full of contentiousness and impudence? He, they say, either voluntarily begat the Son, or else involuntarily. Next, as they think, they bind us on both sides with cords; these however are not strong, but very weak. For, they say, if it was involuntarily he was under the sway of some one, and who exercised this sway; And how is He, over whom it is exercised, God? But if voluntarily, the Son is a Son of Will; how then is He of the Father?—and they thus invent a new sort of Mother for him,—the Will,—in place of the Father. There is one good point which they may allege about this argument of theirs; namely, that they desert Passion, and take refuge in Will. For Will is not Passion.

Secondly, let us look at the strength of their argument. And it were best to wrestle with them at first at close quarters. You yourself, who so recklessly assert whatever takes your fancy; were you begotten voluntarily or involuntarily by your father? If involuntarily, then he was under some tyrant's sway (O terrible violence!) and who was the tyrant? You will hardly say it was nature,—for nature is tolerant of chastity. If it was voluntarily, then by a few syllables your father is done away with, for you are shewn to be the son of Will, and not of your father. But I pass to the relation between God and the creature, and I put your own question to your own wisdom. Did God *create* all things voluntarily or under compulsion? If under compulsion, here also is the tyranny, and one who played the tyrant; if voluntarily, the creatures also are deprived of their God, and you before the rest, who invent such arguments and tricks of logic. For a partition is set up between the Creator and the creatures in the shape of Will. And yet I think that the Person who wills is distinct from the Act of willing; He who begets from the Act of begetting; the Speaker from the speech, or else we are all very stupid. On the one side we have the mover, and on the other that which is, so to speak, the motion. Thus the thing willed is not the child of will, for it does not always result therefrom; nor is that which is begotten the child of generation, nor that which is heard the child of speech, but of the Person who willed, or begat, or spoke. But the things of God are beyond all this, for with Him perhaps the Will to beget is generation, and there is no intermediate action (if we may accept this altogether, and not rather consider generation superior to will).

VII. Will you then let me play a little upon this word Father, for your example encourages me to be so bold? The Father is God either willingly or unwillingly; and how will you escape from your own excessive acuteness? If willingly, when did He begin to will? It could not have been before He began to be, for there was nothing prior to Him. Or is one part of Him Will and another the object of Will? If so, He is divisible. So the question arises, as the result of your argument, whether He Himself is not the child of Will. And if unwillingly, what compelled Him to exist, and how is He God if He was compelled—

and that to nothing less than to be God? How then was He begotten, says my opponent. How was He created, if as you say, He was created? For this is a part of the same difficulty. Perhaps you would say, By Will and Word. You have not yet solved the whole difficulty; for it yet remains for you to shew how Will and Word gained the power of action. For man was not created in this way.

VIII. How then was He begotten? This Generation would have been no great thing, if you could have comprehended it who have no real knowledge even of your own generation, or at least who comprehend very little of it, and of that little you are ashamed to speak; and then do you think you know the whole? You will have to undergo much labour before you discover the laws of composition, formation, manifestation, and the bond whereby soul is united to Body,—mind to soul, and reason to mind; and movement, increase, assimilation of food, sense, memory, recollection, and all the rest of the parts of which you are compounded; and which of them belongs to the soul and body together, and which to each independently of the other, and which is received from each other. For those parts whose maturity comes later, yet received their laws at the time of conception. Tell me what these laws are? And do not even then venture to speculate on the Generation of God; for that would be unsafe. For even if you knew all about your own, yet you do not by any means know about God's. And if you do not understand your own, how can you know about God's? For in proportion as God is harder to trace out than man, so is the heavenly Generation harder to comprehend than your own. But if you assert that because you cannot comprehend it, therefore He cannot have been begotten, it will be time for you to strike out many existing things which you cannot comprehend; and first of all God Himself. For you cannot say what He is, even if you are very reckless, and excessively proud of your intelligence. First, cast away your notions of flow and divisions and sections, and your conceptions of immaterial as if it were material birth, and then you may perhaps worthily conceive of the Divine Generation. How was He begotten?—I repeat the question in indignation. The Begetting of God must be honoured by silence. It is a great thing for you to learn that he was begotten. But the manner of His generation we will not admit that even Angels can conceive, much less you. Shall I tell you how it was? It was in a manner known to the Father Who begat, and to the Son Who was begotten. Anything more than this is hidden by a cloud, and escapes your dim sight.

IX. Well, but the Father begat a Son who either was or was not in existence. What utter nonsense! This is a question which applies to you or me, who on the one hand were in existence, as for instance Levi in the loins of Abraham; and on the other hand came into existence; and so in some sense we are partly of what existed, and partly of what was nonexistent; whereas the contrary is the case with the original matter, which was certainly created out of what was non-existent, notwithstanding that some pretend that it is unbegotten. But in this case "to be begotten," even from the beginning, is concurrent with "to be." On what then will you base this captious question? For what is older than that which is from the beginning, if we may place there the previous existence or non-existence of the Son? In either case we destroy its claim to be the Beginning. Or perhaps you will say, if we were to ask you whether the Father was of existent or non-existent substance, that he is twofold, partly pre-existing, partly existing; or that His case is the same with that of the Son; that is, that He was created out of non-existing matter, because of your ridiculous questions and your houses of sand, which cannot stand against the merest ripple.

I do not admit either solution, and I declare that your question contains an absurdity, and not a difficulty to answer. If however you think, in accordance with your dialectic assumptions, that one or other of these alternatives must necessarily be true in every case, let me ask you one little question: Is time in time, or is it not in time? If it is contained in time, then in what time, and what is it but that time, and how does it contain it? But if it is not contained in time, what is that surpassing wisdom which can conceive of a time which is timeless? Now, in regard to this expression, "I am now telling a lie," admit one of these alternatives, either that it is true, or that it is a falsehood, without qualification (for we cannot admit that it is both). But this cannot be. For necessarily he either is lying, or so is telling the truth, or else he is telling the truth, and so is lying. What wonder is it then that, as in this case contraries are true, so in that case they should both be untrue, and so your clever puzzle prove mere foolishness? Solve me one more riddle. Were you present at your own generation, and are you now present to yourself, or is neither the case? If you were and are present, who were you, and with whom are you present? And how did your single self become thus both subject and object? But if neither of the above is the case, how did you get separated from yourself, and what is the cause of this disjoining? But, you will say, it is stupid to make a fuss about the question whether or no a single individual is present to himself; for the expression is not used of oneself but of others. Well, you may be certain that it is even more stupid to discuss the question whether That which was begotten from the beginning existed before its generation or not. For such a question arises only as to matter divisible by time.

X. But they say, The Unbegotten and the Begotten are not the same; and if this is so, neither is the Son the same as the Father. It is clear, without saying so, that this line of argument manifestly excludes either the Son or the Father from the Godhead. For if to be Unbegotten is the Essence of God, to be begotten is not that Essence; if the opposite is the case, the Unbegotten is excluded. What argument can contradict this? Choose then whichever blasphemy you prefer, my good inventor of a new theology, if indeed you are anxious at all costs to embrace a blasphemy. In the next place, in what sense do you assert that the Unbegotten and the Begotten are not the same? If you mean that the Uncreated and the created are not the same, I agree with you; for certainly the Unoriginate and the created are not of the same nature. But if you say that He That begat and That which is begotten are not the same, the statement is inaccurate. For it is in fact a necessary truth that they are the same. For the nature of the relation of Father to Child is this, that the offspring is of the same nature with the parent. Or we may argue thus again. What do you mean by Unbegotten and Begotten, for if you mean the simple fact of being unbegotten or begotten, these are not the same; but

142

if you mean Those to Whom these terms apply, how are They not the same? For example, Wisdom and Unwisdom are not the same in themselves, but yet both are attributes of man, who is the same; and they mark not a difference of essence, but one external to the essence. Are immortality and innocence and immutability also the essence of God? If so God has many essences and not one; or Deity is a compound of these. For He cannot be all these without composition, if they be essences.

XI. They do not however assert this, for these qualities are common also to other beings. But God's Essence is that which belongs to God alone, and is proper to Him. But they, who consider matter and form to be unbegotten, would not allow that to be unbegotten is the property of God alone (for we must cast away even further the darkness of the Manichaeans. But suppose that it is the property of God alone. What of Adam? Was he not alone the direct creature of God? Yes, you will say. Was he then the only human being? By no means. And why, but because humanity does not consist in direct creation? For that which is begotten is also human. Just so neither is He Who is Unbegotten alone God, though He alone is Father. But grant that He Who is Begotten is God; for He is *of* God, as you must allow, even though you cling to your Unbegotten. Then how do you describe the Essence of God? Not by declaring what it is, but by rejecting what it is not. For your word signifies that He is not begotten; it does not present to you what is the real nature or condition of that which has no generation. What then *is* the Essence of God? It is for your infatuation to define this, since you are so anxious about His Generation too; but to us it will be a very great thing, if ever, even in the future, we learn this, when this darkness and dullness is done away for us, as He has promised Who cannot lie. This then may be the thought and hope of those who are purifying themselves with a view to this. Thus much we for our part will be bold to say, that if it is a great thing for the Father to be Unoriginate, it is no less a thing for the Son to have been Begotten of such a Father. For not only would He share the glory of the Unoriginate, since he is of the Unoriginate, but he has the added glory of His Generation, a thing so great and august in the eyes of all those who are not altogether grovelling and material in mind.

XII. But, they say, if the Son is the Same as the Father in respect of Essence, then if the Father is unbegotten, the Son must be so likewise. Quite so—if the Essence of God consists in being unbegotten; and so He would be a strange mixture, begottenly unbegotten. If, however, the difference is outside the Essence, how can you be so certain in speaking of this? Are you also your father's father, so as in no respect to fall short of your father, since you are the same with him in essence? Is it not evident that our enquiry into the Nature of the Essence of God, if we make it, will leave Personality absolutely unaffected? But that Unbegotten is not a synonym of God is proved thus. If it were so, it would be necessary that since God is a relative term, Unbegotten should be so likewise; or that since Unbegotten is an absolute term, so must God be . . . God of no one. For words which are absolutely identical are similarly applied. But the word Unbegotten is not used relatively. For to what is it relative? And of what things is God the God? Why, of all things. How then can God and Unbegotten be identical terms? And again, since Begotten and Unbegotten are contradictories, like possession and deprivation, it would follow that contradictory essences would co-exist, which is impossible. Or again, since possessions are prior to deprivations, and the latter are destructive of the former, not only must the Essence of the Son be prior to that of the Father, but it must be destroyed by the Father, on your hypothesis.

XIII. What now remains of their invincible arguments? Perhaps the last they will take refuge in is this. If God has never ceased to beget, the Generation is imperfect; and when will He cease? But if He has ceased, then He must have begun. Thus again these carnal minds bring forward carnal arguments. Whether He is eternally begotten or not, I do not yet say, until I have looked into the statement, "Before all the hills He begetteth Me," more accurately. But I cannot see the necessity of their conclusion. For if, as they say, everything that is to come to an end had also a beginning, then surely that which has no end had no beginning. What then will they decide concerning the soul, or the Angelic nature? If it had a beginning, it will also have an end; and if it has no end, it is evident that according to them it had no beginning. But the truth is that it had a beginning, and will never have an end. Their assertion, then, that that which will have an end had also a beginning, is untrue. Our position, however, is, that as in the case of a horse, or an ox, or a man, the same definition applies to all the individuals of the same species, and whatever shares the definition has also a right to the Name; so in the very same way there is One Essence of God, and One Nature, and One Name; although in accordance with a distinction in our thoughts we use distinct Names; and that whatever is properly called by this Name really is God; and what He is in Nature, That He is truly called— if at least we are to hold that Truth is a matter not of names but of realities. But our opponents, as if they were afraid of leaving any stone unturned to subvert the Truth, acknowledge indeed that the Son is God when they are compelled to do so by arguments and evidences; but they only mean that He is God in an ambiguous sense, and that He only shares the Name.

XIV. And when we advance this objection against them, "What do you mean to say then? That the Son is not properly God, just as a picture of an animal is not properly an animal? And if not properly God, in what sense is He God at all?" They reply, Why should not these terms be ambiguous, and in both cases be used in a proper sense? And they will give us such instances as the land-dog and the dogfish; where the word Dog is ambiguous, and yet in both cases is properly used, for there is such a species among the ambiguously named, or any other case in which the same appellative is used for two things of different nature. But, my good friend, in this case, when you include two natures under the same name, you do not assert that either is better than the other, or that the one is prior and the other posterior, or that one is in a greater degree and the other in a lesser that which is predicated of them both, for there is no connecting link which forces this necessity upon them. One is not a dog more than the other, and one less so; either the dogfish more than the land-dog, or the land-dog than the dogfish. Why should they be, or on what principle? But the community of name is here between things of equal value, though of different nature. But in the case of which we are speaking, you couple the Name of God with adorable Majesty, and make It surpass every essence and nature (an attribute of God alone), and then you ascribe this Name to the Father, while you deprive the Son of it, and make Him subject to the Father, and give Him only a secondary honour and worship; and even if in words you bestow on Him one which is Equal, yet in practice you cut off His Deity, and pass malignantly from a use of the same Name implying an exact equality, to one which connects things which are not equal. And so the pictured and the living man are in your mouth an apter illustration of the relations of Deity than the dogs which I instanced. Or else you must concede to both an equal dignity of nature as well as a common name—even though you introduced these natures into your argument as different; and thus you destroy the analogy of your dogs, which you invented as an instance of inequality. For what is the force of your instance of ambiguity, if those whom you distinguish are not equal in honour? For it was not to prove an equality but an inequality that you took refuge in your dogs. How could anybody be more clearly convicted of fighting both against his own arguments, and against the Deity?

XV. And if, when we admit that in respect of being the Cause the Father is greater than the Son, they should assume the premiss that He is the Cause by Nature, and then deduce the conclusion that He is greater by Nature also, it is difficult to say whether they mislead most themselves or those with whom they are arguing. For it does not absolutely follow that all that is predicated of a class can also be predicated of all the individuals composing it; for the different particulars may belong to different individuals. For what hinders me, if I assume the same premiss, namely, that the Father is greater by Nature, and then add this other, Yet not by nature in every respect greater nor yet Father—from concluding, Therefore the Greater is not in every respect greater, nor the Father in every respect Father? Or, if you prefer it, let us put it in this way: God is an Essence: But an Essence is not in every case God; and draw the conclusion for yourself—Therefore God is not in every case God. I think the fallacy here is the arguing from a conditioned to an unconditioned use of a term, to use the technical expression of the logicians. For while we assign this word Greater to His Nature viewed as a Cause, they infer it of His Nature viewed in itself. It is just as if when we said that such a one was a dead man they were to infer simply that he was a Man.

XVI. How shall we pass over the following point, which is no less amazing than the rest? Father, they say, is a name either of an essence or of an Action, thinking to bind us down on both sides. If we say that it is a name of an essence, they will say that we agree with them that the Son is of another Essence, since there is but one Essence of God, and this, according to them, is preoccupied by the Father. On the other hand, if we say that it is the name of an Action, we shall be supposed to acknowledge plainly that the Son is created and not begotten. For where there is an Agent there must also be an Effect. And they will say they wonder how that which is made can be identical with That which made it. I should myself have been frightened with your distinction, if it had been necessary to accept one or other of the alternatives, and not rather put both aside, and state a third and truer one, namely, the Father is not a name either of an essence or of an action, most clever sirs. But it is the name of the Relation in which the Father stands to the Son, and the Son to the Father. For as with us these names make known a genuine and intimate relation, so, in the case before us too, they denote an identity of nature between Him That is begotten and Him That begets. But let us concede to you that Father is a name of essence, it will still bring in the idea of Son, and will not make it of a different nature, according to common ideas and the force of these names. Let it be, if it so please you, the name of an action; you will not defeat us in this way either. The Homoousion would be indeed the result of this action, or otherwise the conception of an action in this matter would be absurd. You see then how, even though you try to fight unfairly, we avoid your sophistries. But now, since we have ascertained how invincible you are in your arguments and sophistries, let us look at your strength in the Oracles of God, if perchance you may choose to persuade us out of them.

XVII. For we have learnt to believe in and to teach the Deity of the Son from their great and lofty utterances. And what utterances are these? These: God—The Word—He That Was In The Beginning and With The Beginning, and The Beginning. "In the Beginning was The Word, and the Word was with God, and the Word was God," and "With Thee is the Beginning," and "He who calleth her The Beginning from generations." Then the Son is Only-begotten: The only "begotten Son which is in the bosom of the Father, it says, He hath declared Him." The Way, the Truth, the Life, the Light. "I am the Way, the Truth, and the Life;" and "I am the Light of the World." Wisdom and Power, "Christ, the Wisdom of God, and the Power of God." The Effulgence, the Impress, the Image, the Seal; "Who being the Effulgence of His glory and the Impress of His Essence," and "the Image of His Goodness," and "Him hath God the Father sealed." Lord, King, He That Is, The Almighty. "The Lord rained down fire from the Lord;" and "A sceptre of righteousness is the sceptre of Thy Kingdom;" and "Which is and was and is to come, the Almighty"—all which are clearly spoken of the Son, with all the other passages of the same force, none of which is an afterthought, or added later to the Son or the Spirit, any more than to the Father Himself. For Their Perfection is not affected by additions. There never was a time when He was without the Word, or when He was not wise, or not powerful, or devoid of life, or of splendour, or of goodness.

But in opposition to all these, do you reckon up for me the expressions which make for your ignorant arrogance, such as "My God and your God," or greater, or created, or made, or sanctified; Add, if you like, Servant and Obedient and Gave and Learnt, and was commanded, was sent, can do nothing of Himself, either say, or judge, or give, or will. And further these,—His ignorance, subjection, prayer, asking, increase, being made perfect. And if you like even more humble than these; such as speak of His sleeping, hungering, being in an agony, and fearing; or perhaps you would make even His Cross and Death a matter of reproach to Him. His Resurrection and Ascension I fancy you will leave to me, for in these is found something to support *our* position. A good many other things too you might pick up, if you desire to put together that equivocal and intruded god of yours, Who to us is True God, and equal to the Father. For every one of these points, taken separately, may very easily, if we go through them one by one, be explained to you in the most reverent sense and the stumbling-block of the letter be cleansed away—that is, if your stumbling at it be honest, and not wilfully malicious. To give you the explanation in one sentence. What is lofty you are to apply to the Godhead, and to that Nature in Him which is superior to sufferings and incorporeal; but all that is lowly to the composite condition of Him who for your sakes made Himself of no reputation and was Incarnate—yes, for it is no worse thing to say, was made Man, and afterwards was also exalted. The result will be that you will abandon these carnal and grovelling doctrines, and learn to be more sublime, and to ascend with His Godhead, and you will not remain permanently among the things of sight, but will rise up with Him into the world of thought, and come to know which passages refer to His Nature, and which to His assumption of Human Nature.

XIX. For He Whom you now treat with contempt was once above you. He Who is now Man was once the Uncompounded. What He was He continued to be; what He was not He took to Himself. In the Beginning He was, uncaused; for what is the Cause of God? But afterwards for a cause He was born. And that cuase was that you might be saved, who insult Him and despise His Godhead, because of this, that He took upon Him your denser nature, having converse with Flesh by means of Mind. While His inferior Nature, the Humanity, became God, because it was united to God, and became One Person because the Higher Nature prevailed . . . in order that I too might be made God so far as He is made Man. He was Born—but He had been begotten: He was born of a woman—but she was a Virgin. The first is human the second Divine. In His Human nature He had no Father, but also in His Divine Nature no Mother. Both these belong to Godhead. He dwelt in the womb—but He was recognized by the Prophet, himself still in the womb, leaping before the Word, for Whose sake He came into being. He was wrapped in swaddling clothes—but He took off the swathing bands of the grave by His rising again.

He was laid in a manger—but He was glorified by Angels, and proclaimed by a star, and worshipped by the Magi. Why are you offended by that which is presented to your sight, because you will not look at that which is presented to your mind? He was driven into exile into Egypt—but He drove away the Egyptian idols. He had no form nor comeliness in the eyes of the Jews—but to David He is fairer than the children of men. And on the Mountain He was bright as the lightning, and became more luminous than the sun, initiating us into the mystery of the future.

XX. He was baptized as Man—but He remitted sins as God—not because He needed purificatory rites Himself, but that He might sanctify the element of water. He was tempted as Man, but He conquered as God; yea, He bids us be of good cheer, for He has overcome the world. He hungered—but He fed thousands; yea, He is the Bread that giveth life, and That is of heaven. He thirsted—but He cried, If any man thirst, let him come unto Me and drink. Yea, He promised that fountains should flow from them that believe. He was wearied, but He is the Rest of them that are weary and heavy laden. He was heavy with sleep, but He walked lightly over the sea. He rebuked the winds, He made Peter light as he began to sink. He pays tribute, but it is out of a fish; yea, He is the King of those who demanded it.

He is called a Samaritan and a demoniac;—but He saves him that came down from Jerusalem and fell among thieves; the demons acknowledge Him, and He drives out demons, and sinks in the sea legions of foul spirits, and sees the Prince of the demons falling like lightning. He is stoned, but is not taken. He prays, but He hears prayer. He weeps, but He causes tears to cease. He asks where Lazarus was laid, for He was Man; but He raises Lazarus, for He was God. He is sold, and very cheap, for it is only for thirty pieces of silver; but He redeems the world, and that at a great price, for the Price was His own blood. As a sheep He is led to the slaughter, but He is the Shepherd of Israel, and now of the whole world also. As a Lamb He is silent, yet He is the Word, and is proclaimed by the Voice of one crying in the wilderness. He is bruised and wounded, but He healeth every disease and every infirmity. He is lifted up and nailed to the Tree, but by the Tree of Life He restoreth us; yea, He saveth even the Robber crucified with Him; yea, He wrapped the visible world in darkness. He is given vinegar to drink mingled with gall. Who? He who turned the water into wine, who is the destroyer of the bitter taste, who is Sweetness and altogether desire. He lays down His life, but He has power to take it again; and the veil is rent, for the mysterious doors of Heaven are opened; the rocks are cleft, the dead arise. He dies, but He gives life, and by His death destroys death. He is buried, but He rises again; He goes down into Hell, but He brings up the souls; He ascends to Heaven, and shall come again to judge the quick and the dead, and to put to the test such words as yours. If the one give you a starting point for your error, let the others put an end to it.

XXI. This, then is our reply to those who would puzzle us; not given willingly indeed (for light talk and contradictions of words are not agreeable to the faithful, and one Adversary is enough for us), but of necessity, for the sake of our assailants (for medicines exist because of diseases), that they may be led to see that they are not all-wise nor invincible in those superflous arguments which make void the Gospel. For when we leave off believing, and protect ourselves by mere strength of argument, and destroy the claim which the Spirit has upon our faith by questionings, and then our argument is not strong enough for the importance of the subject (and this must necessarily be the case, since it is put in motion by an organ of so little power as is our mind), what is the result? The weakness of the argument appears to belong to the mystery, and thus elegance of language makes void the Cross, as Paul also thought. For faith is that which completes our argument. But may He who proclaimeth unions and looseth those that are bond, and who putteth into our minds to solve the knots of their unnatural dogmas, if it may be, change these men and make them faithful instead of rhetoricians, Christians instead of that which they now are called. This indeed we entreat and beg for Christ's sake. Be ye reconciled to God, and quench not the Spirit; or rather, may Christ be reconciled to you, and may the Spirit enlighten you, though so late. But if you are too fond of your quarrel, we at any rate will hold fast to the Trinity, and by the Trinity may we be saved, remaining pure and without offence, until the more perfect shewing forth of that which we desire, in Him, Christ our Lord, to Whom be the glory for ever.

Amen.

THE FOURTH THEOLOGICAL ORATION, WHICH IS THE SECOND CONCERNING THE SON

I. Since I have by the power of the Spirit sufficiently overthrown the subtleties and intricacies of the arguments, and already solved in the mass the objections and oppositions drawn from Holy Scripture, with which these sacrilegious robbers of the Bible and thieves of the sense of its contents draw over the multitude to their side, and confuse the way of truth; and that not without clearness, as I believe all candid persons will say; attributing to the Deity the higher and diviner expressions, and the lower and more human to Him Who for us men was the Second Adam, and was God made capable of suffering to strive against sin; yet we have not yet gone through the passages in detail, because of the haste of our argument. But since you demand of us a brief explanation of each of them, that you may not be carried away by the plausibilities of their arguments, we will therefore state the explanations summarily, dividing them into numbers for the sake of carrying them more easily in mind.

II. In their eyes the following is only too ready to hand "The *Lord* created me at the beginning of His ways with a view to His works." How shall we meet this? Shall we bring an accusation against Solomon, or reject his former words because of his fall in after-life? Shall we say that the words are those of Wisdom herself, as it were of Knowledge and the Creator-word, in accordance with which all things were made? For Scripture often personifies many even lifeless objects; as for instance, "The Sea said" so and so; and, "The Depth saith, It is not in me;" and "The Heavens declare the glory of God;" and again a command is given to the Sword; and the Mountains and Hills are asked the reason of their skipping. We do not allege any of these, though some of our predecessors used them as powerful arguments. But let us grant that the expression is used of our Saviour Himself, the true Wisdom. Let us consider one small point together. What among all things that exist is unoriginate? The Godhead. For no one can tell the origin of God, that otherwise would be older than God. But what is the cause of the Manhood, which for our sake God assumed? It was surely our Salvation. What else could it be? Since then we find here clearly both the Created and the Begetteth Me, the argument is simple. Whatever we find joined with a cause we are to refer to the Manhood, but all that is absolute and unoriginate we are to reckon to the account of His Godhead. Well, then, is not this "Created" said in connection with a cause? He created Me, it so says, as the beginning of His ways, with a view to his works. Now, the Works of His Hands are verity and judgment; for whose sake He was anointed with Godhead; for this anointing is of the Manhood; but the "He begetteth Me" is not connected with a cause; or it is for you to shew the adjunct. What argument then will disprove that Wisdom is called a creature, in connection with the lower generation, but Begotten in respect of the first and more incomprehensible?

III. Next is the fact of His being called Servant and serving many well, and that it is a great thing for Him to be called the Child of God. For in truth He was in servitude to flesh and to birth and to the conditions of our life with a view to our liberation, and to that of all those whom He has saved, who were in bondage under sin. What greater destiny can befall man's humility than that he should be intermingled with God, and by this intermingling should be deified, and that we should be so visited by the Dayspring from on high, that even that Holy Thing that should be born should be called the Son of the Highest, and that there should be bestowed upon Him a Name which is above every name? And what else can this be than God?—and that every knee should bow to Him That was made of no reputation for us, and That mingled the Form of God with the form of a servant, and that all the House of Israel should know that God hath made Him both Lord and Christ? For all this was done by the action of the Begotten, and by the good pleasure of Him That begat Him.

IV. Well, what is the second of their great irresistible passages? "He must reign," till such and such a time . . . and "be received by heaven until the time of restitution," and "have the seat at the Right Hand until the overthrow of enemies." But after this? Must He cease to be King, or be removed from Heaven? Why, who shall make Him cease, or for what cause? What a bold and very anarchical interpreter you are; and yet you have heard that Of His Kingdom *there shall be no end.* Your mistake arises from not understanding that Until is not always exclusive of that which comes after, but asserts *up to* that time, without denying what comes *after* it. To take a single instance—how else would you understand, "Lo, I am with you always, even unto the end of the world?" Does it mean that He will no longer be so afterwards. And for what reason? But this is not the only cause of your error; you also fail to distinguish between the things that are signified. He is said to reign in one sense as the Almighty King, both of the willing and the unwilling; but in another as producing in us submission, and placing us under His Kingship as willingly acknowledging His Sovereignty. Of His Kingdom, considered in the former sense, there shall be no end. But in the second sense, what end will there be? His taking us as His servants, on our entrance into a state of salvation. For what need is there to Work Submission in us when we have already submitted? After which He arises to judge the earth, and to separate the saved from the lost. After that He is to stand as God in the midst of gods, that is, of the saved, distinguishing and deciding of what honour and of what mansion each is worthy.

V. Take, in the next place, the subjection by which you subject the Son to the Father. What, you say, is He not now subject, or must He, if He is God, be subject to God? You are fashioning your argument as if it concerned some robber, or some hostile deity. But look at it in this manner; that as for my sake He was called a curse, Who destroyed my curse; and sin, who taketh away the sin of the world; and became a new Adam to take the place of the old, just so He makes my disobedience His own as Head of the whole body. As long as I am disobedient and rebellious, both by denial of God and by my passions, so long Christ also is called disobedient on my account. But when all things shall be subdued unto Him on the one hand by acknowledgment of Him, and on the other by a reformation, then He Himself also will have fulfilled His submission, bringing me whom He has saved to God. For this, according to my view, is the subjection of Christ; namely, the fulfilling of the Father's Will. But as the Son subjects all to the Father, so does the Father to the Son; the One by His Work, the Other by His good pleasure, as we have already said. And thus He Who subjects presents to God that which he has subjected, making our condition His own. Of the same kind, it appears to me, is the expression, "My God, My God, why hast Thou forsaken Me?" It was not He who was forsaken either by the Father, or by His own Godhead, as some have thought, as if It were afraid of the Passion, and therefore withdrew Itself from Him in His Sufferings (for who compelled Him either to be born on earth at all, or to be lifted up on the Cross?) But as I said, He was in His own Person representing us. For we were the forsaken and despised before, but now by the Sufferings of Him Who could not suffer, we were taken up and saved. Similarly, He makes His own our folly and our transgressions; and says what follows in the Psalm, for it is very evident that the Twenty-first Psalm refers to Christ.

VI. The same consideration applies to another passage, "He learnt obedience by the things which He suffered," and to His "strong crying and tears," and His "Entreaties," and His "being heard," and His "Reverence," all of which He wonderfully wrought out, like a drama whose plot was devised on our behalf. For in His character of the Word He was neither obedient nor disobedient. For such expressions belong to servants, and inferiors, and the one applies to the better sort of them, while the other belongs to those who deserve punishment. But, in the character of the Form of a Servant, He condescends to His fellow servants, nay, to His servants, and takes upon Him a strange form, bearing all me and mine in Himself, that in Himself He may exhaust the bad, as fire does wax, or as the sun does the mists of earth; and that I may partake of His nature by the blending. Thus He honours obedience by His action, and proves it experimentally by His Passion. For to possess the disposition is not enough, just as it would not be enough for us, unless we also proved it by our acts; for action is the proof of disposition.

And perhaps it would not be wrong to assume this also, that by the art of His love for man He gauges our obedience, and measures all by comparison with His own Sufferings, so that He may know our condition by His own, and how much is demanded of us, and how much we yield, taking into the account, along with our environment, our weakness also. For if the Light shining through the veil upon the darkness, that is upon this life, was persecuted by the other darkness (I mean, the Evil One and the Tempter), how much more will the darkness be persecuted, as being weaker than it? And what marvel is it, that though He entirely escaped, we have been, at any rate in part, overtaken? For it is a more wonderful thing that He should have been chased than that we should have been captured;—at least to the minds of all who reason aright on the subject. I will add yet another passage to those I have mentioned, because I think that it clearly tends to the same sense. I mean "In that He hath suffered being tempted, He is able to succour them that are tempted." But God will be all in all in the time of restitution; not in the sense that the Father alone will Be; and the Son be wholly resolved into Him, like a torch into a great pyre, from which it was reft away for a little space, and then put back (for I would not have even the Sabellians injured by such an expression); but the entire Godhead . . . when we shall be no longer divided (as we now are by movements and passions), and containing nothing at all of God, or very little, but shall be entirely like.

VII. As your third point you count the Word Greater; and as your fourth, To My God and your God. And indeed, if He had been called greater, and the word equal had not occurred, this might perhaps have been a point in their favour. But if we find both words clearly used what will these gentlemen have to say? How will it strengthen their argument? How will they reconcile the irreconcilable? For that the same thing should be at once greater than and equal to the same thing is an impossibility and the evident solution is that the Greater refers to origination, while the Equal belongs to the Nature; and this we acknowledge with much good will. But perhaps some one else will back up our attack on your argument, and assert, that That which is from such a Cause is not inferior to that which has no Cause; for it would share the glory of the Unoriginate, because it is from the Unoriginate. And there is, besides, the Generation, which is to all men a matter so marvellous and of such Majesty. For to say that he is greater than the Son considered as man, is true indeed, but is no great thing. For what marvel is it if God is greater than man? Surely that is enough to say in answer to their talk about Greater.

VIII. As to the other passages, My God would be used in respect, not of the Word, but of the Visible Word. For how could there be a God of Him Who is properly God? In the same way He is Father, not of the Visible, but of the Word; for our Lord was of two Natures; so that one expression is used properly, the other improperly in each of the two cases; but exactly the opposite way to their use in respect of us. For with respect to us God is properly our God, but not properly our Father. And this is the cause of the error of the Heretics, namely the joining of these two Names, which are interchanged because of the Union of the Natures. And an indication of this is found in the fact that wherever the Natures are distinguished in our thoughts from one another; the Names are also distinguished; as you hear in Paul's words, "The God of our Lord Jesus Christ, the Father of Glory." The God of Christ, but the Father of glory. For although these two terms express but one Person, yet this is not by a Unity of Nature, but by a Union of the two. What could be clearer?

IX. Fifthly, let it be alleged that it is said of Him that He receives life, judgment, inheritance of the Gentiles, or power over all flesh, or glory, or disciples, or whatever else is mentioned. This also belongs to the Manhood; and yet if you were to ascribe it to the Godhead, it would be no absurdity. For you would not so ascribe it as if it were newly acquired, but as belonging to Him from the beginning by reason of nature, and not as an act of favour.

X. Sixthly, let it be asserted that it is written, The Son can do nothing of Himself, but what He seeth the Father do. The solution of this is as follows:—Can and Cannot are not words with only one meaning, but have many meanings. On the one hand they are used sometimes in respect of deficiency of strength, sometimes in respect of time, and sometimes relatively to a certain object; as for instance, A Child cannot be an Athlete, or, A Puppy cannot see, or fight with so and so. Perhaps some day the child will be an athlete, the puppy will see, will fight with that other, though it may still be unable to fight with Any other. Or again, they may be used of that which is Generally true. For instance,—A city that is set on a hill cannot be hid; while yet it might possibly be hidden by another higher hill being in a line with it. Or in another sense they are used of a thing which is not reasonable; as, Can the Children of the Bridechamber fast while the Bridegroom is with them; whether He be considered as visible in bodily form (for the time of His sojourning among us was not one of mourning, but of gladness), or, as the Word. For why should they keep a bodily fast who are cleansed by the Word? Or, again, they are used of that which is contrary to the will; as in, He could do no mighty works there because of their unbelief,—i.e. of those who should receive them. For since in order to healing there is need of both faith in the patient and power in the Healer, when one of the two failed the other was impossible. But probably this sense also is to be referred to the head of the unreasonable. For healing is not reasonable in the case of those who would afterwards be injured by unbelief. The sentence The world cannot hate you, comes under the same head, as does also How can ye, being evil, speak good things? For in what sense is either impossible, except that it is contrary to the will? There is a somewhat similar meaning in the expressions which imply that a thing impossible by nature is possible to God if He so wills; as that a man cannot be born a second time, or that a needle will not let a camel through it. For what could prevent either of these things happening, if God so willed?

XI. And besides all this, there is the absolutely impossible and inadmissible, as that which we are now examining. For as we assert that it is impossible for God to be evil, or not to exist—for this would be indicative of weakness in God rather than of strength—or for the non-existent to exist, or for two and two to make both four and ten, so it is impossible and inconceivable that the Son should do anything that the Father doeth not. For all things that the Father hath are the Son's;

and on the other hand, all that belongs to the Son is the Father's. Nothing then is peculiar, because all things are in common. For Their Being itself is common and equal, even though the Son receive it from the Father. It is in respect of this that it is said I live by the Father; not as though His Life and Being were kept together by the Father, but because He has His Being from Him beyond all time, and beyond all cause. But how does He see the Father doing, and do likewise? Is it like those who copy pictures and letters, because they cannot attain the truth unless by looking at the original, and being led by the hand by it? But how shall Wisdom stand in need of a teacher, or be incapable of acting unless taught? And in what sense does the Father "Do" in the present or in the past? Did He make another world before this one, or is He going to make a world to come? And did the Son look at that and make this? Or will He look at the other, and make one like it? According to this argument there must be Four worlds, two made by the Father, and two by the Son. What an absurdity! He cleanses lepers, and delivers men from evil spirits, and diseases, and quickens the dead, and walks upon the sea, and does all His other works; but in what case, or when did the Father do these acts before Him? Is it not clear that the Father impressed the ideas of these same actions, and the Word brings them to pass, yet not in slavish or unskilful fashion, but with full knowledge and in a masterly way, or, to speak more properly, like the Father? For in this sense I understand the words that whatsoever is done by the Father, these things doeth the Son likewise; not, that is, because of the likeness of the things done, but in respect of the Authority. This might well also be the meaning of the passage which says that the Father worketh hitherto and the Son also; and not only so but it refers also to the government and preservation of the things which He has made; as is shewn by the passage which says that He maketh His Angels Spirits, and that the earth is founded upon its steadfastness (though once for all these things were fixed and made) and that the thunder is made firm and the wind created. Of all these things the Word was given once, but the Action is continuous even now.

XII. Let them quote in the seventh place that The Son came down from Heaven, not to do His own will, but the Will of Him That sent Him. Well, if this had not been said by Himself Who came down, we should say that the phrase was modelled as issuing from the Human Nature, not from Him who is conceived of in His character as the Saviour, for His Human Will cannot be opposed to God, seeing it is altogether taken into God; but conceived of simply as in our nature, inasmuch as the human will does not completely follow the Divine, but for the most part struggles against and resists it. For we understand in the same way the words, Father, if it be possible, let this cup pass from Me; Nevertheless let not what I will but Thy Will prevail. For it is not likely that He did not know whether it was possible or not, or that He would oppose will to will. But since, as this is the language of Him Who assumed our Nature (for He it was Who came down), and not of the Nature which He assumed, we must meet the objection in this way, that the passage does not mean that the Son has a special will of His own, besides that of the Father, but that He has not; so that the meaning would be, "not to do Mine own Will, for there is none of Mine apart from, but that which is common to, Me and Thee; for as We have one Godhead, so We have one Will." For many such expressions are used in relation to this Community, and are expressed not positively but negatively; as, e.g., God giveth not the Spirit by measure, for as a matter of fact He does not *give* the Spirit to the Son, nor does He *measure* It, for God is not measured by God; or again, Not my transgression nor my sin. The words are not used because He has these things, but because He has them not. And again, Not for our righteousness which we have done, for we have not done any. And this meaning is evident also in the clauses which follow. For what, says He, is the Will of My Father? That everyone that believeth on the Son should be saved, and obtain the final Resurrection. Now is this the Will of the Father, but not of the Son? Or does He preach the Gospel, and receive men's faith against His will? Who could believe that? Moreover, that passage, too, which says that the Word which is heard is not the Son's but the Father's has the same force. For I cannot see how that which is common to two can be said to belong to one alone, however much I consider it, and I do not think any one else can. If then you hold this opinion concerning the Will, you will be right and reverent in your opinion, as I think, and as every right-minded person thinks.

XIII. The eighth passage is, That they may know Thee, the only true God, and Jesus Christ Whom Thou hast sent; and There is none good save one, that is, God. The solution of this appears to me very easy. For if you attribute this only to the Father, where will you place the Very Truth? For if you conceive in this manner of the meaning of To the only wise God, or Who only hath Immortality, Dwelling in the light which no man can approach unto, or of to the king of the Ages, immortal, invisible, and only wise God, then the Son has vanished under sentence of death, or of darkness, or at any rate condemned to be neither wise nor king, nor invisible, nor God at all, which sums up all these points. And how will you prevent His Goodness, which especially belongs to God alone, from perishing with the rest? I, however, think that the passage That they may know Thee the only true God, was said to overthrow those gods which are falsely so called, for He would not have added and Jesus Christ Whom Thou hast sent, if The Only True God were contrasted with Him, and the sentence did not proceed upon the basis of a common Godhead. The "None is Good" meets the tempting Lawyer, who was testifying to His Goodness viewed as Man. For perfect goodness, He says, is God's alone, even if a man is called perfectly good. As for instance, A good man out of the good treasure of his heart bringeth forth good things. And, I will give the kingdom to one who is good above Thee. . . . Words of God, speaking to Saul about David. Or again, do good, O Lord, unto the good . . . and those of us who are praised, upon whom it is a kind of effluence from the Supreme Good, and has come to them in a secondary degree. It will be best of all if we can persuade you of this. But if not, what will you say to the suggestion on the other side, that on your hypothesis the Son has been called the only God. In what passage? Why, in this:—This is your God; no other shall be accounted of in comparison with Him, and a little further on, after this did He shew Himself upon earth, and conversed with men. This addition proves

clearly that the words are not used of the Father, but of the
Son; for it was He Who in bodily form companied with us,
and was in this lower world. Now, if we should determine to
take these words as said in contrast with the Father, and not
with the imaginary gods, we lose the Father by the very terms
which we were pressing against the Son. And what could be
more disastrous than such a victory?

XIV. Ninthly, they allege, seeing He ever liveth to make
intercession for us. O, how beautiful and mystical and kind.
For to intercede does not imply to seek for vengeance, as is
most men's way (for in that there would be something of
humiliation), but it is to plead for us by reason of His Medi-
atorship, just as the Spirit also is said to make intercession for
us. For there is One God, and One Mediator between God and
Man, the Man Christ Jesus. For He still pleads even now as Man
for my salvation; for He continues to wear the Body which
He assumed, until He make me God by the power of His Incarnation; although He is no longer known after the flesh—I mean,
the passions of the flesh, the same, except sin, as ours. Thus
too, we have an Advocate, Jesus Christ, not indeed prostrating
Himself for us before the Father, and falling down before
Him in slavish fashion . . . Away with a suspicion so truly
slavish and unworthy of the Spirit! For neither is it seemly
for the Father to require this, nor for the Son to submit
to it: nor is it just to think it of God. But by what He suffered
as Man, He as the Word and the Counsellor persuades Him to
be patient. I think this is the meaning of His Advocacy.

XV. Their tenth objection is the ignorance, and the statement that Of the last day and hour knoweth no man, not even
the Son Himself, but the Father. And yet how can Wisdom be
ignorant of anything—that is, Wisdom Who made the worlds,
Who perfects them, Who remodels them, Who is the Limit of
all things that were made, Who knoweth the things of God as
the spirit of a man knows the things that are in him? For what
can be more perfect than this knowledge? How then can you
say that all things before that hour He knows accurately, and
all things that are to happen about the time of the end, but of
the hour itself He is ignorant? For such a thing would be like
a riddle; as if one were to say that he knew accurately all that

was in front of the wall, but did not know the wall itself; or that, knowing the end of the day, he did not know the beginning of the night—where knowledge of the one necessarily brings in the other. Thus everyone must see that He knows as God, and knows not as Man;—if one may separate the visible from that which is discerned by thought alone. For the absolute and unconditioned use of the Name "The Son" in this passage, without the addition of whose Son, gives us this thought, that we are to understand the ignorance in the most reverent sense, by attributing it to the Manhood, and not to the Godhead.

XVI. If then this argument is sufficient, let us stop here, and not enquire further. But if not, our second argument is as follows:—Just as we do in all other instances, so let us refer His knowledge of the greatest events, in honour of the Father, to The Cause. And I think that anyone, even if he did not read it in the way that one of our own Students did, would soon perceive that not even the Son knows the day or hour otherwise than as the Father does. For what do we conclude from this? That since the Father knows, therefore also does the Son, as it is evident that this cannot be known or comprehended by any but the First Nature. There remains for us to interpret the passage about His receiving commandment, and having kept His Commandments, and done always those things that please Him; and further concerning His being made perfect, and His exaltation, and His learning obedience by the things which He suffered; and also His High Priesthood, and His Oblation, and His Betrayal, and His prayer to Him That was able to save Him from death, and His Agony and Bloody Sweat and Prayer, and such like things; if it were not evident to every one that such words are concerned, not with That Nature Which is unchangeable and above all capacity of suffering, but with the passible Humanity. This, then, is the argument concerning these objections, so far as to be a sort of foundation and memorandum for the use of those who are better able to conduct the enquiry to a more complete working out. It may, however, be worth while, and will be consistent with what has been already said, instead of passing over without remark the actual Titles of the Son (there are many of them, and they are concerned with many of His Attributes), to set before you the meaning of each of them, and to point out the mystical meaning of the names.

XVII. We will begin thus. The Deity cannot be expressed in words. And this is proved to us, not only by argument, but by the wisest and most ancient of the Hebrews, so far as they have given us reason for conjecture. For they appropriated certain characters to the honour of the Deity, and would not even allow the name of anything inferior to God to be written with the same letters as that of God, because to their minds it was improper that the Deity should even to that extent admit any of His creatures to a share with Himself. How then could they have admitted that the invisible and separate Nature can be explained by divisible words? For neither has any one yet breathed the whole air, nor has any mind entirely comprehended, or speech exhaustively contained the Being of God. But we sketch Him by His Attributes, and so obtain a certain faint and feeble and partial idea concerning Him, and our best Theologian is he who has, not indeed discovered the whole, for our present chain does not allow of our seeing the whole, but conceived of Him to a greater extent than another, and gathered in himself more of the Likeness or adumbration of the Truth, or whatever we may call it.

XVIII. As far then as we can reach, He Who Is, and God, are the special names of His Essence; and of these especially He Who Is, not only because when He spake to Moses in the mount, and Moses asked what His Name was, this was what He called Himself, bidding him say to the people "I Am hath sent me," but also because we find that this Name is the more strictly appropriate. For the Name εός (God), even if, as those who are skilful in these matters say, it were derived from έεω (to run) or from Αἴθεω (to blaze), from continual motion, and because He consumes evil conditions of things (from which fact He is also called A Consuming Fire), would still be one of the Relative Names, and not an Absolute one; as again is the case with Lord, which also is called a name of God. I am the Lord Thy God, He says, that is My name; and, The Lord is His name. But we are enquiring into a Nature Whose Being is absolute and not into Being bound up with something else.

But Being is in its proper sense peculiar to God, and belongs to Him entirely, and is not limited or cut short by any Before or After, for indeed in him there is no past or future.

XIX. Of the other titles, some are evidently names of His Authority, others of His Government of the world, and of this viewed under a twofold aspect, the one before the other in the Incarnation. For instance the Almighty, the King of Glory, or of The Ages, or of The Powers, or of The Beloved, or of Kings. Or again the Lord of Sabaoth, that is of Hosts, or of Powers, or of Lords; these are clearly titles belonging to His Authority. But the God either of Salvation or of Vengeance, or of Peace, or of Righteousness; or of Abraham, Isaac, and Jacob, and of all the spiritual Israel that seeth God,—these belong to His Government. For since we are governed by these three things, the fear of punishment, the hope of salvation and of glory besides, and the practice of the virtues by which these are attained, the Name of the God of Vengeance governs fear, and that of God of Salvation our hope, and that of the God of Virtues our practice; that whoever attains to any of these may, as carrying God in himself, press on yet more unto perfection, and to that affinity which arises out of virtues. Now these are Names common to the Godhead, but the Proper Name of the Unoriginate is Father, and that of the unoriginately Begotten is Son, and that of the unbegottenly Proceeding or going forth is The Holy Ghost. Let us proceed then to the Names of the Son, which were our starting point in this part of our argument.

XX. In my opinion He is called Son because He is identical with the Father in Essence; and not only for this reason, but also because He is Of Him. And He is called Only-Begotten, not because He is the only Son and of the Father alone, and only a Son; but also because the manner of His Sonship is peculiar to Himself and not shared by bodies. And He is called the Word, because He is related to the Father as Word to Mind; not only on account of His passionless Generation, but also because of the Union, and of His declaratory function. Perhaps too this relation might be compared to that between the Definition and the Thing defined since this also is called Λόγος. For, it says, he that hath mental perception of the Son (for this is the meaning of Hath Seen) hath also perceived the Father; and the Son is a concise demonstration and easy setting forth of the Father's Nature. For every thing that is begotten is a silent word of him that begat it. And if any one should say that this Name was given Him because He exists in all things that are, he would not be wrong. For what is there that consists but by the word? He is also called Wisdom, as the Knowledge of things divine and human. For how is it possible that He Who made all things should be ignorant of the reasons of what He has made? And Power, as the Sustainer of all created things, and the Furnisher to them of power to keep themselves together. And Truth, as being in nature One and not many (for truth is one and falsehood is manifold), and as the pure Seal of the Father and His most unerring Impress. And the Image as of one substance with Him, and because He is of the Father, and not the Father of Him. For this is of the Nature of an Image, to be the reproduction of its Archetype, and of that whose name it bears; only that there is more here. For in ordinary language an image is a motionless representation of that which has motion; but in this case it is the living reproduction of the Living One, and is more exactly like than was Seth to Adam, or any son to his father. For such is the nature of simple Existences, that it is not correct to say of them that they are Like in one particular and Unlike in another; but they are a complete resemblance, and should rather be called Identical than Like. Moreover he is called Light as being the Brightness of souls cleansed by word and life. For if ignorance and sin be darkness, knowledge and a godly life will be Light . . . And He is called Life, because He is Light, and is the constituting and creating Power of every reasonable soul. For in Him we live and move and have our being, according to the double power of that Breathing into us; for we were all inspired by Him with breath, and as many of us as were capable of it, and in so far as we open the mouth of our mind, with God the Holy Ghost. He is Righteousness, because He distributes according to that which we deserve, and is a righteous Arbiter both for those who are under the Law and for those who are under Grace, for soul and body, so that the former should rule, and the latter obey, and the higher have supremacy over the lower; that the worse may not rise in rebellion against the better. He is Sanctification, as being Purity, that the Pure may be contained by Purity. And Redemption, because He sets us free, who were held captive under sin, giving Himself a Ransom for us, the Sacrifice to make expiation for the world. And Resurrection, because He raises up from hence, and brings to life again us, who were slain by sin.

XXI. These names however are still common to Him Who is above us, and to Him Who came for our sake. But others are peculiarly our own, and belong to that nature which He assumed. So He is called Man, not only that through His Body He may be apprehended by embodied creatures, whereas otherwise this would be impossible because of His incomprehensible nature; but also that by Himself He may sanctify humanity, and be as it were a leaven to the whole lump; and by uniting to Himself that which was condemned may release it from all condemnation, becoming for all men all things that we are, except sin;—body, soul, mind and all through which death reaches—and thus He became Man, who is the combination of all these; God in visible form, because He retained that which is perceived by mind alone. He is Son of Man, both on account of Adam, and of the Virgin from Whom He came; from the one as a forefather, from the other as His Mother, both in accordance with the law of generation, and apart from it. He is Christ, because of His Godhead. For this is the Anointing One; the effect of which is that That which anoints is called Man, and makes that which is anointed God. He is The Way, because He leads us through Himself; The Door, as letting us in; the Shepherd, as making us dwell in a place of green pastures, and bringing us up by waters of rest, and leading us there, and protecting us from wild beasts, converting the erring, bringing back that which was lost, binding up that which was broken, guarding the strong, and bringing them together in the Fold beyond, with words of pastoral knowledge. The Sheep, as the Victim: The Lamb, as being perfect: the Highpriest, as the Offerer; Melchisedec, as without Mother in that Nature which is above us, and without Father in ours; and without genealogy above (for who, it says, shall declare His generation?) and moreover, as King of Salem, which means Peace, and King of Righteousness, and as receiving tithes from

Patriarchs, when they prevail over powers of evil. They are the titles of the Son. Walk through them, those that are lofty in a godlike manner; those that belong to the body in a manner suitable to them; or rather, altogether in a godlike manner, that thou mayest become a god, ascending from below, for His sake Who came down from on high for ours. In all and above all keep to this, and thou shalt never err, either in the loftier or the lowlier names; Jesus Christ is the Same yesterday and to-day in the Incarnation, and in the Spirit for ever and ever.

Amen.

St. Gregory of Nyssa
335-394

Gregory of Nyssa was the younger brother of St. Basil the Great. He followed his father's profession as a rhetorician in his early adulthood, but after the death of his wife was persuaded by Gregory Nazianzen to enter the monastery which his brother Basil had founded in Pontus. Of these three great Cappadocians, the youngest has always been known as the philosopher and mystic.

In 371 at Basil's insistence Gregory was consecrated bishop of Nyssa. Unlike Basil he had no special administrative abilities and consequently endured many troubles. Nor was he an exceptional preacher, unlike his friend Gregory Nazianzen. But of the three Cappadocians he was certainly the most gifted in intellectual and literary talents. His was a major voice at the Second Ecumenical Council (Constantinople, 381), and Nazianzen refers to him as "the column supporting the whole Church."

The "Star of Nyssa" can be viewed as bringing the Arian controversy to a close. His book Against Eunomius *was its death knell. Therein he defended the doctrine of his deceased brother Basil against the attack of Eunomius by insisting on greater precision when speaking of essence (ousia) and person (hypostasis). But his success against Arianism did not bring him peace. In his last years he was entangled in a bitter controversy over*

Apollinarianism, repudiating the charge of teaching that there are two Sons of God.

The selection which follows, however, is taken from his most important doctrinal work. It is variously referred to as his "Great Catechism," his "Catechetical Oration," or his "Address on Religious Instruction." "It represents the first attempt after Origen's De Principiis to create a systematic theology" (Quasten). It sets forth the basic Christian teachings and defends them against pagan, Jewish, and heretical attacks. His strong interest in Greek philosophy and in Origen's theology made him suspect among some, but it would be hard to find a better example of the real spirit of Greek theology than this work of Gregory's. In it he demonstrates his ability to adapt Christian doctrine to the Greek environment of his day.

This Address seems to have enjoyed wide circulation in the early Church. Gregory's background in rhetoric is obvious as he multiplies similes and synonyms.

Intended as an aid to Christian teachers, the Address presents Christian doctrine in four main sections: 1) God as Trinity; 2) Man as Created, the Nature of Evil, the Fall; 3) the Restoration of Man, the Incarnation and Atonement; 4) Baptism, Eucharist, Faith and Repentance. We present here the entirety of the third section, which is the largest, the most developed, and the most important. "It answers the stock objections brought against these doctrines, and develops in an original manner the way in which the divine attributes of goodness, power, wisdom, and justice were united in the economy of redemption. The most interesting feature here . . . is his elaboration of the ransom theory of the atonement" (Richardson). Thus Gregory of Nyssa carries us further in the unending effort to find appropriate language and concepts in each new setting for understanding and appreciating the heart of the Gospel. If his choices were not always felicitous, his overall contribution was nonetheless exceptional.

THE CATECHETICAL ORATION

THE RESTORATION OF MAN

Nevertheless a man who is mindful of the dissolution of the body is in any case resentful, and takes it hard that our life is dissolved by death. This, he claims, is the final evil, that death should extinguish our life. Let them, then, reflect upon God's exceeding goodness even in this melancholy prospect. For it may be that this will induce him all the more to marvel at God's gracious care for man. Those who share in life find that life is desirable because they can enjoy what they like. Hence, if a man passes his life in pain, he reckons it far preferable not to exist than to exist in a state of suffering. Let us then inquire whether He who gives us life has any other intention than that we should live under the best possible conditions.

It was by a movement of free will that we became associated with evil. To indulge some pleasure we mingled evil with our nature, like some deadly drug sweetened with honey. By this means we fell from that blessed state we think of as freedom from passion, and were changed into evil. That is the reason that man, like a clay pot, is again resolved into earth; in order that he may be refashioned into his original state through the resurrection, when once he has been separated from the filth now attaching to him.

Such a doctrine, it is, that Moses expounds to us by way of a story and in a veiled manner. But what the veiled allegories teach is quite clear. For since, he says, the first men became implicated in things forbidden and were stripped naked of blessedness, the Lord clothed his first creatures in suits of skins. I do not think he uses the word "skins" in its literal sense. For to what sort of animals, when slain and flayed, did this covering contrived for them belong? But since every skin taken from an animal is a dead thing, I am sure the skins mean the attribute of death. This is the characteristic mark of irrational nature; and in His care for man, He who heals our wickedness subsequently provided him with the capacity to die, but not to die permanently. For a suit is an external covering for us. The body is given the opportunity to use it for a while, but it is not an essential part of its nature.

Mortality, then, derived from the nature of irrational creatures, provisionally clothed the nature created for immortality. It enveloped his outward, but not his inward, nature. It affected the sentient part of man, but not the divine image. The sentient part, to be sure, is dissolved; but it is not destroyed. For destruction means passing into nonbeing, while dissolution means separation once more into those elements of the world from which something was constituted. When this happens, it does not perish, even if we cannot grasp this with our senses.

Now the cause of this dissolution is clear from the illustration we have given. Appropriate to sensation is what is thick and earthly. But by nature the intellect is superior to and transcends the movements of the senses. Hence, since our judgment of the good went astray by the prompting of the senses, and this departure from the good produced a contrary state of things, that part of us which was rendered useless by partaking of its opposite is dissolved. We can put our illustration about the clay pot in this way: Suppose it has been treacherously filled with molten lead, which has hardened and cannot be poured out. Suppose, too, the owner recovers the pot, and being skilled in ceramics, he pounds to pieces the clay surrounding the lead. He then remolds the pot, now rid of the intruding matter, into its former shape and for his own use. In the same way the Creator of our vessel, I mean our sentient and bodily nature, when it became mingled with evil, dissolved the material which contained the evil. And then, once it has been freed from its opposite, he will remold it by the resurrection, and will reconstitute the vessel into its original beauty.

Now there is a certain bond and fellowship in the sinful passions between soul and body, and a certain analogy between bodily and spiritual death. Just as we call the body's separation from sentient life "death," so we give the same name to the soul's separation from genuine life. As we have said, soul and body are observed to share together in evil. For by means of both of them wickedness is translated into action. Yet from being clothed with dead skins the soul is not affected by death which implies dissolution. For how could the soul be dissolved when it is not composite? But since it, too, has to be freed by some remedy from the stains contracted through sin, on this account the medicine of virtue in this present life has to be applied to it to heal these wounds. But if it remains unhealed, provision has been made for its cure in the life to come.

Now there are differences in bodily ailments, some of them readily responding to treatment, others with more difficulty. In the latter case knives, cauteries, and bitter medicines are used to remove the sickness which has attacked the body. Something similar, in reference to the healing of the soul's sickness, is indicated by the future judgment. To thoughtless persons this is a threat and a harsh means of correction, so that by fear of a painful retribution we may be brought to our senses and flee evil. The more thoughtful, however, believe it to be a healing remedy provided by God, who thus restores his own creation to its original grace. Those who, by excisions or cauteries, remove moles and warts which have unnaturally grown on the body do not benefit and heal the patient painlessly, although they do not use the knife to hurt him. In the same way, whatever material excrescences have hardened on the surface of our souls, which have become fleshly through their association with the passions, are, at the time of judgment, cut off and removed by that ineffable wisdom and power of Him who (as the gospel says) heals the sick. For "those who are well," it says, "do not need a doctor, but those who are sick."

Now the excision of a wart causes a sharp pain in the surface of the body, since an unnatural growth on a nature affects the subject by a kind of sympathy. There arises an unexpected union between what is our own and what is foreign to us, so that we feel a stinging pain when the unnatural excrescence is removed. In the same way, due to the fact that the soul has developed a great affinity for evil, it pines and wastes away, being convicted of sin, as prophecy somewhere says. Because of its deep kinship with evil, there necessarily follow unspeakable pangs, which are as incapable of description as the nature of the blessings we hope for. Neither the one nor the other can be put into words nor have we an inkling of either.

Anyone, therefore, who bears in mind the wise purpose of Him who governs the universe could not be so unreasonable and shortsighted as to attribute the cause of evil to the Creator of man. He could not say either that He was ignorant of the future or that by knowing it and by creating man He was involved in the impulse toward evil. For He knew what was going to happen and yet did not prevent what led it to happen. He who is able to grasp all things within his knowledge, and sees the future equally with the past, was not ignorant that man would deviate from the good. But just as He saw man's perversion, so he perceived his restoration once more to the good. Which, then, was better? Not to have brought our nature into being at all, since he knew in advance that the one to be created would stray from the good? Or, having brought him into being, to restore him by repentance, sick as he was, to his original grace?

It is the height of shortsightedness to call God the author of evil because of the body's sufferings, which are a necessary accompaniment of our fluctuating nature; or to imagine that he is not the creator of man at all, in order to avoid attributing to him the cause of our sufferings. Such people distinguish good and evil on the basis of sensation, and do not realize that that alone is good by nature which is unaffected by sensation, and that alone is evil which is alien to what is genuinely good. To judge good and evil on the basis of pain and suffering is appropriate in the case of irrational natures, since by not sharing in intelligence and understanding they are unable to grasp what is genuinely good. But that man is a work of God, created good and for the noblest ends, is evident not only from what we have already said, but for thousands of other reasons, most of which we must disregard since their number is infinite.

When we call God the creator of man, we are not unmindful of the careful distinctions we made in [that part of] our introduction addressed to the Greeks. We showed there that God's Word is a substantial and personal being, and is both God and Word. In himself he embraces all creative power, or rather he is absolute power. His impulses are directed toward everything good, and by having power commensurate with his will, he brings to effect whatever he desires. The life of existing things is his will and his work. By him man was brought to life, and endowed with every noble attribute to resemble God.

Now that alone is unchangeable by nature which does not originate through creation. But whatever is derived from the uncreated nature has its subsistence out of nonbeing. Once it has come into being through change, it constantly proceeds to change. If it acts according to its nature, this continual change is for the better. But if it is diverted from the straight path, there succeeds a movement in the opposite direction. Such was man's condition. His mutable nature lapsed in the opposite direction. His departure from the good at once introduced as a consequence every form of evil. By his turning from life, death came in instead. Privation of light engendered darkness. Absence of virtue brought in wickedness; and in the place of every form of goodness there was now to be reckoned the list of opposing evils. Into just such a condition man fell by his thoughtlessness. For it was not possible for him to be discreet, once he had turned from discretion, or to form any wise decision once he had departed from wisdom. By whom did he have to be restored once more to his original grace? To whom did it belong to raise him up when he had fallen, to restore him when he was lost, to lead him back when he had gone astray? To whom, but to the very Lord of his nature? For only the one who had originally given him life was both able and fitted to restore it when it was lost. This is what the revelation of the truth teaches us, when we learn that God originally made man, and saved him when he had fallen.

THE INCARNATION

One who has followed the course of our argument up to this point will probably agree with it, since we do not appear to have said anything unbefitting a right conception of God. He will not, however, take a similar view of what follows, although it substantiates the revelation of the truth in a special way. I refer to the human birth, the advance from infancy to manhood, the eating and drinking, the weariness, the sleep, the grief, the tears, the false accusations, the trial, the cross, the death, and the putting in the tomb. For these facts included as they are in the revelation, in some way blunt the faith of little minds, so that they do not accept the sequel of our argument because of what precedes. Owing to the unworthiness connected with the death, they do not admit that the resurrection from the dead was worthy of God.

For myself, however, I think we must for a moment divert our thoughts from the coarseness of the flesh, and consider what real goodness and its contrary are, and by what distinctive marks each is known. For I imagine that no one who has seriously thought about it will gainsay that one thing alone in the universe is by nature shameful, viz., the malady of evil, while no shame at all attaches to what is alien to evil. What is unmixed with shame is certainly understood to be comprised in the good, and what is genuinely good is unmixed with its opposite.

Now everything we see included in the good is fitting to God. In consequence, either our opponents must show that the birth, the upbringing, the growth, the natural advance to maturity, the experience of death and the return from it are evil. Or else, if they concede that these things fall outside the category of evil, they must of necessity acknowledge there is nothing shameful in what is alien to evil. Since we have shown that what is good is altogether free from all shame and evil, must we not pity the stupidity of those who claim that the good is unbefitting to God?

But, they object, is not human nature paltry and circumscribed, while Deity is infinite? How, then, could the infinite be contained in an atom? But who claims that the infinity of the Godhead was contained within the limits of the flesh as in a jar? For in our own case the intellectual nature is not enclosed in the limits of the flesh. The body's bulk, to be sure, is circumscribed by its particular parts, but the soul is free to embrace the whole creation by the movement of thought. It ascends to the heavens, sets foot in the depths, traverses the dimensions of the world, and in its constant activity makes its way to the underworld. Often it is involved in contemplating the marvels of the heavens, and it is not loaded down by being attached to the body.

If, then, the soul of man, although united to the body by natural necessity, is free to roam everywhere, why do we have to say that the Godhead is confined in a fleshly nature? Why should we not rather rely on examples we can understand, in order to form some sort of proper conception of God's plan of salvation? To illustrate: We see the flame of a lamp laying hold of the material which feeds it. Now reason distinguishes between the flame on the material, and the material which kindles the flame, though we cannot actually divorce the one from the other and point out the flame as something separate from the material. The two together form a single whole. So it is with the incarnation. (My illustration must not be pressed beyond the point where it is appropriate. What is incongruous must be omitted, and the perishable character of fire must not be taken as part of the example.) Just, then, as we see the flame hugging the material and yet not encased in it, what prevents us from conceiving of a similar union and connection of the divine nature with the human? Can we not preserve a right idea of God even when we hold to this connection, by believing that the divine is free from all circumscription despite the fact he is in man?

If you inquire how the Deity is united with human nature, it is appropriate for you first to ask in what way the soul is united to the body. If the manner in which your soul is joined to your body is a mystery, you must certainly not imagine this former question is within your grasp. In the one case, while we believe the soul to be something different from the body because on leaving the flesh it renders it dead and inactive, we are ignorant of the manner of the union. Similarly in the other case we realize that the divine nature by its greater majesty differs from that which is mortal and perishable; but we are unable to detect how the divine is mingled with the human. Yet we have no doubt, from the recorded miracles, that God underwent birth in human naure. But *how* this happened we decline to investigate as a matter beyond the scope of reason. While we believe that the corporeal and intelligent creation owes its being to the incorporeal and uncreated nature, our faith in this regard does not involve an examination of the source and manner of this. The fact of creation we accept; but we renounce a curious investigation of the way the universe was framed as a matter altogether ineffable and inexplicable.

THE INCARNATION AND THE MIRACLES

One who is looking for proofs that God manifested himself to us in the flesh must look to his activities. For of God's very existence he can get no other proof than the testimony of his actions themselves. When we survey the universe and note the orderly government of the world and the blessings we receive in life from God, we recognize the existence of some transcendent power which both created and maintains existing things. It is the same with regard to God's manifesting himself in our flesh. The wonders evident in this actions we regard as sufficient proof of the presence of the Godhead, and in the deeds recorded we mark all those attributes by which the divine nature is characterized.

It is a mark of God to give man life; to preserve by his providence all existing things; to afford food and drink to those who have been granted life in the flesh; to care for those in want; by health to restore to itself the nature perverted by sickness; to exercise an equal sway over all creation, over land, sea, and air, and over the heavenly regions; to possess power sufficient for everything, and above all to be the vanquisher of death and corruption. If, then, the record about him were defective in any of these or suchlike things, unbelievers would have good reason to take exception to our religion. But if everything by which we know God is evident in the record about him, what stands in the way of believing?

But, it is objected, birth and death belong to the nature of flesh. Yes, indeed. But what preceded His birth and followed his death lies outside the nature we share. When we look at the two limits of our human life, we observe the nature of our beginning and our end. Man begins his existence in weakness and similarly ends his life through weakness. But in God's case, the birth did not have its origin in weakness, neither did the death end in weakness. For sensual pleasure did not precede the birth and corruption did not follow the death.

Do you fail to believe the miracle? I welcome your incredulity. For by your very recognition that what we have said surpasses belief, you acknowledge that the miracles transcend nature. This very fact, then, that the gospel proclamation tran-

178

scends natural categories, should be proof to you that He who was manifested was God. For had the narratives of the Christ been confined within the limits of nature, where would the divine be? But if the account transcends nature, then the proof that the one we preach is God is evident in the very things you disbelieve.

Man is born through copulation, and after death lies in corruption. Were these elements comprised in the gospel preaching, you would certainly not imagine Him to be God of whom it was said he only had the properties of our nature. But since you learn that, while he was born, he transcended our nature both in manner of birth and in not being subject to the change of corruption, it would be well for you to exercise your incredulity in a different direction. It would be consistent for you to refuse to think of him as a mere man, as one instance among others of human nature.

Now by refusing to believe such a one was a mere man, a person is forced to acknowledge him to be God. For the one who recorded his birth, recorded also his birth from a virgin. If, then, the account of his birth is credible, there is surely nothing incredible, in the same account, about its manner. For the one who told of his birth told also of his birth from a virgin. And the one who mentioned his death also bore witness to his resurrection along with the death. If, then, on the basis of what you are told, you grant that he both died and was born, you must similarly admit his birth and death were free from weakness. These things, however, transcend nature. In consequence, he, whom we have shown to be born supernaturally, cannot possibly be confined within nature.

Why, then, they ask, did the divine stoop to such humiliation? Our faith falters when we think that God, the infinite, incomprehensible, ineffable reality, transcending all glory and majesty, should be defiled by associating with human nature, and his sublime powers no less debased by their contact with what is abject.

We are not at a loss to find a fitting answer even to this objection. Do you ask the reason why God was born among men? If you exclude from life the benefits which come from God, you will have no way of recognizing the divine. It is from

179

the blessings we experience that we recognize our benefactor, since by observing what happens to us, we deduce the nature of Him who is responsible for it. If, then, the love of man is a proper mark of the divine nature, here is the explanation you are looking for, here is the reason for God's presence among men. Our nature was sick and needed a doctor. Man had fallen and needed someone to raise him up. He who had lost life needed someone to restore it. He who had ceased to participate in the good needed someone to bring him back to it. He who was shut up in darkness needed the presence of light. The prisoner was looking for someone to ransom him, the captive for someone to take his part. He who was under the yoke of slavery was looking for someone to set him free. Were these trifling and unworthy reasons to impel God to come down and visit human nature, seeing humanity was in such a pitiful and wretched state?

WHY DID NOT GOD REDEEM MAN BY A SOVEREIGN ACT?

But, it is objected, man could have been benefited and yet God could have remained at the same time free from weakness and suffering. By this will he framed the universe: by a mere act of will he brought into existence that which was not. Why, then, if he loved man, did he not wrest him from the opposing power and restore him to his original state by some sovereign and divine act of authority? Why did he take a tedious, circuitous route, submit to a bodily nature, enter life through birth, pass through the various stages of development, and finally taste death, and so gain his end by the resurrection of his own body? Could he not have remained in his transcendent and divine glory, and saved man by a command, renouncing such circuitous routes?

To such objections we must oppose the truth, so that those who are seriously searching for the rational basis of our religion may find no obstacle in the way of their faith.

We must inquire first—and we have already done this in part—what it is that stands in opposition to virtue. As darkness is the contrary of light and death of life, so it is clear that vice and nothing else is the contrary of virtue. We observe many things in the created order, but none of them—not stone, wood, water, man, or anything else—is the contrary of light and life except their precise opposites, i.e., darkness and death. So it is with respect to virtue. One cannot say that any created thing is to be thought of as its opposite, except the idea of vice.

Did, then, our teaching represent the divine as born in a state of evil, our opponents would have occasion to criticize our faith, on the ground that we hold views inconsistent and incongruous with the divine nature. For it certainly would not be right to say that he who is wisdom itself and goodness and incorruption and every other sublime idea and title had been changed into the opposite. God is genuine virtue, and vice alone is by nature opposed to virtue. If, then, God entered not a state of evil but human nature, and if shame and indecency alone attach to the weakness of vice and God neither entered such a state nor can by his nature enter it, why are our opponents ashamed to acknowledge God's contact with human nature? There is nothing in man's constitution which is opposed to the principle of virtue. Neither his capacity for reason or thought or understanding nor any similar attribute peculiar to his nature stands opposed to the principle of virtue.

But, it is urged, our body is subject to change and hence to weakness. He who is born in such a state is born in weakness; but the divine is above weakness. It is therefore an idea foreign to God to contend that he who is by nature above weakness came to share in weakness.

In answering this objection we shall use an argument already employed, viz., that "weakness" can be used in a strictly proper sense and also in an extended sense. What affects the will and perverts it toward evil and away from virtue is weakness, properly speaking. On the other hand, the successive changes we observe in nature as it proceeds on its way are more properly referred to as modes of activity than of weakness. I mean birth, growth, continuance of life through taking in and expelling food, the union, and then later the dissolution, of the body's constituent parts, and its return to its kindred elements. With that, then, does our religion contend the divine came into contact? Was it weakness in its strict sense, that is, evil, or was it the changing movement of nature? Were our teaching to affirm that the divine entered a state which is morally forbidden, it would be our duty to avoid such a preposterous doctrine, implying, as it does, an unsound view of the divine nature. But if we affirm that he had contact with our nature, which derived its original being and subsistence from him, in what way does the gospel proclamation fail to have a fitting conception of God? In our faith we introduce no element of weakness in our ideas of God. For we do not say that a doctor incurs weakness when he heals someone in a state of weakness. Even though he comes into contact with sickness, the doctor remains free from such weakness.

If birth in itself is not weakness, one cannot call life weakness. It is the sensual pleasure which precedes human birth that is weakness, and it is the impulse to evil in living beings that is the sickness of our nature. But our religion claims He was pure from both of these. If, then, his birth was free from sensual pleasure and his life from wickedness, what weakness remains for God to have shared in, according to our devout religion? If you call the separation of the body from the soul weakness, you would be much more justified in so naming their union. For if the separation of united elements is weakness, then the union of separated elements will equally be weakness. For the union of things that are separate and the separation of things conjoined or united implies motion and change.

The name, therefore, we give to the final change ought also to apply to that which precedes it. And if the first change, which we call birth, does not involve weakness, neither can the second change, which we call death and which dissolves the union of body and soul, be logically called weakness.

We hold that God was involved in both these changes of our nature, by which the soul is united to the body and separated from it. He was united with both elements in man's make-up—I mean the sensible and intelligible elements. And by means of this ineffable and inexpressible union he brought it about that, once these elements of soul and body were united, the union would remain permanent. For when, in his case too, soul and body had been separated by that successive movement of change our nature undergoes, he joined the parts together again with a kind of glue—I mean by divine power. And so he united what was separated in an unbreakable union. This is what the resurrection means—the restoration of elements into an indissoluble union after their separation, so that they can grow together. In this way man's primal grace was restored and we retrieved once more eternal life. By our dissolution the wickedness mingled with our nature was poured off like a liquid which, when the vessel holding it is broken to pieces, is dispersed and lost, since there is nothing more to contain it.

Now just as the principle of death had its origin in a single person and passed to the whole of human nature, similarly the principle of the resurrection originated in one Man and extends to all humanity. He who united again the soul he had assumed, with his own body, did so by means of his own power which was fused with each element at their first formation. In the same way he conjoined the intelligible and sensible nature on a larger scale, the principle of the resurrection extending to its logical limits. For when in the case of the man in whom he was incarnate the soul returned once more to the body after the dissolution, a similar union of the separated elements potentially passed to the whole of human nature, as if a new beginning had been made. This is the mystery of God's plan with regard to death, and of the resurrection from the dead. He does not prevent the soul's separation from the body by death in accordance with the inevitable course of nature. But he brings them together again by the resurrection. Thus he becomes the meeting point of both, of death and of life. In himself he restores the nature which death has disrupted, and becomes himself the principle whereby the separated parts are reunited.

But, someone urges, the objection raised to our viewpoint has not yet been answered. Rather has the argument put forward by unbelievers been strengthened by what we have said. For if he was as powerful as we have indicated, so that he could destroy death and gain entrance to life, why did he not do what he wanted to by a mere act of will? Why did he effect our salvation in a devious way, by being born and nurtured and by experiencing death in the process of saving man? He could have saved us without submitting to these things.

In addressing reasonable persons it should suffice to answer such an objection in this way: Sick people do not prescribe to doctors their manner of treatment. They do not argue with their benefactors about the form of their cure, asking why the doctor felt the ailing part and devised this or that remedy to relieve the sickness, when something different was needed. Rather do they keep in view the aim of his kind services and accept them gratefully.

But, as the prophet says, God's abounding goodness aids us in a hidden way, and in the present life it is not clearly evident. For every objection of unbelievers would be removed, could we actually see what we only hope for. But our hopes await the ages to come, so that there may then be revealed what at present our faith alone apprehends. In consequence we must search out, as far as we can, some reasonable solution of the question posed, and one in harmony with our preceding line of thought.

And yet it is perhaps superfluous for us who already believe that God entered human life to criticize the manner of his appearing, on the ground that it lacked something in wisdom and superior judgment. For those who do not strongly oppose the truth have no small proof that God dwelt with us. Even in advance of the life to come, it is evident in this present life; I mean we have the testimony of the facts themselves.

Who does not know that the deceit of demons filled every corner of the world and held sway over man's life by the madness of idolatry? Who does not realize that every people on earth was accustomed to worship demons under the form of idols, by sacrificing living victims and making foul offerings on their altars? But, as the apostle says, from the moment that God's saving grace appeared among men and dwelt in human nature, all this vanished into nothing, like smoke. The madness of their oracles and prophecies has ceased. Their annual processions and foul and bloody hecatombs have been done away. Among many peoples altars, temple porches, and precincts and shrines have entirely disappeared, along with the ceremonies practiced by the devotees of demons for their own deceit and that of their friends. The result is that in many places where such things were once current they are not even remembered. Throughout the world, churches and altars have been erected instead in the name of Christ; and the holy and bloodless priesthood and the sublime philosophy which consists in deeds rather than words now flourish. The life of the body is held in contempt; death is despised. Those who were forced by tyrants to renounce their faith gave clear testimony to this. Bodily torture and the sentence of death they reckoned as nothing. Clearly they would not have endured such things had they not had a clear and indubitable proof of the incarnation.

For Jews the following fact is a sufficient indication of the presence of Him whom they renounce. Up to the time that God appeared in Jesus Christ they could see in Jerusalem the splendor of royal palaces, the famous Temple, and the customary sacrifices through the year. And all that the law enjoined in mysteries for those who grasp their inner meaning up to that moment went on unhindered in accordance with the ritual originally imposed on them by their religion. But when they saw the One they expected (for they had already learned of him through the Prophets and the Law), they held what from now on was a mere superstition in higher esteem than faith in him who had come. For they misconstrued their religion. They kept the letter of the law and were in bondage to custom rather than to right reason. As a consequence they refused to accept the grace made manifest; and all that is left of their holy religion is barren narratives. Not a trace of their Temple remains. The splendor of their city is left in ruins. There survives to the Jews none of their ancient customs the law enjoined; and access to their holy city, Jerusalem, is denied them by imperial decree.

However, neither Hellenists nor the leaders of Judaism are willing to regard these things as proof of God's presence. Hence it will be well, in the face of the objections urged, to give a more particular reason why the divine nature became joined to ours, and saved man by its own presence and did not execute its purpose by a mere command. What starting point, then, shall we adopt in order to bring our argument satisfactorily to the proposed conclusion? What other starting point is there than to give a brief review of spiritual conceptions of God?

THE UNION OF GOD'S GOODNESS, WISDOM, JUSTICE, AND POWER IN THE INCARNATION

It is universally agreed that we should believe the Divine to be not only powerful, but also just and good and wise and everything else that suggests excellence. It follows, therefore, in the plan of God we are considering, that there should not be a tendency for one of his attributes to be present in what happened, while another was absent. For not a single one of these sublime attributes by itself and separated from the others constitutes virtue. What is good is not truly such unless it is associated with justice, wisdom, and power. For what is unjust and stupid and impotent is not good. Power, too, if it is separated from justice and wisdom, cannot be classed as virtue. Rather is it a brutal and tyrannical form of power. The same holds good of the other attributes. If wisdom exceeds the bounds of justice, or if righteousness is not associated with power and goodness, one would more properly call them wickedness. For how can we reckon as good what is deficient in excellence?

If, then, in our idea of God all the attributes must be combined, let us inquire whether his plan for man is deficient in any of these appropriate conceptions. We seek above all, in the case of God, signs of his goodness. Now what could be clearer evidence of this than the fact that he reclaimed him who had deserted to the enemy's side, and did not allow the fickleness of man's will to influence his own immutable nature with its constant purpose of goodness? For, as David says, he would not have come to save us, had his intention not been rooted in goodness. But the goodness of his intention would have availed nothing had not wisdom made his love of man effective. In the case of the sick there are probably many who wish the patient were not sick; but only those can bring their good intentions for the sick to effect who have the technical capacity actually to cure them. Wisdom, then, certainly needs to be allied with goodness. How is this alliance of wisdom with goodness evident in what happened [in the incarnation]? A good purpose, to be sure, cannot be detected in the abstract. How, then, can it be evident except in the actual facts that occurred? These facts proceed in a logical chain and sequence, and exhibit the wisdom and skill of God's plan.

As we have already indicated, it is the union of justice with wisdom that really constitutes virtue. Separated and taken by itself, justice is not goodness. Accordingly it will be well for us to take the two together (I mean wisdom and justice) in our consideration of God's plan for man.

What, then, is justice? We recall, doubtless, the points we made in the early course of our argument, that man was created

186

in the image of the divine nature, and along with other blessings he retains this divine likeness by having free will. Yet his nature is necessarily mutable. For it was not possible that one who derived his existence from change could be altogether free from it. The passage from nonbeing to being is a kind of change, nonexistence being transformed into existence by God's power. In another way, too, we observe that man is necessarily subject to change. For he is the image of the divine nature; and an image would be entirely identical with what it resembled, were it not in some way different from it. The difference between the one made "in the image" and the archetype lies in this: that the latter by nature is not subject to change, while the former is. Through change it derived its subsistence, as we have shown; and being subject to change, its being is not entirely permanent.

Now change is a perpetual movement toward a different state. And it takes two forms. In the one case it is always directed toward the good; and here its progress is continual, since there is no conceivable limit to the distance it can go. In the other case it is directed toward the opposite, the essence of which lies in nonexistence. For the opposite of the good, as we have already indicated, implies some such notion of oppositon as we intend when we oppose being to nonbeing and existence to nonexistence. By reason, then, of its impulse toward change and movement, our nature cannot remain essentially unchanged. Rather does the will drive it toward some end, desire for the good naturally setting it in motion.

Now the good is of two kinds: what is really good in the nature of things, and what is not such, but has only an outward and artificial appearance of the good. It is the mind, with which we have been endowed, that discriminates between these. In this we run the risk either of gaining what is essentially good, or else, by being diverted from it by some misleading prospect, of lapsing into the opposite. This is what happened in the pagan fable about the dog which saw in the water the reflection of what it had in its mouth. It let go the real food, and, opening its mouth to swallow the reflection, remained hungry.

Being cheated of the desire for the genuine good, the mind was thus diverted to nonbeing. By the deceit of the advocate and contriver of wickedness, it was convinced that good was its opposite. Nor would this deception have succeeded, had not the fishhook of evil been furnished with an outward appearance of good, as with a bait. Of his own free will man fell into this misfortune, and through pleasure became subject to the enemy of life.

Let us now, in this connection, study all the appropriate attributes of God—goodness, wisdom, justice, power, incorruption, and everything else that indicates excellence. As good he has pity on him who has fallen; as wise he is not ignorant of the way to restore him. For it belongs to wisdom to make just decisions, since one would not associate genuine justice with stupidity.

Wherein, then, did [God's] justice consist in this matter? In His not exercising an arbitrary authority over him who held us in bondage. Also, in His not wresting us from him who held us, by His superior power, and so leaving him who had enslaved man through pleasure, with a just cause of complaint. Those who give up their liberty for money become the slaves of their purchasers. By their selling themselves, neither they nor anyone else can reclaim their freedom, even when those who reduce themselves to this wretched state are nobly born. And should anyone, out of concern for one so sold, exercise force against the purchaser, he would seem unjust in dictatorially freeing one legally acquired. On the other hand, no law stands in the way of his buying back the man's freedom, if he wants to. In the same way, when once we had voluntarily sold ourselves, he who undertook out of goodness to restore our freedom had to contrive a just and not a dictatorial method to do so. And some such method is this: to give the master the chance to take whatever he wants to as the price of the slave.

What, then, was it likely that our overlord would choose to take? It is possible to make a reasonable guess about his wishes, if we proceed from facts already clear. We argued at the beginning that he envied man his happiness and closed his eyes to the good. He begot in himself the darkness of wickedness, and sickened with the love of power. This was the origin of his decline toward evil, and the foundation and, as it were, the mother of all other wickedness. What, then, would he exchange for the one in his power, if not something clearly superior and better?

Thus, by getting the better of the bargain he might the more satisfy his pride.

Among those whom history records from the beginning, he was aware of none who was connected with such circumstances as he saw in His appearance. There was conception without sexual union, birth without impurity, a virgin suckling a child, and heavenly voices witnessing to his eminence. The healing of natural diseases was performed by him without technical skill, but by a mere word and act of will. There was the restoration of the dead to life, the rescue of the condemned, the fear inspired in demons, and authority over the elements. He walked across the sea so that the water was not parted to lay bare the bottom for those who passed over (as happened in Moses' miracle); but the surface of the water became like land to his tread, and supported his footsteps by offering a firm resistance. He ignored food as long as he wished. There were abundant feasts in the desert, which fed many thousands. Heaven did not rain down manna; nor did the earth naturally bring forth wheat to fill their need. But from the secret storehouses of God's power this abundance proceeded. Bread was produced ready-made in the hands of those who served it, and, indeed, increased as it satisfied those who ate of it. Then there were the relishes of fish—not that the sea supplied their need, but He who sowed the sea with its different kinds of fish.

But how can we recount in detail each of the gospel miracles? When the enemy saw such power, he recognized in Christ a bargain which offered him more than he held. For this reason he chose him as the ransom for those he had shut up in death's prison. Since, however, he could not look upon the direct vision of God, he had to see him clothed in some part of that flesh which he already held captive through sin. Consequently the Deity was veiled in flesh, so that the enemy, by seeing something familiar and natural to him, might not be terrified at the approach of transcendent power. So when he saw this power softly reflected more and more through the miracles, he reckoned that what he saw was to be desired rather than feared.

You observe here how the goodness is combined with justice, and wisdom is not separated from them. Through the covering of the flesh the divine power is made accessible, so that the enemy will not take fright at God's appearing and so thwart his plan for us. All God's attributes are at once displayed in this—his goodness, his wisdom, and his justice. That he decided to save us is proof of his goodness. That he struck a bargain to redeem the captive indicates his justice. And it is evidence of his transcendent wisdom that he contrived to make accessible to the enemy what was [otherwise] inaccessible.

It is likely, however, that one who has followed our train of thought will inquire where the power of the Godhead and the incorruptible nature of divine power can be seen in the account we have given. That this too may be clear, let us penetrate the successive events of the gospel story, in which the union of power with love for man is displayed.

In the first place, that the omnipotent nature was capable of descending to man's lowly position is a clearer evidence of power than great and supernatural miracles. For it somehow accords with God's nature, and is consistent with it, to do great and sublime things by divine power. It does not startle us to hear it said that the whole creation, including the invisible world, exists by God's power, and is the realization of his will. But descent to man's lowly position is a supreme example of power—of a power which is not bounded by circumstances contrary to its nature.

It belongs to the nature of fire to shoot upwards; and no one would think it wonderful for a flame to act naturally. But if he saw a flame with a downward motion like that of heavy bodies, he would take it for a marvel, wondering how it could remain a flame and yet contravene its nature by its downward motion. So it is with the incarnation. God's transcendent power is not so much displayed in the vastness of the heavens, or the luster of the stars, or the orderly arrangement of the universe or his perpetual oversight of it, as in his condescension to our weak nature. We marvel at the way the sublime entered a state of lowliness and, while actually seen in it, did not leave the heights. We marvel at the way the Godhead was entwined in human nature and, while becoming man, did not cease to be God.

As we have already observed, the opposing power could not, by its nature, come into immediate contact with God's presence and endure the unveiled sight of him. Hence it was that

St. Gregory of Nyssa

God, in order to make himself easily accesible to him who sought the ransom for us, veiled himself in our nature. In that way, as it is with greedy fish, he might swallow the Godhead like a fishhook along with the flesh, which was the bait. Thus, when life came to dwell with death and light shone upon darkness, their contraries might vanish away. For it is not in the nature of darkness to endure the presence of light, nor can death exist where life is active.

SUMMARY

Let us then, by way of summary, review our argument about the gospel revelation, and so make an effective reply to those who criticize God's plan because he personally intervened to save man. Throughout we must have fitting notions of God. We must not attribute to him one transcendent attribute, and then exclude another which equally befits him. But our faith must certainly include every sublime and devout thought of God, and these must be properly related to each other.

We have shown that God's goodness, wisdom, justice, power, and incorruptible nature are all to be seen in his plan for us. His goodness is evident in his choosing to save one who was lost. His wisdom and justice are to be seen in the way he saved us. His power is clear in this: that he came in the likeness of man and in the lowly form of our nature, inspiring the hope that, like man, he could be overcome by death; and yet, having come, he acted entirely in accordance with his nature. Now it belongs to light to dispel darkness, and to life to destroy death. Seeing, then, we have been led astray from the right path, with the result we were diverted from the life we once had and were involved in death, what is there improbable in what we learn from the gospel revelation? Purity lays hold of those stained with sin, life lays hold of the dead, and guidance is given to those astray, so that the stain may be cleansed, the error corrected, and the dead may return to life.

There is good reason for those who do not take too narrow a view of things to find anything strange in the fact that God assumed our nature. For when he considers the universe, can anyone be so simple-minded as not to believe that the Divine is present in everything, pervading, embracing, and penetrating it?

191

For all things depend on Him who is, and nothing can exist which does not have its being in Him who is. If, then, all things exist in him and he exists in all things, why are they shocked at a scheme of revelation which teaches that God became man, when we believe that even now he is not external to man? For, granted that God is not present in us in the same way as he was in the incarnation, it is at any rate admitted he is equally present in us in both instances. In the one case he is united to us in so far as he sustains existing things. In the other case he united himself with our nature, in order that by its union with the Divine it might become divine, being rescued from death and freed from the tyranny of the adversary. For with *his* return from death, our mortal race begins *its* return to immortal life.

DID GOD USE DECEIT?

But perhaps someone who has examined the justice and wisdom apparent in this plan is driven to conclude that such a scheme as God contrived for us involved deceit. For in a way it was a fraud and deception for God, when he placed himself in the power of the enemy who was our master, not to show his naked deity, but to conceal it in our nature, and so escape recognition. It is the mark of deceivers to divert the hopes of those they plot against to one thing, and to do something different from what is expected. But he who penetrates the truth of the matter will agree that we have here a crowning example of justice and wisdom.

Now it is the character of justice to render to each his due. It belongs to wisdom, on the other hand, neither to pervert justice nor to divorce its just decisions from the noble end of the love of man. Both must be skillfully combined. By justice due recompense is given; by goodness the end of the love of man is not excluded. Let us then inquire whether the two are to be seen in what happened. Justice is evident in the rendering of due recompense, by which the deceiver was in turn deceived. The purpose of the action, on the other hand, testifies to the goodness of him who brought it about. For it is the mark of justice to render to everyone the results of what he originally planted, just as the earth yields fruits according to the types of seed sown. It is the mark of wisdom, however, by the way in which it returns

192

like for like, not to exclude a higher aim. The conspirator and the one who cures the victim both mix a drug with the man's food. In the one case it is poison; in the other it is an antidote for poison. But the mode of healing in no way vitiates the kindly intention. In both instances a drug is mixed with the food; but when we catch sight of the aim, we applaud the one and are incensed at the other. So it is with the incarnation. By the principle of justice the deceiver reaps the harvest of the seeds he sowed with his own free will. For he who first deceived man by the bait of pleasure is himself deceived by the camouflage of human nature. But the purpose of the action changes it into something good. For the one practiced deceit to ruin our nature; but the other, being at once just and good and wise, made use of a deceitful device to save the one who had been ruined. And by so doing he benefited, not only the one who had perished, but also the very one who had brought us to ruin. For when death came into contact with life, darkness with light, corruption with incorruption, the worse of these things disappeared into a state of nonexistence, to the profit of him who was freed from these evils.

When a baser metal is mixed with gold, refiners restore the more precious metal to its natural brightness by consuming the alien and worthless substance with fire. The separation, indeed, does not occur without difficulty, for it takes time for the fire to consume the base element and effect its disappearance. Yet the melting away of the substance embedded in it, which detracts from its beauty, is a kind of healing of the gold. In the same way, when death, corruption, darkness, and the other offshoots of vice have attached themselves to the author of evil, contact with the divine power acts like fire and effects the disappearance of what is contrary to nature. In this way the nature is purified and benefited, even though the process of separation is a painful one. Hence not even the adversary himself can question that what occurred was just and salutary—if, that is, he comes to recognize its benefit. In this present life patients whose cure involves surgery and cautery grow incensed at their physicians when they smart under the pain of the incision. But if by these means they are restored to health and the pain of the cautery passes off, they will be grateful to those who effected their cure. It is the same with the evil which is now mingled with our nature and has become a part of it. When, over long periods of time, it has been removed and those now lying in sin have been restored to their original state, all creation will join in united thanksgiving, both those whose purification has involved punishment and those who never needed purification at all.

WHY GOD ASSUMED HUMAN NATURE

This is the sort of teaching we derive from the mighty revelation of God's becoming man. By his intimate union with humanity, he shared all the marks of our nature. He was born, reared, grew up, and went so far as even to taste death. Thus he brought about all we have mentioned. He freed man from evil, and healed the very author of evil himself. For the healing of an infirmity involves doing away with the disease, even if the process is painful.

Certainly it was in keeping with his intimate union with our nature that he should be united with us in all our characteristics. Those who wash off dirt from garments do not leave some of the stains and remove others. But, from top to bottom, they cleanse the whole garment of the stains, to give it a consistent character with a uniform brightness from the washing. It is the same with our human life, which from beginning to end and throughout was stained with sin. The cleansing power had to penetrate it entirely. One part could not be healed by cleansing while another was overlooked and left uncured. That is why, in view of the fact that our life is bounded by two extremities (I mean its beginning and end), the power which amends our nature had to reach to both points. It had to touch the beginning and extend to the end, covering all that lies between.

Now for every man there is only one way of entering life. Whence, then, did he have to take up his abode in it who was coming to us? "From heaven," is perhaps the reply of one who despises the method of human birth as something shameful and disgraceful. But in heaven there was no human nature, nor was the disease of evil prevalent in that transcendent life. He who united himself with man did so with the aim of helping him. How, then, will anyone seek in that sphere where there was no evil and man did not live his life the particular human nature

194

which God assumed—or rather, not the human nature, but some imitation of it? For how could our nature be restored if it was some heavenly being, and not this sick creature of earth, which was united with the Divine? For a sick man cannot be healed unless the ailing part of him in particular receives the cure. If, then, the diseased member was on earth, and the divine power, to preserve its own dignity, did not come into contact with it, its concern with creatures with which we have nothing in common would not have benefited man.

Indeed, if it is permissible to conceive of anything, except evil, as unworthy of God, such a situation is as unworthy of him as any other. For to one who is so narrow-minded as to define God's majesty from its inability to share the properties of our nature, his union with a heavenly body rather than an earthly would not detract less from his dignity. For every created thing is equally inferior to the Most High who, by reason of his transcendent nature, is unapproachable. The whole universe is uniformly beneath his dignity. For what is totally inaccessible is not accessible to one thing and inaccessible to another. Rather does it transcend all existing things in equal degree. Earth is not more below his dignity, and heaven less. Nor do the creatures inhabiting each of these elements differ in this respect, that some have a direct contact with his inaccessible nature, while others are distant from it. Otherwise we could not conceive of the power that governs the universe as equally pervading all things. In some it would be unduly present, in others it would be lacking. Consequently, from these differences of more and less, the divine nature would appear to be composite and inconsistent with itself, were we to conceive of it in principle as remote from us while it was near some other creature and easily accessible by this proximity.

The true way, however, of regarding the transcendent dignity does not have in view comparisons in terms of "lower" and "higher." Everything is equally beneath the power that rules the universe. In consequence, if our opponents imagine that the earthly nature is unworthy of union with the Divine, they will never discover any other nature worthy of it. If, then, everything equally falls short of this dignity, the one thing which really befits God's nature still remains, namely, to come to the aid of those in need. By acknowledging, therefore, that the healing power had recourse to the very place where the disease was, what conception unworthy of God does our faith entertain?

But our opponents ridicule human nature, and keep stressing the manner of our birth. They imagine, by so doing, that they hold our faith up to derision, as if it were unbecoming to God to share in, and to have contact with, human life by entering it in such a way. But we have already treated this point by our previous contention that evil, and what is akin to it, are alone essentially shameful. But the whole course of our nature has been arranged by God's will and law, and hence it is far removed from the censure of evil. Otherwise the condemnation of our nature would reflect upon the Creator, if any aspect of it could be charged with being disgraceful or improper.

The only thing alien to the Divine is evil. Nature is not evil; and our religion teaches that God was incarnate in man, not that he entered a state of evil. There is only one way for a man to enter life, viz., to be gotten and brought into existence. Now our opponents acknowledge that it was right for the divine power to visit the nature which was weakened by evil, but they are offended at the means of the visitation. What other method, then, of entering life do they prescribe for God? They fail to realize that the whole anatomy of the body is uniformly to be valued, and that no factor which contributes to the maintenance of life can be charged with being dishonorable or evil. The whole organic structure of the body is devised for a single end, and that is to preserve the human race in existence. The other organs support man's present life, and are distributed among different activitites by which man exercises his faculties of perception and action. But the generative organs have the future in view, and it is by them that the succession of the race is maintained. If, then, we have in mind their usefulness, to which one of the organs we generally consider honorable can they be inferior? Indeed, to which of them should we not with good reason reckon them to be superior? For it is not by means of the eye or the ear or the tongue or any of our senses that our race is constantly carried on. As we have said, such senses serve our present enjoyment. But by the generative organs the immortality of the human race is preserved, and death's perpetual moves against us are, in a way, rendered futile and ineffectual. By her successive generations nature is always filling up the deficiency. What unfitting notion, then, does our religion contain, if God was united with human life by the very means by which our nature wars on death?

WHY WAS THE INCARNATION DELAYED?

But taking a different line, they try to calumniate our teaching in another way. Granting, they say, that what occurred was good and worthy of God, why did he delay this act of his goodness? Why did he not cut short the further progress of evil at its very first appearance? We have a brief reply for this: viz., that it was wise and foreseeing to delay the benefit, for this served to the advantage of our nature. In the case of diseases of the body, when some corrupting humor spreads under the skin, the skillful physician does not bind the body up with drugs before the underlying trouble is brought completely to the surface. Rather does he wait until the hidden humor is altogether out, and so applies his remedy to the disease when it is uncovered. And so, when once the disease of wickedness had infiltrated human nature, the universal Physician waited until no form of evil remained concealed in our nature. In consequence, he did not apply his cure to man immediately on Cain's jealousy and murder of his brother. For the wickedness of those destroyed in Noah's time had not yet broken out. Nor had there come to light the terrible disease of Sodom's transgression, or the battle of the Egyptians with God, or the arrogance of the Assyrians, or the murder of God's saints by the Jews, or Herod's iniquitous slaughter of the children, or all the other things which history records or which were wrought by successive generations and left unrecorded. For the root of wickedness produced in men's wills a great variety of shoots. When, then, evil had reached its highest pitch and no form of wickedness had been daringly attempted by man, he healed the disease. Not, indeed, as its onset but when it had fully developed, so that the healing might encompass the total ailment.

If anyone, furthermore, imagines he can refute our argument because human life still continues to go astray through sin, even after the application of the remedy, he may be led to the truth by means of a familiar example. In the case of a snake, should it receive a deadly blow on the head, its coil is not at once killed with its head. While the latter is dead, the tail still remains pulsing with its own life, and is not deprived of vital movement. Similarly it is possible for evil to have been struck a mortal blow, and yet for life still to be harassed by its vestiges.

WHY DO NOT ALL BELIEVE?

When, however, they give up reproaching our religious teaching on this point, they introduce another charge, viz., that our faith does not extent to all mankind. Why is it, they say, that the grace of the gospel has not reached all men? While some have attached themselves to its teaching, the remainder constitute no small number. Either God is unwilling to distribute his benefits ungrudgingly to everyone or else he is quite incapable of doing so. Both alternatives are open to censure. For it does not befit God's nature to be defective either in willing what is good or in executing it. Why is it, then, they ask, that the grace of the gospel has not reached all men, seeing that faith is something good?

Now had we, in the course of our argument, contended that the divine will allots faith to men in such a way that some are called, while others fail to share in the calling, there would be occasion to prefer such a charge against our religion. But all are equally called without respect to rank, age, or nationality. It was, indeed, for this reason that from the very first when the gospel was preached the ministers of the Word were at once divinely inspired to speak every language, so that no one might fail to share in the blessings of their teaching. In the light of this, how can anyone rightly charge God with responsibility for the fact that the Word has not prevailed with all men? Out of his high regard for man, the Sovereign of the universe left something under our own control and of which each of us is the sole master. I mean the will, a faculty which is free from bondage and independent, and is grounded in the freedom of the mind. Such a charge, then, might with greater justice be transferred to those who have not attached themselves to the faith rather than be brought against him who solicited their assent to it. When Peter first preached the gospel before a large gathering of Jews, three thousand at once embraced the faith. But the disbelievers, who were more numerous than those who believed, did not blame the apostle for their lack of conviction. For, seeing the grace of the gospel had been offered to all, it was not reasonable that those who held aloof of their own free choice should put the blame for their hard luck on another, rather than on themselves.

Our opponents, however, are not at a loss for a captious reply to such arguments. For they contend that, had God wanted to, he could have compelled those who were stubborn to accept the gospel preaching. What freedom of choice would they then have had? Wherein would virtue lie? Wherein the praise for those who triumphed? It is a mark only of inanimate or irrational creatures to be induced by another's will to do his bidding. But were a reasonable and intelligent nature to abandon its freedom of choice, it would at the same time lose the boon of intelligence. For what use would such a one's mind be, if his power of free choice were at the disposal of another? If the will is inactive, virtue of necessity vanishes, being precluded by the inertness of the will. With the absence of virtue, life loses its honor, the praise of the victorious is done away, sin is no longer a peril, and different ways of life are indistinguishable. For who any longer could reasonably censure the dissolute, or praise the self-controlled? For everyone would be ready with this answer: that nothing we intend is in our power, but the wills of men are induced by a higher power to do its bidding. The fact, then, that the faith has not taken root in all men is not to be charged against God's goodness, but against the disposition of those to whom the gospel is preached.

WHY DID GOD DIE?

What further objection do our opponents bring forward? In its extreme form this: that the transcendent nature ought never to have experienced death. Rather could He, with his excessive power, have easily accomplished his purpose without this. But even if, for some ineffable reason, this actually had to happen, he at least did not have to be humiliated by a shameful manner of death. For, they urge, what death could be more shameful than that on a cross?

What do we reply to this? That the birth makes the death necessary. He who had once decided to share our humanity had

199

to experience all that belongs to our nature. Now human life is encompassed within two limits, and if he had passed through one and not touched the other, he would only have half fulfilled his purpose, having failed to reach the other limit proper to our nature.

But someone, perhaps, with an accurate grasp of our religion might more reasonably claim that the death did not occur because of the birth, but that, on the contrary, the birth was accepted by Him for the sake of the death. For he who eternally exists did not submit to being born in a body because *he* was in need of life. Rather was it to recall *us* from death to life. Our whole nature had to be brought back from death. In consequence he stooped down to our dead body and stretched out a hand, as it were, to one who was prostrate. He approached so near death as to come into contact with it, and by means of his own body to grant our nature the principle of the resurrection, by raising our total humanity along with him by his power.

Not from another source, but from the lump of our humanity, came the manhood which received the Divine. By the resurrection it was exalted along with the Godhead. In the case of our own bodies the activity of one of our senses is felt throughout the whole system which is united to it. In just the same way, seeing that our nature constitutes, as it were, a single living organism, the resurrection of one part of it extends to the whole. By the unity and continuity of our nature it is communicated from the part to the whole. If, then, He who stands upright stoops to raise up one who has fallen, what is there in our religious teaching which is outside the realm of probability?

Regarding the cross, whether it contains some other, deeper meaning, those familiar with mystical interpretations may know. But what has come down to us from tradition is as follows: Everything spoken and done in the gospel has a higher, divine meaning. There is no exception to this principle whereby a complete mingling of the divine and the human is indicated. The word and the act proceed in a human way, but the secret meaning reveals the divine. It follows, therefore, that in this instance we should not regard the one aspect and overlook the other. In the death we should see the human element; but from its manner we should seek to penetrate its divine significance.

It is the mark of Deity to pervade everything and to extend to every part of the nature of existing things. Nothing, indeed, could continue in existence did it not have its being in that which exists. Now that which is essential and primary being is the divine nature; and the continuance of existing things compels us to believe that it pervades all that is. We learn this from the cross. In shape it is divided into four parts in such a way that the four arms converge in the middle. Now He who was extended upon it at the time God's plan was fulfilled in his death is the one who binds all things to himself and makes them one. Through himself he brings the diverse natures of existing things into one accord and harmony. For we conceive of things as either above or below, or else we think of them as extended sideways. If, then, you consider the constitution of things in heaven or beneath the earth or at either limit of the universe, everywhere the Godhead anticipates your thought. It alone is observed in every part of existence and maintains the universe in a state of being. Whether we should call this nature Godhead or Word or Power or Wisdom, or any other sublime term that better expresses transcendence, makes no difference to our argument. We shall not quibble about a name or title or mode of expression.

The eyes of all creation are set on Him and he is its center, and it finds its harmony in him. Through him the things above are united with those below, and the things at one extremity with those at the other. In consequence it was right that we should not be brought to a knowledge of the Godhead by hearing alone; but that sight too should be our teacher in these sublime matters. This was also the starting point of the great Paul when he initiated the people of Ephesus [into the Christian mysteries]. By his teaching he implanted in them the power to know what is "the depth and height and breadth and length." In fact he designates each projection of the cross by its proper term, calling the top one "height," the bottom one "depth," and the side arms "breadth" and "length." It seems to me, moreover, that he brings out this idea still more clearly when he writes to the Philippians and says to them, "At the name of Jesus every knee shall bow, of things in heaven and on earth and under the earth." There he uses a single term to refer to the crossbar, designating by "on earth" everything in between the things in heaven and the things under the earth.

Such, then, is the mystical meaning of the cross as we have been taught it. The succeeding events, moreover, in the gospel account are consistently of such a kind that even unbelievers would admit they involve no unfitting conception of God. He did not remain dead; and the wounds the spear inflicted on his body did not prevent his living. After the resurrection he appeared at will to the disciples. Whenever he wished, he was present with them, though unobserved. He came into their midst without needing doors to give him entrance. He strengthened the disciples by breathing on them the Spirit. He promised to be with them and that nothing would separate him from them. Visibly he ascended to heaven, but to their minds he was everywhere present. These facts, and whatever the gospel story contains of a similar nature, need no supporting arguments to prove their divine quality and their connection with sublime and transcendent power. I do not think it necessary to dwell upon them in detail. The mere mention of them at once indicates their supernatural character. But since a part of our revealed teaching concerns God's plan regarding washing (whether we call this baptism or enlightenment or regeneration—we will not quibble about the word), we may as well briefly discuss this too. 33. For our opponents are incredulous when they hear us speak about it in the following way.

St. Hilary of Poitiers
315-367

Hilary, the "Athanasius of the West," was born of a noble pagan family and received a classical education. He was married and had a daughter named Abra when he was converted to Christianity in 345. He was chosen bishop of Poitiers by both clergy and people, probably in 353. At the Council of Béziers in 356 he refused to condemn Athanasius in the Arian controversy and was deported to Phrygia by order of Emperor Constantius II. He used his time in exile to study Greek theology and to write two important books, including the one excerpted here.

Hilary's contribution would be much more appreciated if he had not been followed so soon by the Western giants: Jerome, Ambrose, and Augustine, all of whom were his younger contemporaries. As Irenaeus before him, Hilary too was a bridge between East and West. One difference, however, was that the language in Christian Gaul had in the meantime switched from Greek to Latin. His work on The Trinity was thus the first extensive study of this doctrine in Latin and in it he combined the language of Tertullian, Novatian, and Cyprian with the more speculative Greek ideas, especially stemming from Origen. Less than two decades after his death Jerome was sure that "the splendor of his (Hilary's) eloquence will be celebrated wherever the name of Rome is heard."

The main enemies combatted in his work are always the Arians, but he only mentions them by name two or three times, and he does not bother with historical aspects. His first purpose was ever to prove that the Son was of the same substance as the Father, so he never really made a careful study of the human nature of Christ. Two points he insisted upon: 1) Jesus was one and only one divine person, but 2) he had both a divine and a human nature.

In coining the Latin vocabulary for speaking about Jesus in a non-Arian way, Hilary is usually credited with having introduced the very term "Incarnatio." While his expertise in Latin rhetoric is evident, he impregnates his work with a vivid awareness of faith, frequently acknowledging that one is treading in the realm of sacred mystery. His constant preference is thus to appeal to the Word of God Himself in the Scriptures for all his arguments.

"This work of St. Hilary is his masterpiece and upon it rests his fame as a theologian. It is generally regarded as one of the finest writings that the Arian controversy produced. Augustine and Leo the Great are among the early writers who praise it, and St. Thomas Aquinas frequently appeals to it when settling disputes about the Trinity" (S. McKenna). He explains his rather intricate outline for all twelve books in book one. Books 2 and 3 elaborate the positive meaning of the three Persons in God, each being really distinct from the other but united in nature. Books 4 through 12 then focus on the "homoousious" doctrine, the consubstantiality of the Son with the Father. For our selection we have chosen book 7 in its entirety, convinced that it conveys well the style, approach, and eloquence of Hilary in defending the divinity of Christ for the Latin-speaking Church.

THE TRINITY

BOOK SEVEN

We are writing this seventh Book against the insane audacity of the new heresy. In number, it is true, it comes after the others that have preceded, but it is the first or the greatest in regard to the understanding of the mystery of the complete faith. In it we realize how difficult and how arduous is the journey of the evangelical doctrine which we are ascending. Although the consciousness of our weakness inspires us with fear and seeks to call us back, we are inspired by the ardor of faith, aroused by the fury of the heretics, and disturbed by the peril of the ignorant, and we cannot remain silent about those matters of which we do not dare to speak.

The fear of a twofold danger overwhelms us, that either by our silences or by our preaching we shall be guilty of betraying the truth. The cunning heretics have girded themselves with the unbelievable devices of a depraved ingenuity in order that they may claim, first of all, to possess the true worship of God; then, to disturb the confidence of all the uneducated by means of their world; and finally, to hinder the comprehension of the truth by the specious reasons which they allege. By expressing their belief in the one God they have misrepresented the true worship of God; again, by acknowledging the Son they have deceived the hearers by the name; they have also gratified the wisdom of the world by stating that He was not before He was born; and by asserting that God is immutable and incorporeal they have excluded the birth of God from God by the subtle manner in which they have explained their arguments. They have employed our doctrines against us, have fought the faith of the Church with the faith of the Church, and have brought us into the gravest danger, whether we make a reply or remain silent, because they preach those doctrines which are denied by means of those doctrines that are not denied.

We recall, of course, the warning that we addressed to our readers in the preceding Books that, while perusing the manifesto of the entire blasphemy, they should take note that it has no other aim than to inculcate the belief that our Lord Jesus Christ is neither the Son of God nor God, and, while conceding to Him only the names derived from a sort of adoption, they deny that He has the nature of God and the nature of a son, since they assert, therefore, that God is immutable and incorporeal in order that the Son to whom He gave birth may not be God; hence, in their confession only God the Father is the one God, in order that Christ may not be God in our faith, for an incorporeal nature does not admit the ideal of a birth, and the confession of only one God destroys our faith in God from God.

In the preceding Books, where we have already taught, in accordance with the Law and the Prophets, that this teaching of theirs was both deceitful and futile, we mapped out that plan in our reply which, in the explanation of God from God and in our confession of the one true God, would not be found wanting by creating a union in the one true God, nor would it go too far by professing our faith in a second God, since in our confession God is neither alone, nor are there two gods. Meanwhile, as we neither denied nor affirmed that He is one, we preserved the perfection of faith. For, that they are one in nature is referred to both of them, and both are not one person. Accordingly, we who are about to give a complete explanation of this indescribable mystery of the perfect faith in conformity with the teaching of the Gospels and the Apostles must in the first place bring to our readers' attention nothing else than the nature of the Son of God, who subsists by a true birth, and to make known that the Son is not from anywhere else or from anything except from God. In accordance with that which we have brought out in the preceding Books, there is no doubt that He is the Son of God by the true nature of His birth, and that the name of adoption may not be applied we shall now prove these same things from the Gospels so that we may also recognize Him as the true God, because He is the true Son, for He will not be a true Son unless He is also the true God, nor will He be the true God unless He is also the true Son.

There is nothing more oppressive to human nature than the consciousness of danger (for those things which take place unknown to us, or suddenly, leave our peace of mind in a truly pitiable state, but no fear of the future accompanies them), because the anxiety itself brings the pain of suffering with it to one who is aware of the coming misfortunes. I do not now set sail from port without being familiar with shipwreck, nor do I enter upon the journey unaware that the forests are infested with robbers, nor do I pass across the deserts of Libya without realizing that scorpions, asps, and basilisks are present everywhere. Nothing eludes my care or my knowledge. I speak under the watchful eyes of all the heretics who hang upon every word from my mouth, and the entire journey of my treatise is either difficult to ascend because of the narrow passages, or is filled with pitfalls, or covered with traps. I do not complain very much about the fact that the journey is already arduous and difficult, because I am ascending not by own steps but by those of the Apostles. I am, however, always in danger, ever fearful of going aside from the narrow paths, or of falling into the ditches, or of being ensnared by the traps. For, as I am about to explain the one God according to the Law, the Prophets, and the Apostles, Sabellius confronts me; if I proclaim this term, his most savage bite will devour me completely as a choice morsel. Again, if I oppose Sabellius, deny the one God and acknowledge the Son of God as the true God, a new heresy is ready to accuse me of teaching that there are two gods. If I shall say that the Son of God was born from Mary, then Ebion, that is, Photinus, will derive prestige for his lie from the confession of the truth. I pass over the others in silences, because everyone knows that they are outside of the Church.

Although this one has been frequently condemned and rejected, it is a deeply rooted evil even at the present day. Galatia has nourished many who have made this impious confession of God. Alexandria has maliciously proclaimed throughout almost the whole world the two gods whom it denies. Pannonia offers a damaging defense of the doctrine that

Jesus Christ has been born from Mary. And amid these arguments the Church is in peril of not clinging to the truth by means of the truth, since those doctrines by which the true worship of God is confirmed and destroyed are introduced for the sake of godlessness. We cannot teach about the one God in a pious manner if we teach that He is alone, because God the Son will not belong in the faith of a God who is in isolation. But, if we acknowledge that the Son of God is God, as He truly is, we are in danger of not preserving the faith in the one God, and it is as equally dangerous to deny the one God as it is to admit a solitary God. The folly of the world does not grasp these things, since it does not believe that He can be designated as one unless He is alone, nor can it conceive how He is not alone if He is one.

But the Church, as I hope, shall cast that light of her doctrine even upon the folly of the world so that, although it may not accept the mystery of faith, it realizes that we are teaching the mystery of faith to the heretics. For, great is the power of truth which, although it can be comprehended by itself, shines forth by the very teachings which are opposed to it, so that, while it remains steadfast in its nature, its nature daily acquires strength while it is being attacked. It is characteristic of the Church that she conquers when she is undergoing assault, that she is then understood when she is blamed, and that she gains then when she is abandoned. She desires, of course, that all should persevere with her and within her, nor is it her wish either to cast the others from her most peaceful bosom or to destroy them, when they become unworthy of dwelling with so great a mother. But, when the heretics have left her, or when they have rejected her, inasmuch as she loses the opportunity for dispensing her salvation, she gains confidence that blessedness is to be sought from her.

This is perceived most readily from the endeavors of the heretics themselves. Since the Church, instituted by the Lord and strengthened by the Apostles, is the one Church of all men, from which the raging error of the different blasphemous teachings has cut itself off, and it cannot be denied that the separation from the faith has come about as the result of a defective and perverted understanding, while that which was read was adapted to one's views rather than one's views being submissive to what was read, still, while the individual groups contradict one another, she is to be understood not only by her own teachings but also by those of her adversaries, so that, while all are directed against her alone, she refutes the most godless error of all of them by the very fact that she is alone and is one. All the heretics, therefore, rise up against the Church, but, while all the heretics mutually conquer themselves, they gain no victories for themselves. Victory in their case is the triumph of the Church over each of them, while one heresy wages war against that teaching in another heresy which the faith of the Church condemns in the other heresy (for there is nothing which the heretics hold in common), and, meanwhile, they confirm our faith while they contradict one another.

By doing away with the birth of the Son, Sabellius proclaims the one God, while he does not doubt that the power of the nature which produced its effect in the man is God. Since he does not know the mystery of the Son, he has lost the faith in the true generation of the Son through his admiration for the deeds, and while he hears: 'He who has seen me has seen also the Father,' he grasps at the union of the undivided and indistinguishable nature in the Father and the Son, not perceiving that a natural unity is revealed by the designation of a birth, since from the fact that the Father is seen in the Son we have a confirmation of the divinity and not the abolition of the birth.

Accordingly, the knowledge of the one is in the other, because the one does not differ from the other in nature, and, where there is no difference between them, then the study of the true essence of the nature does not reveal any distinction. There can be no doubt that He who remained in the form of God caused the outward appearance of the form of God to be recognized in Himself. Even this saying of the Lord: 'I and the Father are one,' also leads to the absurd madness of this sinful opinion. For, the unity of the identical nature has developed in a godless manner into the error of a union, and by understanding this passage in the sense of power alone they have lost sight of its meaning. For, 'I and the Father are one' does not indicate one who is in isolation. The conjunction 'and' which designates the Father does not permit us to think of one, and the word 'are' is incompatible with a single person, but, while this phrase, 'are one,' does not do away with the birth, it does not make any distinction in the nature, since 'one' is not a suitable word where there is a difference, nor 'are' where one person is concerned.

Join the rage of the present heretics to the rage of this man in order that they may defend themselves against Sabellius! They will declare that they have read: 'The Father is greater than I,' and, since they understand nothing either of the mystery of the birth or the mystery of the God who emptied Himself and assumed our flesh, they effect a lessening of the nature by acknowledging a great nature. They contend that He is a Son to such an extent that He is less than the Father, that He demands a restoration of His former glory, that He is afraid to die, and has died. On the contrary, that one defends the nature of God from His deeds, and since this new heresy will not now deny the one God in order that it may not believe that the Son is God, Sabellius will retain the one God in his profession in order that the Son may not exist at all. This one [Arius] will introduce the Son as working, and this one [Sabellius] will contend that God is present in the works. The latter [Sabellius] will speak of the one God, the former [Arius] will deny the one God.

Sabellius will defend himself in this manner: 'Nothing except the nature of God produces the miracles which have been performed. From God alone come the forgiveness of sins, the cure of diseases, the walking of the paralytics, the sight of the blind, the dead coming back to life. No other nature, except that which is conscious of what it is, would say: "I and the Father are one." Why do you force me into another substance? Why do you endeavor to make me another God? The one God has performed the deeds which are characteristic of God.' But, with a mouth that is no less venomous, these men will cry out against these things, and proclaim that the Son is unlike God the Father: 'You do not know the mystery of your salvation. We must believe that He is the Son, through whom the worlds were made, through whom man was formed, who gave the Law through the angels, who was born from Mary, who was sent by the Father, who was crucified, died, and was buried, who rose from the dead, is at the right hand of God, and who is the judge of the living and the dead. We must be born again into this one, we must acknowledge this one, we must merit this one's kingdom.' Each enemy of the Church is doing the work of the Church, and, while Sabellius preaches that He is God by nature because of His works, these men, on the other hand, acknowledge that He is the Son of God in accordance with the mystery of faith.

Furthermore, what a victory it is for our faith when Ebion, that is, Photinus, either conquers or is conquered, while he reproves Sabellius because he denies that the Son of God is man, and while the Arian fanatics refute him because he knows nothing about the Son of God in man. In opposition to Sabellius he claims the Gospels for the Son of Mary, but Arius does not concede to him that the Gospels belong to the Son of Mary alone. In opposition to him [Sabellius] who denies the Son, he [Photinus] unlawfully assumes a man into the Son. He [Photinus] who does not know that the Son exists before the world is contradicted by this one [Arius] who denies that the Son of God is only from man.

Let them conquer, as they will, because they are conquered by mutually conquering one another. While these men of the present time are also refuted by the nature of God, Sabellius is overthrown by the mystery of the Son, and Photinus is blamed either for his ignorance or his denial of the Son of God who was born before the world. Meanwhile, the faith of the Church, that rests upon the doctrines of the Gospels and the Apostles, clings to the confession of the Son against Sabellius, to the nature of God against Arius, and to the creator of the world against Photinus, and she does so with all the more right because these men are not in mutual agreement about their denial of these doctrines. Sabellius teaches that the nature of God is in the miracles, but he does not recognize the Son who works in them. On the other hand, these men give Him the title of Son, but they do not acknowledge that the nature of God is within Him. Photinus, however, refers to the man, but he is unaware that the man of whom he speaks has been born from God. Thus, while they are either defending or condemning they manifest the truth of our faith, which defends or condemns these doctrines in a God-fearing manner, just as they really are.

I have made these things known in a few words, not from any desire to be diffuse, but for safety's sake, in order that we should realize, first of all, that all the assertions of the heretics are ambiguous and false, since it is to our advantage when they mutually disagree, and furthermore, when I contradict the blasphemous statements of these men of the present day, and proclaim God the Father and the Son of God as God, and next confess that by the identical kind of divinity the Father and the Son have the same name and nature, no one may believe that I have been ensnared either by the error of two gods, or the contrary error of a God who is unique and alone, since no union will be found in our teaching about God the Father and God the Son, and no diversity of gods will result from our explanation of the undivided nature. Since in the preceding Book we based our reply to those who deny that the Son of God subsists from God on the true nature of the birth, we must now prove that He who is truly the Son of God by His nature is also truly God by His nature, but in such a manner that our faith may not deteriorate into an unique God nor into a second God, since it will not teach about the one God in such a manner as if He were alone, nor will it confess the God who is not alone as if He were not one.

We know, therefore, that our Lord Jesus Christ is God in these ways: by His name, birth, nature, power, confession. And in regard to His name I do not believe that there is any ambiguity, for we read: 'In the beginning was the Word and the Word was with God; and the Word was God.' What kind of a slander is it that He should not be what He is called? Or does not the name designate the nature? Since there is a motive behind every contradiction, I shall now inquire into the reason for this denial of God. It is a simple word and nothing strange is added that might be a stumbling-block. For, the Word that was made flesh is nothing else than God. Here we find no indication that this title was assigned to or assumed by Him, so that the name that is God is not His by nature.

Look at the other names that were either bestowed or appropriated. It was said to Moses: 'I have given thee as the God of Pharao.' But is not the reason for the name brought out when 'Pharao' is mentioned? Or has He bestowed the nature of

God upon him and not, rather, the power to inspire terror, when the serpent of Moses, which became a rod shortly afterwards, devours the serpents of the magicians, when he drives away the plague of flies which he had brought in, when he puts a stop to the hail with the power with which he had called it upon them, when he drives away the locusts with the strength with which he had admitted them, when the magicians acknowledge that the finger of God is present.

In this manner Moses was given as the God of Pharao, while He is feared, while petitions are addressed to him, while he punishes, and while he cures. It is one thing to be given as God, and it is another thing to be God. God was given to Pharao. Besides, the nature and the name do not belong to Him in such a manner that He is God. I also recall another use of this title, where it is stated: 'I have said: you are gods.' Here the meaning indicates a name that has been conferred. And when the expression 'I have said' is used, the words refer to the speaker rather than to the name of the thing, because the name of the thing brings us an understanding of the thing, but the title is dependent on the will of another. And where the author of the title reveals himself, there the title comes from the pronouncement of the author, and not as a true name derived from the nature.

But, here, the Word is God; the thing exists in the Word; the thing of the Word is expressed in the name. The name 'Word' belongs to the Son of God from the mystery of the birth just as do the names of wisdom and power. And even if they have been transmitted to the Son of God with the substance of the true birth, they are not wanting to God as attributes that are proper to Him, although they have been born from Him into God. As we have often declared, we do not teach the mystery of a division in the Son, but the mystery of the birth. There was not an imperfect separation but a perfect begetting, for the birth does not lead to any loss on the part of the begetter, while it includes a gain for the one who is born. For this reason, the surnames of those things are suitable to the only-begotten God which still inhere in the Father by the power of His unchangeable nature, while they perfect Him who subsists by the birth. The only-begotten God is the Word, but the unborn God is never wholly without the Word, not that the nature of the Son is the utterance of a voice, but He was designated as the Word, while He subsists as God from God with the true nature of the birth, in order that we might proclaim Him as the proper Son of the Father and inseparable from Him by the identity of nature.

As Christ is the wisdom and power of God, so He is not that efficacious movement of an internal power or thought, as He is wont to be understood, but His nature, which preserves the truth of His substance by His birth, is indicated by these names of the internal natures. For, it is impossible for that which is always internal for everyone. But, in order that we may know that He is not a stranger to the nature of the Father's divinity, the only-begotten Son, who has been born from the eternal God the Father into a God of the same substance, has been revealed as subsisting in the names of these attributes, which are not wanting to Him from whom He subsists. When I hear: 'And the Word was God,' I understand that He is not only called God, but is shown to be God. As we have pointed out above, the name has been added as a title to Moses and to those who are called gods, but here the nature of the substance is indicated. Being is not an accidental name, but a subsistent truth, an abiding principle, and an essential attribute of the nature.

Let us see whether the confession of the Apostle Thomas agrees with this teaching of the Evangelist, when he says: 'My Lord and my God.' He is therefore his God whom he acknowledges as God. And certainly he was aware that the Lord had said: 'Hear, O Israel, the Lord thy God is one.' And how did the faith of the Apostle become unmindful of the principal commandment, so that he confessed Christ as God, since we are to live in the confession of the one God? The Apostle, who perceived the faith of the entire mystery through the power of the resurrection, after he had often heard: 'I and the Father are one' and 'All things that the Father has are mine' and 'I in the Father and the Father in me,' now confessed the name of the nature without endangering the faith. For, the true religion, which acknowledges the Son of God as God, does not conflict with the confession of the one God the Father, since it believes that nothing except the true nature of the Father is in the Son of God, nor is the faith of the one nature imperiled by the impious confession of a second God, because the perfect birth of God does not lead to the nature of a second God.

Since Thomas, therefore, comprehended the true nature of the mystery of the Gospel, he acknowledged Him as his Lord and his God. This is not an honorary name, but the confession of a nature, for he believes that He was God because of the things and the powers themselves. And the Lord taught that this God-fearing confession was not a matter of honor, but of faith, when He said: 'Because thou hast seen, thou hast believed. Blessed are they who have not seen, and yet have believed.' Thomas believed when he saw. But you ask: What did he believe? And did he believe anything else than what he confessed: 'My Lord and my God'? He could not rise from the dead into life by Himself except through the nature of God, and the faith of the orthodox religion has believed and has confessed that He is God. And will not the name of God, therefore, be regarded as the essence of the nature, since the confession of the name follows the faith of the nature that is believed? For, the God-fearing Son, who would do not His own will but the will of Him who sent Him, and who would not seek His own honor but that of Him from whom He had come, would surely have rejected the glory of the name for Himself in order that He might not contradict what He Himself had preached about the one God. But, since He has indeed confirmed the mystery of the apostolic faith, and has admitted that the name of the Father's nature was in Him, He taught that those were blessed who, even though they had not seen Him rising from the dead, believed that He was God because they knew of His resurrection.

The name of the nature, therefore, is not wanting in the profession of our faith. For, the name, which designates everything, also makes known a thing of the same nature, and there are no longer two things but a thing of the same nature. The Son of God is God, since that is what the name indicates. One name does not add up to two gods, for God is the one name of a nature that is one and identical. Since the Father is God and the Son is God and the name of the divine nature is proper to each, the two of them are one, for, although the Son subsists by the birth of the nature, the unity is preserved in the name, nor does the birth of the Son, which claims that the Father and the Son have the one name just as they have the one nature, force the faith of the believers to acknowledge two gods. Hence, the name of God belongs to the Son by His birth. This is the second step in our exposition, that He is God by reason of His birth. Although the authority of the Apostle about the true nature of the name is still available to me, nevertheless it is my intention for the time being to discuss the statements of the Gospel.

First of all, I raise the question: What new element could the birth have introduced into the nature of the Son so that He is not God? The judgment of the human mind rejects this opinion, that anything by its birth is distinct from the nature of its origin, unless, perhaps, it has been conceived by natures that are different and something new comes into the world (and thus that which comes from two natures belongs to neither one), a thing that is customary among animals and wild beasts. But, even that new element is in it only because of the qualities that have been born together with it from the distinction of the natures, and their birth did not cause but accepted the distinction, and from the two of them it held fast to that which it combined into one in itself. Since these things are so in these corporeal processes and occurrences, what madness is it, I ask, to connect the birth of the only-begotten God with a spurious nature, since birth comes only from the essence of the nature, and there will no longer be a birth if the essence of the nature is not in the birth?

Hence, the purpose of all that heat and fury is that there may not be a birth but a creation in the Son of God, and that He who subsists may not preserve the origin of His nature, but may receive from non-existing matter a different nature from God. Since God is a Spirit, there is no doubt that the one born from Him has nothing in Him that is different from or alien to Him from whom He has been born, in accordance with the saying: 'That which is born of the flesh is flesh; and that which is born of the Spirit is spirit.' Consequently, the birth of God perfects God, so that we realize that God is not one who has begun to be but one who has been born, for that which has begun cannot be the same as that which has been born, since that which has a beginning either begins to exist from nothing into something or it develops from one thing into something else and ceases to be, as gold from the earth, as liquids from solids, as heat from cold, as red from white, as animate creatures from water, as living beings from those that are lifeless. The Son of God, however, does not begin to be God from nothing, but was born, nor was He anything else before He was God. Thus, He who is born into God did not begin to be, nor did He develop into that which God is. The birth, therefore, maintains the nature from which it subsists, and the Son of God does not subsist as anything else than that which God is.

If anyone raises doubts at this point, let him learn the knowledge of the nature from the Jews, or, rather, let him recognize the true nature of the birth from the Gospel, wherein it is written: 'This is why the Jews were seeking the more to put him to death; because he was not only breaking the Sabbath, but was also calling God his own Father, making himself equal to God.' The words of the Jews are not recorded here, as generally happens in other places; rather, this is the explanation by the Evangelist, who points out the reason why the Jews wanted to kill Him.

Hence, the excuse of an inadequate knowledge no longer holds for the godless blasphemers, since, according to the testimony of the Apostle, the true meaning of His nature is revealed when His birth is indicated, 'but he was also calling God his own Father, making himself equal to God.' Is there not a natural birth where the equality of the nature is manifested by the name of His own Father? There is no question regarding the fact that they do not differ in equality. Besides, will anyone deny that a birth gives rise to an identical nature? From this alone can come that which is true equality, because only birth can bestow an equality of nature. But, we shall never believe that equality is present where there is a union; on the other hand, it will not be found where there is a distinction. Thus, the equality of likeness does not admit either of solitude or of diversity, because in every case of equality there is neither a difference nor is it by itself.

Although the judgment of our reasoning, therefore, agrees with universal opinion of men, that birth brings about an equality of nature, and where there is equality there can be nothing strange nor can it be alone, still, the faith of our testimony should be ratified by the words of the Lord Himself, so that the reckless spirit of contradiction, by its lack of restraint in comprehending differences in the names, may not dare oppose the assertions of the divine testimony about Himself. The Lord replied: 'The Son can do nothing of himself, but only what he sees the Father doing. For whatever he does, the Son also does the same in like manner. For the Father loves the Son and shows him all that he himself does. And greater works than these he will show him that you may wonder. For as the Father raises the dead and gives them life, even so the Son also gives life to whom he will. For neither does the Father judge any man, but all judgment he has given to the Son, that all men may honor the Son even as they honor the Father. He who does not honor the Son, does not honor the Father who sent him.'

The order of what we have proposed required us, it is true, to discuss every single aspect of every single subject, so that, because we have learned that our Lord Jesus Christ is God in accordance with His name, birth, nature, power, and confession, our exposition should consider the specific steps in the proposed arrangement, but the nature of the birth, which embraces within it the name, the nature, the power, and the confession, does not allow this. For, without these there will be no birth, because by being born it contains all these things in itself. Accordingly, when we treat this subject we are necessarily placed in such a position that it is impossible to postpone the above-mentioned subjects in accordance with our plan of devoting a special treatise to each of them.

In replying to the Jews, who were the more eager to kill Him on this account, because He made Himself equal to God by calling God His Father, He explained the complete mystery of our faith while He rebuked their sinful passions. He had previously declared, after He had cured the paralytic and been judged worthy of death for this violation of the Sabbath: 'My father works even until now, and I work,' and by these words all were inflamed with hatred, because He had placed Himself on an equality with God by using the name of Father. And since He wished, therefore, to confirm His birth, and to confess the power of His nature, He stated: 'This Son can do nothing of himself, but only what he sees the Father doing.' The beginning of His answer was directed toward the godless fury of the Jews by which they were so aroused that they even determined to put Him to death.

To their accusation that He was guilty of violating the Sabbath He had declared: 'My Father works even until now, and I work,' in order that it might be understood that He acted thus by the authority of His example, but He indicated that what He had done was to be regarded as the work of His Father, because the latter Himself was working in whatever He did. Again, He added these words in reference to that hatred which He had stirred up by placing Himself on an equality with God when He gave Him the name of Father: 'Amen, amen I say to you, the Son can do nothing of himself, but only what he sees the Father doing.' In order that that equality, therefore, which was derived from the name and the nature of the Son might not do away with the faith in His birth, He said that the Son can do nothing of Himself except what He sees the Father doing. And that the salutary order of our confession in the Father and the Son might remain, He revealed the nature of His birth, which was the power to work not by an increase of strength, that would be granted for each specific task, but would be possessed beforehand by reason of His knowledge. He possesses it beforehand, however, not after the example of a material work, so that the Father would first do something that the Son would do later on, but He had come into existence with the nature of God into the nature of God, that is to say, the Son had been born from the Father. Because He was aware of the Father's power and strength that was with Him, the Son asserted that He could do nothing by Himself except what He saw the Father doing. And since the only-begotten God would do His work through the operations of His Father's power, He would claim that He could do as much as he was conscious of, that He could do it by His nature which was inseparable from that of God the Father, and which He had received by His legitimate birth. God does not see in a material way, but sees everything by the power of His nature.

Then He continued: 'For all things that the Father does, the Son also does the same in like manner.' He added 'in like manner' to indicate the birth, but He mentioned 'all things' and 'the same' when He was referring to the truth of the nature that He was to reveal. In these words, 'all things whatever' and 'the same,' there can be no distinction, nor can there be anything that is passed over. Thus, He to whose nature it belongs to do all the same things possesses the same nature. But, where all the same things are done by the Son 'in like manner,' the similarity of the works excludes the solitude of the one who does the work, so that all the things that the Father does the Son does in like manner. This is the understanding of the true birth and the most complete mystery of our faith, which confesses the true nature in the Father and the Son, and that arises from the unity of the divine nature and the one and identical Godhead, so that the Son, while He is doing the same things, does them in like manner, and that, while He is doing them in like manner, He is doing the same things, because by the designation of the things that are done in like manner He bears witness to the birth, and by the designation of the same things that are done He bears witness to the nature.

The order of the Lord's response, therefore, keeps intact the order of the Church's faith, so that it does not make any distinction in the nature, and indicates the birth. These words follow: 'For the Father loves the Son, and shows him all that he himself does. And greater works than these he will show him, that you may wonder. For as the Father raises the dead and gives them life, even so the Son also gives life to whom he will.' Does the manifestation of the works in this instance point out anything else to use than the faith in His birth so that we believe that the Son subsists from the Father who subsists? Unless, perhaps, we are to believe that the only-begotten God needed to be instructed in the doctrine that was to be made known because of His ignorance, but the rashness of this godless opinion is not permissible. It is not necessary for Him to be taught who knows whatever He must teach. He said later on: 'The Father loves the Son and shows him all that he himself does,' in order to make known that this complete manifestation of the Father was the doctrine of our faith, that is to say, that we should acknowledge the Father and the Son. And in order that no ignorance might be here attributed to the Son, to whom the Father would show everything that He would do, He immediately continued: 'And greater works than these he will show him, that you may wonder. For as the Father raises the dead and gives them life, even so the Son also gives life to whom he will.'

Hence, the revelation of the coming work is not unknown to the Son, to whom this was to be shown in order that He might bring back the dead to life in accordance with the example of His Father's nature. He declares that the Father will show these things to the Son which they will admire, and He at once taught us what these same things were: 'For as the Father raises the dead and gives them life, even so the Son also gives life to whom he will.' The power is made equal through the unity of an indistinguishable nature. And the manifestation of the works is not for the instruction of ignorance but for our faith. This did not acquaint the Son with the knowledge of things unknown, but acquainted us with the confession of His birth, while it confirms it by the fact that all things would be shown to Him that He could do.

The heavenly statement was not lacking in caution in order that the meaning of a distinct nature might not creep in under the pretext of ambiguous words. It declared that the works of the Father were shown rather than that the nature of the power was added in order to perform them, to teach us that the manifestation was the substance of the birth itself, and because of the Father's love there would be born with it the knowledge of the works of the Father which He wished Him to perform. Furthermore, in order that no one might conclude from this reference to the manifestation that there was a difference of nature in Him who did not know, He already knows the things themselves which, as He asserts, are to be made known. So far removed is He from having to act by the authority of an example that He gives life to those to whom He wills. For, to will is the liberty of a nature, which subsists together with the freedom of choice for the blessedness of perfect omnipotence.

And, then, in order that it might not appear, because He gives life to those whom He wills, that He does not possess the nature of a birth in Him, but that He subsists rather by the permission of the unborn power, He immediately declared: 'For neither does the Father judge any man, but all judgment he has given to the Son.' And from the fact that all judgment has been given to Him, His nature and His birth are shown, for on the one hand only an identical nature can possess everything, and on the other hand birth cannot have anything unless it is given.

But all judgment has been given, because He vivifies those whom He wills. Nor can it be claimed that all judgment has been taken away from the Father, since He Himself does not judge, because the judgment of the Son comes from the judgment of the Father, for from Him all judgment has been given. But the reason why the judgment has been given is not passed over in silence. For there come the words: 'But all judgment he has given to the Son, that all men may honor the Son even as they honor the Father. He who does not honor the Son, does not honor the Father who sent Him.' Is there anything left to us, I ask, that might give grounds for suspicion, or is there anything remaining here that might afford a pretext for impiety? For, neither does the Father judge any man, but all judgment He has given to the Son. The reason why the judgment was given, however, was that the Son might be equally honored with the Father, so that he who does not honor the Son does not honor the Father. And after these words, how can the nature of the birth be understood as being different, which has been made equal not only by the work, the power, the honor, but also by the insult, if the honor is denied? Accordingly, the statement in the Lord's reply now reveals nothing else than the mystery of the birth. Nor can we, nor must we, distinguish the Son from the Father in anything except that we teach that He is born, but is not distinct.

The Father, therefore, works even until now, and the Son works. You have the names of the nature, since both the Father as well as the Son work. Grasp the fact that the nature of God also works through which God works! And in order that you may not believe that the operation of two unlike natures is perhaps to be understood, recall what was said about the blind man: 'But that the works of God were to be made manifest in him. I must do the works of him who sent me.' Accordingly, in the work that the Son does there is the work of the Father, and the work of the Son is the work of God. And the words that follow are still on the subject of these works. Meanwhile, the reply in this instance has had no other aim than to refer every work to the two of them, but the nature of the operation would not be different in either of them, since from the fact that the Father works even until now the Son also works, in order that He who is the Lord of the Sabbath (for the Son of Man is the Lord of the Sabbath) might not be regarded as working in a godless manner on the Sabbath, and the sanction for His work would be the Father, who works in Him through the nature of His birth.

Accordingly, there is no confusion or destruction of nature so that He is not the Son, but, again, the nature is not taken away so that He is not God. They are not separated by any distinction so that they are not one, and the fact that they are one cannot bring it about that there are not two of them. In the first place, recognize the Son when it is said: 'The Son can do nothing of himself, but only what he sees the Father doing.' You have the birth of the Son, who can do nothing of Himself except that which He sees. But from the fact that He can do nothing of Himself He does away with the error that He has not been born, for birth cannot come from itself, but the fact that He sees indicates that He possesses in Himself the knowledge of a nature that is aware of what it is. And from this fact now recognize the true nature of God: 'For, whatever He does, the Son also does the same in like manner.' But after the power of the nature, then learn from it about the unity of the identical nature: 'that all men may honor the Son even as they honor the Father who sent him.' And in order that the unity of the nature may not involve you in the union of one who is alone, learn about the mystery of faith from the words: 'He who does not honor the Son, does not honor the Father who sent him.'

Everything is sealed against the ingenuity of heretical fury. He is the Son because He can do nothing of Himself; He is God because He Himself does the same things that the Father does. They are one because they are equal in honor; He does the same things, not other things. He Himself is not the Father, because He was sent. Hence, the mystery belongs to the birth alone, so that it includes the name, the nature, the power, and the confession, because the entire birth cannot but have that nature from which it was born. It does not offer the substance of an extraneous nature, because a nature alien to it does not come into existence from one. But, that which is not different from it is one in nature. Whatever is one by birth does not include solitude, because solitude pertains to a single individual, and the unity of birth refers to both of them.

Besides, let the evidence of the divine teaching be its own defense! It states: 'Those who are my sheep hear my voice, and I know them and they follow me. And I give them everlasting life; and they shall never perish, neither shall anyone snatch them out of my hand. What the Father has given me is greater than all; and no one will be able to snatch anything out of the hand of my Father. I and the Father are one.' What dullness of the sluggish mind, I ask, deadens our understanding so that these words so clearly expressed do not penetrate our consciousness? Or what vain and arrogant spirit deludes our human infirmity so that, although they have received the knowledge of God from these words, they imagine that God is not to be recognized by the words whereby He is known? For, either other Gospels must be produced which are to teach us, or, if these alone have taught us, why do we not believe them as we are taught? And if our knowledge has been received from them alone, why does not our faith come from these words whence our knowledge is derived?

But, if the faith is found to be contrary to the knowledge, that faith no longer proceeds from knowledge, but from sin, since it arrogates a godless faith to itself in opposition to the orthodox teaching about the knowledge that is confessed. Hence, the only-begotten God, conscious of His nature in Himself, nevertheless reveals the ineffable mystery of His birth in words as clear as possible for the confession of our faith, so that we may know that He was born, and may believe that the nature of God is in Him, and that He is one with the Father, and, while he acknowledges Himself as one with the Father, He is not one in such a way that we may regard Him as being only alone, and as the Father Himself, and that He ceases to be that which the Son is. In the first place, He bears witness to the power of His nature when He says of His sheep: 'Neither shall anyone snatch them out of my hand.' This is the voice of a self-reliant power, to confess the independence of an invincible strength because no one may snatch the sheep out of His hands. Although in the nature of God, still, in order that we might realize that this is the birth of the nature from God, He added: 'What the Father has given me is greater than all.' He does not conceal His birth from the Father, for what He has received from the Father 'is greater than all.'

And He who has received is in that which He has received from His birth, not later on, and still He is from the other while He has received. But He who is from the other has received and in order that no one may believe that He is something else and that He does not exist in the nature of Him from whom He has received, He said: 'No one will be able to snatch anything out of the hand of my Father.' No one snatches from His hand, because that which He has received from the Father is greater than all. What is the meaning of so different a statement that again no one can snatch anything from the hand of His Father? It is the hand of the Son which has received from the Father; it is the hand of the Father which has given to the Son, and how is that which is not taken from the hand of the Son not taken from the hand of the Father? If you ask how, then learn: 'I and the Father are one.'

The hand of the Son is the hand of the Father. The nature does not lose its nobility by its birth, so that it would not be the same, and, again, since it is the same, there is no obstacle to the understanding of a birth, because a birth does not admit anything alien to itself. But, that you may be able to recognize the power of the same nature by means of a corporeal illustration, He mentions that the hand of the Son is the hand of the Father, because the nature and the power of the Father would be in the Son. Finally, that you may become acquainted with the truth of an identical nature by the mystery of the birth, it was said: 'I and the Father are one,' so that because they are one you should believe that they are not different or solitary, and that the same nature exists in both of them through the true significance of birth and generation.

The determination of the insane spirits remains, in so far as we can perceive, even though it has not attained its goal, and the desire of malevolence does not desert the evil mind when the occasion for the performance of an evil work is not present. Although the raging heretics cannot now lead Him to the cross after the example of the Jews, since the Lord is already seated in heaven, they are equally guilty of unbelief in denying that He is what He is. And since they cannot deny what has been said, still, since they are not submissive to His words, they reveal their hatred of God, cast the stones of words, and, if they could, would again drag Him from His throne in heaven to the cross.

Thus, it is written concerning the Jews, who were indeed enraged by the novelty of these words: 'The Jews therefore took up stones to stone him. He answered them, "Many good works have I shown you from the Father. For which of these works do you stone me?" The Jews answered him, "Not for a good work do we stone thee, but for blasphemy, and because thou, being a man, makest thyself God." But you, O heretic, take note of what you are doing and acknowledging, and realize that you are the companion of those whose unbelieving example you are copying. For, when the words were spoken: 'I and the Father are one,' the Jews took up stones, and their godless sorrow, which could not endure the mystery of the salutary faith, burst forth with such violence that they were ready to put Him to death. Are you who cannot stone Him doing anything less by your denial? Your will does not differ, but the heavenly throne renders your will ineffective. And how much greater is your godlessness than that of the Jew! He raises his stones against the body, you against the soul; he against One whom he considers as a man, you against God; he against One living on earth, you against One seated on the throne of power; he against One whom he does not acknowledge, you against One whom you know; he against One who will die, you against the Judge of the ages. He says: 'because thou art a man,' you say: 'because thou art a creature'; both of you declare in unison: 'thou makest thyself God.' This is the customary taunt that comes from your godless mouth. For, you deny that He is God by His birth from God; you deny that He is the Son by a real birth. You deny that these words, 'I and the Father are one,' are an avowal of the one and similar nature in both of them. You set up in His place a God of a new, strange, and alien substance, so that He is either a God of another nature or no God at all, because He does not subsist by His birth from God.

Because you are enraged at the mystery of the words, 'I and the Father are one,' so that, as the Jew declares: 'Because thou, being a man, makest thyself God,' you assert with equal impiety: 'Because thou, being a creature, makest thyself God' (for you declare: 'Thou art not the Son by thy birth, thou art not God by thy true nature, thou art a creature more excellent than the others, but thou hast not been born into God, because I do not admit the birth of a nature from an incorporeal God, not only art thou and the Father not one, but neither art thou the Son, nor art thou like Him, nor art thou God').

The Lord indeed replied to the Jews, but this entire response is better suited to your impiety: 'Is it not written in the Law, "I said you are gods"? If he called them gods to whom the Word of God was addressed (and the Scripture cannot be broken), do you say of him whom the Father has made holy and sent into this world, "Thou blasphemest," because I said, "I am the Son of God'? If I do not perform the works of the Father, do not believe me. But if I do perform them, and if you are not willing to believe me, believe the works, that you may know and believe that the Father is in me and I in Him.' The charge of blasphemy that was brought against Him caused Him to make this reply. For, it was regarded as a crime that, since He was a man, He made himself God. He was accused of making Himself God, therefore, because He had said: 'I and the Father are one.' Accordingly, since He will prove that He employed these words by reason of the nature of His birth, He first refutes the absurdity of this ridiculous reproach of which He was alleged to be guilty, that He, being a man, made Himself God. Since the Law decided upon the designation of this name for holy persons, and the indestructible Word of God ratified this statement about the name that was bestowed, how will this one whom the Father had sanctified, and whom He had sent into the world, be a blasphemer for asserting that He was the Son, since the Word of God, which cannot be broken, had established through the Law that they should be given the name of God?

Hence, it can no longer be regarded as a reproach that He, being a man, makes Himself God, since the Law declares that those who are men are gods. And if the use of this name by others is not blasphemous, then it seems that that man whom the Father has sanctified (for the entire discourse centers about the man because the Son of God is also the Son of Man) is not guilty of any rashness in making use of it when He said that He was the Son of God, since He excels the others, who may call themselves God in a reverential manner, by the fact that He was sanctified into the Son, for blessed Paul imparts the knowledge of this sanctification when he says: 'Which he promised before-hand through his prophets in the holy Scriptures, concerning the Son who was born according to the flesh of the offspring of David; who was ordained Son of God by an act of power in keeping with the holiness of his spirit.' The charge of blasphemy, that He, being a man, makes Himself God, comes to an end, since the Word of God has bestowed this name upon many, and He who was sanctified and sent by the Father confessed that He was nothing else than the Son of God.

There is no longer any reason to doubt, I believe, that the words, 'I and the Father are one,' were spoken in reference to the birth. For, since the Jews had based their accusation against Him on these words, that He Himself, who was a man, made Himself God, His reply corroborates the revelation of Himself as the Son of God from the fact that 'I and the Father are one,' first by the name, then by the nature, and finally by the birth. For, 'I and the Father' are the names of things, but 'one' is the acknowledgment of a nature, because the two of them do not differ in that in which they are, but 'are' does not permit a union. And where there is no union, because they 'are one,' it is the birth that has caused them to be one. All this proceeds from the fact that He who was sanctified by the Father confesses that He is the Son of God, and this assertion of the Son of God is ratified by the words, 'I and the Father are one,' because birth cannot bring any other nature with it except that from which it subsists.

But the discourse of the only-begotten God has completed the mystery of our entire faith. After He had made His reply to the accusation why He, who was a man, made Himself God, in order that the words, 'I and the Father are one,' might provide us with a clear and complete knowledge, He added the following words: 'You say, "Thou blasphemest" because I said, "I am the Son of God"'? If I do not perform the works of the Father, do not believe me. But, if I do perform them, and if you are not willing to believe me, believe the works, that you may know and believe that the Father is in me and I in Him.' Unrestrained audacity now follows when people despair of salvation because of their evil conscience, and every profession of godlessness is beyond the reach of shame. For, when the true religion is lost, no one blushes any longer at his folly; it is not ignorance but madness to oppose these words.

The Lord had said: 'I and the Father are one.' This is the mystery of the birth that the Father and Son possess a unity of nature. And because the claim of nature would be cited as an accusation, the reason for the lawfulness of the claim is offered as proof. For He said: 'If I do not perform the works of the Father do not believe me.' If He does not perform the works of the Father, we should not believe Him when He asserts that He is the Son of God. Hence, His birth does not bring Him a new and alien nature, because we must believe that He is the Son from the fact that He carries out the works of his Father. How can an adoption or the bestowal of the name occur here so that He would not be the Son of God by nature, since we are to believe in Him as the Son of God by the works of the paternal nature?

A creature is not made equal or similar to God; no power of an alien nature is compared to Him; we believe without any blasphemy that only the birth of the Son is similar to or equal to Him. For, whatever is outside of Him will be made equal to Him by a mockery of the power honored in Him. If anything can be found which is not from Him and is similar to Him and possesses the same power, He has lost the privilege of God by the partnership of one who is His co-equal, and there will no longer be one God since there is another God who is His equal. But the equality proceeding from His own true nature does not lead to any insult, because that which is similar to Him is His, and that which is compared to Him by reason of its likeness is from Him, and that which can complete what is His is not outside of Him, and it is an exaltation of the divinity to have begotten the power and not to have changed the nature.

The Son carries out the works of the Father and therefore He asks us to believe in Him as the Son of God. This is no arrogant presumption, which asks that He be tested only by those deeds that He performs. He testifies, however, that He does not perform His own works, but those of His Father, in order that the birth of His nature may not be taken away by the splendor of His deeds. And because the Son of God was not understood in the mystery of the assumed body and in the man born from Mary, the faith in His name was taught by His deeds, since He said: 'But if I do not perform them, and if you are not willing to believe me, believe the works.' First of all, He does not wish that we believe in Him as the Son of God except through the works of the Father which He does. And if He performs the works, and is regarded as unworthy of what He professes because of the abasement of His body, He asks us to believe His actions. For, why should the mystery of Him who is born as man be an obstacle to the understanding of the divine birth, since the divine birth fulfills its entire work during the ministry of the body which He assumed? If, therefore, you do not believe that the man is the Son of God because of the works, then believe that the works are indicative of the Son of God, because it cannot be denied that they are characteristic of God. For, by His birth the Son of God possesses everything in Himself that is God, and, as a consequence, the work of the Son is the work of the Father, because the birth is not outside of the nature from which it subsists, and includes that nature within itself from which it subsists.

Since He therefore performs the works of His Father and asks that, if we do not believe Him, at least we should believe His works, He must show us what we are to believe from the works, and He does so surely in the words that follow: 'But if I do perform them, and if you are not willing to believe me, believe the works, that you may know and believe that the Father is in me and I in Him.' To this statement belong the words: 'I am the Son of God'; to it belong these words: 'I and the Father are one.' This is the nature of the birth, this is the mystery of the salutary faith, not to make a division because they are one, nor to take away the nature from the birth, and to confess the truth of the living God from the living God. God, who is the life, does not subsist by tangible and inanimate things, nor is He who is the power limited by weak things, nor is He who is the light composed of what is dark, nor is He who is a spirit formed out of disparate things.

Everything that is in Him is one, so that what is spirit is also light, power, and life, and what is life is light, power and spirit. He who says: 'I am and I change not,' cannot be changed by parts, nor become different in nature. All these things, which have been pointed out above, are not found within Him as portions, but all are one and perfect within Him, for everything is the living God. Accordingly, there is the living God. and the eternal power of the living nature, and that which is born from Him with the mystery of His own knowledge could not be born as anything else than from a living being. Since He says: 'As the living Father has sent me, and as I live because of the Father,' He taught that life was in Him by the living Father. Hence, when He states: 'For as the Father has life in himself, even so he has given to the Son also to have life in himself,' He gives evidence that everything living within Him is from the living. But that which was born alive from the living has the advantage of birth without the novelty of nature. That is not new which is generated from the living one into the living one, because life was not sought for among non-existing things to bring about the birth, and the life which receives its birth from life by reason of the unity of nature and the mystery of the perfect and unutterable birth must live in the living and have the living life in itself.

We recall the warning that we issued at the beginning of our treatise, that human analogies do not afford an adequate description of their divine counterparts; yet it is through material images that our mind acquires some knowledge of them. I turn for guidance to those who have knowledge of human birth, whether the origin of those who are born does not remain in their parents. For although these inanimate and ignoble elements, which are the primary causes of birth, are passed on to another man, they remain mutually in themselves by the power of nature, while he who begets follows him who is begotten through the origin of the same nature that has been given, and he who is born remains in him who begot him through the birth that has been received, for the power, although transmitted, has not been lost. Of course, we have merely stressed these facts for the sake of understanding a human birth; we do not offer them as an explanation of the perfect example of a birth in the only-begotten God, because the weakness of human nature takes its origin from unlike things, and its life is maintained by lifeless matter.

And that which is begotten does not live in it at once, nor does the whole live from the life because there are many parts in it, which, when they have grown, are cut off without their nature being conscious of it. But in God everything that is lives. God is the life, and nothing can come from life except what is alive. And His birth does not come about through an emanation, but through power. Thus, while everything that is lives, and while everything that is born from Him is power, He possesses the birth and does not experience any change, and He bestows an increase but does not lose His nature, while He follows the birth, which He has given by the similarity of an indistinguishable nature, and the birth, which is the living one from the living one, does not abandon its nature when it is born.

But fire, which is fire in itself and which remains in fire, offers us a partial understanding of this faith. For, while in it there is the brightness of light, the natural warmth, the power of burning, and the fluctuating movement of the flame, it is totally a fire, and this totality is one nature. It has, of course, this weakness, that matter provides it with its sustenance and life, and it dies out with that through which it has received life. But by means of a comparison we have a partial knowledge of that which admits of no comparison in God, so that which is found to some extent in the elements of earth is not incredible when applied to God. I now raise the question whether there is any division and separation when there is a fire from a fire? Or is the nature cut off so that it does not endure, or is it that the nature does not follow so that it is not present within it, since, when a light is enkindled from a light by a sort of increase, as if it were a birth, there is no separation from the nature and yet a light is from a light? Or does it not remain in that which has come into existence from it, without any separation? Or is it not present within that from which it has not been cut off, but has proceeded from it with the unity of the natural substance? And I ask whether they are not one since a light from a light cannot be separated either by a division or by nature?

These things, as I have stated, are only brought in for the sake of a comparison, in order to impart to us a knowledge of the faith, and not as things suitable to the dignity of God, in order that we may the more easily derive our understanding of invisible things from those that are material, not, indeed, that any comparison does adequate justice to the nature of God, since it is fitting and just to believe God when He testifies regarding Himself. But, because the rage of the heretics disturbed the faith of the unlearned so that they should not believe these things about God, which could not be grasped without difficulty except through a material illustration, therefore, in harmony with the saying of the Lord which we have already mentioned in a previous place: 'That which is born of the flesh is flesh; and that which is born of the Spirit is spirit,' because God is a spirit, we have judged it useful to insert these examples as a partial illustration in order that no one may believe that He is guilty of any deception in His assertions about Himself, since the natural examples of created objects would provide us with some insight into this divine confession.

Hence, when the living Son of God from the living one and the God from God revealed the unity of the inseparable and identical nature, as well as the mystery of the birth, He said: 'I and the Father are one.' And because a false accusation arose on account of this statement, as if it were presumptuous, in order to manifest even more emphatically the consciousness of His nature when He uttered these words, He said: 'You say that I have blasphemed because I said, "I am the Son of God," while He thereby affirmed that the unity of nature proceeded from His birth. But, in order that an unmistakable declaration might strengthen the faith in the birth, and the confession of the birth might not cause any conflict with the nature, He concluded this whole response in the following manner: 'Believe the works that the Father is in me, and I in the Father.' Is there anything here in the mystery of the birth that is not natural and proper? They are mutually contained in each other, while there is no birth except from the Father, while He does not subsist as a second God, either outside of Him or unlike Him in nature, while the God who exists from God is that which God is from nowhere else.

Bring two gods into the faith, if occasion offers, or at least invent a solitary God by offering a false claim! Separate the Son from the Father, if you can, excepting only the truth of the birth which you confess! The Son is in the Father and the Father in the Son, not by a mutual transfusion and flowing, but by the perfect birth of a living nature. Thus, in God the Father and God the Son you will not count either two gods because both are one, nor will you proclaim a unique God because the two are not one [person]. The apostolic faith, therefore, does not have two gods, because it does not have two fathers and two sons. When it acknowledges the Father it has acknowledged the Son. When it believes in the Son it has also believed in the Father, because the name of the Father likewise contains the name of the Son in itself. There is no father except through a son; the designation of a son reveals the father to us because there is no son except from a father. There is not one person, therefore, in the confession of the one God, while the Son also completes the Father and the birth of the Son is from the Father. The nature, however, is not changed by the birth so that it would not be the same according to the likeness of the nature. It is the same in such a manner that by reason of the birth and generation we must confess the two as one [nature] and not as one [person].

Let him, therefore, proclaim the two gods who can proclaim the one God without proclaiming the unity, or let him teach that there is a unique God who can deny that the one is in the one by the power of nature and the mystery of the generation and birth! Let him also ascribe a different nature to the two who does not know that in our teaching the Father and the Son are one! Let the heretics suppress the statement of the Son about Himself in the Gospel: 'I and the Father are one,' so that they may teach either that there are two gods or a unique God! For, there are no designations of natures in the proper meaning of one nature, nor does the truth of God from God result in two gods, nor does the birth of God admit of a unique God, nor are they not one who are interchangeable. But they are interchangeable since the one is from the one, because the one has not given anything else to the one by generation except that which is His own, nor has the one obtained by His birth from the one anything else except that which belongs to the one. Consequently, if the apostolic faith will proclaim the Father it will proclaim the Son, or if it will confess the Son it will confess the one God, because the same and identical nature of God is in both, and because the one denotes both while the Father is God and the Son is God, and the nature of both has the one name. The God from God or the God in God does not result in two gods, since the one from the one remains in the nature and the name of the one, nor does it go astray into a solitary God, since the meaning of one and one is not one who is alone.

The Lord has not left us an uncertain or dubious doctrine about so great a mystery, nor has He abandoned us in a labyrinth of hazy ideas. Let us hear Him as He reveals the complete knowledge of his faith to His Apostles, for He says: 'I am the way, and the truth, and the life. No one comes to the Father but through me. If you know me, you would also know my Father. And henceforth you do know him, and you have seen him.' Philip said to him, 'Lord, show us the Father and it is enough for us.' Jesus said to him, 'Am I so long a time with you and you do not know me? Philip, he who has seen me has seen also the Father. How canst thou say, "Show us the Father?" Do you not believe me that I am in the Father and the Father in me? The words that I speak to you I speak not on my own authority. But the Father dwelling in me, it is he who does his works. Believe me that I am in the Father and the Father in me; otherwise believe because of the works themselves.'

He who is the way does not guide us to the wrong roads or to those that are impassable, nor does He who is the truth deceive us by falsehoods, nor does He who is the life leave us in the error of death. Since He Himself has determined upon the gracious names of His dispensation for the sake of our salvation, so that He might be as the way that would lead us to the truth and as the truth that would lead us to life, we must grasp what that mystery is which He has revealed to us for obtaining life. 'No one comes to the Father but through me.' The road to the Father is through the Son. And we must ascertain whether this is to be found in the doctrines of which He warns us or in the faith of His nature, because it might appear as if we are to go to the Father through the doctrine of the Son rather than reach Him by acknowledging the Godhead of the Father in Him. Let us seek for the sense in which this is to be understood in the words that follow. For, we must enter the faith not by our own decisions, but by the meaning of what has been said.

These words follow: 'If you know me, you would also know my Father.' The man Jesus Christ is seen. And if they know Him, how will they know His Father, since the Apostles recognize the outer form of His nature, that is, the nature of man in Him, and since God is not subject to a material body, He cannot be recognized in the weakness of a human body? But, when the Lord confirmed the nature of the Father's divinity in Him in the mystery of the body which He had assumed, He followed this order: 'If you know me, you would also know my Father. And henceforth you do know him, and have seen him.' He draws a distinction between the time of seeing him and the time of knowing Him. In regard to Him whom, as He said, they should know, He also declared that the same one had already been seen, in order that now, from the time of this revelation, they might receive the knowledge of the nature which they had seen in Him for a long time.

The novelty of the expression, however, disturbs the Apostle Philip. A man is seen and confesses that He is the Son of God. He asserts that when He is known the Father must be known. He says that the Father has been seen, and therefore must be known since He has been seen. The weakness of the human spirit does not grasp this and a statement about natures so different does not gain acceptance, so that He who was then seen must now be known since the sight is knowledge, so that if the Son is known the Father is also known, since the mere bodily sight and contact had brought the knowledge of the Son according to His human nature, but the knowledge of the Father that comes from Him was not granted by the nature itself of the visible man that differed from His [the Father's], and the Son often testified that no one had seen the Father.

Hence, Philip, with the informality and confidence of an Apostle, blurted out and asked the Lord: 'Lord, show us the Father and it is enough for us.' His faith does not waver now, but here the mistake is the result of ignorance. The Lord declared that the Father had already been seen and therefore must be known, but the Apostle had not realized that He had been seen. Finally, he did not deny that He had been seen, but asked that He might be revealed to him, nor did he desire the manifestation, as it were, of a bodily appearance but he asked for such a manifestation that would enable him to comprehend Him who had been seen. He had indeed seen the Son under the appearance of man, but he does not understand how he had thereby seen the Father. For, when uttering the words, 'Lord, show us the Father,' he had added 'and it is enough for us,' in order that that revelation might make known how He was to be comprehended rather than how He was to be seen. He did not refuse to believe His words, but asked for a manifestation of Him who was to be known that would be sufficient to place reliance upon His words, because there would be a certain guarantee of the faith from the Lord's assertion. From this arose the request to make the Father known, because He said that He had been seen, and as a consequence must be known because He had been seen. Nor was he guilty of insolence in asking for a revelation of Him who had been seen.

The Lord, therefore, made this reply to Philip: 'Am I so long a time with you, and you do not know me?' He rebukes the Apostle's lack of knowledge in not comprehending Him, because He had previously stated that when He was known the Father would also be known. But, what is the meaning of His complaint that He has not been known for a long time? That is to say, because, if He were known, the divinity of the Father's nature within Him must be understood. For, since those things which He did were proper to God—to walk upon the waters, to command the winds, to perform actions in the changing of water into wine and in the multiplication of the loaves that were incomprehensible and completely credible, to put the demons to flight, to drive out disease, to repair bodily injuries, to correct the defects of birth, to forgive sins, to restore the dead to life, and to do these things in the flesh, and meanwhile to declare that He was the Son of God—the whole basis of His accusation and complaint arose from this fact that in the deeds which were performed during the mystery of the human birth the divine nature was not perceived in the manhood which He had assumed.

Consequently, while He blames him for not knowing Him, since He had been performing these deeds for so long a time, in order to manifest the Father to those who asked Him, He said: 'He who has seen me has seen also the Father.' He is not referring here to His bodily appearance, to that which their earthly eyes gazed upon, but to those of which He had said: 'Do you not say, "There are yet four months, and then comes the harvest"? Well, I say to you, lift up your eyes and behold that the fields are already white for the harvest.' The time does not allow, nor does the allusion to the fields white for the harvest justify us in believing that anything earthly and material was intended here, but He commanded them to lift up the eyes of their soul in order to gaze upon the blessedness of the perfect fruits, so that, as He now says: 'He who has seen me has seen also the Father.'

For this, which is carnal from the birth of the Virgin, does not help us to contemplate the divinity and the image of God within Him, nor is the form of man which He assumed an example of the nature of the immaterial God which we are to behold. God is recognized in Him, if, indeed, He will be recognized by anyone at all, by the power of His nature, and when God the Son is perceived He allows us to perceive the Father, while He is the image in such a manner that He does not differ in nature, but manifests His author. Other images of different colors or materials of different kinds and classes reproduce the appearance of those whose images are placed before them. But, in order that you may have true images, can those that are lifeless be placed on equality with those that are living, or can those that are painted, carved, or molten equal those that are natural? The Son is not the image of the Father after the manner of these things, because He is the living image of the living One, and He who has been born from Him does not have a different nature, and He who does not differ in anything preserves the power of His nature from whom He does not differ. That He is the image, therefore, proceeds from the fact that the birth of the only-begotten God points to God the Father, but it points to Him in such a manner that He Himself is the form and the image of the invisible God; hence, He does not lose the united similarity of the nature, because He is not lacking in the power of the nature.

Therefore, we have those words: 'Am I so long a time with you, and you do not know me? Philip, he who has seen me has seen also the Father. How canst thou say, "Show us the Father"? Do you not believe me that I am in the Father and the Father in me?' Human language has been left with no other choice than to express the things of God in the words of God. Everything else is restricted, confined, cumbersome, and obscure. If anyone should wish to make this known in any other words than those in which God has spoken, either he himself does not understand it or he does not offer an intelligible explanation of it to his readers.

When He was asked to show the Father, the Lord said: 'He who has seen me has seen also the Father.' It is characteristic of Antichrist to change this, of the Jew to deny this, of the Gentile to be ignorant of this. But perhaps the perception of our intelligence is at fault. It may be that the defect lies with our faith, if the words of God are involved in obscurity. His statement does not designate a solitary God, yet His revelation teaches that there is no difference in nature. The Father, who is seen in Him, cannot be unique or unlike Him, because that one who is seen through this one cannot but be one nature in the confession of the mystery, nor can they be one person. And I ask what are we to believe was the meaning of the Lord's words when He said: 'He who has seen me has seen also the Father?'

You do not have a union where the addition of the Father's name is indicated by the conjunction. For when you say 'also the Father' you exclude the idea of one who is isolated and unique. And what else is there left except that the Father is seen through the Son by means of the united likeness of their nature? And in order that our faith in this matter might not remain uncertain, the Lord continued: 'How canst thou say, "Show us the Father"?' What compelling reason was still left for not knowing the Father, or for revealing Him to those who were ignorant of Him, since the Father was seen in the Son?

But, He was seen to such an extent in the property of His nature, while, as a consequence of the identity and the nature of the Godhead, the one who was born and the one who begot are one, that this statement of the Lord follows: 'Do you not believe that I am in the Father and the Father in me?' We cannot teach that the Father and the Son are inseparable because of their natural likeness in any other words except those of the Son. For, by changing His name and appearance, this Son, who is the way, the truth, and the life, is not playing a theatrical role here, so that in the manhood which He assumed He calls Himself the Son of God, but He calls Himself God the Father in His nature, and He who is one and alone now falsely represents Himself as someone else by a change of disguise.

Accordingly, He Himself is not isolated: now He is a Son to Himself, now he acknowledges Himself as His own Father, and He brings in the names of the nature when the nature is not present. Here the candor of the words is quite different, for the Father is also the Father, and the Son is also the Son. These names and natures do not contain within them anything that is new, or different, or strange. The truth of the nature retains its proper meaning, so that what is from God is God and the birth does not bring about any lessening or distinction, while the Son does not subsist in a nature outside of or unlike that of God the Father, nor does the Father acquire anything alien to Himself by the birth of the Son; rather, He has granted everything that is His without any loss to the giver.

Thus, He is not in want of the nature of God, while He is God from nowhere else than from God, nor does He differ from God while He Himself is nothing else than God, because the birth of God takes place in the Son, nor has the nature of God deprived itself of that which God is by the birth of God. The Father, therefore, is in the Son, the Son is in the Father, and God is in God, not by a twofold union of natures that are in harmony, nor through the superimposed nature of a larger substance, because through bodily necessity things that are within cannot be outside of those things by which they are enclosed, but through the birth of a living nature from a living nature, while the nature does not differ, while birth does not deprive the nature of God of its nobility, while God is born as nothing else than God from God, while there is nothing new, nothing strange, nothing separable in these things, while it is impious to believe that there are two gods in the Father and the Son, while it is sacrilegious to preach that the Father and the Son are one unique God, and while it is blasphemy to deny that they are one in the likeness of nature as God from God.

And in order that the evangelical faith might not look upon this mystery as uncertain and ambiguous, the Lord followed this plan in His instruction: 'Do you not believe me that I am in the Father and the Father in me? The words that I speak to you I speak not on my own authority. But the Father dwelling in me, it is he who does his works.' By what other words, I ask, could and can the true significance of the nature in the Father and the Son be revealed than by these very words, while the reference to the birth shines forth prominently in all of them? Since He declares: 'The words that I speak to you I speak not on my own authority,' He does not exclude the person nor does He deny that He was the Son, nor does He conceal the nature of the Father's power within Him. For while He Himself is speaking (and this is indicated by the pronoun 'I') He speaks while He abides in the substance, but, while He does not speak of Himself, He bears testimony to the birth of God in Him from God the Father.

He Himself is inseparable from Him and indistinguishable from Him by the unity of nature, because, although He speaks by His authority, it is He Himself who speaks. He, who does not speak by His own authority, yet speaks, cannot but be while He is speaking, and while He does not speak of Himself He reveals that it is not He alone who speaks. For, He added:

'But the Father dwelling in me, it is he who does His works.' For the Father to remain in the Son does not denote a being that is alone and unique, but for the Father to work through the Son is not characteristic of a nature that is different from or outside of Him—just as it is a sign of one who is not alone not to speak by His own authority on the subjects whereof He speaks, and again it is not an indication of one who is alien to or separable from Him to speak through Him who is speaking, but this is the mystery of those who are one. Both, who are in each other by the property of their nature, are not something else. Their unity consists in this, that the speaker does not speak of Himself, nor does He not speak, who does not speak of Himself. And because He had taught that the Father speaks and works in Him, He established the faith of this perfect unity when He declared: 'But the Father dwelling in me, it is he who does His work. Believe me, that I am in the Father and the Father in me. Otherwise believe because of the works themselves.' The Father works in the Son, but the Son also performs the work of the Father.

Consequently, in order that no one might believe that the Father works and speaks in the Son through the energy of His own power and not through the property of the nature, which is in accordance with the birth, He said: 'Believe me, that I am in the Father and the Father in me.' What, I ask, does the phrase 'believe me' mean? It refers, of course, to what had been said: 'Show us the Father.' The faith is strengthened by the command to believe, and it was that faith that had asked that the Father be shown to it. It was not sufficient to declare: 'He who has seen me has seen also the Father,' if He did not increase our knowledge to such an extent that, since we know the Father in the Son, we would still remember that the Son was in the Father, in order that we might not look upon it as a transfusion of one into another rather than as the unity of the same nature in both of them through the generation and birth.

Hence, the Lord wishes us to believe Him in order that our consciousness of the faith might not be imperiled, perhaps, through the dispensation of the man who was assumed. Indeed, if the flesh, the body, and the passion should give rise to any doubts, then at least we should believe from His works that God is in God and God is from God, that they are one, while by the power of the nature each one is in Himself, and neither one is without the other, while the Father loses nothing of Himself in the Son, and the Son takes everything from the Father that a son is. Material natures are not so constituted that they mutually inhere in one another, that they possess the perfect unity of a subsistent nature, and that the abiding birth of the Only-begotten is inseparable from the true nature of the Godhead in the Father. That is proper only to the only-begotten God, and that faith is rooted in the mystery of the true birth, and it is to the spiritual power that this work belongs, so that there is no distinction between to be and to inhere, but to inhere not as the one thing in another as a body in a body, but to be and to subsist in such a manner that He inheres in Him who subsists but inheres in such a manner that He Himself subsists. Hence, we have those sayings: 'I and the Father are one,' and 'He who has seen me has seen also the Father' and 'I in the Father and the Father in me,' because the birth did not bring about any distinction or loss of nobility, because the nature of the birth completes the mystery of the Godhead in the Father and the Son, while the Son of God is nothing else than that which God is. For this reason, the generation of the Only-begotten does not result in a separation into two gods, because, when the Son of God was born into God, He revealed in Himself the nature of the God who begot Him.

St. Cyril of Alexandria
d. 444

Cyril succeeded his uncle Theophilus in 412 as bishop of Alexandria. Virtually nothing is known about his earlier life, and very little about his first 15 or so years as a bishop. But as of 428, when Nestorius became bishop of Constantinople, an acrimonius controversy broke out. Nestorius began to teach that Mary should not be called Mother of God (Theotokos), and that it was wrong to speak of God being wrapped in swaddling clothes or dying on a cross. Cyril replied in a letter in 429. Both of them then appealed to Pope Celestine and in 430 at a synod held in Rome Nestorius was condemned as heretical and Cyril was deputed to convey the decision and to excommunicate him in case of contumacy. Before doing so Cyril added a profession of faith approved in Alexandria in 430 and 12 Anathemas describing the errors Nestorius was to reject.

As a diplomat, Cyril was a good theologian. The long-standing rivalry between Alexandria and Antioch/Constantinople was at its aggravated worst. All involved appealed to Caesar and a general Council was called to assemble in Ephesus in June, 431. Nestorius arrived with 16 supporting bishops, and Cyril appeared with 50 Eygptian bishops. They waited two weeks, but the delegations from Rome and Antioch still had not arrived, so Cyril connived to start without them. Nestorius, who refused to appear, was condemned, deposed, and excommunicated.

When the Antioch delegation arrived, they formed their own council and condemned Cyril. When the Romans came, their message was that the condemnation of Nestorius at the Roman synod of the previous year was simply to be carried out. The Third Ecumenical Council thus hardly presented a picture of brotherhood or harmony for the Christian world.

The following selection offers the two "ecumenical letters" of Cyril involved in the above-described happenings. The former one, numbered 4 in his general collection, is the one he sent directly to Nestorius in 429, and which on June 22, 431 the first meeting of the Council of Ephesus solemnly approved by a unanimous vote as being in full agreement with the Nicene Creed and a true expression of Catholic doctrine. It was to be reaffirmed by the Council of Chalcedon in 451 and again by II Constantinople in 553 for the same reasons. Seldom has the letter of a single individual had such a celebrated history, unless we think of those of St. Paul.

The latter letter is less illustrious. Numbered 17 in his general collection, it is the one which Cyril sent in the name of the Alexandrian synod at the end of 430. The 12 anathemas attached to it and the peculiar terminology employed created great difficulties. "Although it was added to the Acta *of the Council of Ephesus, it did not receive formal ratification by vote. Nevertheless, the opinion prevailed later on that this letter and the anathemas had been adopted by the Councils of Ephesus and Chalcedon" (Quasten).*

Cyril is thus an ambiguous figure. He came to be looked upon as the ultimate authority in Christology, and indeed his contributions were significant, especially in clearing away some of the confusion caused by Nestorius. But his own terminology left further precision to be desired, so the debate would not be resolved until seven years after Cyril's death, 451, when the Fourth Ecumenical Council took up the issue in Chalcedon.

LETTERS TO NESTORIUS

C ertain persons, as I hear, are making free with my reputation before your Holiness, and that repeatedly,
watching the occasion especially when councils are
being held, thinking, it may be, to bring welcome news to your
ears. And they utter ill-advised speeches, though they have
suffered no wrong at my hands, except that they have been
reprehended, and that deservedly—one for having defrauded the
blind and the poor, another for having drawn his sword upon
his mother, and a third for having stolen money, with a maid-
servant for an accomplice, and as having always borne such a
character as no one would wish his worst enemy to bear.

But I make no great account of these matters lest I should
stretch the measure of my littleness beyond my Lord and Master,
or even beyond the Fathers. For it is impossible to escape the
perverseness of bad men, however one may order one's life.
But they, *having their mouth full of cursing and bitterness*, shall
give account to the Judge of all.

But I shall return to what specially becomes me, and
admonish you as a brother in the Lord, to use all possible cir-
cumspection in teaching the people, and in setting forth the
doctrine of the faith, bearing in mind that to offend even *one of
these little ones who believe in Christ,* subjects the person guilty
of it to intolerable punishment. And if so great numbers of persons have been thus injured, how do we need all possible care
and study that we may do away the offences, and rightly expound
the doctrine of the faith to those who are seeking the truth! And
in this we shall succeed, if, betaking ourselves to the statements
of the holy Fathers, we are careful to esteem them highly, and,
proving ourselves whether we be in the faith, as it is written,

thoroughly conform our own beliefs to their sound and unexceptionable doctrines.

The holy and great council then affirmed that the "only-begotten Son", according to nature "begotten of the Father", "true God of true God", "Light of Light", by whom the Father made all things, "came down, was incarnate, and was made man, suffered, rose again the third day, and ascended into heaven". We too must also adhere to these words and these doctrines considering what is meant when it is said that the Word which is of God "was incarnate and was made man".

For we do not affirm that the nature of the Word underwent a change and became flesh, or that it was transformed into a complete human being consisting of soul and body; but rather this, that the Word, having in an ineffable and inconceivable manner personally ($\kappa\alpha\theta$' $\dot{\upsilon}\pi\dot{o}\sigma\tau\alpha\sigma\iota\nu$) united to himself flesh animated with living soul, became man and was called Son of Man, yet not of mere will or favour, nor again by the simple assumption to himself of a human person, and that while the natures which were brought together into this true unity were diverse there was of both one Christ and Son: not as though the diverseness of the natures were done away by this union, but rather Godhead and Manhood completed for us the one Lord and Christ and Son by their unutterable and unspeakable concurrence into unity. And thus, although he subsisted and was begotten of the Father before the worlds, he is spoken of as having been born also after the flesh of a woman: not that his divine nature had its beginning of existence in the holy Virgin, or needed of necessity on its own account a second generation after its generation from the Father, for it is foolish and absurd to say that he who subsisted before all worlds, and was coeternal with the Father, stood in need of a second beginning of existence, but forasmuch as the Word having "for us and for our salvation", personally united to himself human nature, came forth of a woman, for this reason he is said to have been born after the flesh. For he was not first born an ordinary man of the holy Virgin, and then the Word descended upon him, but having been made one with the flesh from the very womb itself, he is to have submitted to a birth according to the flesh, as appropriating and making his own the birth of his own flesh.

In like manner we say that he "suffered" and "rose again". Not as though God the Word suffered in his own divine nature either stripes or the piercing of nails, or the other wounds inflicted on him, for the Godhead is impassible because it is incorporeal. But forasmuch as that which had become his own body suffered these things, therefore again he himself is said to have suffered them for us. For the Impassible was in the suffering body.

So likewise we conceive of his death. For the Word of God is by nature both incorruptible, and Life, and Life-giving, but forasmuch as his own body *by the grace of God,* as Paul says, *tasted death for every man,* therefore once more he himself is said to have suffered death for us. Not as though he experienced death as regards his own (divine) nature—to say or hold which is madness—but that, as I said, just now, his flesh tasted death.

So likewise when his flesh was raised, the resurrection again is spoken of as his resurrection, not as though he had seen corruption, God forbid, but because once more it was his own body that was raised.

Thus we confess one Christ and Lord, not as worshipping a man conjointly with the Word, that there may not through this phrase "conjointly" be insinuated the semblance of division—but as worshipping one and the same (Lord), because the body of the Lord is not alien from the Lord, with which body also he sits with the Father himself: not again as though two sons do sit with the Father, but one united to his own flesh. But if we reject this personal union either as impossible or unseemly, we fall into the error of making two sons. For in that case we must needs distinguish and speak of the man in his own person dignified with the appellation of Son, and again of the Word which is of God in his own Person possessing by nature the Sonship, both name and thing.

We must not then divide the one Lord Jesus Christ into two sons. To hold this will nowise contribute to soundness of faith, even though some make a show of acknowledging a union of person (προσώπων ἔνωσις). For Scripture does not say that the Word united to himself the person of man, but that *he became flesh.* But this expression *the Word became flesh* is nothing else than that *he became partaker of flesh and blood, like us* and made our body his own, and came forth a man of a woman, not casting aside his being God, and his having been begotten of God the Father, but even in the assumption of flesh remaining what he was.

This is the doctrine which strict orthodoxy everywhere prescribes. Thus shall we find the holy Fathers to have held. So did they make bold to call the holy Virgin *Theotocos.* Not as though the nature of the Word or his Godhead had its beginning from the holy Virgin, but forasmuch as his holy Body, endued with a rational soul, was born of her, to which Body also the Word was personally united, on this account he is said to have been born after the flesh.

Thus, writing even now out of love which I have in Christ, I entreat thee as a brother, and charge thee before Christ, and the elect angels, to hold and teach these things with us, that the peace of the Churches may be preserved, and that the bond of harmony and love between the priests of God may remain unbroken. (C. A. Heurtley, *On Faith and the Creed,* pp. 156-61, altered.)

LETTER DATED NOVEMBER 430

To Nestorius, most religious, and most dear to God, our fellow-minister, Cyril and the synod assembled at Alexandria from the province of Egypt send greeting in the Lord.

When our Saviour says in plain terms, *He that loveth father or mother more than me is not worthy of me, and he that loveth son or daughter more than me is not worthy of me,* what should be our feelings who are asked by your Religiousness to love you more than Christ, our common Saviour? Who shall be able to succour us in the day of judgement, or what apology shall we find for our so long silence under your blasphemies against him? If indeed it were only yourself whom you were injuring in holding and teaching such things, it would be of less consequence, but seeing that you have given offence to the universal Church, and have cast the leaven of a novel and strange heresy among the laity, and not the laity at Constantinople only but everywhere (for copies of your sermons have been circulated), what satisfactory account can any longer be given of our silence, or how are we not bound to remember Christ's words, *Think not that I am come to send peace on the earth; I did not come to send peace but a sword; for I have come to set a man against his father, and a daughter against her mother.* For when the faith is being tampered with, perish reverence for parents as a thing unseasonable and pregnant with mischief, and let the law of natural affection to children and brethren be set aside, and let religious men count death better than life, that, as it is written, *they may obtain a better resurrection.*

Take notice then that in conjunction with the holy synod which was assembled in great Rome, under the presidency of our most pious and religious brother and fellow-minister, Bishop Coelestine, we conjure and counsel you, in this third letter also, to abstain from these mischievous and perverse doctrines, which you both hold and teach, and to adopt in place of them the correct faith delivered to the Churches from the beginning by the holy Apostles and Evangelists, *who were both ministers and eye-witnesses of the Word.* And unless your Religiousness does this by the time prescribed in the Epistle of our aforementioned, most pious and religious brother and fellow-minister, Coelestine, bishop of the Romans, know that you have neither part nor lot with us, nor place nor rank among the priests and bishops of God. For it is impossible that we should bear to see the Churches thus thrown into confusion, and the laity scandalized, and the correct faith set aside, and the flocks scattered abroad by you who ought rather to save them, if you were, as we are, a lover of correct doctrine, treading in the pious footsteps of the holy Fathers. But with all, both laity and clergy, who have been excommunicated or deposed for faith's sake by your Religiousness, we all are in communion. For it is not just that those who hold the true faith should be wronged by your sentence, for having rightly withstood you. For this same thing you signified in your letter to our most holy fellow-bishop Coelestine, bishop of great Rome.

[It is not enough for Nestorius to acknowledge the Creed of Nicaea; he must also abjure his erroneous interpretation of that creed, and hold to the universal teaching of both East and West. The Creed of Nicaea is quoted in full].

Following in every particular the confessions of the holy Fathers, which they have drawn up under the guidance of the

251

Holy Spirit speaking in them, and keeping close to the meaning which they had in view, and journeying, so to speak, along the king's highway, we affirm that the very only-begotten Word of God, begotten of the very substance of the Father, true God of true God, Light which is from Light, by whom all things were made, both in heaven and on earth, for our salvation came down, and of his condescension emptied himself, and became incarnate and was made man, that is, having taken flesh of the Holy Virgin, and made it his own from the womb, he vouchsafed to be born as we, and proceeded forth, a human being from a woman, not having cast away what he was, but even in the assumption of flesh and blood, still continuing what he was—God in nature and truth. Neither do we say that the flesh was converted into the divine nature, nor surely that the ineffable nature of God the Word was debased and perverted into the nature of flesh, for he is unchangeable and unalterable, ever continuing altogether the same according to the Scriptures: but we say that the Son of God, while visible to the eyes, and a babe and in swaddling clothes, and still at the breast of his Virgin Mother, filled all creation as God, and was seated with his Father. For the divinity is without quantity and without magnitude and without limit.

Confessing then the personal ($\kappa\alpha\theta$' $\dot{\upsilon}\pi\delta\sigma\tau\alpha\sigma\iota\nu$) union of the Word with the flesh, we worship one Son and Lord, Jesus Christ, neither putting apart and sundering man and God, as though they were connected with one another by a unity of dignity and authority (for this is vain babbling and nothing else), nor surely calling the Word of God Christ in one sense, and in like manner him who is of the woman Christ in another sense; but knowing only one Christ, the Word which is of God the Father with his own flesh. For then (i.e. when he took flesh) he was anointed with us as man, while yet to those who are worthy to receive it himself gives the Holy Spirit, and *not by measure*, as says the blessed Evangelist John.

But neither again do we say that the Word which is of God dwelt in him who was born of the Holy Virgin as in an ordinary man, lest Christ should be understood to be a man who carries God within him, for though the Word *dwelt in us*, and, as it is said, *all the fullness of the Godhead dwelt in Christ bodily,* yet we understand, that when he became flesh the indwelling was not in the same manner as when he is said to dwell in the saints, but that having been united by a union of natures and not converted into flesh, he brought to pass such an indwelling as the soul of man may be said to have with its own body.

There is then one Christ, and Son and Lord, not as though he were a man possessing a conjunction with God simply by a unity of dignity or authority, for equality of honour does not unite natures—Peter and John are equal in honour in that they are apostles and holy disciples, but the two are not one (person).

Nor certainly do we understand the mode of conjunction to be that of juxtaposition, for this does not suffice to express a union of natures.

Nor do we understand the union to be in the way of relative participation as we, *being joined to the Lord,* as it is written, *are one spirit with him,* but rather we reject the term "conjunction" altogether, as insufficient to signify the union.

Nor do we call the Word which is of God the Father the God or Master of Christ, lest we should again openly divide the one Christ and Son and Lord, into two, and incure the charge of blasphemy, by making him the God and Master of himself. For the Word of God being personally united with flesh, as we said, is God of the universe and Master of the whole world. Neither is he his own servant or his own Master; for it is silly, or rather impious to hold or say this. He did indeed speak of God as his own Father, though yet himself God by nature, and of his Father's essence. But we are not ignorant, that while he continued God he also became man subject under God, as befits the law of man's nature. But how could he become the God or Master of himself? Therefore as man, and as befits the measure of his emptying, he speaks of himself as subject under God with us. So also he became under the Law, though as God himself spake the Law, and is the Lawgiver.

We refuse also to say of Christ, "For the sake of him who assumes I worship him who is assumed; for the sake of him who is unseen I worship him who is seen." One must shudder also to say, "He that is assumed shares the name of God with him who assumed." For he who speaks again makes two Christs, one God and one man. For he confessedly denies the union, according to which there is understood one Christ Jesus—not one jointly worshipped with another, or jointly sharing the name of God with another, but one Christ Jesus, one only-begotten Son, honoured with one worship with his own flesh.

We confess also that the very Son, which was begotten of God the Father, and is the only-begotten God, though being in his own nature impassible, suffered for us in the flesh, according to the scriptures, and was in his Crucified Body impassibly appropriating and making his own the sufferings of his own flesh. And *by the grace of God he tasted death also for every man,* yielding to death his own body, though originally and by nature Life, and himself the Resurrection. For *he tasted death for every man,* as I said, and returned to life again on the third day, bringing with him the spoils of Hell, that having trampled upon death by his ineffable power, he might in his own flesh first become *the first-born from the dead,* and the *first-fruits of them that sleep,* and might prepare the way for the return of man's nature to immortality. So that, though it be said, *By man came the resurrection of the dead,* yet by *man* we understand the Word which was begotten of God, and that by him has the dominion of death been destroyed. And he will come at the appointed time, as one Son and Lord, in the glory of the Father, to judge *the world in righteousness,* as it is written.

And we must add this also. For showing forth the death in the flesh of the only-begotten Son of God, that is, of Jesus Christ, and confessing his return to life from the dead, and his assumption into heaven, we celebrate the service of bloodless sacrifice in the Churches, and so approach the mystic Benedictions, and are sanctified, being made partakers of the holy flesh and precious blood of Christ the Saviour of us all, receiving it not as ordinary flesh, God forbid, nor as the flesh of a man sanctified and associated with the Word by a unity of dignity, or as having God dwelling in him, but as Life-giving of a truth and the very own flesh of the Word himself. For being, as God, life by nature, when he became one with his own flesh, he made that flesh life-giving. So that though he says to us, *Verily, verily I say unto you, Except ye eat the flesh of the Son of Man and drink his blood,* yet we shall not account it as though it were the flesh of an ordinary man (for how could the flesh of a man be life-giving of its own nature?) but as having become of a truth

254

the own flesh of him, who for our sakes became and was called Son of Man.

Moreover we do not distribute the Words of our Saviour in the Gospels to two several subsistences or Persons. For the one and sole Christ is not twofold, although we conceive of him as consisting of two distinct elements inseparably united, even as a man is conceived of as consisting of soul and body, and yet is not twofold but one out of both. But if we hold the right faith we shall believe both the human language and the divine to have been used by one Person.

[Cyril quotes John 14.9 and 10.30 to show the divinity of Christ, John 8.40 to show the humanity. The use of "human" language on the part of one who "being God by nature, became flesh, i.e. man endowed with a rational soul" need not surprise us.]

To one Person, therefore, must be attributed all the expressions used in the Gospels, the one incarnate *hypostasis* of the Word, for the Lord Jesus Christ is one according to the Scriptures.

And if he be called also *Apostle and High-Priest of our confession,* as ministering to God the Father the confession of faith which is offered from us both to him, and through him to God the Father, and assuredly to the Holy Spirit also, again we aver that he is by nature the only-begotten Son of God, and we do not attribute the Priesthood, name and thing, to another man beside him. For he is become a Mediator between God and man, and a reconciler unto peace having offered up himself for a smell of sweet savour to God the Father. For this cause also he said, *Sacrifice and offering thou wouldest not. In whole burnt-offerings and sacrifices for sin thou hadst no pleasure, but a body thou hast prepared for me. Then said I, Lo, I come. In the volume of the book it is written of me, to do thy will, O God.* For he hath offered his own body for a sweet-smelling savour for us, and not for himself. For what offering or sacrifice did he need for himself, being as God above all sin? For though *all have sinned and do come short of the glory of God,* even as we are prone to turn aside, and man's nature is diseased with the disease of sin (it is not so with him), and failed, therefore, of his glory, how could any doubt remain that the true Lamb of God has been slain on our account, and in our behalf? To say that "he offered himself both for himself and for us" is nothing short of blasphemy. For in nothing was he an offender or a sinner. Of what offering then did he stand in need, there being no sin for which offering should be made with any show of reason?

And when he says of the Spirit, *He shall glorify Me*, if we understand the words rightly, we shall not say that the one Christ and Son received glory from the Holy Ghost, as being in need of glory from another, for the Holy Ghost is not superior to him and above him. But since for the manifestation of his Godhead, he made use of the Holy Ghost for the working of miracles, he says that *he was glorified by him*, just as any one of us might say, of his strength, for instance, or his skill in any matter, "they shall glorify me". For though the Holy Spirit has a personal existence (ὑπόστασις) of his own, and is conceived of by himself, in that he is the Spirit and not the Son, yet he is not therefore alien from the Son. For he is called *the Spirit of Truth*, and Christ is *the Truth*, and he is poured forth from him just as he is also from God the Father.

For this cause the Holy Ghost glorified him when he wrought miracles by the hands of the holy Apostles also, after our Lord Jesus Christ had gone up to heaven. For himself working miracles by his own Spirit, he was believed to be God by nature. For which reason also he said, *He shall take of mine and shall show it unto you*. On the other hand, we do not say for a moment, that the Holy Spirit is wise and powerful by participation. For he is perfect in every respect, and wanting of no possible good. But since he is the Spirit of the Father's Power and Wisdom, that is, of the Son's, he is in very deed Wisdom and Power himself.

But since the Holy Virgin brought forth after the flesh God personally united to flesh, for this reason we say of her that she is *Theotocos*, not as though the nature of the Word had its beginning of being from the flesh, for he was *in the beginning*, and *the Word was God, and the Word was with God*, and he is the Maker of the worlds, coeternal with the Father, and the Creator of the universe, but, as we said before, because having personally united man's nature to himself, he vouchsafed also to be born in the flesh, from her womb. Not that he needed of necessity, or for his own nature, to be born in time and in the last ages of the world, but that he might bless the very first element of our being, and that, a woman having borne him united to flesh, there might be made to cease thenceforward the curse lying upon our whole race, which sends to death our bodies which are of the earth, and that, the sentence, *In sorrow shalt thou bring forth children,* being annulled by him, the words of the Prophet might be verified, *Death prevailed and swallowed up, and then again God wiped away every tear from every face.* For this cause we affirm also that he blessed marriage in accordance with the dispensation by which he became man, and went with his holy Apostles to a marriage-feast when invited at Cana of Galilee.

To these things we have been taught to assent by the holy Apostles and Evangelists, and by all the inspired Scripture, and from the true confession of the blessed Fathers. To all of them it behoves thy Religiousness also to assent and consent without dissimulation of any sort.

Now the statements which your Religiousness must anathematize are subjoined to this letter of ours.

1. If anyone does not confess Emmanuel to be very God, and does not acknowledge the Holy Virgin consequently to be *Theotocos,* for she brought forth after the flesh the Word of God became flesh, let him be anathema.

2. If anyone does not confess that the word which is of God the Father has been personally united to flesh, and is one Christ with his own flesh, the same (person) being both God and man alike, let him be anathema.

3. If anyone in the one Christ divides the personalities, i.e. the human and the divine, after the union, connecting them only by a connection of dignity or authority or rule, and not rather by a union of natures, let him be anathema.

4. If anyone distributes to two Persons or Subsistences ($\dot{v}\pi\dot{o}\sigma\tau\alpha\sigma\iota\varsigma$) the expressions used both in the Gospels and in the Epistles, or used of Christ by the Saints, or by him of himself, attributing some to a man conceived of separately, apart from the Word which is of God, and attributing others, as befitting God, exclusively to the Word which is of God the Father, let him be anathema.

5. If anyone dares to say that Christ is a man who carries God (within himself), and not rather that he is God in truth, as one Son even by nature, even as the Word became flesh, and became *partaker in like manner as ourselves of blood and flesh,* let him be anathema.

6. If anyone dares to say that the Word which is of God the Father is the God or Master of Christ, and does not rather confess the same to be both God and man alike, the Word having become flesh according to the Scriptures, let him be anathema.

7. If anyone says that Jesus as a man was actuated by God the Word, and that he was invested with the glory of the only-begotten, as being other than he, let him be anathema.

8. If anyone dares to say that the man who was assumed ought to be worshipped jointly with God the Word, and glorified jointly, and ought jointly to share the name of God, as one in another (for the word "jointly" which is always added obliges one to understand this), and does not rather honour Emmanuel with one worship, and offer to him one ascription of Glory, inasmuch as the Word has become flesh, let him be anathema.

9. If anyone says that the one Lord, Jesus Christ, was glorified by the Spirit, as though the power which he exercised was another's received through the Spirit, and not his own, and that he received from the Spirit the power of countervailing unclean spirits, and of working divine miracles upon men, and does not rather say that it was his own Spirit by whom he wrought divine miracles, let him be anathema.

10. Divine Scripture says, that Christ became *High Priest and Apostle of our confession,* and that he *offered up himself for us for a sweet-smelling savour to God the Father.* If then anyone says that it was not the very Word of God himself who became our High-Priest and Apostle, when he became flesh and man as we, but another than he, and distinct from him, a man born of a woman; or if anyone says that he offered the sacrifice for himself also, and not rather for us alone, for he who knew no sin had no need of offering, let him be anathema.

11. If anyone does not confess that the Lord's flesh is life-giving, and that it is the own flesh of the Word of God the Father, but affirms that it is the flesh of another than he, connected

with him by dignity, or as having only a divine indwelling, and not rather, as we said, that it is life-giving, because it has become the own flesh of the Word who is able to quicken all things, let him be anathema.

12. If anyone does not confess that the Word of God suffered in the flesh, and was crucified in the flesh, and tasted death in the flesh, and became *the first-born from the dead,* even as he is both Life and Life-giving, as God, let him be anathema. (C. A. Heurtley, *On Faith and the Creed,* pp. 162-76, altered.)

Pope St. Leo the Great
400-461

Leo was probably of Tuscan origin and was ordained a deacon in the pontificate of Celestine I. He was on a peace mission in Gaul in 440 when Pope Sixtus III died and the Roman populace elected him pope. It was a difficult period for Church and State. Barbarian incursions in the West and the Monophysite heresy in the East called for special leadership if any kind of unity were to be maintained. Leo was equal to the challenge and brought such prestige to the papacy during his 21 year reign that he opened a new era and was himself dubbed Leo the Great by posterity.

Leo's pastoral emphasis is reflected in the fact that his surviving works consist of some 96 sermons and over 120 letters, dealing with the chief problems of the day. "He is admittedly the greatest administrator of the ancient Church, the man who truly amalgamated ecclesiastical procedure with Roman law and put a juridical structure under the Roman primacy that has withstood the toll of 16 centuries" (F. X. Murphy).

It is noteworthy that in the fifth-century christological disputes thus far the chief developments took place in the Greek-speaking East. But in the crisis of 449 Leo intervened decisively with the most important document of its kind ever produced by the Latin Church. An old monk of Constantinople named Eutyches had started preaching the exact opposite of Nestori-

anism by claiming that in the Incarnation the humanity of Jesus was totally swallowed up by the divinity. This "Monophysitism" (single-nature theory) was condemned by a synod in Constantinople in 448, but supporters of Eutyches persuaded the Emperor to call a new council at Ephesus. It was at this point that Leo took the initiative and intervened with his famous letter to Bishop Flavian of Constantinople.

That letter (or "Tome") is still today considered the finest expression of orthodox teaching about the meaning of Christ, but circumstances required that it wait two years before it could be used to draw up the definition adopted by the Council of Chalcedon. Meantime, the "Robber Council" of Ephesus took place with all its political machinations, and only the unexpected death of Emperor Theodosius II in 450 cleared the way for the turning of the tables and the condemnation of Monophysitism.

Chalcedon made use of the basic expressions of Leo. It confessed classical Christian faith for subsequent centuries: one single Christ, Son, Lord, Only-Begotten, without confusion, without change, without division, without separation, the difference of natures being in no way suppressed by the union, but rather the properties of each being safeguarded and reunited in a single person and a single hypostasis. In little more than a century four great threats had arisen: Arianism, Apollinarianism, Nestorianism, and Monophysitism. Each had forced clarification in Christian thought about Jesus and the Father. At Chalcedon in 451 the phrases of Leo the Great were acknowledged as the most accurate among the various options, and were thereupon endorsed for the subsequent instruction of the Christian world.

THE TOME

28. Bishop Leo, to his dearly beloved brother, Flavian, Bishop of Constantinople (June 13, 449).

We have read your Charity's letter (we are amazed that it came so late) and have reviewed the proceedings of the council of bishops. At last we have found out about the obstacle to the integrity of the faith which arose in your area; what before seemed obscure has now been disclosed and clarified for us. Eutyches, who appeared to be honorable because of his priestly title, is revealed by your letter to be quite rash and ignorant. Hence, the saying of the Prophet also fits him: 'He would not understand that he might do well. He hath devised iniquity on his bed.' What is more iniquitous than to hold blasphemous opinions and not yield to those who are more learned and informed? Those men fall into this foolishness who, when they are impeded by some lack of intelligence from learning the truth, have recourse, not to the voice of prophecy, not to the epistles of the Apostles, not to the authority of the Scriptures, but to themselves. Hence, they are teachers of error because they were not pupils of the truth. For, what knowledge of the Old and New Testaments has he acquired who does not even comprehend the elements of the Christian Creed itself and in his heart, even as an old man, does not understand the words which everywhere in the world are exacted from those about to be baptized?

Not knowing, therefore, what he ought to believe about the Incarnation of the divine Word and being willing to labor in order to enlighten his mind from the breadth of holy Scripture, he might at least by careful attention have learned the common and uniform profession of faith which all the faithful make: namely that they believe in one God, the Father Almighty, and in Jesus Christ, His only Son, our Lord, who was born of the Holy Spirit and the Virgin Mary. It is by these three ideas that the machinations of almost all heretics are destroyed. For, when there is belief in God and the omnipotent Father, then the Son is shown to be co-eternal with Him, in no way differing from the Father, because He was born God from God, the Omnipotent from the Omnipotent, the Co-eternal from the Eternal, not coming later in time or inferior in power, not of unequal glory, not separate in essence. This same only-begotten Son of the eternal Father was truly born eternal of the Holy Spirit and the Virgin Mary. This birth in time in no way minimized His divine and eternal birth, nor did it add thereto. He sacrificed His entire self in order to redeem man (who had been deceived), to overcome death, and by His power to destroy the Devil, who held sway over death. We could not overcome the author of sin and death had not Christ taken on our nature and made it His; sin could not defile Him nor death hold Him in bondage. He was truly conceived of the Holy Spirit within the womb of His Virgin Mother, who bore Him while preserving her virginity just as, preserving her virginity, she conceived Him.

But, if Eutyches was unable to draw from this most pure fount of Christian faith a clear understanding, because he had darkened the light of clear truth by his blindness, he might have betaken himself to the teaching of the Scriptures, where Matthew says: 'The book of the origin of Jesus Christ, the son of David, the son of Abraham.' He might also have sought instruction from the Apostle's teaching, reading in the Epistle to the Romans: 'Paul, the servant of Jesus Christ, called to be an apostle, set apart for the gospel of God, which he had promised beforehand through his prophets in the holy Scriptures, concerning his Son who was born to him according to the flesh of the offspring of David.' He might have applied pious study to the writings of the Prophets, and coming upon the promise of God to Abraham, where He says: 'In thy offspring shall all nations be blessed,' in order not to have doubts about the proper significance of this 'offspring,' he might have followed the Apostle saying: 'The promises were made to Abraham and to his offspring. He does not say, "And to his offsprings," as of many; but as of one, "And to thy offspring," who is Christ.' He might also have understood by deeper attention the teaching of Isaias saying: ' "Behold, the virgin shall be with child, and shall bring forth a son; and they shall call his name Emmanuel"; which is, inter-

preted, "God with us." ' He might have read the words of the
same Prophet: 'A child is born to us, and a son is given to us,
and the government is upon his shoulders: and they shall call his
name, Angel of the Great Counsel, God the Mighty, the Prince
of Peace, Father of the world to come.' And he would not
speak nonsense, saying that the Word was flesh in such a way
that Christ, born from the Virgin's womb, had a man's form, yet
did not have the reality of His Mother's body. Or did Eutyches
by chance think that our Lord Jesus Christ was not of our
nature because the angel sent to the blessed Mary said: 'The
Holy Spirit shall come upon thee and the power of the Most High
shall overshadow thee; and therefore the Holy One to be born
shall be called the Son of God"; that is, because the Virgin's conceiving was a divine work, the flesh of Him who was conceived
was not taken from the nature of her who conceived Him? But
that birth, singularly wonderful and wonderfully singular, must
not be understood as meaning that, because of the new type of
procreation, the intrinsic quality of birth was changed. Fecundi-
ty was given to the Virgin by the Holy Spirit, but the reality of
the body was taken from her body; and with Wisdom building a
dwelling for Himself, 'The Word was made flesh, and dwelt
among us"; that is, in that flesh which He took from a human
being and which He animated with the breath of rational life.

In this preservation, then, of the real quality of both natures, both being united in one person, lowliness was taken on
by majesty, weakness by strength, mortality by the immortal.
And in order to pay the debt of our fallen state, inviolable nature was united to one capable of suffering so that (and this is
the sort of reparation we needed) one and the same mediator
between God and men, the man Jesus Christ, could die in the
one nature and not die in the other. In the whole and perfect
nature of the true man, then, the true God was born, complete
in His own nature, complete in ours. But by ours we mean that
which the Creator formed in us at the beginning and which He
took upon Himself, to redeem it. That part which the Deceiver
added and man, deceived, accepted left no traces in the Saviour.
He did not share in our sins just because He undertook to share
in our weaknesses. He took on the aspect of servitude without
the stain of sin; He added to the humanity but did not lessen

the divinity. For that putting off of self whereby He the invisible made Himself visible and as Creator and Lord of all things wished to become one of the mortals was an inclination to mercy, not a failure of power. He who keeping the form of God created man, the same was made man in an aspect of servitude. Both His natures keep their intrinsic quality without defect; and, just as the aspect of God does not remove the aspect of servitude, so also this latter does not lessen the aspect of God. Because the Devil boasted that man, deceived by his trickery, lacked help from God; that man, deprived of the gift of immortality, had undergone the hard sentence of death; and that man had found a sort of solace in his misfortunes by associating with the Deceiver; that God, also, because the course of justice demanded it, had changed His own design in regard to man, whom He had created with so much honor—for these reasons God had to arrange a secret design whereby the unchanging God, whose will cannot be deprived of its clemency, might actually fulfill His original plan of fatherly care towards us by a much hidden mystery; and man, led into sin by the cleverness of the Devil's iniquity, might not perish contrary to the plan of God.

The Son of God, then, enters into this weakness of the world, coming down from His heavenly throne, begotten in a new type of birth, but not departing from His Father's glory in the new order. The 'order was new' in that, being invisible in His own nature, He became visible in ours; incomprehensible, He desired to be comprehended; enduring before time began, He began to exist in time; the Lord of the universe assumed the aspect of servitude with a shadow veiling the immensity of His majesty. A God incapable of suffering, He deigned to become a man who could suffer, and, being immortal, to become subject to the laws of death. He was born in a 'new type of birth' in that undefiled virginity experienced no concupiscence, yet supplied the material for the flesh. From the Mother the Lord took His nature, but no fault; and the Lord Jesus Christ, born from a virgin's womb, does not have a nature different from ours just because His birth was an unusual one. He who is true God is also man; there is no falsity in this union, wherein the lowliness of man and the greatness of the divinity are mutually united. Just as God is not changed by His show of mercy, so the man is not changed by being swallowed up in majesty. Each aspect performs its own acts in co-operation with the other; that is, the Word doing what is proper to the Word, the flesh pursuing what pertains to the flesh. The first of these is ablaze with the miraculous, the other is overpowered by injuries. And just as the Word does not give up any of His equality in the Father's glory, so also the flesh does not abandon the nature of our species. He is one and the same, truly Son of God and truly Son of man. He is God because of the fact that 'in the beginning was the Word, and the Word was with God, and the Word was God'; and man through the fact that 'the Word was made flesh, and dwelt among us'; God, because 'all things were made through him, and without him nothing was made'; a man through the fact that 'He was born of a woman, born under the Law.' The birth of flesh is a manifestation of human nature; that a virgin should give birth is a show of divine power. The infancy of the babe is displayed by the lowliness of the cradle; the greatness of the Almighty is proclaimed by the voices of angels. He has a man's helpless infancy in that Herod impiously tries to kill him; but He is the Lord of all, before whom the Magi rejoice to kneel in supplication. Already when He came to be baptized by John, the precursor, lest it be unknown that divinity was being covered by a veil of flesh, the voice of the Father thundering from heaven said: 'This is my beloved Son, in whom I am well pleased.' And so, He whom the cleverness of the Devil tempts, as if He were a man, is accompanied by the ministration of angels, as to God. To hunger, to thirst, to grow tired, and to sleep: these are evidently human. But to satisfy 5,000 men with five loaves of bread and to give the Samaritan woman living water, to drink which frees the one drinking from further thirst, to walk on top of the sea without sinking, and to calm the waves stirred up by a storm—are doubtless the work of God. Hence, to skip over many other items, just as it is not part of the same nature to weep over a dead friend from the emotion of pity and then by the command of His voice to call forth this same man alive, after rolling back the stone from a tomb closed for four days; or to hang on a cross of wood, and yet turn day into night and cause the elements to tremble; or to have been pierced with nails, yet to open the doors of paradise to the faithful thief—so also to say: 'I and the

Father are one' and to say: 'The Father is greater than I' are not both pertinent to the same nature. Although in the Lord Jesus Christ there is one person, of God and man, it is only from one of these sources that contempt comes to both in common and from the other source that glory comes to both in common. From us He has a humanity less than the Father; from the Father, a divinity equal to the Father's.

Because, then, of this union of personality (to be understood of both natures) 'the Son of man', as we read, came down from heaven when the 'Son of God' assumed flesh from that Virgin through whom He was born. And again, the 'Son of God' is said to have been crucified and buried, although this did not pertain to His divinity as such, in which the Only-begotten is co-eternal and consubstantial with the Father; but He endured this in the weakness of His human nature. Hence, too, we all profess in the Creed that the only-begotten 'Son of God' was crucified and buried, according to that statement of the Apostle: 'For had they known it, they never would have crucified the Lord of glory.' When our Lord and Saviour Himself was teaching the faith to His disciples, He questioned them, saying: 'Who do men say that I the Son of man am?" And when they had given Him various opinions of others, He said: 'But who do you say that I am?' That is, I, who am the Son of man and one whom you see in a condition of servitude and the reality of the flesh, whom do you say that I am? When blessed Peter by divine inspiration said (and by his profession he would be of service to all peoples): 'Thou art the Christ, the Son of the living God,' not undeservedly he was called 'blessed' by the Lord and derived from the word *rock* that solidity associated with his virtue and his name. It was Peter who, through the revelation of the Father, professed that Christ and the Son of God were the same. For to have possessed one of these without the other was of no value for salvation; it was equally dangerous to believe that the Lord Jesus Christ was either God only without man, or man only without God. After the Lord's resurrection (which, of course, was the resurrection of His real body, since the one who came to life was the same as He who had been crucified and died), why did He delay on earth for forty days except to clear away every cloud from the fullness of our faith? Speaking with His disciples and living and eating with them, He allowed Himself to be touched by the attentive and curious hand of those who were afflicted by doubt. For the same reason He also entered into a room with His disciples while the doors were shut and by breathing on them He gave them the Holy Spirit. And having bestowed light on their intelligence, He explained the mysteries of holy Scripture. And once more He pointed out the same wound in His side, the holes left by the nails, and all the marks of His quite recent passion, saying: 'See my hands and feet that it is I myself. Feel me and see; for a spirit does not have flesh and bones, as you see I have.' This was to show us that there remained in Him the particular qualities of both the divine and human natures, and that we might thus realize that the Word is not the same as the flesh and might therefore confess that the one Son of God is both the Word and flesh. That man Eutyches must be considered as totally lacking in this mystery of the faith. He did not recognize our nature in the only-begotten Son of God, neither through the lowliness of His mortal state nor through the glory of His Resurrection. And Eutyches did not fear the sentence of the blessed Apostle and Evangelist John, saying: 'Every spirit that confesses that Jesus Christ has come in the flesh, is of God. And every spirit that severs Jesus, is not of God, but is of Antichrist.' What is meant by 'severing' Jesus if not the taking away from Him of His human nature and nullifying by the foulest imaginings the mystery through which alone we have been saved? But, being in the dark about the nature of Christ's body, he is of necessity also ignorant about the passion because of the same blindness. If he does not think the cross of Christ was false and does not doubt that it was endured as a real satisfaction for the salvation of the world, then let him admit the flesh of the one whose death he believes in. Let him not deny that one, by his admission, was capable of suffering was a man with a body like ours. For a denial of the actual flesh is also a denial of bodily suffering. If, then, he accepts the Christian faith and does not turn away his ear from the teaching of the Gospel, let him see which nature it was that, pierced with nails, hung on the wood of the cross; let him realize whence the blood and water flowed, when the side of Christ was opened by the soldier's spear, so that God's Church might be wet therewith by washing and drinking. Let him also listen to the blessed Apostle Peter preaching that sanctification of the spirit is effected by sprinkling with the blood of Christ. Let him read, not cursorily, the statement of the same Apostle saying: 'You know that you are redeemed from the vain manner of life handed down from your fathers, not with perishable things, with silver or gold, but with the precious blood of Christ, as of a lamb without blemish and without spot.' Let him likewise not resist the testimony of blessed John the Apostle saying: 'And the blood of Jesus, the Son of God, cleanses us from all sin'; and again: 'And this is the victory that overcomes the world, our faith'; and: 'Who is there that overcomes the world if not he who believes that Jesus is the Son of God? This is he who came in water and in blood, Jesus Christ; not in the water only, but in the water and in the blood. And it is the Spirit that bears witness that the Spirit is the truth. For there are three that bear witness . . . the Spirit, and the water, and the blood; and these three are one.' This means the Spirit of sanctification and the blood of redemption and the water of baptism, which three are one and remain distinct, and none of them is separated from union with the others. This is the faith by which the Catholic Church lives and progresses, namely, that humanity is believed to exist in Jesus Christ not without real divinity, and divinity, but without real humanity.

But when Eutyches answered the questions put to him at your investigation, saying, 'I confess that our Lord had two natures before they were united, but I confess that after the union He had one nature,' I am amazed that so absurd and so perverse a profession was not corrected by any rebuttal on the part of the judges and that a totally insipid and blasphemous statement was passed over as if nothing to give offense was heard. The fact is that it was as impious to say that the only-begotten Son of God had two natures before the Incarnation as it was blasphemous to assert that He had a single nature after the Word was made flesh. Hence, in order that Eutyches may not think that what he said was right or tolerable on the grounds that it was not refuted by any opinion of yours, we strongly exhort your Charity's zeal so that, dearest brother, if ever this case is satisfactorily concluded through the intervention of God's mercy, the folly of an ignorant may may also be purged of this pernicious item of belief. As the record of the proceedings made clear, Eutyches had indeed made a good start toward giving up his views at the time when, pressed by your ideas, he admitted that he was saying what he had not said previously and that he was yielding to a belief that previously was not his. But when he was unwilling to agree to a condemnation of the impious doctrine, it was your Fraternities' understanding that he was remaining in his perfidious belief and deserved to have a judgment of condemnation passed against him. If he faithfully and profitably repents this action and recognizes, even at this late date, how justly episcopal authority was aroused against him, or if he makes the fullest satisfaction by a condemnation read aloud and signed by him personally against all his heretical opinions, then no fault will be found with any show of mercy toward him who has repented. For our Lord, the true and good Shepherd, who laid down His life for His sheep and who came to save the souls of men, not to destroy them, wishes us to be imitators of His fatherly care. That is, sinners are indeed to be restrained by justice, but through mercy they are not to be driven away when converted. The true faith is then at last most fruitfully defended when a false opinion is condemned even by its supporters.

We are sending our brothers, Julius the bishop and Renatus the priest, as well as my son Hilary the deacon, to represent us in seeing that the entire problem is settled with piety toward and faith in God. With these we are associating Dulcitius, our notary, whose faith has been proved to us. We are confident that God's assistance will be present so that he who erred may be saved through the condemnation of his heretical ideas. May God keep you safe, dearest brother.

Issued on the thirteenth of June in the consulship of the most illustrious Asturius and Protogenes.

St. John Damascene
675-749

    After the Council of Chalcedon (451) a period of decline in theological thought took place, covering over two and a half centuries. As of the 7th century much of the "Christian East" became the "Muslim East." In Damascus, while that city was under the caliphs, the civil head of the Christian population was a nobleman named John. Around 716 he gave up his civil position and entered the monastery of St. Sabas near Jerusalem, where he was ordained a priest. The unique role of this man was to be one of salvage and summary. As the last of the Greek Fathers he gathered the wisdom of the previous five centuries and tried to sift out the best of posterity.

    John Damascene systematised the teachings and testimony of the Councils and Fathers and undertook to capture the essence of the Greek Christian heritage. His work, The Fount of Wisdom, *is thus intentionally traditional; it is the faithful echo of patristic tradition, especially in Christology. It was written at the request of his good friend Cosmas, bishop of Maiuma. It consists of three quite different parts: 1) The* Philosophical Chapters, *commonly known in the West as the* Dialectica; *his purpose here is to set forth "the best contributions of the philosophers of the Greeks." This is the first example of a philosophy manual composed as an aid to the study of theology. 2)* Heresies in Epitome *contains descriptions of 103 different heresies. It is especially interesting to note heresy number 101—the Ishmaelites, his term for the Muslims, in treating which he reveals a thorough knowledge of the Koran.*

But 3) The Exact Exposition of the Orthodox Faith *is the most important, the longest, and the best known part of the* Fount of Knowledge. *It is quite a remarkable synthesis of Greek theology (the only Western writing he uses is Leo's* Tome). *His chief authority frequently cited by name, is "the Theologian," Gregory Nazianzen, but all the others are there as well, back to the Council of Nicaea (325). Curiously enough, the ante-Nicene writers are absent.*

If the content is traditional, the originality of the Orthodox Faith *is in its being a synthesis of exceptional clarity. After dealing with the mystery of God in unity and trinity in book one, John presents the realms of creation in book two; book three, the bulk of which is given in the following excerpt, is his synthesis of Christology, which is concluded in book four, which also has treatments of faith, the Eucharist, and several lesser topics. "Whatever defects the* Orthodox Faith *may have, it still remains an incomparable summa of theology and an indispensable aid to the study of the Greek Christian tradition. And the* Fount of Knowledge *as a whole remains a fitting monument and landmark to mark the close of the patristic age, of which it is one of the greatest single achievements." (F. H. Chase).*

John Damascene, the last of the Greek Fathers, firmly disallowed any kind of ignorance or growth in Christ, extending His human wisdom to the maximum. But he also stressed the necessity of His having a true, fully human will without which He could not have been our Savior. The following excerpts present the highlights of Book Three.

ORTHODOX FAITH

BOOK THREE

CHAPTER 1

A nd so, man succumbed to the assault of the demon, the author of evil; he failed to keep the Creator's commandment and was stripped of grace and deprived of that familiarity which he had enjoyed with God; he was clothed with the roughness of his wretched life—for this is what the fig leaves signify—and put on death, that is to say, the mortality and grossness of the flesh—for this is what the garment of skins signifies; he was excluded from paradise by the just judgment of God; and was condemned to death and made subject to corruption. Even then the Compassionate One, who had given him his being and had favored him with a blessed existence, did not disregard him. On the contrary, He first schooled him and exhorted him to conversion in many ways—by groaning and trembling, by a flood of waters and the near destruction of the entire race, by the confusion and division of tongues, by the tutelage of angels, by the destruction of cities by fire, by prefigurative and portents, by diverse influences, by the Law and the Prophets, all of which were directed to the destruction of that sin which had abounded under many forms and had enslaved man and heaped every sort of evil into his life, and to his return to the blessed existence. Since it was by sin that death had come into the world like some wild and savage beast to destroy the life of man, it was necessary for the one who was to effect a redemption to be sinless and not liable to the death which is due to sin. And it was further necessary for human nature to be strengthened and renewed, to be taught by experience, and to learn the way of virtue which turns back from destruction and leads to eternal life. Finally, the great sea of His benevolence toward man was made manifest, for the Creator and Lord Himself took up the struggle in behalf of His own creation and became a teacher in deed. And, since the enemy had caught man with the bait of the hope of divinity, he himself was taken with the bait of the barrier of the flesh; and at the same time the goodness and wisdom and justice and power of God were made manifest. His goodness, because He did not despise the weakness of His own handiwork, but, when he fell, had compassion on him and stretched out His hand to him. His justice, because, when man had suffered defeat, He did not have another conquer the tyrant nor did He snatch man away from death by force, but He, the Good and Just, made him victor against whom death had once enslaved through sin; and like He rescued by like, which was most difficult to do. And His wisdom, because He found the most fitting solution for this most difficult problem. For by the good pleasure of God the Father the only-begotten Son and Word of God and God, who is in the bosom of God the Father, consubstantial with the Father, and with the Holy Ghost, existing before the ages, without beginning, who was in the beginning and was with God the Father and was God, He, being in the form of God, bowed down the heavens and descended—that is, without lowering it, He brought down His exalted sublimity and condescended to His servants with an ineffable and incomprehensible condescension, for such is the meaning of the term condescension. And He, while being perfect God, became perfect man and accomplished the newest of all new things, the only new thing under the sun, by which the infinite power of God was clearly shown. For what is greater than for God to become man? So, without suffering change, the Word was made flesh of the Holy Ghost and the holy and ever-virgin Mary, Mother of God. And He stands as mediator between God and men. He, the only loving One, was conceived in the immaculate womb of the Virgin not by the will of man, nor by concupiscence, nor by the intervention of a husband, nor by pleasurable generation, but of the Holy Ghost and the first offspring of Adam. And He became obedient to the Father by healing our disobedience with that which is like to us and which was taken from us, and by becoming to us a model of that obedience without which it is impossible to attain salvation.

CHAPTER 2

Now, an angel of the Lord was sent to the Holy Virgin, who was descended from the tribe of David, 'for it is evident that our Lord sprung out of Juda: of which tribe no one attended on the altar,' as the divine Apostle said and concerning which we shall speak more fully later on. Bringing the good tidings to her, he said: 'Hail, full of grace, the Lord is with thee.' And she was troubled at his saying, and the angel said to her: 'Fear not, Mary, for thou hast found grace with God, and thou shalt bring forth a son and thou shalt call his name Jesus; for he shall save his people from their sins.' It is for this reason that the name Jesus is interpreted as meaning saviour. And she was troubled and said: 'How shall this be done to me, because I know not man?' Again the angel spoke to her: 'The Holy Ghost shall come upon thee and the power of the Most High shall overshadow thee. And therefore also the Holy which shall be born to thee shall be called the Son of God.' Then she said to him: 'Behold the handmaid of the Lord; be it done to me according to thy word.'

And so, after the holy Virgin had given her assent, the Holy Ghost came upon her according to the Lord's word, which the angel had spoken, and purified her and gave her the power both to receive the divinity of the Word and to beget. Then the subsistent Wisdom and Power of the Most High, the Son of God, the Consubstantial with the Father, overshadowed her like a divine seed and from her most chaste and pure blood compacted for Himself a body animated by a rational and intellectual soul as first-fruits of our clay. This was not by seed, but by creation through the Holy Ghost, with the form not being put together bit by bit, but being completed all at once with the Word of God Himself serving as the person to the flesh. For the divine Word was not united to an already self-subsistent flesh, but, without being circumscribed, came in His own person to dwell in the womb of the holy Virgin and from the chaste blood of the ever-virgin made flesh subsist and animated by a rational and intellectual soul. Taking to Himself the first-fruits of the human clay, the very Word became person to the body. Thus, there was a body which was at once the body of God the Word and an animate, rational, intellectual body. Therefore, we do not say that man became God, but that God became man. For, while He was by nature perfect God, the same became by nature perfect man. He did not change His nature and neither did He just appear to become man. On the contrary, without confusion or alteration or division He became hypostatically united to the rationally and intellectually animated flesh which He had from the holy Virgin and which had its existence in Him. He did not transform the nature of his divinity into the substance of His flesh, nor the substance of His flesh into the nature of His divinity, and neither did He effect one compound nature out of His divine nature and the human nature which He had assumed.

CHAPTER 3

The natures were united to each other without change and without alteration. The divine nature did not give up its proper simplicity, and the human nature was certainly not changed into the nature of the divinity, nor did it become non-existent. Neither was there one compound nature made from the two natures. For the compounded nature can in no wise be consubstantial with either one of the natures from which it has been compounded, since from diverse natures it had been made into something else. For example, the body, which is made up of the four elements, is not said to be consubstantial with fire, nor is it called fire, nor is it called water or earth or air either, nor is it consubstantial with any one of these. Accordingly, if Christ had one compound nature after the union, having changed from one simple nature to a compound one, as the heretics say, then He is neither consubstantial with His Father, who has a simple nature, nor with His Mother, because she was not composed of divinity and humanity. Nor, indeed, will He belong to divinity or humanity, nor can He be called God or man, but just Christ alone, and, according to them, 'Christ' will not be the name of the person but the name of the one nature. We, however, declare that Christ has a compound nature, not in the sense of something new made from different things, as man is made up of body and soul or as the body is composed of the four elements, but in the sense of being made up of different things which remain the same. For we confess that from divinity and humanity there is the same

278

perfect God and that He both is and is said to be of two natures and in two natures. We say that the term 'Christ' is the name of the person and that it is not used in a restricted sense, but as signifying what is of the two natures. Thus, He anointed Himself—as God, anointing His body with His divinity, but as man, being anointed, because He is both the one and the other. Moreover, the anointing of the humanity is the divinity. Now, if Christ, who is consubstantial with the Father, has one compounded nature, then the Father, too, will certainly be compounded and consequently consubstantial with the flesh, which is absurd and redolent of every blasphemy.

What is more, how can one nature comprise different substances that are contradictory? How is it possible for the same nature to be at once created and uncreated, mortal and immortal, circumscribed and uncircumscribed?

Now, were they to say that Christ had one nature and that this was simple, then either they would be confessing Him to be pure God and would be introducing a mere appearance that would not be incarnation, or they would be confessing Him to be mere man after the manner of Nestorius. Then, where is the perfection in divinity and the perfection in humanity? How can they ever say that Christ has two natures, while they are asserting that after the union He has one compound nature? For it is obvious to anyone that, before the union, Christ had one nature.

However, the reason for the herectics' error is their saying that nature and hypostasis are the same thing. Now, when we say that men have one nature, it must be understood that we do not say this with the body and soul in mind, because it is impossible to say that the soul and the body as compared to each other have one nature. Nevertheless, when we take a number of human hypostases, all of these are found to admit of the same basis of their nature. All are made up of a soul and a body, all share the nature of the soul and possess the substance of the body, and all have a common species. Thus, we say that several different persons have one nature, because each person has two natures and is complete in these two natures, that is to say, the natures of the soul and of the body.

In the case of our Lord Jesus Christ, however, it is impossible to have a common species, for there never was, nor is, nor ever will be another Christ of divinity and humanity, in divinity and humanity, the same being perfect God and perfect man. Hence, in the case of our Lord Jesus Christ, one cannot speak of one nature made up of divinity and humanity as one can in the case of the individual made up of soul and body. In this last case we have an individual, but Christ is not an individual, because He does not have a predicated species of Christness. It is precisely for this reason that we say that it was of two perfect natures, the divine and the human, that the union was made. It was not made by mixing, or mingling, or blending, or compounding as was asserted by the fatal Dioscorus, by Eutyches, too, and Severus, and their accursed associates; neither was it apparent (προσωπική) nor relative, nor by dignity or harmony of will or equality in honor or identity of name or complaisance as was asserted by that enemy of God, Nestorius, and by Diodorus, too, and Theodore of Mopsuestia, and their hellish band. Rather, it was by composition—hypostatically, that is to say—without change or mingling or alteration or division or separation. And we confess one Person of the Son of God incarnate in two natures that remain perfect, and we declare that the Person of His divinity and of His humanity is the same and confess that the two natures are preserved intact in Him after the union. We do not set each nature apart by itself, but hold them to be united to each other in one composite Person. For we say that the union is substantial; that is to say, true and not imaginary. We do not, however, define the substantial union as meaning that the two natures go to make up one compound nature, but as meaning that they are truly united to each other into one composite Person of the Son of God, each with its essential difference maintained intact. Thus, that which was created remained created, and that which was uncreated, uncreated; the mortal remained mortal and the immortal immortal; the circumscribed remained circumscribed and the uncircumscribed, uncircumscribed; the visible remained visible and the invisible, invisible. 'The one glows with miracles, while the other has succumbed to insults.'

Moreover, the Word makes human things His own, because what is proper to His sacred flesh belongs to Him; and the things which are His own He communicates to His flesh. This after the manner of exchange on account of the mutual immanence of the parts and the hypostatic union and because He who 'with each form co-operating with the other performed' both divine and human acts was one and the same. Wherefore, the Lord of Glory is even said to have been crucified, although His divine nature did not suffer; and the Son of Man is confessed to have been in heaven before His passion, as the Lord Himself has said. For one and the same was the Lord of Glory and He who was naturally and truly Son of Man, that is, He who became man. And we recognize both the miracles and the sufferings as His, even though it was in one nature that He worked miracles and in another that He endured suffering. For we know that His one Person thus preserves for itself the essential difference of the natures. How, indeed, would the difference be preserved, were not those things preserved in which they differ from each other? For difference is that by which things that are different differ. Therefore, we say that Christ is joined to the extremes by the fact of His natures differing from each other, that is, by the fact of His essence. On the one hand, He is joined to the Father and the Spirit by His divinity, while on the other He is joined by His humanity to His Mother and to all men. However, because of the fact that His natures are united, we say that He differs both from the Father and the Spirit and from His Mother and other men. For His natures are united in His Person and have one composite Person, and in this He differs both from the Father and the Spirit and from His Mother and us.

CHAPTER 4

We have repeatedly said that *substance* is one thing and *person* another, and that *substance* means the common species including the persons that belong to the same species—as, for example, God, man—while *person* indicates an individual, as Father, Son, Holy Ghost, Peter, Paul. One must furthermore know that the terms *divinity* and *humanity* are indicative of the substances or natures, but that the terms *God* and *man* are used in reference to the nature, as when we say: 'God is an incomprehensible substance' and 'God is one.' But these are also taken as referring to the persons, with the more particular receiving the name of the more general, as when Scripture says: 'Therefore God, thy God, hath anointed thee,' for in this case it means the

Father and the Son. And again, when it says: 'There was a man in the land of Hus,' for it means Job only.

Since, then, in our Lord Jesus Christ we recognize two natures and one composite Person for both, when we are considering the natures, we call them divinity and humanity. But, when we consider the composite Person of the two natures, we sometimes call Christ both God and Man and God incarnate, naming Him from both; and sometimes we name Him from one of the two and call Him just God and Son of God, or just Man and Son of Man. And also, we sometimes name Him from just the sublime attributes and sometimes from just the more humble ones. For He is one who is alike both the one and the other—the one existing uncaused and eternally from the Father; the other come into being at a later time because of love for men.

Therefore, when we speak of the divinity, we do not attribute the properties of the humanity to it. Thus, we never speak of a passible or created divinity. Neither do we predicate the divine properties of the flesh, for we never speak of uncreated flesh or humanity. In the case of the person, however, whether we name it from both of the parts or from one of them, we attribute the properties of both the natures to it. And thus, Christ—which name covers both together—is called both God and man, created and uncreated, passible and impassible. And whenever He is named Son of God and God from one of the parts, He receives the properties of the co-existent nature, of the flesh, that is to say, and can be called passible God and crucified Lord of Glory—not as being God, but in so far as the same one is also man. When, again, He is named Man and the Son of Man, He is given the properties and splendors of the divine nature. He is called Child before the Ages and Man without beginning, not as a child or a man, but as God, who is before the ages and became a child in latter times. Such, then, is the manner of this exchange by which each nature communicates its own properties to the other through the identity of their person and their mutual immanence. This is how we can say of Christ: 'This is our God, who was seen upon earth and conversed with men,' and: 'This man is uncreated, impassible, and uncircumscribed.'

CHAPTER 5

In the Divinity we confess one nature, while we hold three really existing Persons. And we hold everything belonging to the nature and the essence to be simple, while we recognize the difference of the Persons as residing only in the three properties of being uncaused and Father, of being caused and Son, and of being caused and proceeding. And we understand them to be inseparable and without interval between them, and united to one another and mutually immanent without confusion. And we understand them, while being separated without interval, to be united without confusion, for they are three, even though they are united. For, although each is subsistent in itself, that is to say, is a perfect Person and has its own property or distinct manner of existence, they are united in their essence and natural properties and by their not being separated or removed from the Person of the Father, and they are one God and are so called. In the same way, when it comes to that divine and ineffable Incarnation of one of the Holy Trinity, God the Word and our Lord Jesus Christ, which surpasses all understanding and comprehension, while we confess two natures, a divine and a human, conjoined with each other and hypostatically united, we also confess one composite Person made of those natures. We furthermore hold that, even after the union, the two natures are preserved intact in the one composite person, that is to say, in the one Christ, and that they and their natural properties have real existence, being nevertheless united without confusion, differing without separation, and numbered. Now, just as the three Persons of the Holy Trinity are united without confusion and are distinct without separation and have number without the number causing division, or separation, or estrangement, or severance among them—for we recognize that the Father and the Son and the Holy Ghost are one God—so in the same way the natures of Christ, although united, are united without confusion, and, although mutually immanent, do not suffer any change or transformation of one into the other. For each one keeps its own distinctiveness unchanged. Thus, too, they are numbered, yet the number does not introduce division. For Christ is one and He is perfect both in divinity and humanity. And number is not by nature a cause of division or union, but is, rather a sign of the quantity of the things numbered, whether they be united or divided. Thus, as an example of things that are united, this wall contains fifty stones; or, as an example of things that are divided, there are fifty stones lying in this field. Or again, as an example of things that are united, there are two natures in a coal— that of fire, I mean, and that of wood; or these may be divided, because the nature of fire is one thing and that of wood another. And these are not united or divided by their number but in some other manner. And so, just as it is impossible to say that the three Persons are one Person, even though they are united, without bringing about confusion or suppression of the difference, so it is impossible to say that the two hypostatically united natures of Christ are one nature without our bringing about suppression, confusion, or annihilation of their difference.

CHAPTER 6

Things that are common and universal are predicated of particulars subordinate to them. Now, the substance as a species is a common thing, while the person is a particular. A thing is a particular not in that it possesses a part of the nature, because it does not have such a part, but in that it is particular in number, as an individual. Thus, persons are said to differ in number but not in nature. The substance, moreover, is predicated of the person, because the substance is complete in each of the persons of the same species. For that reason, persons do not differ from one another in substance, but rather in the accidents, which are their characteristic properties—characteristic, however of the person and not of the nature. And this is because the person is defined as a substance plus accidents. Thus, the person has that which is common plus that which is individuating, and, besides this, existence in itself. Substance does not subsist in itself, but is to be found in persons. Accordingly, when one of the persons suffers, then, since the whole nature in which the person has suffered is affected, this whole nature is said to have suffered in one of its persons. This, however, does not necessitate all the persons of the same species suffering together with the one that does suffer.

Thus, then, we confess that the nature of the divinity is entirely and completely in each one of its Persons—all in the Father, all in the Son, all in the Holy Ghost. For this reason, the Father is perfect God, the Son is perfect God, and the Holy Ghost is perfect God. In the same way, we say that in the Incarnation of one of the Holy Trinity, the Word of God, the entire and complete nature of the divinity was united in one of its Persons to the entire human nature, and not a part of one to a part of the other. And so the divine Apostle say that 'in Him dwelleth the fullness of the Godhead corporeally,' that is to say, in His flesh. And his inspired disciple Dionysius, who was most learned in matters divine, says that the Divinity in its entirety has community with us in one of its Persons. But, certainly, let us not be constrained to say that all the Persons of the sacred Godhead, the Three, that is, were hypostatically united to all the persons of humanity. For in no wise did the Father and the Holy Ghost participate in the incarnation of the Word of God except by Their good pleasure and will. We do not say that the entire substance of the Divinity was united to the entire human nature, because God the Word lacked none of those things which He implanted in our nature when He formed us in the beginning; He assumed them all—a body and a rational, intellectual soul, together with the properties of both, for the animal which lacks one of these is not a man. He in His entirety assumed me in my entirety and was wholly united to the whole, so that He might bestow the grace of salvation upon the whole. For that which has not been assumed cannot be healed.

And so, the Word of God is united to the flesh by the intermediary of mind which stands midway between the purity of God and the grossness of the flesh. Now, the mind has authority over both soul and body, but, whereas mind is the purest part of the soul, God is the purest part of mind. And when the mind of Christ is permitted by the stronger, then it displays its own authority. However, it is under the control of the stronger and follows it, doing those things which the divine will desires.

Moreover, the mind became the seat of the Divinity which had been hypostatically united to it, just as, of course, the flesh did—but not an associate, as the accursed opinion of the heretics falsely teaches, when, judging immaterial things in a material way, they say that one measure will not hold two. But, how shall Christ have been said to be perfect God and perfect man and consubstantial both with the Father and with us, if a part of the divine nature is united in Him to a part of the human nature?

Furthermore, when we say that our nature rose from the dead and ascended and sat at the right hand of the Father, we do not imply that all human persons arose and sat at the right hand of the Father, but that our entire nature did so in the Person of Christ. Certainly, the divine Apostle says: 'He hath raised us up together and hath made us sit together in Christ.'

And we also say this: that the union was made of common substances. For every substance is common to the persons included under it. And it is not possible to find a partial and individuating nature of substance, since it would then be necessary to say that the same persons were of the same substance and of different substances, and that the Holy Trinity was in its divinity both of the same substance and of different substances. Consequently, the same nature is found in each one of the Persons. And when, following the blessed Athanasius and Cyril, we say that the nature of the Word became incarnate, we are declaring that the Divinity was united to the flesh. For this reason, we may by no means say: 'The nature of the Word suffered,' because the Divinity did not suffer in Him. But we do say that human nature suffered in Christ without any implication that all human persons did; confessing that Christ suffered in His human nature. Thus, when we say 'the nature of the Word,' we mean the Word Himself. And the Word possesses the community of substance and the individuality of person.

CHAPTER 7

We say, then, that the divine Person of God the Word exists before all things timelessly and eternally, simple and uncompounded, uncreated, incorporeal, invisible, intangible, and uncircumscribed. And we say that it has all things that the Father has, since it is consubstantial with Him, and that it differs from the Person of the Father by the manner of its begetting and by relation, that it is perfect and never leaves the Person of the Father. But, at the same time, we say that in latter times, without leaving the bosom of the Father, the Word came to dwell uncircumscribed in the womb of the holy Virgin, without seed and without being contained, but after a manner known to Him, and in the very same Person as exists before the ages He made flesh subsist for Himself from the holy Virgin.

Thus, He was in all things and above all things, and at the same time He was existing in the womb of the holy Mother of God, but He was there by the operation of the Incarnation. And so, He was made flesh and took from her the first-fruits of our clay, a body animated by a rational and intellectual soul, so that the very Person of God the Word was accounted to the flesh. And the Person of the Word which formerly had been simple was made composite. Moreover, it was a composite from two perfect natures, divinity and humanity. And it has that characteristic and distinctive property of sonship by which God the Word is distinct from the Father and the Spirit, and also had those characteristic and distinctive properties of the flesh by which He is distinct both from His Mother and from the rest of men. It further had those properties of the divine nature in which He is one with the Father and the Spirit, and also had those features of human nature in which He is one with His Mother and with us. Moreover, He differs from the Father and the Spirit and from His Mother and us in yet another way, by His being at once both God and man. For this we recognize as a most peculiar property of the Person of Christ.

And so, we confess that even after the Incarnation He is the one Son of God, and we confess that the same is the Son of Man, one Christ, one Lord, the only-begotten Son and Word of God, Jesus our Lord. And we venerate His two begettings—one from the Father before the ages and surpassing cause and reason and time and nature, and one in latter times for our own sake, after our own manner, and surpassing us. For our own sake, because it was for the sake of our salvation; after our own manner, because He was made man from a woman and with a period of gestation; and surpassing us, because, surpassing the law of conception, He was not from seed but from the Holy Ghost and the holy Virgin Mary. And we do not proclaim Him God alone, stripped of our humanity, nor do we despoil Him of His divinity and proclaim Him man alone. Neither do we proclaim Him one and another; rather, we proclaim Him to be one and the same, at once both God and man, perfect God and perfect man, God entire and man entire—the same being God entire, even with His flesh, and man entire, even with His most sacred divinity. By saying 'perfect God and perfect man' we show the fullness and completeness of the natures, while by saying 'God entire and man entire' we point out the individuality and the indivisibility of the person.

Following the blessed Cyril, we also confess one incarnate nature of the Word of God and by saying 'incarnate' intend the substance of the flesh. So, the Word was made flesh without giving up His own immateriality and He was wholly made flesh while remaining wholly uncircumscribed. With respect to His body He becomes small and contracted, while with respect divinity He is uncircumscribed, for His body is not co-extensive with His uncircumscribed divinity.

The whole He, then, is perfect God, but not wholly God, because He is not only God but also man. Likewise, the whole He is perfect man, but not wholly man, because He is not only man but also God. For the 'wholly' is indicative of nature, while the 'whole' is indicative of person, just as 'one thing' is of nature, while 'another one' is of person.

One must know, moreover, that, although we say that the natures of the Lord are mutually immanent, we know that this immanence comes from the divine nature. For this last pervades all things and indwells as it wishes, but nothing pervades it. And it communicates its own splendours to the body while remaining impassible and having no part in the affections of the body. For, if the sun communicates its own operations to us, yet has no part in our own, then how much more so the Creator of the sun who is the Lord?

* * * * * * * *

CHAPTER 12

And we proclaim the holy Virgin to be properly and truly Mother of God ($\theta\epsilon o\tau\acute{o}\kappa o\varsigma$). For, as He who was born of her is true God, so is she truly Mother of God who gave birth to the true God who took His flesh from her. Now, we do not say that

288

God was born of her in the sense that the divinity of the Word has its beginning of being from her, but in the sense that God the Word Himself, who was timelessly begotten of the Father before the ages and exists without beginning and eternally with the Father and the Holy Ghost, did in the last days come for our salvation to dwell in her womb and of her was, without undergoing change, made flesh and born. For the holy Virgin did not give birth to a mere man but to true God, and not to God simply, but to God made flesh. And He did not bring His body down from heaven and come through her as through a channel, but assumed from her a body consubstantial with us and subsisting in Himself. Now, had the body been brought down from heaven and not been taken from our nature, was there any need for His becoming man? God the Word was made man for this reason: that that every nature which had sinned, fallen, and become corrupt should conquer the tyrant who had deceived it. Thus should it be freed from corruption, as the divine Apostle says: 'For by a man came death: and by a man the resurrection of the dead.' If the first was true, then so is the second.

If, however, he also says: 'The first Adam was, of earth, earthly: the second Adam, the Lord, from heaven,' he is not saying that the body is from heaven. But it is obvious that He is not a mere man, for notice how he called Him both Adam and Lord—thus indicating that He is both together. For Adam is interpreted as meaning born of earth, and it is obvious that man's nature is born of earth because it was formed from dust. On the other hand, the name Lord is expressive of the divine substance.

And again, the Apostle says: 'God sent his only-begotten Son, made of a woman.' He did not say *by* a woman, but *of* a woman. Therefore, the divine Apostle meant that the one made man of the Virgin was Himself the only-begotten Son of God and God, and that the Son of God and God was Himself the one born of the Virgin. And he further meant that, in so far as He was made man, He was born corporeally and did not come to inhabit a previously formed man, as a prophet, but Himself substantially and truly became man, that is, He made flesh animated by a rational and intellectual soul subsist in His person and Himself became to Person to it. Now, that is what 'made of a woman' means for how would the Lord of God Himself have been made under the law, had it not been that He was made a man of the same substance as ourselves?

Hence, it is rightly and truly that we call holy Mary the Mother of God, for this name expresses the entire mystery of the Incarnation. Thus, if she who gave birth is Mother of God, then He who was born of her is definitely God and also definitely man. For, had He not become man, how could God whose existence is before the ages have been born of a woman? And that the Son of Man is a man is quite evident. Moreover, if He who was born of a woman is God, then it is quite evident that the very one who in respect to His divine and unoriginated nature was begotten of God the Father, and the one who in the last times was born of the Virgin in respect to his originated and temporal nature—His human nature, that is—are one. And this means that our Lord Jesus Christ has one Person, two natures, and two begettings.

However, under no circumstances do we call the holy Virgin Mother of Christ (χριστοτόκος). This is because that vessel of dishonor, that foul and loathsome Jew at heart, Nestorius, invented this epithet as an insult to do away with the expression Mother of God and—though he burst with his father Satan—to bring dishonor upon the Mother of God, who alone is truly worthy of honor above all creation. And David is 'Christ,' too, and so is the high priest Aaron, because the royal and priestly offices are both conferred by anointing. Furthermore, any God-bearing (θεοφόρος) man may be called 'Christ,' yet he is not by nature God, which is why the accursed Nestorius was so insolent as to call Him who was born of the Virgin 'God-bearing.' But God forbid that we should ever speak or think of Him as God-bearing; rather, let it be as God incarnate. For the very Word of God was conceived of the Virgin and made flesh, but continued to be God after this assumption of the flesh. And, simultaneously with its coming into being, the flesh was straightway made divine by Him. Thus three things took place at the same time: the assuming of the flesh, its coming into being, and its being made divine by the Word. Hence, the holy Virgin is understood to be Mother of God, and is so called not only because of the nature of the Word but also because of the deification of the humanity simultaneously with which the conception and the coming into being of the flesh were wondrously brought about—the conception of the Word, that is, and the existence of the flesh in the Word Himself. In this the Mother of God, in a manner surpassing the course of nature, made it possible for the Fashioner to be fashioned and for the God and Creator of the universe to become man and deify the human nature which He had assumed, while the union preserved the things united, just as they had been united, that is to say, not only the divinity of Christ but His humanity, also; that which surpassed us and that which was like us. Now, it was not first made like us and then made to surpass us. On the contrary, it was always both from its first beginning of being, because from the first instant of conception it had its existence in the Word Himself. Therefore, while by its own nature it is human, it is also of God and divine in a manner surpassing the course of nature. And what is more, it possessed the properties of the living flesh, since by reason of the Incarnation the Word received them as truly natural in the order of natural motion.

CHAPTER 13

Since we confess our Lord Jesus Christ to be at once both perfect God and perfect man, we declare that this same One has all things that the Father has, except the being unbegotten, and, with the sole exception of sin, all that the first Adam has; namely, a body and a rational and intellectual soul. We furthermore declare that corresponding to His two natures He has the twofold set of natural properties belonging to the two natures—two natural wills, the divine and the human; two natural operations, a divine and a human; two natural freedoms, a divine and a human. For, since He is consubstantial with God the Father, He freely wills and acts as God. And, since He is also consubstantial with us, the same one freely wills and acts as man. Thus, the miracles are His, and so are the sufferings.

CHAPTER 14

Since, then, Christ has two natures, we say that He has two natural wills and two natural operations. On the other hand, since these two natures have one Person, we say that He is one and the same who wills and acts naturally according to both natures, of which and in which is Christ our God, and which are Christ our God. And we say that He wills and acts in each, not independently, but in concert. 'For in each form He wills and acts in communion with the other.' For the will and operation of things having the same substance is the same, and the will and operation of things having different substances is different. Conversely, the substance of things having the same will and operation is the same, whereas that of things having a different will and operation is different.

Thus, in Father and Son and Holy Ghost we discover the identity of nature from the identity of the operation and the will. In the divine Incarnation, on the other hand, we discover the difference of the nature from the difference of the wills and operations, and knowing the difference of the natures we confess the difference of the wills and operations. For, just as the number of the natures piously understood and declared to belong to one and the same Christ does not divide this one Christ, but shows that the difference of the natures is maintained even in the union, neither does the number of the wills and operations belonging substantially to His natures introduce any division—God forbid— for in both of His natures He wills and acts for our salvation. On the contrary, their number shows the preservation and maintenance of the natures even in the union, and this alone. We do not call the wills and operations personal, but natural. I am referring to that very faculty of willing and acting by force of which things which will will and things which act act. For, if we concede these to be personal, then we shall be forced to say that the three Persons of the Holy Trinity differ in will and operation.

Now, one must know that *willing* is not the same thing as *how one wills*. This is because willing, like seeing, is of the nature, since it belongs to all men. How one wills, however, does not belong to nature but to our judgment, just as does how one looks at something, whether it be favorably or unfavorably. All men do not will alike, nor do they see things alike. And this we shall also concede in the case of the operations, for how one wills or sees or acts is a mode of the use of willing or seeing or acting, and this mode belongs to the user alone and distinguishes him from the others in accordance with what is commonly called the *difference*.

Consequently, simple willing is called *will,* or the volitive faculty, which is a natural will and rational appetite. But how one wills, or the subject of the volition, is the object *willed* and will based on judgment. And that is *volitive* which has it in its nature to will. For example, the divine nature is volitive, and so is the human. And finally, he is *willing* who uses the volition, and that is the person; Peter, for example.

Thus, since Christ is one and has one Person, the divinely willing in Him and the humanly willing are one and the same. Nevertheless, since He has two natures which are volitive because they are rational, for everything that is rational is both volitive and free, we shall say that in Him there are two volitions, or natural wills. For the same one is volitive in both of His natures, since He assumed the volitive faculty which is inherent in our nature. Furthermore, since Christ is one and it is the same who wills in either nature, we shall say that the thing willed is the same. In saying this, we do not mean that He willed only what He willed naturally as God, for it is not of the nature of God to will to eat, drink, and the like; we mean that He also willed the things which go to make up human nature, not by any contradiction of judgment, but in accordance with the peculiarity of the natures. For, when His divine will willed and permitted the flesh to suffer and to do what was peculiar to it, He willed these things naturally.

Now, that the will naturally belongs to man is evident from the following consideration. Not counting the divine, there are three kinds of life: the vegetative, the sensitive, and the intellectual. Proper to the vegetative are the motions of nutrition, growth, and reproduction; proper to the sensitive is the motion by impulse; and proper to the rational and intellectual is the free motion. Therefore, if the nutritive motion is proper to the vegetative life and the impulsive to the sensitive, then surely the free motion is proper to the rational and intellectual. But, freedom of motion is nothing else but the will. Consequently, since the Word was made flesh animate, intellectual, and free, He was also made volitive.

Again, things which are natural are not acquired by learning, for no one learns to reason or live or hunger or thirst or sleep. And neither do we learn to will. Hence, it is natural to will.

And again, if, while nature rules in irrational beings, it is ruled in man who is freely moved by his will, then man is by nature volitive.

Still, again, if man has been made after the image of the blessed and supersubstantial Godhead, then, since the divine nature is naturally free and volitive, man as its image is also free and volitive by nature. For the Fathers have defined free will as volition.

Furthermore, if to will is inherent in all men and not present in some while absent in others, then, since what is found to be common to all is a characteristic of a nature in the individuals possessing that nature, man is by nature volitive.

And again, if the nature does not admit of more or less, and if to will is inherent in all and is not more in some while less in others, then man is by nature volitive. And so, if man is by nature volitive, the Lord, too, is by nature volitive, not only in so far as He is God but also in so far as He was made man. For, just as He assumed our nature, so also has He assumed our natural will. And it is in this sense that the Fathers say that He impressed our will in Himself.

If the will is not natural, it will either be personal or be against nature. But, if it is personal, then the Son will have a different will from that of the Father, because that which is personal is characteristic of the person alone. And if it is against nature, there will be a defect in the nature, because what is against nature is destructive of what is according to nature.

Now, the God and Father of all things either wills as Father or as God. But, if He wills as Father, His will will be other than that of the Son, because the Son is not the Father. If, however, He wills as God, and the Son is God and the Holy Ghost is also God, then the will will belong to the nature; that is to say, it will be natural.

Furthermore, if, as the Fathers say, those things that have one will have one substance, and if Christ's divinity and humanity have one will, then the substance of the divinity and that of the humanity will be one and the same.

And again, if, as the Fathers say, the natural difference does not appear in the one will, we must either say that there is one will in Christ and no natural difference, or that there is a natural difference and more than one will.

And still again, as the holy Gospel relates, the Lord went 'into the coasts of Tyre and Sidon: and entering into a house, he would that no man should know it. And he could not be hid.' So, if His divine will was all-powerful and yet He was unable to conceal Himself when He willed to, then it was when willing as man that He was unable to, and as man also He was volitive.

And again, it says: 'Coming to the place he said: I thirst. And they gave him wine to drink mixed with gall. And when he had tasted, he would not drink.' Now, if it was as God that He thirsted and having tasted did not want to drink, then as God He was subject to passion, for thirst is a passion and so is taste. If, however, it was not as God, then it was entirely as man that He thirsted, and as man also He was volitive.

There is also the blessed Apostle Paul, who says: 'Becoming obedient unto death, even to the death of the cross.' This obedience was a submission of what was really His will and not of what really was not, for we may not call an irrational being either obedient or disobedient. However, the Lord became obedient to the Father not in so far as He was God, but in so far as He was man. For, as God, He is neither obedient or disobedient, because obedience or disobedience belong to such as are subject to authority, as the inspired Gregory has said. Then, as man also, Christ was volitive.

Moreover, when we speak of the natural will, we mean that it is not constrained but free—for, if it is rational, it is also absolutely free. For there is not only the uncreated divine nature which is not subject to constraint, but there is also the created intellectual nature which is not so either. And this is obvious, because, although God is by nature good and creative and God, He is not these things by necessity—for who was there to impose the necessity?

It is furthermore necessary to know that the term *freedom of will* is used equivocally—sometimes being referred to God, sometimes to the angels, and sometimes to men. Thus with God it is supersubstantial, but with the angels the execution coincides with the inclination without admitting of any interval of time at all. For the angel has freedom by nature and he is unhampered

295

in its exercise because he has neither the opposition from a body nor has he anyone to interfere with him. With men, however, it is such that the inclination precedes the execution in point of time. This is because, though man is free and has this freedom of will naturally, he also has the interference of the Devil to contend with and the motion of the body. Consequently, because of this interference and the burden of the body, the execution comes after the inclination.

If, then, Adam willingly gave ear, and willed and ate, then the will was the first thing to suffer in us. But, if the will was the first thing to suffer, and if, when the Word became incarnate, He did not assume it, then we have not been made free from sin.

And still further, if the nature's power of free will is His work, and yet He did not assume it, it was either because He condemned His own creation as not being good or because He begrudged us our being healed in it. And while He deprived us of perfect healing, He showed Himself subject to suffering without willing or without being able to save us perfectly.

It is furthermore impossible to speak of one thing composed of two wills in the same way that we speak of a person composed of its natures. This is because, in the first place, compounds are made of things that have their own subsistence and are not found to exist by virtue of another principle than their own; whereas, in the second place, if we are to speak of a composition of wills and operations, we shall be forced to admit a composition of the other natural properties, such as the uncreated and the created, the invisible and the visible, and so on. And besides, what will the will that is composed of the wills be called? For it is impossible for the compound to be given the name of the things of which it is composed, since in such a case we should call that which is composed of the natures a *nature* and not a *person*. And further, should we speak of one compound will in Christ, then we are making Him distinct from the Father in will, because the will of the Father is not compound. Accordingly, it remains for us to say that only the Person of Christ is compound, in so far as it is composed of His natures and his natural properties as well.

And, should we wish to speak literally, it would be impossible to speak of *opinion* (γνώμη) and choice in the Lord. For the opinion resulting from the inquiry and deliberation, or counsel and judgment, in respect to the unknown thing is a disposition toward the thing judged. After the opinion comes the choice which selects and chooses one thing rather than the other. Now, since the Lord was not a mere man, but was also God and knew all things, He stood in no need of reflection, inquiry, counsel, or judgment. He also had a natural affinity for good and antipathy for evil. Thus, it is in this sense that the Prophet Isaias, too, says: 'Before the child shall know to refuse the evil, he will choose the good. For before the child know to refuse the evil, and to choose the good, he will reject the evil by choosing the good.' The 'before' shows that he made no inquiry or investigation in a human manner, but that, since He was God and divinely subsisted in the flesh—that is to say, was hypostatically united to the flesh— by the fact of His very being and His knowing all things He naturally possessed the good. Now, the virtues are natural, and they are also naturally inherent in all men, even though all of us do not act naturally. For, because of the fall, we went from what is according to nature to what is against it. But the Lord brought us back from what is against nature to what is according to it—for this last is what is meant by 'according to his image and likeness.' Now, asceticism and the labors connected with it were not intended for the acquisition of virtue as of something to be introduced from the outside, but for the expulsion of evil, which has been introduced and is against nature—just as the steel's rust, which is not natural but due to neglect, we remove with hard toil to bring out the natural brightness of the steel.

Moreover, one must know that the word γνώμη, or opinion, is used in many ways and with many meanings. Thus, it sometimes means *advice,* as when the divine Apostle says: 'Now, concerning virgins, I have no commandment of the Lord: but I give counsel.' Sometimes it implies *design,* as when the Prophet David says: 'They have taken a malicious counsel against thy people.' Sometimes it means *judgment,* as when Daniel says: 'Why so cruel a sentence had gone forth.' And sometimes it is used in the sense of *faith,* or *notion,* or of *intent*—to put it simply, the word γνώμη has twenty-eight different meanings.

CHAPTER 15

Now, we also say that in our Lord Jesus Christ there are two operations. For, in so far as He was God and consubstantial with the Father, like the Father He had the divine operation; in so far as He was made man and consubstantial with us, He had the operation of the human nature.

However, one must know that operation is one thing, what is operative another, which is operated another, and still another the operator. *Operation,* then, is the efficacious and substantial motion of the nature. And that which is *operative* is the nature from which the operation proceeds. That which is *operated* is the effect of the operation. And the *operator* is the one who performs the operation; the person, that is. However, the term operation is also used for the effect, and the term for the effect for the operation, as 'creation' is used for 'creature.' For in that way we say 'all creation,' meaning 'all creatures.'

One must know that the operation is a motion and that it is operated rather than operating, as Gregory the Theologian says in his sermon on the Holy Ghost: 'But if He is an operation, then He will obviously be operated and will not operate. And, as soon as He has been effected, He will cease.'

It is further necessary to know that life itself is an operation, and the primary operation of the animal. So also is the whole vital process—the motions of nutrition and growth, or the vegetative; the impulsive, or the sensitive; and the intellectual and free motions. Operation, moreover, is the perfection of a potentiality. So, if we find all these things in Christ, then we shall declare that He also has a human operation.

The first thought ($\nu\acute{o}\eta\mu\alpha$) formed in us is called an operation. It is a simple unrelated operation by which the mind of itself secretly puts forth those thoughts of its own without which it could not rightly be called mind ($\nu o\hat{v}\varsigma$). And again, that is also called an operation which is the expression and explanation of what has been thought by means of speech utterance. This, however, is no longer unrelated and simple. On the contrary, since it is composed of thought and speech, it is found to be in a relation. And the very relation which the doer has to the thing done is also an operation. And the thing itself which is effected is called an operation. Now, the first of these belongs to the soul alone, the next to the soul as using the body, the next to the body as endowed with an intellectual soul, and the last of them is the effect. Thus, the mind first considers the thing to be done and then acts accordingly through the body. So, it is to the soul that the control belongs, since it uses the body as an instrument which it guides and directs. The operation of the body as guided and moved by the soul, however, is a different one. And as to the effect, while that of the body is, as it were, the touching, holding, and clasping of the thing made, that of the soul is the thing's formation and configuration. It was also the same with our Lord Jesus Christ. While the power of working miracles was an operation of His divinity, the work of His hands, His willing, and His saying: 'I will. Be thou made clean,' were operations belonging to His humanity. And as to the effect, the breaking of the loaves, the healing the leper, and the 'I will' belong to His human nature, whereas to His divine nature belong the multiplication of the loaves and the cleansing of the leper. Now, by both, that is, by the operation of the soul and that of the body, He showed His divine operation to be one and the same, akin and equal. And just as we know that the natures are united and mutually imma-nent and still do not deny their difference, but even number them, while we know them to be indivisible; so also do we know the connection of the wills and operations, while we recognize their difference and number them without introducing any division. For, as the flesh was made divine, yet suffered no change in its own nature, in the same way the will and operation were made divine, yet did not exceed their proper limits. For He is one who is both the one thing and the other and who wills and acts in both one way and the other, that is to say, both in a divine and in a human fashion.

Accordingly, because of the duality of His nature, it is necessary to affirm two operations in Christ. For things having diverse natures have different operations, and things having diverse operations have different natures. And conversely, things having the same nature have the same operation, and things hav-ing one operation have also one substance, as the inspired Fathers declare. Consequently, we must do one of two things: either we shall say that there is one operation in Christ and then say that

His substance is one; or, if we keep to the truth, we shall confess with the Gospels and the Fathers that there are two substances, and at the same time we shall be confessing that there are also two operations corresponding to these. For, since in His divinity He is consubstantial with God the Father, He will also be equal to Him in His operation. On the other hand, since in His humanity He is consubstantial with us, He will also be equal to us in His operation. Indeed, the blessed Gregory, who was Bishop of Nyssa, says: 'Things having one operation very definitely have the same potentiality. Moreover, it is impossible for there to be one nature, potentiality, or operation belonging both to an uncreated nature and to a created one. And, were we to say that Christ has one nature, we should be attributing the passions of the intellectual soul to the divinity of the Word—fear, I mean, and grief, and anguish.

However, should they say that in discussing the Blessed Trinity the holy Fathers said: 'Things having one substance also have one operation, and things which have different substances also have different operations,' and that one must not transfer to the human nature what belongs to the divine, we shall reply as follows. If this was said by the Fathers in respect to the divinity only, then the Son does not have the same operation as the Father and He is not even of the same substance. And, what is more, to whom shall we attribute the words: 'My Father worketh until now, and I work'; and 'What things soever he seeth the Father doing, these things the Son also doth in like manner'; and 'If you do not believe me, believe my works'; and 'The works which I do give testimony of me'; and 'As the Father raiseth up the dead and giveth life: so the Son also giveth life to whom He will'? For all these show that even after the Incarnation He is not only consubstantial with the Father but also has the same operation.

And again, if the providence exercised over creatures belongs not only to the Father and the Holy Ghost, but also to the Son even after the Incarnation, and if this is an operation, then even after the Incarnation He has the same operation as the Father.

And if from His miracles we perceive Christ to be of the same substance as the Father, and if miracles are an operation of God, then even after the Incarnation He has the same operation as the Father.

And if His divinity and His flesh have one operation, it will be composite, and either He will have a different operation from that of the Father, or the Father's operation will be composite, too. But, if the Father's operation is composite, it is obvious that His nature will be, too.

And, if they were to say that the introduction of the operation requires that of a person along with it, we should reply that, if the introduction of the operation requires that of a person along with it, then by logical conversion the introduction of the person will require that of an operation along with it. In such a case, since there are three Persons, or hypostases, in the Holy Trinity, there will also be three operations; or, since there is one operation, there will also be one Person and one hypostasis. But the holy Fathers were all agreed in declaring that things having the same substance also have the same operation.

What is more, if the introduction of the operation requires that of a person, then those who decreed that neither one nor two operations be affirmed in Christ in doing so ordered that neither one nor two persons be affirmed in Him.

And then, just as the natures of both the fire and the steel are preserved intact in the red-hot knife, so also are there two operations and their effects. For, while the steel has its cutting power, the fire has its power of burning; and the cut is the effect of the operation of the steel, while the burn is that of the operation of the fire. And the distinction between these is preserved in the burnt cut and the cut burn, even though the burning of the cut does not take place separately after the union, and the cut is not made separately from the burn. Neither do we say that because of the twofold natural operation there are two red-hot knives, nor do we destroy their substantial difference because of the singleness of the red-hot knife. In just the same way there is in Christ both the divine and all-powerful operation of His divinity, and that after our own fashion, which is that of His humanity. Thus, the child's being taken by the hand and drawn up was an effect of His human operation whereas her being restored to life was an effect of His divine operation. For the latter is one thing and the former another, even though they are inseparable in the theandric operation. What is more, if, because the Person of the Lord is one, His operation must also be one, then because of the one Person there must also be one substance.

Again, if we were to affirm one operation in the Lord, we should be saying that this was either divine or human or neither. Now, if we say that it is divine, we shall be saying that He is only God and devoid of our humanity. And if we say that it is human, we shall be uttering the blasphemy that He is mere man. But, if we say that it is neither divine nor human, we shall be saying that He is neither consubstantial with the Father nor with us. For the identity of person came from the union, without in any way destroying the difference of the natures. And, if the difference of the natures is kept intact, their operation will plainly be kept so, also, because there is no nature without any operation.

If the operation of the Lord Christ is one, then it will be either created or uncreated; for, just as there is no intermediate nature between the created and the uncreated, neither is there any such operation. Therefore, if it is created, it will show only a created nature; if it is uncreated, it will indicate an uncreated substance only. This is because the natural properties must correspond with the natures absolutely, since the existence of a defective nature is impossible. The natural operation, moreover, does not come from anything outside the nature and it is obvious that the nature can neither exist nor be known without its natural operation. For, by remaining invariable in its operations, each thing gives proof of its own nature.

If Christ's operation is one, then the same operation can do divine and human things. But, no being acting according to nature can do things which are contrary. Thus, fire does not make hot and cold, nor does water make wet and dry. How, then, did He, who is God by nature and who became man by nature, both work the miracles and experience the passions with one operation?

Now, if Christ assumed a human mind, that is to say, a rational and intellectual soul, He certainly thinks and will always think. But, thinking is an operation of the mind. Therefore, Christ acts as a man also and will always so act.

St. John Damascene

The most wise and great St. John Chrysostom in the second homily of his commentary on the Acts says this: 'No one should be wrong in calling His suffering an action. For by suffering all things He did that great and wonderful work of destroying death and working all the rest.'

If every operation is defined as a substantial motion of some nature, as those who are well versed in these matters have clearly laid down, where has anyone seen a nature without a motion or without any operation at all, or where has anyone found an operation which is not a motion of a natural power? And, according to the blessed Cyril, no one in his right mind would hold the natural operation of God and of a creature to be one. It is not the human nature that restores Lazarus to life, nor is it the power of the divinity that sheds tears. For tears are peculiar to humanity, whereas life belongs to the Subsistent Life. Nevertheless, by reason of the identity of the person each one of these actions is common to both natures. For Christ is one, and one is His Person, or hypostasis. Nevertheless, He has two natures: that of His divinity and that of His humanity. Consequently, the glory which proceeds naturally from the divinity became common to both by reason of the identity of person, while the humble things proceeding from the flesh became common to both. For He is one and the same who is both the one thing and the other, that is, both God and man; and to the same one belong both what is proper to the divinity and what is proper to the humanity. Thus, while the divinity worked the miracles but not separately from the flesh, the flesh did the humble things but not apart from the divinity. Thus, also while remaining impassible, the divinity was joined to the suffering flesh and made the sufferings salutary. And the sacred mind was joined to the acting divinity of the Word and thought and knew the things which were being done.

Therefore, the divinity communicates its excellences to the flesh while remaining with no part of the sufferings of the flesh. For His flesh did not suffer through the divinity in the same way that the divinity acted through the flesh, because the flesh served as an instrument of the divinity. So, even though from the first instant of conception there was no divisions whatsoever of either form, but all the actions of each form at all times belonged to one Person, we nevertheless in no way confuse these things which were done inseparably. On the contrary, from the nature of the works we perceive to which form they belong.

And so, Christ acts through each of His natures and in Him each nature acts in communion with the other. The Word does whatever pertains to the kingdom and the principality, which is what belongs to Him by reason of the authority and the power of His divinity, while the body in accordance with the intent of the Word united to it does what has also become proper to it. Now, the body of itself had no inclination for physical suffering, nor yet did it avoid and refuse to accept what was painful. Neither was it affected by external influences; rather, it was moved in accordance with the order of its nature, with the Word wisely willing and permitting it to suffer and do what was proper to it, so that through its works the truth of its nature might be guaranteed.

Moreover, even as He was conceived of a virgin and put on substance in a way that transcended substance, so does He also do human things in a way that transcends the human—as when He walked with His earthly feet upon unstable water which had not become earth but by the supernatural power of His divinity was made firm and did not yield to the weight of material feet. He did not do human things in a human way, because He was not only man, but God, also, which is the reason why His sufferings were life-giving and saving. Neither did He do divine things in a divine way, because He was not only God, but man, also, which is the reason why He worked miracles by touch and word and other such things.

And should someone say that we do not hold one operation in Christ because we do away with the human operation, but because the human operation as contrasted with the divine is called passion, and in this sense we say that there is one operation in Christ—should they say this: We shall reply that by this token they who hold one nature do not do so in the sense of doing away with the human nature, but because the human nature as contrasted with the divine is called passible. God forbid that we should call the human motion passion just because of its contrast with the divine operation. For, generally speaking, nothing is known or defined as having its real existence from

304

contrast or comparison. In such a case, things which exist would be found to be mutually causative of each other. Thus if, because the divine motion is action, the human is passion, then it will definitely follow that, because the divine nature is good, the human will be evil. Conversely, because the human motion is called action; and because human nature is evil, the divine will be good. What is more, all creatures will thus be evil, and he will be a liar who said: 'And God saw all the things that he had made, and they were very good.'

Now we say that the holy Fathers gave the human motion a variety of names, depending upon the fundamental concept in question. Thus, they called it both power, operation, difference, movement, property, quality, and passion. And they did not do this by way of contrast to the divine motion. On the contrary, they called it *power,* in so far as it is sustaining and unchangeable; *operation,* as being distinctive and showing the invariability in all things of the same species; *difference,* as being defining; *motion,* as being indicative; *property,* as being component and as belonging to this alone and not to some other; *quality,* as being specific; and *passion,* as being moved. For all things which are from God and after Him are subject to being moved, since they are not motion or force itself. Consequently, it was not so named by contrast, as has been said, but after the principle that was put in it at its creation by the cause which framed the universe. For this reason, it was called operation, even when mentioned together with the divine motion. For what else did he do, who said: 'For each form acts in communion with the other,' than he who said: 'And he had fasted forty days and forty nights, afterwards he was hungry'—for, when He wished, He permitted His nature to do what was proper to it? Or what else did he do than those who said that there was a different operation in Him, or a twofold operation, or one and another? For by the opposition of terms these expressions signify two natures, since the number is oftentimes indicated by the opposition of terms, just as well as it is by saying 'divine and human.' Thus, the difference is a difference of things which differ. And how can things differ which do not exist?

CHAPTER 16

Since each individual man is made up of two natures—that of the soul and that of the body—and has these unchanged in himself, it will be reasonable to say that he has two natures. For even after the union he retains the natural property of each. Thus, the body is not immortal but corruptible, and the soul is not mortal but immortal. Neither is the body invisible, nor is the soul visible to bodily eyes. On the contrary, the latter is rational and understanding and incorporeal, whereas the former is material and visible and irrational. Moreover, things which are distinct in substance do not have the same nature; consequently, the soul and the body are not of the same substance.

And again, if man is a rational mortal animal, and if every definition designates the natures defined, and if, furthermore, that which is rational is not the same as that which is mortal as respects the concept of nature, then by the norm of his own definition man will not have one nature.

Now, should man at times be said to have one nature, the term 'nature' is being taken in the sense of 'species.' Thus, we say that one man does not differ from another by any difference in nature, because, to the contrary, all men fall under the same definition, in so far as they all are composed of body and soul and have the same makeup, each individual being two constituent natures. And this is not unreasonable, because the divine Athanasius in his discourse against the blasphemers of the Holy Ghost said that all created things have the same nature, when he wrote to the effect that the Holy Ghost is over and above creation and that it is possible to see clearly that, while in relation to the nature of created things He is something else, to the divinity He is proper. Everything that is found to be common to several things without being more in one and less in another is said to be essence. Therefore, since every man is made up of a soul and a body, in this sense men are said to have one nature. As regards the Person of the Lord, however, we cannot speak of one nature, because even after the union each nature retains its natural property and it is not possible to find a species of Christs. For there has been no other Christ made of divinity and humanity, the same being both God and man.

And again, the specific unity of man is not the same thing as the substantial unity of soul and body. For the specific unity of man shows the invariable element in all men, whereas the substantial unity of soul and body destroys their very being and reduces them to absolute non-existence. For either the one will be transformed into the substance of the other, or from two different things a third will be made, or they will remain within their proper limits and be two natures. For it is not by reason of its substance that the body is identical with that which is incorporeal. Consequently, when people speak of one nature in man, not on account of the identity of the substantial quality of the body with that of the soul, but on account of the invariability of the individuals falling under the species, they do not also have to say that in Christ, in whom there is no species comprising several persons, there is one nature.

And further, every composite is said to be composed of those things which have been put together directly. Thus, we do not say that the house is composed of earth and water, but of bricks and wood. Otherwise, we should also have to say that man is made up of five natures at least, of the four elements, that is, and of a soul. So also, in the case of our Lord Jesus Christ we do not consider the part or parts, but those which have been put together directly—the divinity and the humanity.

Further, if by saying that man is two natures we shall be forced to say that there are three natures in Christ, then you, too, by saying that man is of two natures will be teaching that Christ is of three natures. And it will be the same way with the operations, because the operation must correspond with the nature. Witness to the fact that man is said to and does have two natures in Gregory the Theologian, who says: 'God and man are two natures, as, indeed, are soul and body.' Also, in his sermon on baptism he says as follows: 'Since we are twofold, being of soul and body—of the visible and of the invisible nature—so also is the purification twofold: by water and by the Holy Ghost.'

CHAPTER 17

One should know that it is not by a transformation of nature or by change or alteration or mingling that the Lord's flesh is said to have been deified and made identical with God and

God, as Gregory the Theologian says: 'The one of whom did deify, while the other was made divine and, I may confidently say, identical with God. And that which anointed became man, and that which was anointed became God.' This was by no transformation of nature but by the union through dispensation, the hypostatic union, I mean, by which the flesh is inseparably united to God, the Word, and by the mutual indwelling of the natures such as that we also speak of in the case of the heating of the steel. For, just as we confess that the Incarnation was brought about without transformation or change, so also do we hold that the deification of the flesh was brought about. For the Word neither overstepped the bounds of His own divinity nor the divine prerogatives belonging to it just because He was made flesh; and when the flesh was made divine, it certainly did not change its own nature or its natural properties. For even after the union the natures remained unmingled and their properties unimpaired. Moreover, by reason of its most unalloyed union with the Word, that is to say, the hypostatic union, the Lord's flesh was enriched with the divine operations but in no way suffered any impairment of its natural properties. For not by its own operation does the flesh do divine works, but by the Word united to it, and through it the Word shows His own operation. Thus, the steel which has been heated burns, not because it has a naturally acquired power of burning, but because it has acquired it from its union with the fire.

And so the same flesh was mortal in itself and life-giving by its hypostatic union with the Word. Likewise, we say that the deification of the will was not by a transformation of its natural motion, but by its becoming united with His divine and almighty will and being the will of God made man. It was for this reason that, when He wished to be hid, He could not of Himself, because it pleased God the Word that it be shown that in Himself He had the weakness of the human will. However, it was by willing that He worked the cure of the leper, and this because of the union with the divine will.

One must furthermore know that the deification of the nature and the will is very expressive and indicative of the two natures and the two wills. For, just as heating does not transform the nature of the thing heated into that of fire, but, rather, brings out both the thing heated and the thing heating and shows not one thing but two, so neither does the deification produce one compound nature, but, rather, the two natures and their hypostatic union. In fact, Gregory the Theologian says: 'The one of whom did deify, while the other was made divine,' where by saying 'of whom' and 'the one' and 'the other' he showed that there were two.

St. Anselm of Canterbury

1033-1109

The Middle Ages witnessed the emerging of a new kind of theology in the West as a result of the development of the "scholastic method" in the 11th and 12th centuries. It was an attempt to achieve a rational and systematic formulation of the truths of Christian faith, using Aristotle's logic so that questions were placed in a dialectical manner. This resulted in a significant change of style from the "monastic theology" that looked more to Scripture and liturgy than to logic.

Anselm, the "Father of Scholasticism," was born in Aosta, but went to France for his education after his mother died. In 1060 he entered the new abbey of Bec in Normandy, succeeded Lanfranc as prior three years later, and was elected abbot in 1078. In 1093 he was once again called upon to succeed Lanfranc, this time as Archbishop of Canterbury. The remainder of his public life was made miserable by the insoluble conflict first with King William Rufus, then with King Henry I, over the appropriate extent of authority of state over church and of church over state.

Anselm completed his classic masterpiece Why God Became Man *during the summer of 1098 in a mountain village in Italy before he went on to the Council of Bari. He had certainly been working on it for the previous few years. It is written in the form of a dialogue between himself and his friend, Dom Boso who was the principal instigator in getting Anselm to write the book. The best description of its contents is given by Anselm himself in the preface: "I have divided it into two short books. The first of these contains the objections of the unbelievers who reject the Christian faith because they consider it opposed to reason, together with the answers of believers. Later on, leaving Christ aside, as if nothing had ever been known of Him, proof is given by necessary reasons that it is impossible for any person to be saved without Him. In the second book, likewise, as if nothing were known about Christ, it is shown with no less evident argument and truth, that human nature was created for the very purpose that finally the whole person, that is, body and soul, should enjoy a blissful immortality. Proof is given also that it is necessary that man achieve the purpose of his creation— but that it could occur only through a Man-God; and besides, that all that we believe about Christ must of necessity occur." The following selection consists of Book One with all 25 of its chapters.*

As will be evident from the above quote, Anselm places an extremely high value on reason in the realm of faith. He has been accused of rationalism and of compromising God's freedom. In response his defenders have understood him in quite different ways (e.g., Karl Barth and Etienne Gilson, in our own century). All agree that there is a danger of rationalism present in his formulas and that later representatives did not always avoid the pitfalls. But there is no denying that we are here in the presence of a powerful new movement intent upon probing ever more deeply into the mystery of God revealed in Christ. The value and validity of this effort was best demonstrated by the resulting life-style of Anselm.

WHY GOD BECAME MAN

BOOK ONE

CHAPTER ONE

THE QUESTION ON WHICH THE WHOLE WORK DEPENDS.

F requently and most earnestly I have been requested by many persons, both by word of mouth and by letter, to commit to writing for posterity, the proofs I usually give as answers to inquirers, regarding a certain special question of our faith. They say that these arguments appeal to them and they think them adequate. They make this request, not to attain to faith by way of reason, but to find delight in the understanding and contemplation of what they already believe; and also to be, so far as possible, *ready always to satisfy everyone that asks* them *a reason of that hope which is in* us. This is a question regularly thrown at us by unbelievers who deride Christian simplicity as absurd, and it preoccupies the minds of many of the faithful. The question is: for what reason or by what necessity did God become man, and by His death, as we believe and acknowledge, restore life to the world, although He could have accomplished this by means of another person, whether angelic or human, or simply by an act of His will? Not only the learned but also many of the unlearned raise this question and want it answered. Many people, therefore, ask to have this matter treated, and although the investigation seems very difficult, the solution is nevertheless intelligible to all, and attractive because of the utility and beauty of the argument. So, although what has been said by the holy Fathers ought still to be enough, nevertheless I shall make an effort to show the inquirers what God will condescend to make clear to me on this subject. And since those matters which are studied in the style of question and answer are more intelligible and therefore more pleasing to many minds, especially to those who are slower to apprehend, I shall take as a disputant with me one of those persons who earnestly make inquiries about this matter—the one who urges me more insistently than the others to discuss it—so that Boso puts a question and Anselm answers, in the following manner.

Boso: As right order requires that we believe the profound truths of the Christian faith before we presume to analyze them by reason, so it would seem to me a matter of negligence if after we have been confirmed in the faith, we make no effort to understand what we believe. Therefore, since I think that by the prevenient grace of God, I have such firm faith in our redemption that even if I could not rationally grasp what I believe, there would still be nothing that could uproot the constancy of my faith, I beg of you to make clear to me what, as you know, many are asking about, as well as myself. That is, of course, by what necessity and for what reason God, although He is almighty, took on the lowliness and weakness of human nature, to restore it?

Anselm: What you ask of me is above me, and I fear to treat things too high for me, for fear that, should anyone think or even see that I do not give him satisfaction, he might judge that I do not have the true doctrine, rather than that my intellect is not capable of understanding it.

Boso: You should not fear that so much. Rather recall that when we talk over some question it often happens that God makes clear what was obscure before. You should expect from the grace of God that if you generously give of what you have freely received, you will merit to receive higher things to which you have not yet attained.

Anselm: There is still another reason why I think it is totally impossible or barely possible for us to treat fully of this subject at the present time. The reason is that we would have to know about power and necessity and will and certain other subjects which are so interrelated that none of them can be considered fully without the others. A discussion of them, then, would require a treatise by itself, and that would be, in my opinion, not very easy, yet not wholly useless. For ignorance of these things makes certain topics difficult, which become easy when these things are understood.

St. Anselm of Canterbury

Boso: You could speak briefly of these things, each in its relevant context, so that we may know enough to complete the present treatise, and put off to another time what remains to be said.

Anselm: There is another weighty reason for my holding back from what you ask, and it is this: that the subject matter is not only important but, as it is concerned with Him who is, in appearance, *beautiful above the sons of men,* so it is also imposing in intelligibility beyond human understanding. Hence, as I generally become indignant at debased artists when I see the Lord Himself depicted with an ugly figure, I am equally afraid that the same thing may happen to me, if I dare to write on so beautiful a theme in a rough and vulgar style.

Boso: Even this should not deter you. For, as you let anyone express himself better than you, if he can, so you do not dictate that anyone who is not satisfied with your style should not write more beautifully. Anyway, to put an end to all your excuses—what I am asking for, you will be doing not for the learned, but for me and those with me who are making the same request.

CHAPTER TWO

How the things to be said are to be understood.

Anselm: Seeing your insistence and that of those who join you in this request, out of love and zeal for religion, I shall try to the best of my ability—with the help of God and your prayers, which, while making this request, you have often promised me when I asked for them—not so much to show you what you are looking for, as to look for it with you. I would like you to agree, however, to accept all my statements this way: if I should say anything which a greater authority does not confirm—even though I seem to prove it by reason—it is not to be accepted as any more settled than that I think it probable, until God in some way manifests it to me with greater clarity. But if I am able to answer your question with satisfaction up to some extent, it must be beyond all doubt that someone wiser than I will be able to give more complete satisfaction. Indeed, we must acknowledge that however far human statement can go, the more profound explanation of so great a subject remains still hidden.

CHAPTER THREE

Objections of unbelievers and answers of believers.

Boso: Permit me, then, to use the words of unbelievers. For when we strive to find out the reason for our faith, it is only fair to pose the objections of those who are absolutely unwilling to approach that faith without rational arguments. Although they, of course, seek arguments of reason just because they do not believe, while we seek them because we do believe, what we both are seeking is, nevertheless, one and the same. And if you should make any response which sacred authority seems to oppose, let me bring forth that authority until you show me clearly that there is no opposition.

Anselm: Say what you think.

Boso: Unbelievers, ridiculing our simplicity, accuse us of offending and dishonoring God when we assert that He had descended into the womb of a woman, was born of a female body, that He grew up, nourished by milk and human foods, and—not to mention many other things which do not seem fitting for God—that He endured fatigue, hunger, thirst, scourging and crucifixion and death between thieves.

Anselm: We give no offence or dishonor to God, but, giving wholehearted thanks, we praise and proclaim that inexpressible depth of His mercy. For the more marvelous and unexpected is the manner in which He restored us from such great and such deserved evils that had befallen us, to such great and undeserved favors that we had lost, so much the greater are the love and compassion He has shown toward us. If, then, they would carefully consider how fittingly the restoration of man was procured in this way, they would not ridicule our simplicity, but would join us in praising the wisdom and generosity of God. It was fitting, surely, that just as death had entered into the human race because of the disobedience of man, so by the obedience of man, life should be restored. Further, just as the sin that was the cause of our condemnation had its origin in a woman, it was equally fitting that the author of our justification and salvation should be born of a woman. It was also fitting that the devil, who conquered man by tempting him to taste of the fruit of a tree, should be conquered by a man through suffering he endured on the wood of a tree. There are also many other things which, carefully considered, show a certain indescribable beauty in this manner of accomplishing our redemption.

CHAPTER FOUR

These answers may seem unconvincing to unbelievers, and to be like so many pictures.

Boso: All these statements must be accepted as beautiful and like so many pictures. But if there is no solid foundation for them, unbelievers do not think them adequate to show why we ought to believe that God was willing to suffer what we described. Anyone who wants to produce a picture chooses something solid to paint on, so that his painting will last. No one, surely, paints upon water or air, because no traces of the picture would stay there. Hence, when we present to unbelievers these reasons of fitness which you propose as so many pictures of a real event, since they think that what we believe in is not a historical fact but a fiction, they criticize us, so to speak, for painting upon a cloud. Therefore, we must first show the rational soundness of the truth, that is, the necessity of the inference that God should and could abase Himself to the extent that we proclaim. Then, so that the very body of truth, so to speak, may shine more brightly, those reasons of fitness are to be put on view, like pictures of the body.

Anselm: Do you not think this is a sufficiently necessary reason why God should have done what we described: that the human race, that so precious product of His hand, had been totally lost, and that it was not fitting that all that God had planned for man should come to nothing, and that this plan could not be realized unless the human race were liberated by its Creator Himself?

CHAPTER FIVE

The redemption of man could not be brought about by anyone but a Divine Person.

Boso: If you were to say that, in some way or other, this liberation could have been brought about by someone else than a Divine Person, whether by an angel or by a man, the human mind would have accepted this with far less reluctance. It was possible for God, surely, to create some man free of sin, not out of the sinful mass, nor generated by another human being, but as he made Adam; and by this man, it seems, this task could have been accomplished.

Anselm: Do you not understand that, if any other person had redeemed man from eternal death, man would justly be considered his servant? But if that were so, man would not at all have been restored to that dignity he would have had if he had not sinned. For he who was to be the servant of God alone and equal in all things to the good angels would be the servant of one who is not God and whom the angels do not serve.

CHAPTER SIX

How unbelievers criticize our statements that God redeemed us by His death and thus showed His love for us and that He came to conquer the devil for us.

Boso: What they especially wonder at is that we call this liberation "redemption." For in what captivity—they say to us—or in what prison, or in whose power were you held, from which God could not free you, without redeeming you by such great efforts and finally, by his own blood? Suppose we say to them: He redeemed us from sins and from His own wrath and from hell, and from the power of the devil whom He Himself came to conquer for us, since we could not conquer him ourselves; and He bought back for us the kingdom of heaven; and because He has done all these things in this manner, He showed how much He loved us. Then they will retort: If you say that God could not accomplish all this by a simple command, yet say that He created all things by a command, you contradict yourselves, because you make Him powerless. If, on the other hand, you admit that He could have saved man in some other way, but did not wish to, how can you vindicate His wisdom—since you are asserting that He willed to suffer such unbecoming things without any reason? For all these reasons you adduce are dependent on His will. The wrath of God, for example, is nothing but His will to punish. If, then, He does not choose to punish the sins of men, man is free from sins and also from the wrath of God, and from hell and from the power of the devil—all of which he suffers on account of sins—and he regains what he was deprived of because of those very sins. Under whose power is hell, or the devil, or whose is the kingdom of heaven, but His who created everything? Everything you fear or desire, then, is subject to His will, and nothing can resist that will. Hence, if He was unwilling to save the human race except in the way you describe, when He could have done it simply by His will, see—to put it quite mildly—how you depreciate His wisdom. Surely, if a man should, without any reason, do at a cost of greater labor what he could have done easily, no one would consider him wise. As for your statement that God showed in this way how much He loved you, it is rationally indefensible, certainly, unless you prove that He could not have saved man in any other way. Admittedly, if He could not have done it in another way, then perhaps it would have been necessary to show His love in this way. Now, however, since He could have saved man in another way, what reason is there for His doing and undergoing what you describe, to show His love? Does He not show the good angels how much He loves them, without undergoing such things for them? As for your assertion that He came to conquer the devil for you, in what sense do you dare to propose that? Does not the omnipotence of God have sway everywhere? How, then, did God need to descend from heaven, to conquer the devil?—These are the objections unbelievers seem to be able to make against us.

CHAPTER SEVEN

The devil had no justice on his side in opposing man. Why he seems to have had it. Why God should free man in this way.

Boso: We usually say, moreover, that to set man free, God must have acted against the devil more through justice than through fortitude. It would follow that when the devil slew Him who was God, and in whom there was no reason for death, it was through justice that he lost the power he had over sinners. Otherwise God would have inflicted unjust violence on him, since the devil was rightfully in possession of man, for the devil had not dragged man by violence, but man had willingly delivered himself to him. Now, I do not see what value this argument has. Of course, if the devil, or man, belonged to himself or to any other being but God, or remained under any other power than God's, perhaps it would be right to say that. Since the devil, however, or man, belongs to no one but God, and neither one is exempt from the power of God, what case did God have to plead with someone who belonged to Him, regarding another who belonged to Him, in a matter which concerned Himself, except to punish His servant, who, with what he had stolen from his master, had persuaded his fellow servant to desert their common master and go over to his own side, and being a traitor, had received him as a fugitive, and being a thief had received him as a thief? Each one, surely, was a thief, since one persuaded the other to steal himself from his master. What, indeed, would be more just than for God to do this? Or if God, the judge of all, had liberated man, thus possessed, from the power of the one who so unjustly possessed him—either to punish him in another way than by the devil, or to spare him— what injustice would there have been? For although it was just that man be tormented by the devil, yet the devil was unjust in tormenting him. Man, indeed, had deserved punishment, and by no one more fittingly than by the one to whom he gave his consent to commit sin. The devil, though, had deserved no right to inflict the punishment; on the contrary, his action was all the more unjust in that he was not motivated by love of justice, but was driven by an impulse of malice. For he did not do this at the command of God, but by permission of God's incomprehensible wisdom, by which He disposes even evil things toward good.

I believe, moreover, that those who think the devil has some right in justice to hold man in possession, come to this

conclusion because they see that it is just for man to be subjected to abuse by the devil, and that it is just for God to permit
this, and consequently they think it is just for the devil to
inflict it. Sometimes, you know, one and the same thing is just
and unjust, when considered from different points of view, and
for this reason it is judged entirely just or entirely unjust by
those who do not view the matter carefully. It may happen, for
example, that someone unjustly strikes an innocent person, so
that he justly deserves to be struck himself. If, however, the one
who has been struck ought not to avenge himself, yet strikes
the person who has struck him, he acts unjustly. This assault,
therefore, is unjust for the one who strikes the blow, because he
should not avenge himself; but from the standpoint of the one
who receives the blow, it is just, because, for unfairly striking
someone, he has deserved in justice to be struck back. The same
action, then, is just and unjust, from different points of view,
and it can happen that one person will judge the action simply
right and another will judge it simply wrong. In this sense,
therefore, we say it is just for the devil to molest man, because
it is just for God to permit this, and it is just that man suffers
it. But when we say it is just that man suffers, we mean that
he suffers justly, not by reason of any justice proper to himself,
but because he is punished by the just verdict of God.

Suppose, now, someone cites that *handwriting of the
decree* which the Apostle says *was against us* and was blotted
out by the death of Christ. Someone may think this means
that the devil, as if under some sort of signed contract, justly
exacted sin of man, before the passion of Christ, as a sort of
interest on the first sin which he persuaded man to commit and
as a penalty for sin, so that thereby he would seem to prove his
just rights over man. I cannot at all agree with this interpretation. That handwriting, surely, is not the devil's, for it is called
the handwriting of the decree. Now, that decree was not the
devil's, but God's. For it was decreed by a just judgment of God
and confirmed as it were, by a signed document, that man who
had freely sinned could not, by himself, avoid either sin or the
punishment for sin. For he is a *wind that goeth and returneth
not.* Besides, *whosoever committeth sin is the servant of sin* and
whoever sins should not be let go without punishment, unless

mercy spares the sinner and liberates and restores him. There-fore, we should not think that this *handwriting* indicates any possible justice on the devil's part, when he harms man.

Finally, just as there is no injustice at all in a good angel, so in an evil angel there is absolutely no justice. Hence there was nothing in the devil to prevent God from using His power against him to liberate man.

CHAPTER EIGHT

Although the humiliations we attribute to Christ do not affect His divinity, nevertheless unbelievers think it unfitting that they be attributed to Him as man. The reasons why they think this man did not die voluntarily.

Anselm: The will of God must be enough of a reason for us, when He does something, even though we do not see why He wills it. For the will of God is never unreasonable.

Boso: That is true, if it is evident that God wills the thing in question. But many people refuse to admit that God wills something, if it seems to be opposed to reason.

Anselm: What do you think is opposed to reason, when we say that God has willed whatever we believe about His incar-nation?

Boso: To put it briefly: that the Most High is brought down to such an abyss; that the Almighty does something with such great effort.

Anselm: Those who talk like that do not understand our beliefs. We do, beyond doubt, assert that the divine nature is incapable of suffering and absolutely incapable of being brought down from its eminence, and it does not expend effort in doing what it wills to do. But we say that the Lord Jesus Christ is true God and true man, one person in two natures and two natures in one person. Therefore, when we say God is subjected to some abasement or weakness, we do not understand this with regard to the sublimity of His impassible nature, but with regard to the weakness of the human substance He bore. So it is evident there is no rational objection to our faith. For we are not attributing any abasement to the divine substance, but we are showing that the God-Man is one person. Hence in the incarnation of God there is no thought of any abasement of God, but we believe in the exaltation of the nature of man.

Boso: All right; let us not attribute to the divine nature anything said of Christ that implies human weakness. But how will you ever prove that it is just and reasonable for God to treat, or allow to be treated in such a way, that man whom the Father called His *beloved Son,* in whom He was *well-pleased,* and with whom the Son identified Himself? What sort of justice is it to hand over to death the most virtuous man of all, in place of a sinner? What man would not be judged deserving of condemnation if he condemned the innocent to free the guilty? It looks, then, as if the whole thing leads to the same incongruity that we spoke of before. I mean: if He could not save sinners any other way than by condemning the just, where is His omnipotence? If He could, but would not, how shall we defend His wisdom and His justice?

Anselm: God the Father did not treat that man in the way you seem to think, nor did He hand over the innocent to death in place of the guilty. For God did not compel Him to die, or allow Him to be slain, against His will; rather, He Himself, by his own free choice, underwent death, to save men.

Boso: Even if He was not unwilling, since He consented to the Father's will, still it does seem, in a way, that the Father did compel Him by giving Him a command. For it is recorded that Christ *humbled Himself, becoming obedient* to the Father, *unto death, even to the death of the cross, for which cause God also hath exalted Him,* and that *He learned obedience by the things which He suffered* and that *the Father spared not even His own Son, but delivered Him up for us all.* And the Son Himself says: *I came down, not to do mine own will, but the will of Him that sent me.* And when about to go to His passion, He says: *As the Father hath given me commandments, so do I.* Likewise: *The chalice which my Father hath given me, shall I not drink it?* And in another place: *Father, if it be possible, let this chalice pass from me. Nevertheless, not as I will, but as Thou wilt.* Again: *Father, if this chalice may not pass away but I must drink it, Thy will be done.* In all these texts, the impression is given that Christ bore death by the compulsion of obedience rather than by the choice of His own free will.

CHAPTER NINE

*He died voluntarily. The meaning of: "He became obedi-
ent unto death" and "for which cause God also hath exalted
Him," and "I came . . . not to do my own will," as well as:
"God spared not His own Son," and "Not as I will but as thou
wilt."*

Anselm: As I see it, you fail to distinguish between His
doing something under the requirement of obedience, and His
enduring what happened to Him, without obedience requiring
it, because He persevered in obedience.

Boso: I need a clearer explanation of that.

Anselm: Why did the Jews persecute Him to the point
of death?

Boso: Simply because He was unswervingly devoted to
truth and justice in His life and in His speech.

Anselm: This, I believe, is what God requires of every
rational creature, and what this creature owes to God under
obedience.

Boso: We have to admit that.

Anselm: Therefore that man owed this obedience to God
the Father and His humanity owed it to His divinity, and the
Father required it of Him.

Boso: No doubt about that.

Anselm: Here you have something He did under the
requirement of obedience.

Boso: Right! And now I am beginning to see what he endured as imposed upon Him, because he persevered in obedience. Death, surely, was imposed upon Him, because he stood
firm in obedience, and He endured death. But how obedience
did not require this, I do not understand.

Anselm: If man had never sinned, would he have had to
suffer death, or should God have required this of him?

Boso: According to our faith, man would not have died,
and this would not have been exacted of him. But I would like
you to tell me the reason for this.

Anselm: You do not deny that the rational creature was
created in a state of justice, and for the purpose of being happy
in the enjoyment of God.

Boso: No.

Anselm: Now you will never think it fitting for God to compel a creature to be wretched, through no fault of his own, after He created him just and destined for happiness. And surely, it would be wretched for man to have to die, contrary to his desire.

Boso: It is obvious that if man had not sinned, God should not have required him to die.

Anselm: Therefore, God did not compel Christ to die, there being no sin in Him. But Christ freely endured death, not by giving up His life out of obedience, but by obeying a command to preserve justice, in which He persevered so unwaveringly that He incurred death as a result.

It can even be said that the Father commanded Him to die, when He commanded that on account of which He met His death. In this sense, then, He did just as the Father commanded Him and He drank the chalice which the Father gave, *and He became obedient* to the Father *unto death,* and thus *He learned obedience by the things which He suffered,* that is, to what extent obedience must be observed. Now, the expression "He learned" that is used here can be interpreted in two ways. "He learned" means either that "He made others learn," or that He learned by experience what He was not unaware of through infused knowledge. When the Apostle said *He humbled Himself, becoming obedient unto death, even to the death of the cross,* he added: *for which cause God also hath exalted Him, and hath given Him a name which is above all names.* Similar to this is what David said: *He drinks of the torrent in the way, therefore He lifts up his head.* These expressions do not mean that He absolutely could not arrive at this exaltation but by this obedience unto death, and that this exaltation was given only in reward for this obedience. For before He suffered He said that *all things* were *delivered* to Him by the Father and that everything belonging to the Father was His. The meaning rather is that the Son, together with the Father and the Holy Spirit, had determined that He would manifest to the world the height of His omnipotence, in no other way than by death. Surely, since it was determined that this occur only by that death, and since it actually occurred by that death, it is not incorrect to say that it occurs "on account of" it.

For if we intend to do something, but decide to do something else first, by means of which our intended goal may be achieved, then, if our goal is achieved after we have done what we wished to do first, it is correct to say that the intended action occurred precisely *because* that other action occurred which caused a delay in achieving our goal; and the reason is that it was decided that the intended action occur only by means of the other. Suppose, for example, I can cross a river either by horseback or by boat, and I decide to cross it only by boat, and then I defer making the crossing because there is no boat handy. Then, when a boat is available, and I make the crossing, it is correct to say of me: the boat was ready, therefore he went across. Further, we speak in this way when we have decided to do something else not only *by means of* that which we wish to precede, but also when it is not *by means of* it, but only *after* it. If, for instance, someone postpones eating because he has not yet been present at the celebration of Mass on that day, then when he has finished what he wanted to do first, it is not inexact to say to him: "Now take some food, because you have already done that *on account of which* you put off eating." Much less strange, then, is our expression, when we say Christ was exalted *because* He underwent death, since He determined to achieve that exaltation both *by means of* His death and *after* it. This can be understood also, in the same way as the text stating that the Lord *advanced in wisdom and . . . grace with God,* not meaning that He really advanced, but that He acted as if He did so. For He was exalted after death, just as if this occurred *on account of* His death.

Now, His statement: *I came not to do my own will, but the will of Him who sent me,* is of the same sort as: *My doctrine is not mine.* For what a person possesses, not of himself, but from God, he ought not to call his own, so much as God's. And no man has from himself the truth he teaches or rightness of will—but from God. Hence Christ came not to do His own will, but the Father's, because the justness of will which He had was not from His humanity, but from His divinity. The statement that God *spared not His own Son, but delivered Him up for us* means, in fact, only that God did not free Him. Many similar statements are found in Sacred Scripture. Where He says, for example, *Father, if it be possible, let this chalice pass from me; nevertheless, not my will, but thine be done,* and *If this chalice may not pass from me, but that I drink it, thy will be done,* He means by "His own will," the natural desire for well-being by which His human flesh shunned the pain of death. He did, it is true, speak of the will "of the Father," not however, because the Father preferred His Son's death to His life, but because the Father was unwilling that the human race be restored unless man performed some deed as outstanding as that death was to be. Since reason did not require something another could not do, the Son says the Father wills His death, and He would rather endure His own death than the loss of the human race. It is as if He said: "Because You do not will the world to be reconciled in any other way, I declare that in this way You are willing my death. May this will of yours, then, be done—that is, let my death occur, that the world may be reconciled to You." For we often say a person wills something, for the reason that he does not will something else, when, if he did will the other thing, what he is said to will would not occur. We say, for example, that a person wills the lamp to be blown out, if he does not wish to close a window through which a wind enters and blows out the light. In this way, then, the Father willed the death of His Son, because He did not will the world to be saved except by a man performing some outstanding deed, as I have said. Since no one else could perform such a deed, this was equivalent to the Father's commanding the Son to die, since the Son willed the salvation of men. Hence He did *as the Father gave* Him *commandment,* and He drank the chalice which the Father gave Him, being *obedient unto death.*

CHAPTER TEN

It is possible that a different interpretation of the same texts is correct.

Anselm: It can also be correct to interpret these texts to mean that, through that holy will by which the Son was willing to die for the salvation of the world, the Father, without compelling the Son, gave Him a command, and gave Him the chalice of suffering, and did not spare Him, but *delivered Him up for us* and willed His death; and that the Son Himself was *obedient unto death* and *learned obedience by the things which He suffered.* For just as, from the standpoint of His humanity, He had the will to live in the state of justice, not from Himself but from the Father, so also He could have had that willingness to die to bring about so much good, only from *the Father of lights* from whom is *every best gift and every perfect gift.* And as the Father is said to "draw" a person when He confers a willingness on him, it is equally proper to assert that He "moves" him. Just as, for example, the Son says to the Father, *No man comes to me, except the Father . . . draw him.* He could just as well have said: "unless the Father move him." He could also have continued in a similar way: "No one hastens toward death for my name's sake, unless the Father move or draw him." For since it is through the will that a person is drawn or moved to what he unwaveringly chooses, it is not unfitting to assert that God draws or moves him, when He confers this willingness. We are to understand this drawing or moving as implying not any compulsion of violence, but a spontaneous and loving tenacity of the good will that has been received. If in this sense, then, we cannot deny that the Father, in imparting that willingness, drew or moved the Son to death, who would not see that, in the same sense, He gave Him a "commandment" willingly to endure death, and a "chalice" which He would drink without reluctance. And if it is correct to say that the Son did not spare Himself, but delivered Himself up for us with unforced willingness, who can deny it is correct to say that the Father, from whom He had such a willingness, *spared* Him *not, but delivered Him up for us* and willed His death? In this sense, too, by unswervingly and freely persevering in the willingness He received from the Father, the Son became *obedient* to Him *unto death* and *learned obedience by the things which He suffered,* that is to say, He learned how great a result is achieved through obedience. For that is simple and genuine obedience when a rational nature maintains, not by necessity but freely, the willingness it has received from God.

We can interpret the statement that the Father willed the death of the Son in other ways, too, but these can suffice. For as we say that he wills something who influences another to will it, so we also say that he wills something who approves of another person's choice, even though he does not influence the choice. For example, when we see someone resigned to endure hardship bravely, to accomplish something good he intends, although we admit we want him to undergo that pain, it is nevertheless not his pain that we desire and approve, but his willingness. We commonly say, also, that a person who can prevent something and does not prevent it, is willing what he does not prevent. Since, therefore, the Son's desire was acceptable to the Father, and He did not prevent Him either from willing as He did or from fulfilling what he willed, it is right to say that He willed that the Son suffer death so loyally and so fruitfully, even though He did not love the Son's suffering. He said it was not possible for the chalice to pass without His drinking it, not because He could not avoid death if He chose, but because—as has been said—it was impossible to save the world in any other way, and He unwaveringly willed rather to suffer death than let the world be lost. He used that expression, therefore, to point out that the human race could not be saved in any other way than by His death, not to show that He had no power to avoid death. Whatever statements are made of Him, similar to those which have been made, are, of course, to be interpreted as meaning that He died not of necessity, but by free choice. For He was almighty, and we read of Him that *He was offered, because it was His own will.* He Himself also says: *I lay down my life, that I may take it up again. No man taketh it away from me, but I lay it down of myself. And I have power to lay it down and I have power to take it up again.* It is not at all right, then, to say that He is compelled to do what He does by His own power and by His own choice.

Boso: The single fact that God permits Him to be so treated does not seem to be fitting for such a Father with regard to such a Son, even though He is willing.

Anselm: On the contrary, it is eminently fitting for such a Father to give consent to such a Son if He wills something for the glory and honor of God and conducive to the salvation of man, which could not be achieved in any other way.

Boso: We are still concerned with the problem of showing how that death was reasonable and necessary. If it is not such, indeed, it seems that neither the Son ought to have willed it, nor the Father ought to have required or permitted it. For the question is: why God could not have saved man in another way, or, if He could, why He chose to save him in this way? It really seems unfitting for God to have saved man in this way, and further, it is not apparent what that death can accomplish for the salvation of man. It is surely to be wondered at if God so derives delight from, or has need of, the blood of the innocent, that He neither wishes nor is able to spare the guilty without the death of the innocent.

Anselm: Since, in this inquiry, you are playing the role of those who wish to believe nothing unless it is previously proved by reason, I would like to make an agreement with you not to attribute to God anything even slightly unsuitable, and not to reject any explanation, however weak, unless there is a stronger argument contradicting it. For in regard to God, just as whatever is unsuitable, however slightly, is consequently impossible, so a rational argument, however weak, induces certainty unless there is a stronger argument to refute it.

Boso: There is nothing I would rather have than our mutual agreement on this matter.

Anselm: Our inquiry is concerned only with the incarnation of God, and with what we believe regarding that humanity assumed by God.

Boso: That's right.

Anselm: Then let us suppose that the incarnation of God and what we say of that man never occurred. Let us agree that man was made for happiness, which cannot be possessed in this life, also that no one can arrive at happiness unless his sins are forgiven, and that no person passes through this life without sin, and anything else, the belief of which is necessary for eternal salvation.

Boso: Fine! There is nothing in these matters that appears impossible or unsuitable to God.

Anselm: It is necessary, then, that man's sins be forgiven, so he may arrive at happiness.

Boso: That we all hold.

CHAPTER ELEVEN

What "to sin" and "to satisfy for sin" mean.

Anselm: We must inquire, now, into the reason why God forgives the sins of men. And to do this more clearly, let us first see what "to sin" and "to satisfy for sin" mean.

Boso: It is your function to explain, and mine to listen.

Anselm: If an angel or a human being always rendered to God what he should, he would never sin.

Boso: I can only agree.

Anselm: "To sin" then, is nothing else than not to render to God His due.

Boso: What is the debt we owe God?

Anselm: The will of every rational creature must be subject to the will of God.

Boso: Perfectly true.

Anselm: This is the debt which angel and man owe to God, so that no one sins if he pays it and anyone who does not pay it, sins. This is justice or rectitude of will, which makes persons upright or *right in heart,* that is, in will. This is the only and the total honor which we owe to God and which God exacts of us. For only such a will produces works pleasing to God, when it is able to act; and when it is unable to act, it gives satisfaction by itself alone, because no effect of activity gives satisfaction without it. A person who does not render God this honor due Him, takes from God what is His and dishonors God, and this is to commit sin. Now, as long as he does not repay what he has plundered, he remains at fault. Neither is it enough merely to return what was taken away, but on account of the insult committed, he must give back more than he took away. For example, one who harms the health of another does not do enough if he restores his health, unless he makes some compensation for the injury of pain he has inflicted. Similarly, for one who violates the honor of some person, it does not suffice to render honor, if he does not make restitution of something pleasing to the person dishonored, in proportion to the injury of dishonor that has been inflicted. This also must be given attention: when someone pays back what he unjustly pilfered, he must give what could not be demanded of him if he had not defrauded the other person. Thus, therefore, everyone who sins must pay to God the honor he has taken away, and this is satisfaction, which every sinner must make to God.

Boso: Since we have set out to follow reason, I have no objection I can make on any of these points, although you frighten me a bit.

CHAPTER TWELVE

Is it fitting for God to remit sin out of mercy alone, without any payment of the debt?

Anselm: Let us go back and see whether it is fitting for God to remit sin out of mercy alone, without any payment for honor taken away from Him.

Boso: I do not see why it is not fitting.

Anselm: To remit sin in such a way is the same as not to punish it. And since to deal justly with sin, without satisfaction, is the same as to punish it, then, if it is not punished, something inordinate is allowed to pass.

Boso: What you say is reasonable.

Anselm: It is, however, not seemly for God to let pass something inordinate in His kingdom.

Boso: If I wanted to say otherwise, I would be afraid of sinning.

Anselm: Hence it is not fitting for God to remit sin without punishing it.

Boso: That follows.

Anselm: There is another consequence, if an unpunished sin is remitted: one who sins and one who does not sin will be in the same position before God. And that would be unseemly for God.

Boso: I cannot deny that.

Anselm: Look at this, also. Everyone knows that the justice of human beings is subject to the law that the measure of recompense is weighed out by God in proportion to the degree of justice.

Boso: So we believe.

Anselm: But if sin were neither atoned nor punished, it would not fall under any law.

Boso: I cannot disagree.

Anselm: If pardon is given out of mercy alone, injustice is less encumbered than justice. And this appears extremely incongruous. This incongruity even goes so far as to make injustice resemble God, for as God is subject to no law, neither would injustice be.

Boso: I cannot refute your argument. But since God commands us absolutely to forgive those who offend us, it seems to be inconsistent for Him to command us to do what is not fitting for Him to do.

Anselm: There is no inconsistency here, because God gives us this command precisely that we may not usurp what belongs to God alone. For it belongs to no one to carry out vengeance, except to Him who is the Lord of all. Even when earthly rulers exercise vengeance justifiably, the one who is really exercising it is the One who established them in authority for this very purpose.

Boso: You have gotten rid of the inconsistency which I thought was there. But there is another problem for which I would like to have your answer. For since God is so free that He is subject to no law, to no one's judgment, and so kind that nothing kinder can be imagined, and since nothing is right or becoming but what He wills, it does seem extraordinary to say that He absolutely does not will, or has not the freedom, to pardon an injury to Himself, although it is from Him that we are accustomed to ask remission even of the wrongs we do to others.

Anselm: What you say about His freedom and will and kindness is true. But we must understand these things by reason in such a way as not to seem to compromise His dignity. For freedom extends only to what is advantageous or to what is becoming, and a kindness which would bring about something unworthy of God ought not to be called kindness at all. But when we say that what God wills is just and what He does not will is not just, this is not to be understood in the sense that if God should will something unbecoming, it would become right by His willing it. It is not, for example, logical to say: "If God wants to lie, it is right to lie"; rather, one who wants to lie is not God. For a will can never choose to lie unless it be a will in which the truth is impaired, in fact, a will which is itself impaired by deserting the truth. When, then, someone says: "If God wants to lie" all he means is: "If God were of such a nature that He could wish to lie"; and so it does not follow that a lie is right. Perhaps, though, it may be interpreted in the same sense as when we say of two impossible things: "If this is, that is," although neither the one or the other is so. Should a person say, for instance: "If water is dry, then fire is wet," neither statement is true. Therefore, it is true to say: "If God wills this, it is right," only regarding those things which it is not unfitting for God to will. If, for example, God wills that it rain, it is right that it rain, and if He wills that some man be killed, it is right that he be killed. Hence, if it is not fitting for God to do anything unjustly or inordinately, it does not pertain to His freedom or kindness or will to pardon without punishment a sinner who does not make recompense to God for what he took away.

Boso: You are making irrelevant every objection I thought I could make against you.

Anselm: Consider, further, why it is not fitting for God to do this.

Boso: I am gladly listening to whatever you say.

CHAPTER THIRTEEN

Nothing is less tolerable in the order of things than for a creature to take away honor due to the Creator and not make recompense for what he takes away.

Anselm: Nothing is less tolerable in the order of things than for a creature to take away the honor due to the Creator and not make recompense for what he takes away.

Boso: That is perfectly clear.

Anselm: Now, nothing would be less justifiably tolerated than what is least tolerable.

Boso: This is clear, too.

Anselm: Then I think you will not say that God ought to tolerate that than which nothing would be less justifiably tolerated, such as that a creature not restore to God what he takes from Him.

Boso: On the contrary, I see that that is to be denied, absolutely.

Anselm: Likewise, if there is nothing greater or better than God, there is nothing more just than for the supreme justice which is the same as God Himself, to preserve His honor in the order of the universe.

Boso: Nothing is clearer to me than that.

Anselm: Therefore, God preserves nothing with greater justice than the honor of His dignity.

Boso: I have to agree.

Anselm: Do you think He would be preserving it entirely, if He permitted it to be taken away from Him in such a way that there would be no reparation and no punishment for the offender?

Boso: I dare not say yes.

Anselm: Then it is necessary either that the honor taken away be restored, or that punishment follow. Otherwise, either God will not be just to Himself or He will be unable to attain either. And it would be monstrous even to entertain that thought.

CHAPTER FOURTEEN

What kind of honor does the punishment of a sinner give to God?

Boso: I understand that nothing more reasonable can be said. But I want you to tell me if the punishment of a sinner gives honor to God, or rather, what kind of honor it is. For if the punishment of a sinner is not for the honor of God, when the sinner does not repay what he took away, but is punished, then God loses His honor in such a way as not to regain it. But this seems to contradict what we have said.

Anselm: It is impossible for God to be deprived of His honor. For either the sinner freely pays what he owes, or God takes it from him against his will. It may be that a person by free choice shows due subjection to God—either by not sinning or by making reparation for sin—or it may be that God subjects him to Himself, against the person's will, and thus He shows Himself his Lord, which is what the person himself refuses to acknowledge voluntarily. And in this matter, we must observe that just as man, by sinning, plunders what belongs to God, so God, by punishing, takes away what belongs to man. Surely, not only that which he already possesses is said to belong to a person, but also what is in his power to possess. Since, then, man is so made that he could have possessed happiness if he had not sinned, it follows that when, because of sin, he is deprived of happiness and every good, he is paying back what he plundered, out of what belongs to himself, although he is paying unwillingly. For although God does not transfer to His own use, for His own advantage, what He takes away—as a man directs to his own use, money he takes away from another—nevertheless, what He takes away He uses for His own honor, by the very fact that He takes it away. For by taking it away, He shows that the sinner and the things that belong to him are subject to Himself.

CHAPTER FIFTEEN

May God permit His honor to be violated, even in the least degree?

Boso: I like your explanation. But there is still another question I would like you to answer. If God must preserve His own honor, as you are establishing, then why does He allow it to be violated, even in the slightest degree? For what is allowed to be damaged in any measure is not entirely and perfectly protected.

Anselm: Considered in itself, God's honor cannot be increased or diminished. It is itself, by itself, honor incorruptible and absolutely unchangeable. But when each single creature, either by natural impulse or by the use of reason, fulfills its directions toward a goal proper to itself, and, so to speak, prescribed for it, it is said to obey God and to honor Him. This is especially true of rational nature, which has the gift of knowing what it ought to do. When it wills what it should, it honors God—not that it confers anything on Him, but that it freely subjects itself to His will and plans and keeps its place in the order of the universe, and to the best of its power, it preserves the beauty of that universe. But when it does not will what it should, it dishonors God so far as it can, since it does not subject itself freely to His plan, and, to the extent of its power, it disturbs the order and the beauty of the universe, although it does not injure or degrade the power and dignity of God, at all.

If, for example, those things that are contained within the sphere of the sky should wish not to be under the sky or to be released from the sky, they could not at all exist except under it, nor can they flee from the sky except by drawing nearer to it. For no matter where they were to come from or where they were to go, or what direction they took, they would be under the sky, and the greater the distance they would get away from any part of the sky, the closer they would approach to the opposite part. Similarly, even though a man or a fallen angel is unwilling to submit to the divine will and plan, still he cannot escape it; for if he wants to escape the dominion of the will that commands, he rushes under the dominion of the will that punishes. And if you ask how he passes from one state to another, it is only under a permissive will; and supreme wisdom directs his perversity of will or action toward the order and beauty of the universe I have been talking about. For a willing satisfaction for wickedness, or at least the exaction of a penalty from one who refuses satisfaction—granting that God draws good out of evils in many ways—takes its proper place in this same universe, and contributes to the beauty of its order. If divine wisdom did not impose these sanctions where wickedness tries to disturb right order, there would arise in the very universe which God has to keep in order, a certain deformity from the violation of the beauty of order, and God would seem to be deficient in His providence. As these two consequences are unfitting, they are therefore impossible, with the result that it is necessary that satisfaction or punishment follow every sin.

Boso: You have answered my objection satisfactorily.

Anselm: It is evident, then, that no one can honor or dishonor God, as God is in Himself; but to the extent of his own nature, a person appears to do one or the other, when he subjects his own will to God's, or withdraws it from God's.

Boso: I know nothing to say against that.

CHAPTER SIXTEEN

The reason why the number of the angels who fell is to be made up from among human beings.

Anselm: Let me add still more.

Boso: Keep on talking until I am tired of listening.

Anselm: It is certain that God intended to make up the number of angels who had fallen, out of human nature, which He made sinless.

Boso: This we believe, but I would like to have some reason for it.

Anselm: You are tricking me. We intended to treat only of the incarnation of God, and nothing else, and here you are interspersing other questions for me.

Boso: Do not be angry. *God loveth a cheerful giver.* Now, no one gives greater proof that he is cheerfully giving what he promises, than one who gives more than he promises. So tell me with good grace, what I am looking for.

Anselm: It is not to be doubted that rational nature which either is, or is going to be, made happy by the contemplation of God, was known by God before its existence, as having a definite, calculable and perfect number, which cannot fittingly be greater or less. For either God does not know what number of rational creatures would be more appropriate—and that is false—or, if He knows it, He will create it in the number He knows to be more appropriate for His purpose. Therefore, either those angels who fell were created to be within that number, or else, their fall was necessary, since, being excluded from that number, they could not persevere—and it is absurd to think that.

Boso: What you say is evident truth.

Anselm: Therefore, since they must have been included in that number, either their number was necessarily to be substituted, or else the rational nature, which was foreseen to exist in a perfect number, will remain numerically incomplete; and that cannot be.

Boso: Without doubt, there had to be substitutions for them.

Anselm: Then the substitutions had to be made from human nature, since there is no other nature from which they could be made.

CHAPTER SEVENTEEN

Other angels cannot replace the fallen ones.

Boso: Why cannot they themselves be restored, or other angels replace them?

Anselm: After you see the difficulty of our restoration, you will understand that their reconciliation is impossible. As for other angels supplanting them—not to mention how incompatible this seems to be with the perfection of the first creation—it is impossible for the reason that they ought not to replace them unless they could be the same as the fallen angels would have been if they had not sinned. Had the latter persevered, it would have been without their having witnessed any punishment for sin, and after their fall, that would have been impossible for the others who would have been substituted for them. For one who has no knowledge of any punishment for sin, and one who always has in view eternal punishment, are not equally praiseworthy for standing firm in the truth. We ought never to think, surely, that the good angels were confirmed in goodness by the fall of the evil ones; it was rather by their own merit. If the good ones had sinned with the evil ones, they would have been condemned together with them; it is equally true that if the unfaithful ones had stood firm with the virtuous ones, they would likewise have been confirmed. Indeed, if some of the angels were not to be confirmed except by the fall of others, either no one would ever have been confirmed, or it would have been necessary for someone to fall, so that he might be punished for the strengthening of others— and both of these alternatives are absurd. Therefore, those who were steadfast were confirmed in exactly the same way in which all would have been confirmed if they had persevered. What that way is, I have shown, to the best of my ability, when I treated the question why God did not grant perseverance to the devil.

Boso: You have proven that the evil angels were to be replaced from human nature; and it is evident from this reasoning that the elect among human beings will not be less numerous than the reprobate angels. But show, if you can, whether they are to be more numerous.

CHAPTER EIGHTEEN

Are there to be more human saints than evil angels?

Anselm: If the number of angels, before any of them fell, was that perfect one of which we have spoken, human beings were created solely to replace the lost angels, and it is evident that they will not outnumber those angels. But if all the angels did not constitute a perfect number, then human beings were to replace both what was lost and what was lacking from the beginning, and the human beings destined for glory will exceed the reprobate angels in number. And thus we shall say that human beings were created not only to replace the diminished number, but also to make perfect a number that was not yet perfect.

Boso: Which is the better view to hold? Were the angels from the beginning, created in a perfect number, or not?

Anselm: I shall tell you my opinion.

Boso: I cannot ask more of you.

Anselm: If man was created after the fall of the evil angels, as some interpret *Genesis,* I do not see how I can, on that basis, prove either of these alternatives decisively. In my opinion, it is possible that the angels first existed in a perfect number, and afterwards man was created to complete their diminished number. It is also possible they did not exist in a perfect number, because God deferred—as He is still deferring— to complete that number, since He was to create human nature in its own time. It would follow either that He might only make perfect a number that was not yet total, or even that He might restore it if it had been diminished. But if the whole of creation was produced all together and those "days" which Moses mentions, seeming to imply that this world was not created all at once, are to be understood as different from these days of our life, I cannot understand how the angels were created in that complete number. Indeed, if it had been so, it seems to me that of necessity, either some angels or some men were to fall, or else that there were to be more inhabitants in that heavenly city than that suitability of a perfect number would require. Therefore, if all things were created at once, it would seem that angels and the first two human beings were in an imperfect number, so that, if no angel were to fall, only the number that was lacking would be completed from human beings, and if anyone should be lost, the part that fell would also be replaced. Then the nature of man, which was the weaker one, would as it were, vindicate God and confound the devil if he should impute his own fall to his weakness, since a weaker than he remained constant. Should that human nature itself fall, moreover, much more would it show God to be just, against the devil and against itself, since, although it had been made much weaker and mortal, it was to have advanced among the elect from such extreme weakness to an eminence so much more exalted than that from which the devil had fallen—as exalted as that the good angels, with whom it ought to be on the same level, attained after the ruin of the evil ones, because they persevered.

For these reasons, it seems to me more likely that the angels did not constitute that perfect number by which that celestial city will be brought to completion. This view is possible, if man was not created together with the angels. And it seems to be a necessary assumption if they were created together—which many think more likely, since we read: *He that liveth forever created all things together.* But even if the perfection of a created world is to be understood not so much with regard to the number of individuals as with regard to the number of natures, it is necessary that human nature was created either to complete that same perfection or else that it is superfluous to it—which we dare not say regarding the nature of the lowest little worm. Hence, it was created on the earth for its own sake and not merely to replace the individuals of another nature. From this it is evident that even if no angel had been lost, human beings would still have had their own place in the heavenly city. It follows, then, that the number of the angels, before any of them fell, was not that perfect one. Otherwise it would have been necessary that either human beings or certain angels fall, since no one could remain in that city in excess of the perfect number.

Boso: You have accomplished something.

Anselm: There is another reason, also, I think, which gives more than a little support to that opinion that angels were not created in a perfect number.

Boso: Tell me what it is.

Anselm: If angels were created in that perfect number, and human beings were created for no other reason than to replace the lost angels, it is evident that unless some angels had fallen from that blessedness, human beings would not have ascended to it.

Boso: That is clear.

Anselm: If anyone should say, then, that the human beings chosen for blessedness will rejoice in the loss of the angels as much as in their own elevation—since, without doubt, the latter would not occur unless the former occurred—how will it be possible to defend them from this perverse gratification? Or how shall we say that the angels who fell have been replaced by human beings, if the angels, in case they had not fallen, were to have remained free from this vice—that is, free from gratification over the fall of others—although human beings cannot be free from it? What sort of blessedness will they deserve, in fact, having this defect? How rash, then, we would be to say that God is not willing or is not able to bring about this replacement without this defect!

Boso: Is it not similar to the case of the Gentiles who were called to the faith because the Jews rejected it?

Anselm: No. For even if all Jews had accepted the faith, the Gentiles would still have been called, because *in every nation, he that feareth* God *and worketh justice, is acceptable to Him.* But the fact that the Jews despised the apostles was the occasion for the latter to turn to the Gentiles.

Boso: I cannot see the slightest objection to make to this.

Anselm: What do you think is the origin of that joy in individuals over another's fall?

Boso: What, but that every individual will be convinced that he would not possibly be where he is unless another fell from there?

Anselm: Then, if no one had this conviction, there would be no reason for anyone to rejoice over another's loss?

Boso: So it seems.

Anselm: Do you think any one of them will have this conviction if there are many more of them than of those who fell?

Boso: It is simply impossible for me to think that anyone would have it or should have it. For how could anyone know whether he was created to replace what was lost, or to complete what is still lacking to the number required to constitute the city? But all will be certain that they were created to complete that city.

Anselm: Therefore, if they are more numerous than the reprobate angels, none of them will be able to know or ought to know he has been brought up there only because of someone else's fall.

Boso: That is right.

Anselm: Hence no one will have reason for rejoicing over someone else's loss.

Boso: That follows.

Anselm: Since, therefore, we see that if there will be more chosen human beings than reprobate angels, there will not be that unseemly result that would have to follow if there were not more. And since it is impossible that there will be anything unseemly in that city, it appears to be an inescapable conclusion that the number of angels created was not that perfect number, and there were to have been more human beings in blessedness than there were wicked angels.

Boso: I do not see any reason for denying that.

Anselm: I think that still another argument can be given for that same opinion.

Boso: You ought to give that one, too.

Anselm: We believe that this bodily mass of the universe is to be renewed in a better state, and that this will neither occur until the number of human beings destined for eternal life is completed and that blessed city is perfected, nor will it be deferred beyond its perfection. From this we can conclude that God intended from the beginning to bring both to perfection together. Thus the inferior nature which did not see God, would not be brought to perfection before the superior one which ought to enjoy God. Having been changed for the better, it, in its own way, would share in the joy, as it were, of the perfection of the superior nature. Indeed, every creature would derive delight from so glorious and so wonderful an achievement of its own perfection, each one, in its own way, eternally finding joy in its Creator and itself and one another. By God's ordering, even a creature not having sensation would manifest, in accordance with its nature, what the will does freely in a rational nature. For we are accustomed to share the joy of the exaltation of our ancestors, as when we celebrate the birthdays of the saints with festive exultation, taking delight in their glory. It seems that this opinion is bolstered by the fact that, if Adam had not sinned, God would nevertheless have deferred completing that city, until the number He desired was fulfilled from among human beings, and these human beings themselves would also be—so to say—transmuted into the immortal immortality of their bodies. For in paradise they had immortality of a sort, that is, the power of not dying; but this power was not immortal, because it was able to die, with the result that the human beings themselves would be unable not to die.

If all this is true, that is, if God from the beginning determined to bring to perfection together, that intelligent and blessed city and this earthly and irrational nature, it seems that the following alternatives are possible. It may be that the number of angels before the fall of the wicked ones did not fill up that city, but God was waiting to complete it from among human beings, when He would change the bodily nature of the universe into something better. Or it is possible that, although it was numerically complete, it was not complete in having full confirmation, and its confirmation was to be deferred, even if no one in it should sin, until that renewal of the universe which we are awaiting. Another possibility is that if that confirmation was not to be deferred any longer, the renewal of the earth was to be accelerated, so as to take place together with this confirmation. But that God determined to renew the universe right after it was created, and in the very beginning, before the reason for their creation was evident, to destroy those things which will not exist after that renewal— that does not make sense at all. Hence it follows that the number of the angels was not perfect in such a way that their confirmation was not to be long deferred, since it would be necessary for the renewal of the new universe to have taken place at once—and this is not fitting. On the other hand, that God should will to defer that confirmation until some future renewal of the universe also seems unfitting, especially since He had brought about that confirmation so soon in certain creatures, and since we can assume that He would have confirmed the first human beings at the time of their sin, if they had not sinned, as He did the angels who persevered. For, although they would not yet be advanced to that equality with the angels at which human beings were to arrive, when the number to be taken from them was completed, nevertheless, it seems that if they had triumphed by not sinning when they were tempted, they, with all their posterity, would have been so confirmed in that state of justice in which they were, that they would be unable to sin again—just as, for the reason that they were vanquished and have sinned, they were so weakened that, of themselves, they cannot be without sin. Who, indeed, would dare to say that lack of justice has more power to bind man in slavery when he gives consent to its first suggestion, than justice has to confirm in freedom the person who is faithful to it in the same first temptation? Since the whole of human nature was in our first parents, the whole of it was conquered for sin in them—with the single exception of that Man whom God knew how to exempt from Adam's sin, just as He knew how to fashion Him from the Virgin without the seed of a male. In the same way, the whole of human nature would have triumphed in the same parents, if they had not sinned. We are left to conclude, then, that the heavenly city was not completed by that original number of angels, but was to have been completed from among men. If all this is valid, there will be more human beings chosen for salvation than there are reprobate angels.

Boso: What you are saying seems extremely reasonable to me. But how shall we interpret the statement that God *appointed the bounds of people according to the number of the children of Israel?* Some, reading "angels of God" for "children of Israel," expound it to mean that the number of human beings chosen for eternal life corresponds to the number of good angels.

Anselm: This does not contradict the opinion given before, if it is not certain that just as many angels fell as persevered. For if the angels chosen for eternal life are more numerous than the reprobate, it is both necessary that the human beings chosen for eternal life replace the reprobate, and also possible that they be equal in number to the blessed; and thus there will be more human beings in the state of justice than angels in the state of injustice. But remember on what condition I undertook to respond to your questioning, that is, that if I should say anything which higher authority does not confirm—even though I seem to prove it by reason—it is not to be accepted as settled except that it is my present opinion, until God in some way makes known to me something better. For I am certain that if I say anything that is certainly in opposition to Holy Scripture, it is false; and if I knew it was opposed to Scripture, I would not want to hold it. But suppose we are dealing with matters on which different opinions can be held without danger, such as the one we are now discussing. If we do not know, for example, whether or not a greater number of human beings is to be chosen for eternal life than angels were lost, and we consider one of the alternatives more probable than the other, I do not think there is any danger for the soul. If, in matters of this kind, we expound the words of God in such a way that they seem to favor different opinions and no texts are discovered anywhere which indisputably determine what should be held, I do not think we should be censured.

Now for the text you cited: *He appointed the bounds of people* or nations *according to the number of the angels of God,* which, in another translation, reads: *according to the number of the children of Israel.* Since both translations either have the same meaning, or have different but compatible meanings, there are various interpretations possible. Both *angels of God* and *children of Israel* could signify good angels alone, or the chosen human beings alone, or both angels and the chosen human beings together, that is, that whole heavenly city. Again, *angels of God* could mean holy angels alone, and *children of Israel,* virtuous human beings alone. Or *children of Israel* could designate angels alone, and *angels of God* could mean virtuous human beings. If only good angels are designated by both phrases, it is the same as if only the expression *the angels of God* were used. If, however, the whole heavenly city is referred to by both phrases, the meaning here is that people, that is, multitudes of the chosen human beings, will be taken up or that there will be peoples in this world until the predetermined but not yet completed number of residents of that city is brought to completion from among human beings.

But right now, I do not see how *children of Israel* can mean angels alone, or angels and holy human beings taken together. It is not strange, however, to call holy human beings *children of Israel,* as well as *children of Abraham.* They can also be correctly called "angels of God" for the reason that they imitate angelic life, and likeness to the angels and equality with the angels are promised to them in heaven; and because all who live in the state of justice are angels of God. That is the reason why they are called "confessors" or "martyrs." For anyone who acknowledges the truth of God or bears witness to it, is His messenger, that is, His angel. And if a sinful man is called a devil, as Judas was, by the Lord, because of a likeness in malice, why should not a good man be called an angel, because of imitation of justice? Hence we can say, I think, that God established *the bounds of people according to the number* of His chosen human beings, because there will be peoples and procreation of human beings in this world until the number of those chosen ones is completed; and when it is completed, generation of human beings which occurs in this life, will cease.

But if by *angels of God* we understand holy angels alone, and by *children of Israel,* virtuous human beings alone, there are two other ways in which we can interpret the text: *God appointed the bounds of people according to the number of the angels of God.* We may interpret it either in the sense that as great a people, that is, as many human beings, as there are holy angels of God, will be elevated; or else in the sense that the peoples will continue to exist until the number of angels of God is to be completed from among human beings. And I see only one possible way of explaining *he appointed the bounds of people according to the number of the children of Israel,* and that is, as I said before, in the sense that the people in this world will exist up to the point when the number of saintly human beings is elevated; and we may infer from both translations that as many human beings will be elevated as there are angels who remained steadfast. From this, nevertheless, it will not follow that as many angels fell as persevered, even though the lost angels are to be replaced from among human beings. If anyone says that it does follow, however, he will have to find the flaws in the arguments just proposed; since they seem to show that the angels, before some of them fell, did not constitute that perfect number I spoke of before, and that the number of human beings chosen for future eternal life is greater than the number of angels who sinned.

Boso: I am not sorry that I made you discuss these questions about the angels. It certainly has not been useless. Return, now, to the subject from which we have digressed.

CHAPTER NINETEEN

Man cannot be saved without satisfaction for sin.

Anselm: We agree that God has intended to replace with human beings the angels who fell.

Boso: That is certain.

Anselm: Then the human beings in that heavenly city who will be taken up into it in place of angels ought to be in the same condition as those whom they replace, that is, the same condition in which the good angels are now. Otherwise those who have fallen would not be replaced, and it will follow that God is not able to complete the good that He began, or that

He will regret having begun such a blessing. And both of these alternatives are absurd.

Boso: Surely, it is necessary that the human beings be equal to the good angels.

Anselm: Did the good angels ever sin?

Boso: No.

Anselm: Can you imagine that man who once sinned and never made satisfaction to God for sin, but was only pardoned without punishment, would be equal to an angel who never sinned?

Boso: I can imagine and speak those words, but I cannot commit myself to their meaning, any more than I can understand falsity to be truth.

Anselm: Then it is fitting for God to elevate a sinful human being who has made no satisfaction, to replace the lost angels, since truth does not allow him to be raised to equality with the blessed.

Boso: Reason proves it.

Anselm: With regard to man alone, regardless of his having to be the equal of angels, consider also whether God must elevate him in such a way to any happiness, even such as he had before he sinned.

Boso: Say what *you* think, and I shall consider it to the best of my ability.

Anselm: Let us suppose that some rich man is holding in his hand a precious pearl, totally unspotted by the slightest stain. No one else can take it from his hand without his permission. Suppose he decides to store it in his treasury, where his dearest and most precious possessions are.

Boso: I am imagining this as if it were present before us.

Anselm: What if he himself permits some envious person to knock the same pearl out of his hand into the mud, although he could prevent it, and afterwards, picking it up from the mud, puts it away, soiled and unwashed, in some clean and costly receptacle, to preserve it as it is. Would you think him wise?

Boso: How can I? Would it not be much better for him to hold on to his pearl and preserve it while it is clean, rather than when it is soiled?

Anselm: Would not God be doing something similar, if He, so to speak, held in His hand, in Paradise, the human being who was to be in the company of the angels, free from sin, and then allowed the devil, inflamed with envy, to throw him down in the mire of sin, although man gave his consent (for if God chose to prevent him, the devil could not have tempted man)? Would not God, I say, be doing something similar, if He had brought back at least to Paradise from which he had been cast out, the human being now stained with the filth of sin and uncleansed, that is, without making any satisfaction, and always to remain in that condition?

Boso: I dare not deny the similarity, if God were to do this, and for that reason I do not admit He can do it. For it would seem either that He could not bring about what He had planned, or that He regretted His good intention—and these things cannot happen to God.

Anselm: Hold it as most certain, then, that without satisfaction, that is, without voluntary payment of the debt, God cannot remit sin without punishment, nor can the sinner arrive at happiness, even such as he had before he sinned. For man would not have been rehabilitated in this way, not even to the state he had before his sin.

Boso: I am absolutely unable to contradict your arguments. But how is it that we say to God: *Forgive us our debts,* and that every people prays to the God it believes in, to forgive it its sins? For if we have paid what we owe, why do we pray Him to pardon us? Is God unjust, that He demands, a second time, what has already been paid? But if we have not paid our debt, why do we uselessly beseech Him to do what He cannot do because it is unfitting?

Anselm: One who has not paid the debt is uselessly saying "Pardon!" One who has paid, is praying because this very act of praying is part of the payment. For God owes nothing to anyone, but every creature has a debt to Him; and therefore it is not proper for a human being to act toward God as one equal with another. But on this point it is not necessary to answer you now. For when you come to know why Christ has died, perhaps you will see the answer to this question by yourself.

Boso: For the present, then, I am satisfied with your answer to this question. But that no human being in the state of sin can attain happiness or be released from sin unless he repays what he appropriated to himself by sinning, you have so clearly proved that I could not doubt it if I wanted to.

CHAPTER TWENTY

Satisfaction must be made in accordance with the measure of the sin. And man cannot do this by himself.

Anselm: You do not doubt this, either, I suppose: that satisfaction must be made in accordance with the measure of the sin.

Boso: If it were otherwise, sin would remain to some extent outside the rule of order; and this cannot be, if God leaves no disorder in His kingdom. But we have already established the principle that the slightest incongruity in God is impossible.

Anselm: Tell me, then: what will you pay to God for your sin?

Boso: Repentance, a contrite and humbled heart, fasting, and all sorts of bodily work, mercy in giving and forgiving, and obedience.

Anselm: In all these things, what are you giving to God?

Boso: Do I not honor God, when, because of fear and love of Him, in sorrow of heart I give up temporal joy; when by self-denials and labors I trample underfoot the delight and repose of this life; when, in giving and forgiving, I give liberally of what is mine; when, in obedience, I subject myself to Him?

Anselm: When you render to God what you owe to Him, even without having sinned, you ought not to count it as payment for a debt you owe because of sin. Now all those things you mention, you owe to God. In this mortal life, so great must be your love and so great your desire to arrive at the goal for which you were created (this is the purpose of prayer), and so great your sorrow at not being there yet, and your fear that you may not arrive there, that you ought not to experience any joy except from those things which give you either the help or the hope to arrive at your goal. For you do not deserve to have what you do not love and desire in proportion to its nature, and regarding which you are not in sorrow when you do not yet possess it and you are still running such a great risk of never possessing it. This risk also involves fleeing the repose and earthly pleasures which distract the mind from that genuine repose and delight, except to the extent that you know they foster your intention to persevere. But you must regard your giving as a paying of a debt, just as you recognize that what you are giving you have, not from yourself, but from Him whose servant you are—both you and the one to whom you are giving. Nature also teaches you to do for your fellow-servant, that is, as one human being to another, what you want him to do for you; and it makes clear that whoever is not willing to give what he has, ought not to receive what he does not possess. With regard to forgiveness, I say briefly that vengeance does not at all belong to you, as we said before. The reason is that you do not belong to yourself, nor does he who did you any injury belong to you or to himself, but you are servants of one Lord, created by Him out of nothing; and if you have revenge on your fellow-servant, you are proudly arrogating to yourself a right of judgment over him which belongs exclusively to the Lord and Judge of all. As for obedience, now, what do you give to God that you do not owe Him, to whose command you owe all that you are and have and are able to do?

Boso: I do not dare to say now, that in all these cases I give anything to God which I do not owe Him.

Anselm: What payment, then, will you make to God for your sin?

Boso: If, even when I am not in the state of sin, I owe Him myself and whatever I can do, in order to avoid sinning, I have nothing to offer Him in compensation for sin.

Anselm: What, then, will become of you? How can you be saved?

Boso: If I take your arguments into consideration, I do not see how. But if I have recourse to my faith—I hope that in Christian faith *that worketh by love,* I can be saved. Besides, we read: *If the unjust be converted from his injustice and do justice,* all his injustices are forgotten.

Anselm: This is said only to those who either awaited Christ before He came, or who believe in Him after His coming. But we excluded Christ and the Christian faith as if they never existed, when we proposed to seek by reason alone, whether His coming was necessary for the salvation of men.

Boso: So we did.

Anselm: Let us, then, proceed by reason alone.

Boso: Although you lead me into some tight corners, still I greatly desire you to continue as you began.

CHAPTER TWENTY-ONE

How great a burden sin is.

Anselm: Let us suppose that you are not obliged to give all those things you just claimed you are able to give in compensation for sin, and let us see whether they can suffice for the satisfaction of even one slight sin, such as a single glance opposed to the will of God.

Boso: Except for hearing you question it, I should think that I would wipe out such a sin with a single act of remorse.

Anselm: You have not yet considered what a great burden sin is.

Boso: Show me now.

Anselm: Suppose you recognize that God sees you. Suppose someone should say to you: "Look there!" and God, on the contrary, should say: "I absolutely do not want you to look." Now ask yourself in your heart what there is among all the things that exist, for which you ought to cast that glance, in opposition to the will of God.

Boso: I find nothing for the sake of which I ought to do this, unless perhaps I were placed in the necessity of having to commit either this sin or a more grievous one.

Anselm: Disregard this necessity, and regarding this sin alone, consider whether you can commit it to save yourself.

Boso: I clearly see that I cannot.

Anselm: Not to delay you too long—what if the whole world and whatever is not God had to perish and be annihilated, unless you did such a slight thing against the will of God?

Boso: When I consider the action itself, I see it is something very slight. But when I give attention to what "against the will of God" means, I understand that it is something very serious and beyond comparison with any loss. Still, we are accustomed, at times, to act against someone's will, without blame, to preserve his interests, and he against whose will we have acted is afterwards pleased.

Anselm: This occurs in the case of a human being who sometimes does not understand what is useful to himself, or who cannot replace what he loses, but God is in need of nothing, and if all things should perish, He could replace them, just as He has created them.

Boso: I must acknowledge that I should do nothing against the will of God, to preserve the whole of creation.

Anselm: What if there were more worlds like this one, full of creatures?

Boso: If the number of them were multiplied indefinitely, and they were spread out before me in a similar way, my answer would be the same.

Anselm: You could not be more right. But consider also what compensation you could make for that sin, if it should happen that you cast that glance, against the will of God.

Boso: I have nothing more to say than I said before.

Anselm: So we sin seriously, whenever we knowingly do anything, however slight, against the will of God, because we are always within His sight and He is always commanding us not to sin.

Boso: As I understand you, we live in a very dangerous condition.

Anselm: It is evident that God demands satisfaction in proportion to the gravity of the sin.

Boso: I cannot deny that.

Anselm: Therefore, you do not make satisfaction if you do not return something greater than that for whose sake you were bound not to commit the sin.

Boso: I see that reason requires that, and yet I see that it is absolutely impossible.

Anselm: And God cannot admit into happiness anyone who is bound in any way by the debt of sin, because it would not be right for Him.

Boso: This thought is a very crushing one.

CHAPTER TWENTY-TWO

What an affront man gave to God, when he let himself be overcome by the devil, and for this he cannot make satisfaction.

Anselm: Listen to still another reason why it is not less difficult for man to be reconciled with God.

Boso: Unless faith gave me comfort, this one alone would drive me to despair.

Anselm: Listen, anyway.

Boso: Go ahead.

Anselm: Man, created in paradise without sin, was placed, as it were, on God's side, between God and the devil, to overcome the devil by not consenting to his temptations to sin. He was intended, in this way, to vindicate and honor God and confound the devil, since man, although the weaker one, would not sin on the earth when tempted by that very devil, who, despite his greater strength, sinned in heaven, although no one tempted him. And although man could have done this easily, and was not compelled by any force, he freely permitted himself to be overcome, by urging alone, in accordance with the will of the devil and against the will and honor of God.

Boso: What is your drift?

Anselm: Judge for yourself if it is not contrary to the honor of God for man to be reconciled to Him while man still bore the shame of this outrage inflicted on God, without first honoring God by overcoming the devil, just as he had dishonored Him by being overcome by the devil. But the victory must be of this sort. Man, while strong and potentially immortal, easily gave in to the devil, so as to sin, for which reason he justly incurred the penalty of having to die. Now, when he is weak and mortal by his own doing, he should overcome the devil by the hardship of death, so as to be without sin entirely. This he can not do, as long as, due to the wound of the first sin, he is conceived and born in sin.

Boso: I repeat that what you say is proven true by reason—and yet that it is impossible.

CHAPTER TWENTY-THREE

What man, when he sinned, took away from God, which he cannot repay.

Anselm: Take one thing more, without which man is not reconciled in justice, and which is equally impossible.

Boso: You have already proposed to us so many obligations we have to fulfill that nothing else you add can make me more fearful.

Anselm: Listen, anyway.

Boso: I am listening.

Anselm: What did man take away from God, when he allowed himself to be overcome by the devil?

Boso: You give the answer, as you have begun to do, because I do not know what he could add to these evils you have indicated.

Anselm: Did he not take from God whatever He had intended to make out of human nature?

Boso: That cannot be denied.

Anselm: Take strict justice into account, and judge, in accordance with that, whether man gives God satisfaction equivalent to his sin, unless, by overcoming the devil, he restores exactly what he took away from God by allowing himself to be conquered by the devil. Thus, just as by the very fact that man was conquered, the devil stole what belonged to God and God lost it, so by the very fact that man triumphs the devil loses what belonged to God and God regains it.

Boso: I cannot think of anything more strict or more just.

Anselm: Do you think supreme Justice can violate this justice?

Boso: I dare not think so.

Anselm: Hence it is absolutely wrong and even impossible for man to receive from God what God intended to give him, if he does not render back to God all that he took from Him; so that as God has lost it through him, so He was to regain it through him. This cannot occur in any other way than that, as through him who was vanquished, the whole human nature was corrupted and, as it were, leavened, by sin—and God takes no one afflicted by sin to complete that heavenly city—so by his triumph, as many men were justified as were required to total that number which man was created to complete. But it is absolutely impossible for sinful man to do this, because a sinner cannot justify a sinner.

Boso: Nothing is more just, yet nothing is more impossible. But out of all this, the mercy of God and the hope of man seem to vanish, so far as the happiness for which man was created is concerned.

CHAPTER TWENTY-FOUR

As long as man does not render to God what he ought, he cannot be happy, and he is not excused by inability.

Anselm: Wait a little longer.

Boso: What more do you have to say?

Anselm: If a man is called unjust for not repaying what he owes to a man, he is much more unjust who does not render to God what he ought.

Boso: If he is able to render it, and does not, he is indeed unjust. But if he is unable to do it, how is he unjust?

Anselm: If the reason for the inability is not something within himself, perhaps he can be to some extent excused. But if the source of his inability is a fault, then, as it does not mitigate his sin, so it does not excuse him from paying his debt. Suppose someone, for example, assigns some task to his servant and directs him not to throw himself into a pit which he points out to him, and from which he simply cannot escape. Suppose that servant, having no regard for the command and the warning of his master, voluntarily throws himself into the pit that has been pointed out to him, so that he cannot perform the task assigned. Do you think this inability can in any way excuse him from not performing the assigned task?

Boso: Not at all. Rather, it would increase his guilt, since he brought that inability on himself. For he sinned in two ways: in not doing what he was commanded to do, and in doing what he was commanded not to do.

Anselm: Thus, man is inexcusable, for he voluntarily incurred that debt which he could not pay, and by his own fault lapsed into the inability, so that he could neither fulfill the obligation he had before sin—that is, to avoid sin—nor pay the debt he owes because he sinned. For his very inability is a fault because he ought not have it; indeed, he was obliged not to have it. Just as it is a fault, of course, not to have what one should have, so it is a fault to have what one should not have. Therefore, as it is a fault for man not to have that ability to avoid sin which he was given, so it is a fault for him to have that inability either to preserve justice and guard against sin, or to give due compensation for sin. For he voluntarily did that on account of which he lost that inability and lapsed into that inability. Not to have an ability one ought to have is the same, surely, as to have an inability one ought not have. Hence, the inability to render to God what is His due, which prevents man from rendering it, does not excuse him if he does not render it, since the effect of sin does not excuse the sin he commits.

Boso: This is extremely hard to accept, and yet it must be so.

Anselm: Man, then, is unjust if he does not render to God what he owes Him.

Boso: That is all too true. For he is at fault for not rendering it and at fault for not being able to render it.

Anselm: No one, however, who is unjust will be admitted into happiness, since happiness is a state of sufficiency in which there is nothing lacking, and it is not suitable for anyone, unless his justice is so pure that there is not a speck of injustice in him.

Boso: I dare not believe otherwise.

Anselm: But if you wish to say: "The merciful God remits the debt of one who supplicates Him, for the very reason that he cannot repay it"—well, God cannot be said to remit a debt except in two senses. Either He remits what a human being ought voluntarily to return to Him, but cannot, that is, some compensation for the sin he should not have committed even to preserve everything which is not God; or else He remits the punishment which, as I said before, is the deprivation of happiness, against the person's will. If, however, He remits what man is obliged to render voluntarily for the reason that he cannot render it, what else would that mean but that God is remitting what He cannot obtain? But to attribute such "mercy" to God would be to deride Him. And if He remits what He was to take away from man against his will, on account of man's inability to repay what he should voluntarily repay, then God is relaxing the penalty and making a man happy on account of his sin, because he would be possessing what he should not possess. For he ought not have that inability and so, as long as he has it without making satisfaction, it is a sin for him. But divine "mercy" of this sort is quite opposed to God's justice which allows nothing but punishment to be the return for sin. Therefore, just as it is impossible for God to contradict Himself, so is it impossible for Him to be merciful in this way.

Boso: I see we are to look for a different kind of divine mercy than this one.

Anselm: Let us suppose it were true that God pardons him who does not pay his debt for the reason that he cannot.

Boso: That is the way I would like it to be.

Anselm: But as long as he will not make restoration, he is either willing or unwilling to make it. Now, if he is willing but unable to make it, he will be in a state of insatiable desire. If, however, he is unwilling, he will be unjust.

Boso: Nothing is clearer than that.

Anselm: Now, if he is in a state of insatiable desire, or if on the other hand, he is unjust, he will not be happy.

Boso: This is also evident.

Anselm: Therefore, so long as he does not make restoration, he cannot be happy.

Boso: If God follows the rule of justice, there is no way for miserable little man to escape, and the mercy of God seems to come to an end.

Anselm: You have asked for a reason; accept the reason. I do not deny that God is merciful, since He saves *men and beasts* as he has *multiplied* His mercy. But we are speaking of that ultimate mercy by which He makes man happy after this life. That this happiness must not be granted to anyone except to one whose sins are totally forgiven, and that this forgiveness must not be granted except after payment of the debt which is due for sin in proportion to the magnitude of the sin, I think I have adequately shown by the arguments given before. If you think any objection can be brought against these arguments, you ought to say so.

Boso: Indeed, I do not see that any of your arguments can be weakened in the least degree.

Anselm: Neither do I, if they are carefully examined. Nevertheless, if only one of all that I have proposed is confirmed as indisputably true, that must satisfy us. For whether truth is proven indisputably by one or many arguments, it is equally well defended against every doubt.

Boso: Quite so.

CHAPTER TWENTY-FIVE

It is necessarily through Christ that man is saved.

Boso: How, then, will man be saved, if he does not pay what he owes, and if he should not be saved without paying? Moreover, how shall we dare to assert that God, who is rich in mercy beyond human understanding, is not able to exercise this mercy?

Anselm: You ought, at this point, to demand of those in whose place you are speaking, who believe Christ is not necessary for that salvation of man, that they tell you how man can be saved without Christ. But if they absolutely cannot do this, let them stop deriding us and let them approach and join us who do not doubt that man can be saved by Christ, or else let them despair of man's being saved at all. But if they dread this alternative, let them believe in Christ as we do, that they may be saved.

Boso: I shall ask you, as I did in the beginning, to show me in what way man is saved through Christ.

Anselm: Is there not adequate proof that man can be saved through Christ, since even unbelievers do not deny that man can in some way attain happiness, and it has been sufficiently shown that if we suppose Christ does not exist, it is absolutely impossible to find a means of human salvation? For man can be saved either through Christ or by someone else or not at all. Consequently, if it is false that salvation is impossible, or that it can be due to another, it is necessary that it be accomplished through Christ.

Boso: If someone, seeing the reason why man cannot be saved in another way, yet not understanding just how we can be saved through Christ, wants to assert that human salvation is impossible, either through Christ or in any way at all—what answer shall we give him?

Anselm: What answer is to be given to him who maintains that something which has to be is impossible, for the simple reason that he does not know how it occurs?

Boso: That he is out of his mind.

Anselm: Therefore, what he says is to be met with disdain.

Boso: Yes. But we ought to show him precisely how what he thinks impossible really exists.

Anselm: Do you not understand from what we said before, that it is necessary that some human beings attain to happiness? For if it is unfitting for God to bring a human being with some stain upon him to that for which He created him free from stain, lest He seem either to regret having undertaken something good or to be unable to fulfill His plan, much more is it impossible, because of the same unsuitableness, that no man at all attain to the goal for which he was created. Therefore, the satisfaction for sin such as we showed before to be necessary, is either to be found outside the Christian faith—which cannot be proved by any argument—or we are to believe without the slightest doubt that it exists within that faith. For what is proved to be true on the basis of a necessary reason cannot at all be called into doubt, even if we do not see the reason why it is so.

Boso: You are right.

Anselm: Then what more do you ask for?

Boso: I have come to you, not to have you remove doubts about the faith from me, but to have you show me the reason for my certitude. Hence, now that you have led me along the way of reason to the point of seeing that a human sinner owes to God, for sin, a debt which he cannot repay, and cannot be saved without repaying, I would like you to lead me further. Help me to understand by rational necessity how all those things which the Catholic faith requires us to believe regarding

Christ, if we wish to be saved, must be true, and what value they have for the salvation of man, and how it is that God saves man by mercy when He does not forgive his sin unless man pays back what he owes on account of it. And to make your arguments more certain, begin from far enough back to establish them upon a firm foundation.

Anselm: May God help me now, since you are not sparing me at all, and are not taking into consideration the weakness of my knowledge, in imposing such a great task upon me. I shall make the effort, however, now that I have started, trusting not in myself but in God, and by His help I shall do what I can. But for fear of causing repugnance in anyone who wants to read this, by too long and uninterrupted a discourse, let us separate what remains to be said from what has already been said, by a new introduction.

St. Bonaventure
1217-1274

Bonaventure was born in Italy and studied under Alexander of Hales in Paris. After joining the Franciscans he was quickly identified as a man of unusual intelligence as well as piety, and excelled in his studies and his teaching until 1257 when he was elected general of his Order. His relatively short life was thus divided into an academic followed by an administrative career, although he continued to write throughout both periods.

In the dynamic theological development of the 13th century, it was the theologians of the mendicant orders who were the chief contributors. The productive rivalry between Franciscans and Dominicans has often been interpreted as the clash of two conflicting syntheses, Augustinianism versus Aristotelianism. There is some truth in this, but in our own days several studies have made it clear that this is an oversimplification. "Augustinians" like Bonaventure made great use of Aristotle, and "Aristotelians" like Aquinas made great use of Augustine. Yet there certainly were distinctive differences in the theologies of these two great thinkers that led to later difficulties.

The realm of Christology, however, is not an area in which there was striking disagreement. The Sentences of Peter Lombard, which Alexander of Hales had introduced as the textbook for young theologians, summarized the work of earlier centuries and, in a famous section, described three different ways in *which the statement "God is man" could be understood. They are known as the "assumptus" theory, the "subsistence" theory, and the "habit" theory, and it is not clear what Peter Lombard's own position was. But both Bonaventure and Aquinas defended the second as the only formulation compatible with the doctrine set forth by the Fathers and Councils. It states that the Word, who subsists from all eternity in the divine nature, after the Incarnation subsists also in a human nature.*

It is not surprising that Bonaventure's whole theology has been described as Christocentric. In the spirit of Francis of Assisi, his followers emphasized the way in which Jesus is the unique Master in Christian life. It is especially his reflections on the human knowledge of Christ that are usually pointed to as Bonaventure's most original contribution.

The profound way in which Bonaventure synthesizes all and makes practical application while keeping Christ absolutely central can be seen in his intriguing treatment of contemplation: "The key to contemplation is the threefold understanding, viz., the understanding of the uncreated Word, through which all things are produced; the understanding of the Incarnate Word, through which all things are restored, the understanding of the inspired Word, through which all things are revealed."

The following selection is from his theological gem, The Breviloquium. *It contains Book Four in its entirety (all ten chapters). It should not be overlooked how Bonaventure has in this work even structurally remained Christocentric, for there are three books before his treatment of "The Incarnation of the Word" (God, Creation, and Sin), and three books after it (Grace, Sacraments, and Judgment). The work is one of the models of simplicity and clarity in the theological tradition of the West. To appreciate all that Bonaventure has condensed into it one would really have to turn to his earlier, more academic work on Peter Lombard's* Sentences. *Only thus could one get a real sense of what he has achieved in* The Breviloquium.

THE BREVILOQUIUM

CHAPTER 1

ON THE REASON WHY THE INCARNATION OF THE WORD
WAS NECESSARY, OR FITTING

A fter speaking of the Trinity of God, the creation of the world, and the corruption of sin, we must consider briefly the incarnation of the Word; for through this Word Made Flesh was wrought the salvation and restoration of mankind. Nor was this because God could not have saved and freed the human face in some other way; but because no other way would have been so fitting and so adapted, alike to the Redeemer, the redeemed, and the nature of redemption itself.

This should be understood as follows. The creative Principle of all things could not have been, and could not fittingly be conceived as being, any other than God. Now, the restoration of the universe is no lesser task than that of bringing it into existence; for to exist fittingly is no less important than simply to exist. It was entirely right, then, that the restorative Principle of all things should be the supreme God. In this way, just as God had created all things through the Word Not Made, even so He restored all things through the Word Made Flesh.

Again, God does all things with complete power, wisdom, and goodness or benevolence. It was fitting, then, that He so restore all things as to display His power, wisdom, and benevolence. What greater act of power than to combine within a single Person two extremely distant natures. What more suitable act of wisdom than to bring the universe to full perfection by uniting the First and the last: the Word of God, origin of all things, and the human creature, last to be made? What greater act of benevolence than for the Master to redeem the slave by *taking the nature of a slave*? This is, in truth, a deed of such unfathomable goodness that no greater proof of mercy, care, and love can be conceived.

Assuredly, then, this was the most fitting way for God the Restorer to reveal His power, wisdom, and benevolence.

When man sinned, he went astray, rejecting the most mighty, wise, and benevolent Principle. As a result, he fell headlong into weakness, ignorance, and malice. From having been spiritual, he became carnal, animal, and sensual. He could no longer imitate divine power, behold divine light, or love divine goodness. The most perfect way for man to be raised out of this misery was for the first Principle to come down to man's level, offering Himself to him as an accessible object of knowledge, love, and imitation. Man, carnal, animal, and sensual, could not know, love, or imitate anything that was not both proportionate and similar to himself. So, in order to raise man out of this state, *the Word was made flesh*; that He might be known and loved and imitated by man who was flesh, and that man, so knowing and loving and imitating God, might be healed of the disease of sin.

Finally, man could not be completely healed unless he recovered purity of soul, the friendship of God, and his proper excellence whereby he had been subject to none but God. Since such a thing could not be brought about except by God in *the nature of a slave*, it was fitting that the Word be made flesh.

Man could not have recovered *excellence* through any Restorer other than God. Had it been a mere creature, man would have been subject to this mere creature, and thus could not have recovered the state of excellence.

Nor could man have recovered the *friendship of God* except through a fitting Mediator, who would be the likeness and the friend of both: God in His divinity, and man in His humanity.

Nor, again, could man have recovered *purity of soul* if his sin had not been blotted out, which divine justice could not fittingly bring about except after condign atonement had been made. And because God alone *could* provide atonement for the whole of mankind, and man alone *must* provide it, for man had sinned: therefore the best of ways was that mankind be restored by the God-man, born of Adam's race.

Now, since man could not have recovered excellence except through the most excellent Restorer, nor friendship except through the most friendly Mediator, nor purity of soul except through the most superabundant Satisfier; and the most excellent Restorer could be none but God, the most friendly Mediator, none but a man, and the most superabundant Satisfier, none but Him who was both God and man: therefore, it was absolutely the most fitting thing for our restoration that the Word become incarnate. For as the human race came into being through the Word Not Made, and as it sinned because it failed to heed the Word Inspired, so it would rise from sin through the Word Made Flesh.

CHAPTER 2

ON THE INCARNATION AS REGARDS THE UNION OF NATURES

Concerning the incarnate Word, there are three points to consider: the union of natures, the fullness of gifts, and the endurance of sufferings for the redemption of man.

In order to clarify the mystery of the incarnation, we must consider the union of natures under three subheads: what was done; how it was done; and when it was done.

In regard to what was done in the incarnation, Christian faith obliges us to hold the following. The incarnation was brought about by the Trinity, through whom the Godhead assumed flesh, and a union was accomplished between Godhead and flesh in such a way that the assuming was not only of the material flesh, but also of the rational spirit in its three functions, vegetative, sensitive, and intellective; and that the union occurred through oneness, not of nature, but of person; not of a human person, but of a divine; not of the assumed, but of the Assuming; not of any [divine] Person indifferently, but of the Word alone, in whom the oneness is so absolute that whatever may be said of the Son of God may be said also of the Son of Man, and vice versa: excepting, however, such matters as designate the union itself or imply some contradiction.

This should be understood as follows. The incarnation is the work of the first Principle seen not only in His creative power but also in His restorative power as the Healer, the

Atoner, and the Reconciler. In so far as it means something performed, the incarnation is the work of the first Principle, the Doer by His omnipotence of all that is done. Now substance, power, and operation are absolutely one in the three Persons. That is why the work of the incarnation must necessarily proceed from the whole Trinity.

The incarnation derives from the first Principle as it expresses the *restorative power of God the Healer.*

The whole human race had fallen into sin, and was vitiated not only in spirit but also in flesh. Hence, the whole composite had to be assumed so that the whole might be cured. Now, the flesh, the part of our being more evident to us, is the part more distant from God. In order to use the more expressive term, to indicate a greater humiliation and a deeper condescension, we call this work, not "in-animation," but "in-carnation."

Again, the incarnation derives from the first Principle as it expresses the *restorative power of God the Atoner.*

Atonement can be offered only by a person both obliged to atone and able to do so; and none but man is obliged, and none but God is able. Both natures, then, the divine and the human, must concur in this atonement. Divine nature, however, could not so concur with another nature as to become part of a third that would arise from this concurrence; nor could divine nature change into some other; nor could another nature change into the divine: for divine nature is utterly perfect, simple, and immutable. Hence, divinity and humanity can be joined, not in a union of nature or of accident, but in one that is personal and hypostatic. Now, divine nature cannot subsist in any subject other than its own hypostasis. The union, then, cannot occur in the hypostasis or person of man, but only in that of God. By this union, therefore, the first Principle, in one of His hypostases, became the supposit of human nature. Hence, there is here but one Person, and one personal unity, that is, of the Person who assumed humanity.

Finally, the incarnation derives from the first Principle as it expresses the *restorative power of God the Reconciler.*

Such a reconciler is a mediator, and as mediation is proper to the Son of God, so is incarnation also. For it pertains to a mediator to be the channel between man and God for the restoration of man to the knowledge, the likeness, and the sonship of God. But there could be no more fitting mediator than the Person who both is produced and Himself produces, the intermediate One of the Three Persons; nor could there be a more fitting restorer of man to the knowledge of God than the Word through whom the Father reveals Himself, the Word able to be combined with flesh, even as a word with the voice. Nor again could there be a more fitting restorer of man to the likeness of God than He who is the Image of the Father. Nor, finally, could there be a more fitting restorer of man to adopted sonship than He who is the Son by nature. Most fittingly, then, did He become the Son of Man who was the very Son of God.

In the incarnation, the Son of God and the Son of Man are the same identical Person, since "whenever two things are identical to a third, they are identical to each other." Thus any predicate of one applies to both, unless it is a term that betokens incompatibility, such as those which express the very union of one nature with the other—for instance, to unite, to be made flesh, to assume, to be assumed; or those which express a negation as regards one nature of something pertaining to the other nature—for instance, to begin to be, to be created, and so forth. In these cases, for the reason here explained, there is an exception to the given rule.

CHAPTER 3

ON HOW THE INCARNATION CAME ABOUT

Concerning how the incarnation came about, the following must be held. When the angel announced to the Blessed Virgin Mary the mystery of the incarnation to be accomplished within her, she believed it, desired it, and consented to it: whereupon she was sanctified and made fruitful by the overshadowing of the Holy Spirit. Through His power, "virginal was her conceiving of the Son of God, virginal her birth-giving, and virginal her state after deliverance." She conceived not only a body, but a body with a soul, a body united to the Word and free from the stain of sin, a body all-holy and immaculate. That is why she is called the Mother of God, and is yet also the most sweet Virgin Mary.

This should be understood as follows. The incarnation is the work of the first Principle, whose restorative power is utterly congruous, universal, and complete: for by the law of His essence, His divine wisdom acts congruously, His divine generosity universally, and His divine power perfectly.

The incarnation is the work of the first Principle in that He uses the most *congruous* means of restoration. The means are congruous when the medicine specifically corresponds to the disease, the restoration to the fall, and the remedy to the injury. The human race had fallen through the suggestion of the devil, through the consent of a deceived woman, and through a begetting become lustful that handed down original sin to the offspring. Conversely, and most fittingly, there was here a good angel persuading to what was good, a Virgin believing him and consenting to the proposed good, and the love of the Holy Spirit making her both holy and fruitful for a virginal conception. Thus, "evils were healed by their opposites."

As it was a woman deceived by Satan and carnally known and corrupted by her husband's lust who handed down sin, sickness, and death to all, so it was a woman instructed by an angel and made holy and fruitful by the Holy Spirit who gave birth without taint of soul or body to an Offspring, the Giver of grace, health, and life to all who come to Him.

Again, the incarnation is the work of the first Principle in that He uses the most *universal* means of restoration, for through the Word made flesh the fall of both men and angels is repaired: that is, the fall of the dwellers of heaven and earth. And the fall of man is repaired in both sexes. Hence, if the cure was to be universal, it was wholly becoming that angel, woman, and man should concur in the mystery of the incarnation: the angel as the herald, the Virgin as the conceiver, and the Man as the conceived Offspring. The angel Gabriel was the herald of the eternal Father, the immaculate Virgin was the temple of the Holy Spirit, and the conceived Offspring was the very Person of the Word. The representatives of all three hierarchies—divine, angelic, and human—concurred in this way in the universal restoration, suggesting not only the Trinity of God, but also the universality of the boon, and the generosity of the supreme Restorer. Now, generosity is appropriated to the Holy Spirit, and so is the sanctification of the Virgin in whose womb the Word was conceived. Therefore, although the incarnation is the work of the whole Trinity, by appropriation we say that the Virgin conceived of the Holy Spirit.

Finally, the incarnation is the work of the first Principle in that He uses the most *complete* means of restoration. Hence, the conception must be complete as regards the Offspring, the manner of conceiving, and the power that effected it.

First, there must be completeness in the Offspring. Hence, at the very instant of conception, the seed was not only individuated but also organized, shaped, and vivified by the soul, and deified through union with the Godhead. Thus, the Virgin truly conceived the Son of God, because the flesh was united to the Divinity through the rational soul that rendered the flesh susceptible of such union.

Next, there must be completeness in the manner of conceiving. Of the four possible ways of producing man, three had already been followed: first, out of neither man nor woman, as with Adam; then, out of man but not woman, as with Eve; third, out of both man and woman, as with those born of concupiscence. For the completion of the universe, a fourth way must be introduced: out of woman without the seed of man, through the power of the supreme Maker.

Again, there must be completeness in the power itself. Hence, in the production of the Son of God, three powers concurred: the natural, the infused, and the uncreated. The natural power furnished the material element; the infused power set it apart by cleansing it; the uncreated power brought about instantly what a created power can achieve only gradually.

Thus, the Blessed Virgin became a Mother in the most complete sense, for, without man, she conceived the Son of God through the action of the Holy Spirit. Because the love of the Holy Spirit burned so intensely in her soul, the power of the Holy Spirit wrought marvels in her flesh, by means of grace prompting, assisting, and elevating her nature as required for this wondrous conception.

CHAPTER 4

ON THE INCARNATION AS REGARDS THE FULLNESS OF TIME

Concerning the time of the incarnation, the following must be held. While God could have become man at any time from the very beginning, He chose not to do so before the ages of the law of nature and of prefiguration had ended; that is, the ages of the patriarchs and prophets, to whom and through whom the incarnation had been promised. Then only did He deign to become flesh, in the consummation and fullness of time, as the apostle says: *But when the fullness of time came, God sent His Son, born of a woman, born under the Law, that He might redeem those who were under the Law.*

This should be understood as follows. The incarnation is the work of the first Principle acting as the Restorer. Necessarily and fittingly, then, it would come about in a manner consonant with free will, with the sublimity of the remedy, and with the final completion of the universe; for, in acting, the Artificer most wise takes all of these into account.

Free will requires that there be no compulsion. God was to restore mankind in such a way that those who willed to find the Saviour would be saved, while those who refused to seek Him would not. Now, no one calls a physician unless he knows he is sick; no one employs a teacher unless he knows he is ignorant; no one seeks a helper unless he knows he needs help. Because fallen man yet retained pride of intellect and power, God first established the age of the law of nature to convince him of his ignorance. And because man, convinced of his ignorance, still gloried in his power (as in the saying, "Here is the one who can do, but where is the one who should command?"), God added a law teaching moral precepts and multiplying ritual practices. Thereby man, made aware at last of both his duty and his weakness, was led to implore divine mercy and grace: and these were given to us by the coming of Christ. That is why the laws of nature and of Scripture had to precede the incarnation of the Word.

Again, such a *sublime remedy* must be accepted with the strongest faith and cherished with the most ardent love, as a deep and life-giving mystery. It was most fitting, then, that before the coming of Christ the prophets should appear with their manifold proofs, both explicit in words and implicit in figures. By these numerous and powerful testimonies, what had been hidden became clear and unshakable to belief. Repeated promises and intense longing also were to precede the coming of Christ. As the promised Blessing, He would be expected; as the Expected, He would be long awaited; as the Long Awaited, He would be more intensely desired; as the Desired of the Ages, He would be loved more fervently, received more thankfully, and heeded with greater care.

Finally, the perfection and *completion of the universe* require in all things an order of time and place. Since development must proceed from the imperfect to the perfect, and not conversely, the incarnation—the most perfect of all God's works—was to occur in the last age. As the first man, the crowning glory of the whole material world, had been made last, that is, on the sixth day for the completion of that world, so also the Second Man, the Completer of the whole world redeemed—in whom the first Principle is joined to the last, "God, to dust"—was to be born in the sixth and last age: the age meet for the exercise of wisdom and the curbing of concupiscence and the passage from turmoil to peace. These blessings belong to the sixth age of the world's course because of the incarnation in that age of the Son of God.

Christ came in the time of the law of grace; as a fulfillment of the promised mercy; and at the beginning of the sixth age. Each of these circumstances indicates plenitude: the law of grace fulfills the law of nature; the giving of what was promised fulfills the promise; and the sixth age—the number six being the number symbolical of perfection—is in itself a sign of completeness. That is why the coming of the Son of God marks the fullness of time: not because time ends with His coming, but because the hidden prophecies of all ages have been fulfilled. Had Christ come at the beginning of time, He would have come too soon; and had His coming been delayed until the very end, He would have come too late. It belonged to Him as the true Saviour to provide the healing—time between the time of sickness and the time of judgment; as the true Mediator, to come midway, some of His elect preceding and others following Him; as the true Leader, to come at a time when it was still possible for man *to press on toward . . . the prize*—that is, in the last age, when the end had not yet come, but the final judgment was close at hand: so that moved by fear of the judgment and urged on by hope of the reward and inspired by perfect example, we may follow our Leader vigorously and wholeheartedly *from virtue to virtue* until we attain the prize of everlasting happiness.

CHAPTER 5

ON THE FULLNESS OF THE GRACE OF CHRIST CONSIDERED IN THE GIFTS OF HIS WILL

After examining the union of natures within the incarnate Word, we shall go on to consider the fullness of His spiritual gifts. First, we shall speak of the fullness of grace in His will; then, of the fullness of wisdom in His intellect; lastly, of the fullness of merit in His actions, that is, in the work He performed.

Concerning the fullness of grace in Christ's will, the following must be held. From the instant of His conception, Christ wholly possessed all graces: the grace of the particular Person, the grace of headship, and the grace of union. By reason of the *grace of the particular person,* He was immune to any actual or possible sin, for neither did He sin nor could He have sinned. By reason of the *grace of union,* He merited not only the beatitude of glory, but also the adoration of latria, that is, the reverential worship due to God alone. By reason of the *grace of headship,* He prompts and enlightens all those who turn to Him either in simple faith, or through the sacraments of faith; that is, all the just, whether they live before or after His coming. *Those who went before Him, and those who followed, kept crying out, saying, —"Hosanna to the Son of David!"*

This should be understood as follows. Since restoration is the work of the first Principle, flowing from generosity and leading back to Him through conformation, it must be wrought through a gift and through a likening. Now grace, as it flows generously from God, also makes man like unto Him. Because, therefore, it is through grace that the restoring Principle brings about restoration, and because any perfection exists more fully

374

and completely in its fountainhead or origin than elsewhere, our restoring Principle, Christ the Lord, must have possessed the fullness of all grace. Because, moreover, this restoring Principle, in the act of restoration, proceeds not only as the Source, but also as the Means and as the End—as the End, in providing satisfaction; as the Means, in effecting reconciliation; and as the Source, in exercising superabundant influence—there was in Christ of necessity the fullness of grace alike in being the atoning End, the reconciling Means, and the Source of superabundant influence. Now, since what is capable of supplying full atonement must be pleasing to God and therefore free from all sin; and since this can come about only as a gift of divine grace conferred upon an individual man: of necessity, we must posit the the presence in Christ of a grace sanctifying and strengthening Him: that grace which we call *grace of the particular person.*

Again, because no being could be a means of reconciliation had he not possessed both natures, the higher and the lower, the adorable and the adoring, the only way this could be done was through a union supremely imparting dignity and grace. Thus, we must posit in Christ a grace above all grace, a grace worthy of all worship. This is what we call the *grace of union,* whereby Christ the Man *is, over all things, God blessed forever,* and is to be adored.

Finally, in order to have an effective influence, a being must possess fullness, original and fontal: a fullness not merely sufficient but superabundant. Hence, the Word made flesh was necessarily *full of grace and of truth,* so that *of His fullness* all the just might receive, as all members receive the impulse of motion and feeling from the head. That is why we call this the *grace of headship.* For as the head has in itself the fullness of the senses, and is coordinated with the other members of the body, presiding over them and giving them the benefit of direction, so also Christ, possessing grace in superabundance and being like unto us in nature, yet holy and just above others, confers upon those who turn to Him the spiritual benefit of grace, through which love and knowledge are given to spiritual beings.

The way to Christ is either through faith, or through the sacrament of faith. Yet, faith in Christ is the same in all believers, past, present, and future; and thus Christ's influencing power affects all men—those who are gone no less than those living now, or yet to come into being: alike those believing in Christ and those reborn in Him; those bound to Christ by faith, and those who, through an inpouring of grace, become His members and temples of the Holy Spirit, and thus sons of God the Father, joined to one another by the unbreakable bond of love. This bond is not destroyed by the passing of time any more than by distance in space: the just of all times and places constitute the one mystical body of Christ in that they receive both perception and motion from the one Head that influences them, through the fontal, radical, and original fullness of all grace that dwells in Christ the Fountainhead.

CHAPTER 6

ON THE FULLNESS OF WISDOM IN THE INTELLECT OF CHRIST

Concerning the fullness of wisdom in the intellect of Christ, the following must be held. Christ our Lord, the incarnate Word, not only knew all things, but knew them in every possible way. As God, Christ knew eternally; as a sensitive being, He knew sensorially; as a rational and spiritual being, He knew intellectually, this latter knowledge being threefold: of nature, of grace, and of glory. Thus He was endowed with wisdom both as God and as man, as possessing the beatific vision and as living on earth, as enlightened by grace and as gifted by nature. Christ, then, knew in five distinct ways. One, by His divinity, He knew actually and comprehensively all things, actual and possible, finite and infinite. Two, by glory, He knew actually and comprehensively all things actual and finite: but the infinite He did not know, except perhaps through a knowledge that was virtual or excessive. Three, by grace, He knew everything related to the salvation of mankind. Four, by integrity of nature, as it was in Adam, He knew everything related to the structure of the universe. Five, by sensible experience, He knew all that falls under the senses. It is by this last mode that He is said to have *learned obedience from the things that He suffered.*

This should be understood as follows. The Principle of our restoration restores us as much through provident wisdom as through bounteous grace. What was created according to an order of wisdom cannot be restored without the light and order of that same wisdom. Hence, as Christ was necessarily immune from all sin, so He was free from all ignorance, and thus completely filled with the clarity and all-embracing radiance of divine wisdom itself. Wherefore He enjoyed perfect knowledge according to both natures in their proper cognitive powers, and according to every mode of existence of beings.

Since beings have existence in eternal Art, in the human mind, and in their own concrete reality, Christ accordingly possessed this threefold knowledge. Now, in art, things are known in two different ways: by the artificer, and by the one who sees the work. In the mind, also, besides acquisition which, because of its imperfection, is not characteristic of Christ, things exist and may be known in two different ways: by innate and by infused dispositions. That is why the fullness of wisdom in Christ, God and man, requires a knowledge that is fivefold, as indicated above: in eternal Art, a twofold knowledge, through His divine nature and through the vision of glory; in His created intellect, a twofold knowledge, through innate science due to nature, as had by Adam and the angels, and through infused science due to grace, as had by the saints of God enlightened by the Holy Spirit; finally, in terms of the concrete reality of things, knowledge through sense-perception, memory, and intelligence which, in us, makes known some things not known before, whereas in Christ it made known in one way things already known in another.

Because God's substance, power, and action are immeasurable, Christ has in the first way, *through His divine nature*, an actual knowledge of all the countless possibles: for in some ineffable manner, the supremely Infinite sees all the countless possibles as actual.

But because even the loftiest creature is limited in its substance, power, and action, and the human mind, though it does not rest except in infinite Good, cannot naturally comprehend that Good—since, to use the term "comprehension" in its full meaning, the infinite cannot be comprehended by the finite: it follows that, in the second way, *through the vision of glory,* the intellect of Christ grasps everything within the reach of finite nature beatified by the infinite Good to which it is supremely united. Hence, the intellect of Christ knows the finite by actually comprehending it; but the infinite it does not know, except perhaps through a knowledge that is virtual and also excessive. For neither in the act of knowing nor in any other act can the created mind be equated with the Word.

Now, grace concerns primarily the work of restoration. Wherefore, in the third way, *through perfect grace*, Christ knew everything that had to do with our redemption; and He knew it far better and more completely than any prophet or angel could.

Furthermore, man *in the state of natural integrity* was designed to be higher than any other [material] creature, and to know that every other [material] creature was intended for his service. This appears clearly in the creation of the first man. Wherefore in the fourth way Christ understood, much more fully than Adam did, everything that had to do with the organization of the universe.

Finally, sense perception is limited to objects actually present. Through *sense knowledge*, therefore, Christ perceived things, not simultaneously, but successively, as much as needed for the work of man's salvation.

CHAPTER 7

ON THE PERFECTION OF MERIT IN THE ACTIONS OF CHRIST

In regard to Christ's plenitude of merit, the following must be held. In Christ our Lord, merit was perfect and complete [for seven reasons]. One, the Person who acquired merit was not only Man but also God. Two, the time for His acquiring merit ran from the instant of conception to the instant of death. Three, the means for acquiring merit were the perfect disposition of charity and the perfect practice of virtue in praying, acting, and suffering. Four, the benefit of this merit went not only to Christ Himself but also to us, indeed to all the just. Five, the result for us of this merit was not only glory but also grace and pardon; and not only glory of the soul but also glory of the flesh and the opening of the gates of heaven.

Six, the result for Christ of this merit was not glorification of soul which He already possessed, but the glorification of His body, the hastening of His resurrection, the honor of His name, and the exaltation of His judicial power. Seven, the manner in which He merited. There are three ways in which a man may be said to merit: by acquiring a claim he did not have before; by increasing his right to what is his due; by acquiring a further claim to what he already has by right. Christ merited in all three ways in our behalf, but for Himself, He merited only in the third way. All this He did through the fullness of the grace of the Holy Spirit, which established Him in beatitude, and at the same time in the state of meriting, so that all our merits are based on His.

This should be understood as follows. Christ our Lord, the Principle of our restoration, necessarily possessed the *fullness of grace* and wisdom which are for us the source of upright and holy living. Necessarily, then, He also possessed the fullness and perfection of all merit in every way such plenitude was possible. From the instant of His conception, Christ possessed in full the grace of union by which He was God. He enjoyed from this instant both the vision of glory and the use of free will. Hence, His merit was perfect both because of the high dignity of His Person and because His acquisition of merit began so soon.

Again, Christ possessed in fullness the grace of the particular Person which established Him firmly in charity and in the perfection of all the virtues, both as habits and as acts. Hence, His merit was necessarily complete through the very means by which it was gained: fundamental charity and the acts of a manifold virtue.

Furthermore, He possessed completely the grace of headship, through which He acted with fullest power upon His members. Hence, He acquired full merit, not only for Himself but also for us. As, in His divinity, He poured into us all the spiritual goods we possess, so, in His assumed humanity, He merited for us both the graces of the present life and the beatitude of the life to come.

Finally, the fullness of such great gifts necessarily implied in the soul of Christ a *supreme and perfect beatitude,* even though, providentially, for our sake, He lived in the state of pilgrimage. Hence, the merit He acquired for Himself was perfect. He did not merit the glory and beatitude which had been concreated with His soul and existed in Him naturally before any meritorious act: He merited only those things which could not coexist with the state of pilgrimage, that is, the glory of the body along with its exaltation to a high dignity.

His merit was perfect also because of the *mode of meriting*. From the very instant of His conception, He was established in full perfection. He instantly merited all that He was to merit for Himself. He thus acquired a further title to what was already due to Him for a different reason. He could not grow in holiness because He was utterly holy from the very beginning. Hence it would not be possible for Him to earn *for Himself* some reward to which He had no previous right, or to increase the right He would have had to it. These things, however, He did *for us* who, through His merit, are justified by grace, advance in righteousness, and are crowned with eternal glory.

The merit of Christ, then, is the root of all our merits, both those which offset penalties, and those which gain for us eternal life. For we are not worthy to be absolved from an offense against the supreme Good, nor do we deserve to be rewarded with the immensity of the eternal Reward which is God Himself, except through the merit of the God-Man, of whom we can and should say: *Lord, . . . it is You who have accomplished all we have done.* And He indeed is the Lord of whom the prophet speaks: *I say to the Lord, "My Lord are You. Apart from You I have no good."*

CHAPTER 8

ON THE STATE OF THE SUFFERING CHRIST

We have seen so far the union of natures and the fullness of gifts in the incarnate Word. Let us now consider His suffering. In this regard, we shall examine the condition of the Sufferer, the nature of the suffering, and its issue.

As regards the condition of the Sufferer, the following must be held. Christ assumed not only the nature of man, but also the defects of that nature, for He assumed such penalties of the body as hunger, thirst, and fatigue, and such penalties of the soul as sorrow, anguish, and fear. He did not, however, assume all the penalties of body and soul, for He was unaffected by physical disease of any kind, by ignorance, or by the body's war upon the spirit. Nor did He assume unqualifiedly those penalties to which He did consent: for He accepted the necessity of suffering, but no pain was to touch Him against either His divine or His rational will, although the passion did violence to his sensorial and carnal will, as appears from His prayer: *"Not as I will, but as Thou willest."*

This should be understood as follows. The restoring Principle, in His work of reconciliation, was to act as a Mediator. He needed, therefore, to be in harmony with both the estranged parties, as regards not only their natures but also their circumstances. Now, God is in the state of perfect righteousness, beatitude, impassibility, and immortality, while fallen man is in the state of sin, wretchedness, and liability to pain and death. For man to be led back to God, the *Mediator between God and men* had to share with God the state of righteousness and beatitude, and with man the state of passibility and mortality. "Transiently mortal, but permanently in the state of beatitude," Christ could lead man out of his wretchedness into beatific life: just as, conversely, the angel of evil, being immortal but living in the state of wretchedness and malice, became the means of leading man, by suggestion, into sin and misery. Since it belonged to Christ the Mediator to enjoy innocence and the bliss of fruition while being liable to death and suffering, He must have been at one and the same time a pilgrim and a possessor. Something of both states existed in Him: wherefore we say that He assumed the sinlessness of the state of innocence, the mortality of the state of fallen nature, and the perfect blessedness of the state of glory.

Again: since the damaging penalties, which are ignorance, weakness, malice, and concupiscence—four of the punishments incurred by original sin—are incompatible with perfect innocence, Christ could not be subject to them, nor did He in fact assume them. Other penalties, however, which give occasion for the practice of perfect virtue and testify to a humanity that is true, not feigned—penalties such as hunger and thirst in the absence of nourishment, sorrow and fear in the face of opposition—are characteristic of men in common; hence it was fitting for Christ to be subject to them, and He did in fact assume them.

Finally, no innocent person is morally obliged to suffer against his will, since this would contradict the order of divine justice; also, no mortal being wishes for death and suffering by natural impulse, for it is his nature to flee death. Christ, then, could assume these penalties only in a qualified manner: He was not to suffer against His rational will, since He not only lived in the state of beatitude and of union with the omnipotent Godhead through which He could repel any evil, but He also possessed perfect innocence which, according to the order of natural justice, cannot be obligated to suffer. Yet He was to suffer against His instinctive will: that is, against the sensible impulse and desire of His flesh. He expressed in His prayer— a rational act—the will of the flesh through which He shrank from suffering, when He said: *"Let this cup pass away from Me"*; but He conformed His rational will to the will of His Father, thus placing reason above instinct, when He said: *"Not My will but Thine be done."* One will was not opposed to the other, for "in His divine will, He wished what was just; in His rational will, He consented to justice; and in His natural instinct, while averse to pain, yet He did not contest justice. Each will acted in its field, tending toward its proper object: divine will to justice, rational will to obedience, and sensible will to nature." And so there was in Christ no conflict or struggle, but peaceful order and orderly peace.

CHAPTER 9

ON THE NATURE OF CHRIST'S SUFFERING

Now, concerning the nature of Christ's suffering, the following must be held. Christ suffered a passion most comprehensive, most bitter, and most shameful, a passion deadly yet life-giving. I repeat that, even though He could not suffer in His divine nature, He suffered in His human nature a passion most comprehensive, for not only every part of His body was affected, but every power of His soul as well. He suffered a passion most bitter, for besides enduring the anguish of His wounds, He endured the added anguish of grieving for our sins. He suffered a passion most shameful, alike because crucifixion was a punishment set aside for the worst criminals, and because He was placed in the company of evildoers, that is, robbers: He *was counted among the wicked*. He also suffered a passion that was deadly, for it separated body and soul, although both remained united with the Godhead. Accursed indeed is he who says that the Son of God ever relinquished the nature He had assumed.

This should be understood as follows. As the restoring Principle created man in orderly fashion, so must He also restore him in orderly fashion. He must restore him in such a way as to respect not only the freedom of the will, but also the honor of God and the harmonious functioning of the universe.

First, the work of restoration must *respect freedom of the will*. Christ, therefore, restored man through His all-efficacious example. An example is all-efficacious when it both invites to the summit of virtue and shows the way thither. Now, nothing could show man the way to virtue more clearly than the example of a death endured for the sake of divine justice and obedience: a death, moreover, not of the ordinary sort but agonizing in the extreme. Nothing could move man to virtue more strongly than the benignity with which the most high Son of God *laid down His life for us* who were not only undeserving, but actually full of guilt. This benignity appears all the greater in that the sufferings He endured for us, indeed, willed to endure, were so cruel and humiliating. For how could God, *who has not spared even His own Son but has delivered Him for us all . . . fail to grant us also all things with Him?* We are invited, then, to love Him, and loving Him, to follow His example.

Again, the work of restoration must *respect the honor of God*. Christ, therefore, brought it about by offering to the Father a fully satisfactory obedience. "Satisfaction means the repayment of the honor due to God." Now, the honor taken away from God through pride and disobedience in a matter in which man was obligated could be restored in no better way than through humiliation and obedience in a matter in which man was not bound in the least. Jesus Christ, as God, was equal to the Father through His divine nature; as man, He was innocent, and hence utterly undeserving of death. When, therefore, He *emptied Himself, . . . becoming obedient to death,* He paid back to God through a fully satisfactory obedience that which He Himself had not stolen, and offered for God's perfect appeasement a supremely pleasing sacrifice.

Finally, the work of restoration must *respect the harmonious functioning of the universe.* Wherefore it was achieved by means wholly consonant to that end, for it is most fitting that evils should be healed through their opposites. Man had sinned, aspiring to be as wise as God, desiring to enjoy the forbidden tree; hence, he who had risen in presumption was brought down to the level of lust; and through his sin, the whole of mankind was infected, forfeiting immortality and incurring inevitable death. To heal man by the appropriate remedy, God-made-man willed to be humiliated and to suffer on a tree. As an antidote to universal infection, He willed to suffer a passion most comprehensive; as an antidote to lust, a passion most bitter; as an antidote to pride, a passion most ignominious: as an antidote to death incurred but not willed, He chose to suffer a death not deserved but freely willed.

So thorough was the corruption within us that it not only affected our body and soul in a general way but penetrated to every part of the body and every power of the soul. Christ, therefore, suffered in every part of His body and in every power of His soul, even in the loftier part, reason. While this power, as a spiritual principle united with things above, supremely enjoyed the presence of God, as a principle of nature attached to things below, it supremely suffered: for Christ was both pilgrim and possessor.

Again, lust had powerfully infected us in body and soul, giving rise to sins of both flesh and spirit. Christ, therefore, suffered not only the cruelest physical pain, but also the bitterest mental torment. As His body was in a state of perfect health, and His senses thus to the highest degree alive, as His soul burned with perfect love for God and supreme concern for His neighbor, His anguish in both body and soul was immeasurable.

Furthermore, the disease of swollen pride arises sometimes from within, because of presumption, sometimes from without, because of vanity and the praise of others. To cure all pride, Christ endured both kinds of debasement: within Himself, as suffering, and from the companions with whom He had to suffer.

Finally, since Christ's divine nature was beyond the reach of pain, all this affected only His humanity; therefore, when He died, though His soul left His body, the oneness of His Person remained, and neither body nor soul was separated from the Godhead. Since it is the union of body and soul that makes a living man, it follows that, during those three days, Christ was not a man, although both body and soul were united with the Word. But because death in Christ's human nature could not bring death to the Person who never ceases to live, death itself perished in life. Through the death of Christ, *death is swallowed up in victory;* the prince of death has been vanquished.

Thus man has been freed from death and from the cause of death by the most efficacious means: the merit of the death of Christ.

CHAPTER 10

ON THE ISSUE OF THE PASSION OF CHRIST

Concerning now the issue of the passion of Christ and its fruit, the following must be held with undoubting faith. After the passion, the soul of Christ descended into the nether world or limbo, for the liberation, not of all, but of those who had died as members of Christ through living faith or through the sacraments of faith. Then, on the third day, He rose from the dead, assuming the same body He had quickened before, but a body no longer in the same state: for what had been subject to pain and death had risen impassible and immortal, to live forever. Forty days later, Christ ascended into heaven where, exalted above all creatures, He is enthroned at the right hand of the Father. These words are not to be understood as having a reference to place, which would not apply to God the Father: they refer, rather, to the summit of all good, meaning that Christ is established in the choicest riches of the Father. Finally, after ten more days, Christ sent down upon the apostles the Holy Spirit, as promised: by Him the Church was gathered out of all nations and set to function in accordance with the diverse offices and graces given to it.

This should be understood as follows. As Christ the uncreated Word had formed all things in perfection, so Christ the incarnate Word must have reformed all things in the same perfection. As the utterly perfect Principle could not allow an imperfect work to leave His hands, so the Principle of man's redemption must have made the remedy fully perfect. And if it was perfect, it must have been utterly sufficient and efficacious.

The means used for man's redemption was *utterly sufficient,* for it embraced heaven, earth, and the nether world. Through Christ, the souls in the lower regions were recovered, those on earth restored, and the heavenly ranks replenished. The first deed was achieved through mercy, the second through grace, and the third through glory. After the passion, the soul of Christ descended into hell in order to release the souls detained there; then He rose from the dead in order to restore life to those dead in sin; He ascended into heaven and *led captivity captive* in order to fill the ranks of the heavenly Jerusalem; finally, He sent the Holy Spirit in order to establish Jerusalem on earth. All these acts were necessary conditions and prerequisites of the full restoration of mankind.

The remedy was *utterly efficacious* in those who preceded the coming of Christ and those who followed it, those who served Him in the past and those who serve Him now, those who became His members and those who are so now: and such are those who cleave to Him through faith, hope, and love. The remedy, therefore, had to act first upon those who had faith in Christ, hoped out of faith, and loved out of hope. Hence it was fitting that Christ should descend into hell at once to set them free. And so the gates of heaven were opened through the atoning passion of Christ who, by making satisfaction, removed the sword, and by commuting the divine sentence, led His members out of hell.

In addition, this remedy must be particularly efficacious for those who were to be born after the coming of Christ; by attracting them to faith, hope, and love, it was finally to lead them into heavenly glory.

His purpose, then, was to establish in us the *faith* whereby we believe that Christ is true man and true God; whereby we also believe that He has willed to redeem us through His death, and is able to lead us back to life through His resurrection. It was to this end that He willed to rise to an immortal life only after a proper lapse of time—that is, thirty-six hours—thus proving that His death was real. If this period had been shortened and He had risen sooner, it might have been believed that He had not died at all, but had merely feigned death; if it had been longer, and He had continued to lie in death, He might have seemed powerless, and unable to lead others back to life. That is why *He rose again the third day.*

Next, that He might excite us to *hope,* He rose to that heavenly glory to which we also aspire. Since hope, however, is born only of faith in future immortality, He did not ascend at once, but allowed forty days to elapse during which, through many signs and proofs, He demonstrated the truth of His resurrection; for it was that by which the soul would be strengthened in faith and lifted up to the hope of heavenly glory.

Lastly, that He might inflame us with *love,* He sent down the fire of the Holy Spirit on the day of Pentecost. And since no one is filled with this fire who does not ask, seek, and knock with the importunate insistence of desire, He did so, not immediately after His ascension, but ten days later. During this interval the disciples, through fasting, prayers, and groanings, prepared themselves for the reception of the Spirit.

Thus, even as Christ had chosen the right time to suffer, so also He appointed the right time to rise from the dead, to ascend into heaven, and to send the Holy Spirit. The times were right both for establishing the three virtues mentioned above, and because of the many mysteries implied in the choice of such times.

The Holy Spirit, who is love and is possessed through love, is the origin of all charismata. When He came down, the fullness of these flowed out for the final perfecting of the mystical body of Christ. And because in a perfect body there must be a diversity of members, each member having its own function and office, and each office having its own charisma, it comes about that *to one through the Spirit is given the utterance of wisdom; and to another the utterance of knowledge, according to the same Spirit; to another faith, in the same Spirit; to another the gift of healing, in the one Spirit; to another the working of miracles; to another prophecy; to another the distinguishing of spirits; to another various kinds of tongues; to another interpretation of tongues. But all these things are the work of one and the same Spirit, who allots to everyone according as He will:* following in this His most generous providence and most provident generosity.

St. Thomas Aquinas
1225-1274

Thomas Aquinas has received in our own century due recognition for his extraordinary achievement in Christian theology. He was "a man of almost unparalleled power of mind, a man whose scope, precision, and vigor in clarification of ideas are seldom to be met with in the history of human thought" (Pieper). He constructed two different "summas," the first one in his mid-thirties, and the second more famous one in his forties, the Summa Theologica *that was incomplete at the time of his death.*

The first great systematic effort on which he ventured was his Summa Contra Gentiles, *in which—despite the title—he was doing something much more positive than merely polemics. The work would surely have received much greater attention over the years if it had not been overshadowed by his second magisterial* Summa. *It is from the earlier* Summa *that the following selection is taken.*

The Summa Contra Gentiles *has two main parts: Books I-III "seek to make known that truth which faith professes and reason investigates," whereas Book IV proceeds to "make known that truth which surpasses reason." This creative, even revolutionary, approach was admirably suited to the needs of the day. Contact between Christian thought and that of the Greeks and Arabs was on the increase, and the precise role and potential of human reason was coming under scrutiny.*

Book IV is thus open to misunderstanding; in it Thomas is building upon what he did in the first three books, but here the authority of Scripture can be (and is) appealed to. Faith is now taken for granted, the acceptance of divine revelation that "surpasses reason." So, he is setting out to enlighten those who already believe. With this new dimension, therefore, he doubles back and repeats the general structure of the earlier books, but now appealing to Scripture, the privileged source of new and deeper knowledge.

The first 26 chapters deal with God and His perfections, especially the mystery of the Trinity. Then the things that God has done which surpass reason are dealt with in chapters 27 to 78, especially the mystery of the Incarnation and what follows from it. And finally chapters 79 to 97 deal with the things surpassing reason which concern the ultimate end of man, such as the resurrection and glorification of bodies and the everlasting happiness of souls.

What follows is an excerpt consisting of chapters 39 to 49, the middle section of Book IV, showing Thomas' treatment of the mystery of the Incarnation in some of its key points. It stands as the basic truth of Christian faith that functions as a principle from which the others flow. Everything else is contained in it: salvation from despair, healing of frailty, remedy for sin, model for virtue, and assurance of God's friendship. Thomas' proverbial powers of synthesis are already well demonstrated here.

The triple strength of Aquinas is illustrated on every page of this work. He draws on his thorough familiarity with the Bible, he demonstrates his mastery of the thought of the Fathers and Councils, and he relentlessly applies his razor-edged power of reason. Thus it is theology in the grand tradition, faith in pursuit of understanding, with a focus on the central meaning of Christ that would mark Western theology for centuries to come.

SUMMA CONTRA GENTILES

CHAPTER 39

WHAT THE CATHOLIC FAITH HOLDS ABOUT
THE INCARNATION OF CHRIST

F rom what has been set down above it is clear that
according to the tradition of the Catholic faith we
must say that in Christ there is a perfect divine nature
and a perfect human nature, constituted by a rational soul and
human flesh; and that these two natures are united in Christ not
by indwelling only, nor in an accidental mode, as a man is
united to his garments, nor in a personal relation and property
only, but in one hypostasis and one supposit. Only in this way
can we save what the Scriptures hand on about the Incarnation.
Since, then, sacred Scripture without distinction attributes the
things of God to that man, and the things of that man to God
(as is plain from the foregoing), He of whom each class is said
must be one and the same.

But opposites cannot be said truly of the same thing in
the same way: the divine and human things said of Christ are, of
course, in opposition, *suffering* and *incapable of suffering,*
for example, or *dead* and *immortal,* and the remainder of this
kind; therefore, it is necessarily in different ways that the
divine and the human are predicated of Christ. So, then, with
respect to the "about which" each class is predicated no distinction must be made, but unity is discovered. But with respect
to "what" is predicated, a distinction must be made. Natural
properties, of course, are predicated of everything according to
its nature; thus to be borne downward is predicated of this
stone consequently on its nature as heavy. Since, then, there are
different ways of predicating things human and divine of Christ,
one must say there are in Christ two natures neither confused
nor mixed. But that about which one predicates natural properties consequently on the proper nature pertaining to the genus

of substance is the hypostasis and supposit of that nature. Since, then, that is not distinct and is one about which one predicates things divine and human concerning Christ, one must say that Christ is one hypostasis and one supposit of a human and a divine nature. For thus truly and properly will things divine be predicated of that man in accord with the fact that the man bears the supposit not only of the human but of the divine nature; conversely, one predicates things human of God's Word in that He is the supposit of the human nature.

It is clear also from this that, although the Son is incarnate, neither the Father nor the Holy Spirit, for all that, need be incarnate, since the Incarnation did not take place by a union in the nature in which the three divine Persons are together, but in hypostasis or supposit, wherein the three Persons are distinguished. And thus, as in the Trinity there is a plurality of Persons subsisting in one nature, so in the mystery of the Incarnation there is one Person subsisting in a plurality of natures.

CHAPTER 40

OBJECTIONS AGAINST FAITH IN THE INCARNATION

But against this statement of the Catholic faith many difficulties come together, and by reason of these the adversaries of the faith attack the Incarnation.

We showed in Book I that God is neither a body nor a power in a body. But, if He assumed flesh, it follows either that He was changed into a body or that He was a power in a body after the Incarnation. It seems, then, impossible that God was incarnate.

Again, whatever acquires a new nature is subject to substantial change; for in this is a thing generated, that it acquires a nature. Then, if the hypostasis of the Son of God becomes a subsistent anew in human nature, it appears that it was substantially changed.

Furthermore, no hypostasis of a nature extends outside that nature; rather, indeed, the nature is found outside the hypostasis, since there are many hypostases under the nature. If, then, the hypostasis of the Son of God becomes by the Incarnation the hypostasis of a human nature, the Son of

God—one must conclude—is not everywhere after the Incarnation, since the human nature is not everywhere.

Once again; one and the same thing has only one *what-it-is*, for by this one means a thing's substance and of one there is but one. But the nature of any thing at all is its *what-it-is*, "for the nature of a thing is what the definition signifies." It seems impossible, then, that one hypostasis subsist in two natures.

Furthermore, in things which are without matter, the quiddity of a thing is not other than the thing, as was shown above. And this is especially the case in God, who is not only His own quiddity, but also His own act of being. But human nature cannot be identified with a divine hypostasis. Therefore, it seems impossible that a divine hypostasis subsist in human nature.

Once again; a nature is more simple and more formal than the hypostasis which subsists therein, for it is by the addition of something material that the common nature is individuated to this hypostasis. If, then, a divine hypostasis subsists in human nature, it seems to follow that human nature is more simple and more formal than a divine hypostasis. And this is altogether impossible.

It is, furthermore, only in matter and form composites that one finds a difference between the singular thing and its quiddity. This is because the singular is individuated by designated matter, and in the quiddity and nature of the species the latter is not included. For, in marking off Socrates, one includes this matter, but one does not in his account of human nature. Therefore, every hypostasis subsisting in human nature is constituted by signate matter. This cannot be said of the divine hypostasis. So, it does not seem possible that the hypostasis of God's Word subsist in human nature.

Furthermore, the soul and body in Christ were not less in power than in other men. But in other men their union constitutes a supposit, an hypostasis, and a person. Therefore, in Christ the union of soul and body constitutes a supposit, hypostasis, and person of the Word of God; this is eternal. Therefore in Christ there is another supposit, hypostasis, and person beside the supposit, hypostasis, and person of the Word of God. Or so it seems.

There is more. Just as soul and body constitute human nature in common, so this soul and this body constitute *this man*, and this is the hypostasis of a man. But this soul and this body were in Christ. Therefore, their union constitutes an hypostasis, it seems. And we conclude exactly as before.

Again, this man who is Christ, considered as consisting of soul alone and body, is a certain substance; not, of course, a universal one; therefore, a particular one. Therefore, it is an hypostasis.

Moreover, if the supposit of the human and the divine nature in Christ is identified, then in one's understanding of the man who is Christ there ought to be a divine hypostasis. Of course, this is not in one's understanding of other men. Therefore, *man* will be said equivocally of Christ and others. Hence, He will not belong to the same species with us.

In Christ, what is more, one finds three things, as is clear from what was said: a body, a soul, and divinity. The soul, of course, since it is nobler than the body, is not the supposit of the body, but its form. Neither, then, is what is divine the supposit of the human nature; it is, rather, formally related to that nature.

Furthermore, whatever accrues to something after its being is complete accrues to it accidentally. But, since the Word is from eternity, plainly the flesh assumed accrues to Him after His being is complete. Therefore, it accrues to Him accidentally.

CHAPTER 41

HOW ONE SHOULD UNDERSTAND THE INCARNATION OF THE SON OF GOD

Now, to get at the solution of these objections, one must begin somewhat more fundamentally. Since Eutyches set it down that the union of God and man took place in nature; Nestorius, that it was neither in nature nor in person; but the Catholic faith holds this: that the union takes place in Person, not in nature—it seems necessary to know first what it is "to be made one in nature," and what it is "to be made one in person."

Grant, then, that *nature* is a word used in many ways: the generation of living things, and the principle of generation and of motion, and the matter and the form are all called nature. Sometimes, also, nature is said of the *what-it-is* of a thing, which includes the things that bear on the integrity of the species; in this way we say that human nature is common to all men, and say the same in all other cases. Those things, therefore, are made one in nature from which the integrity of a species is established; just as the soul and human body are made one to establish the species of the animal, so, universally, whatever the parts of a species are.

Of course, it is impossible that to a species already established in its integrity something extrinsic be united for the unity of its nature without losing the species. For, since species are like numbers, and in these any unity added or substracted makes the species vary, if to a species already perfected something be added, necessarily it is now another species; thus, if to animate substance one adds only *sensible,* one will have another species, for animal and plant are different species. It does happen, nonetheless, that one finds something which is not integral to the species; in an individual included under that species—white and dressed, for instance, in Socrates or in Plato, or a sixth finger, or something of the sort. Hence, nothing prevents some things being made one in the individual which are not united in one integrity of species; thus, human nature and whiteness and music in Socrates; and things of this kind are united and are called "one by subject." Now, the individual in the genus of substance is called *hypostasis,* and even in rational substances is called *person;* therefore, all things such as those mentioned are suitably said to be united "in the hypostasis" or even "in the person." Clearly, then, nothing prevents some things not united in nature from being united in hypostasis or person.

But, when the heretics heard that in Christ a union of God and man took place, they approached the exposition of this point in contrary ways, but neglected the way of the truth. For some thought of this union after the mode of things united into one nature: so Arius and Apollinaris, holding that the Word stood to the body of Christ as soul or as mind; and so Eutyches, who held that before the Incarnation there were two natures of God and man, but after the Incarnation only one.

But others, seeing the impossibility of this position, went off on a contrary road. Now, the things which accrue to one having a nature, but do not belong to the integrity of that nature, seem either to be accidents—say, whiteness and music; or to stand in an accidental relation—say, a ring, a garment, a house, and the like. Of course, they weighed this: Since the human nature accrues to the Word of God without belonging to the integrity of His nature, it is necessary (so they thought) that the human nature have an accidental union with the Word. To be sure, it clearly cannot be in the Word as an accident: both because God is not susceptible to an accident (as was previously proved); and because human nature, being in the genus of substance, cannot be the accident of anything. Hence there appeared to be this remaining: Human nature accrues to the Word, not as an accident, but as a thing accidentally related to the Word. Nestorius, then, held that the human nature of Christ stood to the Word as a kind of temple, so that only by indwelling was the union of the Word to the human nature to be understood. And because a temple possesses its individuation apart from him who dwells in the temple, and the individuation suitable to human nature is personality, this was left: that the personality of the human nature was one, and that of the Word another. Thus, the Word and that man were two persons.

To be sure, others wished to avoid this awkwardness. So, regarding the human nature they introduced a disposition such that personality could not be properly suitable to it. They said that the soul and the body, in which the integrity of human nature consists, were so assumed by the Word that the soul was not united to the body to establish any substance, lest they be forced to say that the substance so established fulfilled the account of person. But they held the union of the Word to soul and body to be like a union to things in an accidental relation, for instance, of the clothed to his clothes. In this they were somehow imitating Nestorius.

Now, with these accounts set aside by the foregoing, it must be laid down that the union of the Word and the man was such that one nature was not breathed together out of two; and that the union of the Word to the human nature was not like that of a substance—a man, say—to those externals which are accidentally related to him, like a house and a garment. But let the Word be set down as subsisting in a human nature as in one made His very own by the Incarnation; and in consequence that body is truly the body of the Word of God, and the soul in like manner, and the Word of God is truly man.

And although to explain this union perfectly is beyond man's strength, nonetheless, in accord with our measure and power, we will try to say something "for the upbuilding of the faith" (cf. Eph. 4:29), so that concerning this mystery the Catholic faith may be defended from the infidels.

Now, in all created things nothing is found so like this union as the union of soul to body. And the likeness would be greater, as Augustine also says, in *Against Felician,* if there were one intellect in all men. So some have held, and according to them one ought to say that the pre-existing intellect is in such wise united anew to a man's conception that from each of these two a new person is made; just as we hold that the pre-existing Word is united to the human nature in a unity of person. Accordingly, and by reason of the likeness of these two unions, Athanasius says in the Creed: "as the rational soul and flesh are one man, so God and man are one Christ."

However, since the rational soul is united to the body both as to matter and as to an instrument, there cannot be a likeness so far as the first mode of union is concerned, for thus from God and man one nature would be made, since the matter and the form properly establish the nature of a species. Therefore, what is left is to look upon the likeness so far as the soul is united to the body as an instrument. With this, also, there is the concordance of the ancient Doctors, who held that the human nature in Christ was "a kind of organ of the divinity," just as the body is held to be an organ of the soul.

Now, the body and its parts are the organ of the soul in one fashion; external instruments in quite another. For this axe is not the soul's very own instrument, as this hand is, for by an axe many can operate, but this hand is deputy to this soul in its very own operation. For this reason the hand is an instrument of the soul united to it and its very own, but the axe is an instrument both external and common. This is the way, then, in which even the union of God and man can be considered. For all men are related to God as instruments of a sort, and by these He works: "for it is God who worketh in you both to will and to accomplish according to His good will" (Phil. 2:3), as the Apostle says. But other men are related to God as extrinsic and separated instruments, so to say; for God does not move them only to operations which are His very own, but to the operations common to every rational nature, to understand the truth, for example, to love the good, to do what is just. But the human nature in Christ is assumed with the result that instrumentally He performs the things which are the proper operation of God alone: to wash away sins, for example, to enlighten minds by grace, to lead into the perfection of eternal life. The human nature of Christ, then, is compared to God as a proper and conjoined instrument is compared, as the hand is compared to the soul.

Nor is there departure from the course of natural things because one thing is by nature the proper instrument of another, and this other is not its form. For the tongue, so far as it is the instrument of speech, is the intellect's very own organ; and the intellect is nevertheless, as the Philosopher proves, not the act of any part of the body. In like manner, too, one finds an instrument which does not pertain to the nature of the species, which is, nevertheless, on the material side fitted to this individual; a sixth finger, for example, or something of the sort. Therefore, nothing prevents our putting the union of the human nature to the Word in this way: that the human nature be, so to speak, an instrument of the Word—not a separated, but a conjoined, instrument; and the human nature, nonetheless, does not belong to the nature of the Word, and the Word is not its form; nevertheless the human nature belongs to His person.

But the examples mentioned have not been set down so that one should look in them for an all-round likeness; for one should understand that the Word of God was able to be much more sublimely and more intimately united to human nature than the soul to its very own instrument of whatever sort, especially since He is said to be united to the entire human nature with the intellect as medium. And although the Word of God by His power penetrates all things, conserving all, that is, and supporting all, it is to the intellectual creatures, who can properly enjoy the Word and share with Him, that from a kind of kinship of likeness He can be both more eminently and more ineffably united.

CHAPTER 42

THAT THE ASSUMPTION OF HUMAN NATURE WAS MOST SUITED TO THE WORD OF GOD

From this it is also clear that the assumption of human nature was outstanding in suitability to the person of the Word. For, if the assumption of human nature is ordered to the salvation of men, if the ultimate salvation of man is to be perfected in his intellective part by the contemplation of the First Truth, it should have been by the Word who proceeds from the Father by an intellectual emanation that human nature was assumed.

There especially seems to be, furthermore, a kind of kinship of the Word for human nature. For man gets his proper species from being rational. But the Word is kin to the reason. Hence, among the Greeks "word" and "reason" are called *logos*. Most appropriately, then, was the Word united to the reasonable nature, for by reason of the kinship mentioned the divine Scripture attributes the name "image" to the Word and to man; the Apostle says of the Word that He is "the image of the invisible God" (Col. 1:15); and the same writer says of man that "the man is the image of God" (I Cor. 11:7).

The Word also has a kind of essential kinship not only with the rational nature, but also universally with the whole of creation, since the Word contains the essences of all things created by God, just as man the artist in the conception of his intellect comprehends the essences of all the products of art. Thus, then, all creatures are nothing but a kind of real expression and representation of those things which are comprehended in the conception of the divine Word; wherefore all things are said (John 1:3) to be made by the Word. Therefore, suitably was the Word united to the creature, namely, to human nature.

CHAPTER 43

THAT THE HUMAN NATURE ASSUMED BY THE WORD DID NOT PRE-EXIST ITS ASSUMPTION, BUT WAS ASSUMED IN THE CONCEPTION ITSELF

However, since the Word assumed the human nature into a unity of person (this is clear from the things already said), necessarily the human nature did not pre-exist before its union to the Word.

Now, if it were pre-existing, since a nature cannot pre-exist except in an individual, there would have had to be some individual of that human nature pre-existing before the union. But the individual of human nature is an hypostasis and person. Then one will be saying that the human nature to be assumed by the Word had pre-existed in some hypostasis or person. If, then, that nature had been assumed with the previous hypostasis or person remaining, two hypostases or persons would have remained after the union: one of the Word, the other of a man. And thus the union would not have taken place in the hypostasis or person. This is contrary to the teaching of the faith. But if that hypostasis or person in which the nature to be assumed by the Word had pre-existed were not remaining, this could not have happened without corruption, for no singular ceases to be what it is except through corruption. Thus, then, would that man have had to be corrupted who pre-existed the union and, in consequence, the human nature, as well, which was existing in him. It was impossible, then, that the Word assume into a unity of person some pre-existing man.

But at the same time it would detract from the perfection of the incarnation of God's Word, if something natural to man were lacking to it. But it is natural to man to be born in a human birth. But God's Word would not have this if He had assumed a pre-existing man, for that man in his birth would have existed as pure man, and so his birth could not be attributed to the Word, nor could the Blessed Virgin be called the Mother of the Word. But what the Catholic faith confesses regarding natural things is that He is "in all things like as we are, without sin" (Heb. 4:15); and it says that the Son of God was "made of a woman," following the Apostle (Gal. 4:4), that He was born and that the Virgin is the Mother of God. This, then, was not seemly, that He assume a pre-existing man.

Hence, also, it is clear that from the first moment of conception He united human nature to Himself. Just as God's Word's being human demands that the Word of God be born by a human birth, in order to be a true and natural man in complete conformity with us in respect to nature, so, too, it requires that God's Word be conceived by a human conception, for, in the order of nature, no man is born unless first he be conceived. But, if the human nature to be assumed had been conceived in any state whatever before it was united to the Word, that conception could not be so attributed to the Word of God that one might call Him conceived by a human conception. Necessarily, then, from the first moment of conception the human nature was united to the Word of God.

Again, the active power in human generation acts toward the completion of human nature in a determined individual. But, if the Word of God had not assumed human nature from the first moment of His conception, the active power in the generation would, before the union, have ordered its action to an individual in human nature, and this is a human hypostasis or person. But after the union the entire generation would have had to be ordered to another hypostasis or person, namely, to God's Word who was being born in the human nature. And such a generation would not have been numerically one, if thus ordered to two persons. Neither would it—in its entirety—have been one in form; this seems foreign to the order of nature. Therefore, it was not suitable that the Word of God assume human nature after the conception, but in the conception itself.

Once again, this seems to be required by the order of human generation: the one who is born must be the same as the one conceived, not another, for conception is ordered to birth. Hence, if the Son of God was born by a human birth, it must be that it was the Son of God who was conceived in a human conception, and not a pure man.

CHAPTER 44

THAT THE HUMAN NATURE ASSUMED BY THE WORD IN THE CONCEPTION ITSELF WAS PERFECT IN SOUL AND BODY

Now, this further point is also clear: In the very beginning of conception the rational soul was united to the body.

The Word of God, of course, assumed the body through the soul's mediation, for the body of a man is not more subject to assumption by God than other bodies except because of the rational soul. The Word of God, then, did not assume the body without the rational soul. Therefore, since the Word of God assumed the body in the very beginning of conception, necessarily the rational soul was united to the body in the very beginning of conception.

Moreover, one who grants what is posterior in a generation must grant also that which is prior in the order of generation. But the posterior in a generation is that which is most perfect. But the most perfect is the generated individual, and this in human generation is an hypostasis or person, and it is toward constituting this that the body and soul are ordered. Granted, then, a personality of the man generated, there must needs exist a body and a rational soul. But the personality of the man Christ is not different from the personality of God's Word. But the Word of God united a human body to Himself in the very conception. Therefore, the personality of that man was there. Therefore, the rational soul must also have been there.

It would also have been awkward if the Word, the fount and origin of all perfections and forms, were united to a thing not formed, which still was lacking the perfection of nature. Now, anything corporeal that comes into being is, before its animation, formless and still lacking the perfection of nature. It was, therefore, not fitting for the Word of God to be united to a body not yet animated. Thus, from the moment of conception that soul had to be united to the body.

Hence, this point, too, is clear: The body assumed in the moment of conception was a formed body, if the assumption of something not formed was improper for the Word. But the soul demands its proper matter, just as any other natural form does. But the proper matter of the soul is the organized body, for a soul is "the entelechy of a natural organic body having life potentially." If, then, the soul from the beginning of the conception was united to the body (this has been shown), the body from the beginning of the conception was of necessity organized and formed. And even the organization of the body precedes in the order of generation the introduction of the rational soul. Here, again, if one grants what is posterior, he must grant what is prior.

But there is no reason why a quantitative increase up to the due measure should not follow on the body's being animated. And so, regarding the conception of the man assumed, one should hold that in the very beginning of conception the body was organized and formed, but had not yet its due quantity.

CHAPTER 45

THAT IT BECAME CHRIST TO BE BORN OF A VIRGIN

It is, of course, now plain that of necessity that man was born from a Virgin Mother without natural seed.

For the seed of the man is required in human generation as an active principle by reason of the active power in it. But the active power in the generation of the body of Christ could not be a natural power, in the light of the points we have seen. For the natural power does not of a sudden bring about the entire formation of the body; it requires time for this, but the body of Christ was in the first moment of conception formed and organized as was shown. Therefore, one concludes that the generation of Christ was without natural seed.

Again, the male seed, in the generation of any animal at all, attracts to itself the matter supplied by the mother, as though the power which is in the male seed intends its own fulfillment as the end of the entire generation; hence, also, when the generation is completed, the seed itself, unchanged and fulfilled, is the offspring which is born. But the human generation of Christ had as ultimate term union with the divine Person, and not the establishment of a human person or hypostasis, as is clear from the foregoing. In this generation, therefore, the active principle could not be the seed of the man; it could only be the divine power. Just as the seed of the man in the common generation of men attracts to its subsistence the matter supplied by the mother, so this same matter in the generation the Word of God has assumed into union with Himself.

In like manner, of course, it was manifestly suitable that, even in the human generation of the Word of God, some spiritual property of the generation of a word should shine out. Now, a word as it proceeds from a speaker—whether conceived within or expressed without—brings no corruption to the speaker; rather, the word marks the plenitude of perfection in the speaker. It was in harmony with this that in His human generation the Word of God should be so conceived and born that the wholeness of His Mother was not impaired. And this, too, is clear: It became the Word of God, by whom all things are established and by whom all things are preserved in His wholeness, to be born so as to preserve His Mother's wholeness in every way. Therefore, suitably this generation was from a virgin.

And for all that, this mode of generation detracts in nothing from the true and natural humanity of Christ, even though He was generated differently from other men. For clearly, since the divine power is infinite, as has been proved, and since through it all causes are granted the power to produce an effect, every effect whatever produced by every cause whatever can be produced by God without the assistance of that cause of the same species and nature. Then, just as the natural power which is in the human seed produces a true man who has the human species and nature, so the divine power, which gave such power to the seed, can without its power produce that effect by constituting a true man who has the human species and nature.

But let someone object: a naturally generated man has a body naturally constituted from the seed of the male and what the female supplies—be that what it may; therefore, the body of Christ was not the same in nature as ours if it was not generated from the seed of a male. To this an answer may be made in accordance with a position of Aristotle; he says that the seed of the male does not enter materially into the constitution of what

404

is conceived; it is an active principle only, whereas the entire matter of the body is supplied by the mother. Taken thus, in respect of matter the body of Christ does not differ from ours; for our bodies also are constituted materially of that which is taken from the mother.

But, if one rejects the position of Aristotle just described, then the objection just described has no efficacy. For the likeness or unlikeness of things in matter is not marked off by the state of the matter in the principle of generation, but by the state of the matter already prepared as it is in the term of the generation. There is no difference in matter between air generated from earth and that from water, because, although water and earth are different in the principle of generation, they are nonetheless reduced by the generating action to one disposition. Thus, then, by the divine power the matter taken from the woman alone can be reduced at the end of the generation to a disposition identical with that which matter has if taken simultaneously from the male and female. Hence, there will be no unlikeness by reason of diversity of matter between the body of Christ which was formed by the divine power out of matter taken from the mother alone, and our bodies which are formed by the natural power from matter, even though they are taken from both parents. Surely this is clear; the matter taken simultaneously from a man and a woman and that "slime of the earth" (Gen. 2:7) of which God formed the first man (very certainly a true man and like us in everything) differ more from one another than from the matter taken solely from the female from which the body of Christ was formed. Hence, the birth of Christ from the Virgin does not at all diminish either the truth of His humanity or His likeness to us. For, although a natural power requires a determined matter for the production of a determined effect therefrom, the divine power, the power able to produce all things from nothing, is not in its activity circumscribed within determinate matter.

In the same way, that she was a virgin conceived and gave birth diminishes not at all the dignity of the Mother of Christ—so that she be not the true and natural mother of the Son of God. For, while the divine power worked, she supplied the natural matter for the generation of the body of Christ—and this alone is required on the part of the mother; but the things which in other mothers contribute to the loss of virginity belong not to the process of being a mother, but to that of being a father, in order to have the male seed arrive at the place of generation.

CHAPTER 46

THAT CHRIST WAS BORN OF THE HOLY SPIRIT

Although, of course, every divine operation by which something is accomplished in creatures is common to the entire Trinity (as has been shown in the points made above), the formation of Christ's body, which was perfected by the divine power, is suitably ascribed to the Holy Spirit although it is common to the entire Trinity.

Now, this seems to be in harmony with the Incarnation of the Word. For, just as our word mentally conceived is invisible, but is made sensible in an external vocal expression, so the Word of God in the eternal generation exists invisibly in the heart of the Father, but by the Incarnation is made sensible to us. Thus, the Incarnation of God's Word is like the vocal expression of our word. But the vocal expression of our word is made by our spirit, through which the vocal expression of our word takes place. Suitably, then, it is through the Spirit of the Son of God that the formation of His flesh is said to have taken place.

This is also in harmony with human generation. The active power which is in the human seed, drawing to itself the matter which flows from the mother, operates by the spirit, for this kind of power is founded on the spirit, and by reason of its control the seed must be cloudy and white. Therefore, the Word of God taking flesh to Himself from the Virgin is suitably said to do this by His Spirit—to form flesh by assuming it.

This also helps to suggest a cause moving to the Incarnation of the Word. And this could, indeed, be no other than the unmeasured love of God for man whose nature He wished to couple with Himself in unity of person. But in the divinity it is the Holy Spirit who proceeds as love, as was said. Suitably, then, was the task of Incarnation attributed to the Holy Spirit.

Sacred Scripture, too, is accustomed to attributing every grace to the Holy Spirit, for what is graciously given seems bestowed by the love of the giver. But no greater gift has been bestowed on man than union with God in person. Therefore, suitably is this work marked as the Holy Spirit's own.

CHAPTER 47

THAT CHRIST WAS NOT THE SON OF THE HOLY SPIRIT IN THE FLESH

Now, although Christ is said to be conceived of the Holy Spirit and of the Virgin, one cannot for all that say that the Holy Spirit is the father of Christ in the human generation as the Virgin is His mother.

For the Holy Spirit did not produce the human nature of Christ out of His substance, but by His power alone operated for its production. It cannot, therefore, be said that the Holy Spirit is the father of Christ in His human generation.

It would, furthermore, be productive of error to say that Christ is the son of the Holy Spirit. Plainly, God's Word has a distinct Person in that He is the Son of God the Father. If, then, He were in His human nature called the son of the Holy Spirit, one would have to understand Christ as being two sons, since the Word of God cannot be the son of the Holy Spirit. And thus, since the name of *sonship* belongs to a person and not to a nature, it would follow that in Christ there are two Persons. But this is foreign to the Catholic faith.

It would be unsuitable, also, to transfer the name and the authority of the Father to another. Yet this happens if the Holy Spirit is called the father of Christ.

CHAPTER 48

THAT CHRIST MUST NOT BE CALLED A CREATURE

It is clear, moreover, that, although the human nature assumed by the Word is a creature, it cannot, for all that, be said without qualification that Christ is a creature.

For to be created is to become something. Now, since becoming is terminated in being simply, a becoming is of that which has subsistent being, and it is a thing of this kind which is a complete individual in the genus of substance, which, indeed in an intellectual nature is called a person or even an hypostasis. But one does not speak of forms and accidents and even parts becoming, unless relatively, since they have no subsistent being in themselves, but subsist in another; hence, when one becomes white, this is not called becoming simply, but relatively. But in Christ there is no other hypostasis or person save that of God's Word, and this person is uncreated, as is clear from the foregoing. Therefore, one cannot say without qualification: "Christ is a creature," although one may say it with an addition, so as to say a creature "so far as man" or "in His human nature."

Granted, however, that one does not, in the case of a subject which is an individual in the genus of substance, refer to that as becoming simply which belongs to it by reason of accidents or parts, but that one calls it becoming only relatively, one does predicate simply of the subject whatever follows naturally on the accidents or parts in their own intelligibility; for one calls a man "seeing" simply: this follows the eye; or "curly" because of his hair; or "visible" because of his color. Thus, then, the things which follow properly on human nature can be asserted of Christ simply: that He is "man"; that He is "visible"; that He "walked," and that sort of thing. But what is the person's very own is not asserted of Christ by reason of His human nature, unless with some addition whether expressed or implied.

CHAPTER 49

SOLUTION OF THE ARGUMENTS AGAINST
THE INCARNATION GIVEN ABOVE

With what has now been said the points made previously against faith in the Incarnation are easily disposed of.

For it has been shown that one must not understand the Incarnation of the Word thus: that the Word was converted into flesh or that He is united to the body as a form. Hence, it is not a consequence of the Word's Incarnation that He who is truly God is a body or a power in a body as the first argument was trying to proceed.

Neither does it follow that the Word was substantially changed by the fact that He assumed human nature. For no change was made in the Word of God Himself, but only in the human nature which was assumed by the Word, in accord with which it is proper that the Word was both temporally generated and born, but to the Word Himself this was not fitting.

What is proposed in the third argument is also without necessity. For an hypostasis is not extended beyond the limits of that nature from which it has subsistence. The Word of God, of course, has no subsistence from the human nature; rather, He draws the human nature to His subsistence or personality. It is not through, but in, human nature that He subsists. Hence, nothing prevents the Word of God from being everywhere, although the human nature assumed by the Word of God is not everywhere.

Thus, also, the fourth is answered. For in any subsistent thing there must be only one nature by which it has being simply. And so, the Word of God has being simply by the divine nature alone, not, however, by the human nature; by human nature He has being *this*—namely, being a man.

The fifth also is disposed of in the very same way. For it is impossible that the nature by which the Word subsists be other than the very person of the Word. Of course, He subsists by the divine nature and not by the human nature, but He draws the latter to His own subsistence that He may subsist in it, as was said. Hence, it is not necessary that the human nature be identical with the person of the Word.

From this also follows the exclusion of the sixth objection. For an hypostasis is less simple—whether in things or in the understanding—than the nature through which it is established in being: in the thing, indeed, when the hypostasis is not its nature; or in the understanding alone in the cases in which the hypostasis and the nature are identified. The hypostasis of the Word is not established simply by the human nature so as to have being through the human nature, but through it the Word has this alone: that He be man. It is, then, not necessary that the human nature be more simple than the Word so far as He is the Word, but only so far as the Word is this man.

From this also the way is open to solving the seventh objection. For it is not necessary that the hypostasis of the Word of God be constituted simply by signate matter, but only so far as He is this man. For only as this man is He constituted by the human nature, as was said.

Of course, that the soul and body in Christ are drawn to the personality of the Word without constituting a person other than the person of the Word does not point to a lessened power, as the eighth argument would have it, but to a greater worthiness. For everything whatever has, when united to what is worthier, a better being than it has when it exists through itself; just so, the sensible soul has a nobler being in man than it has in the other animals in which it is the principal form, for all that it is not such in man.

Hence, also, comes the solution to the ninth objection. In Christ there was, indeed, this soul and this body, for all that there was not constituted from them another person than the person of God's Word, because they were assumed unto the personality of God's Word; just as body, too, when it is without the soul, does have its own species, but it is from the soul, when united to it, that it receives its species.

Thus, also, one answers what the tenth argument proposed. It is clear that this man who is Christ is a certain substance which is not universal, but particular. And He is an hypostasis; nevertheless, not another hypostasis than the hypostasis of the Word, for human nature has been assumed by the hypostasis of the Word that the Word may subsist in human as well as in divine nature. But that which subsists in human nature is this man. Hence, the Word itself is supposed when one says "this man."

But, let one move the very same objection over to human nature and say it is a certain substance, not universal but particular and consequently an hypostasis—he is obviously deceived. For human nature even in Socrates or Plato is not an hypostasis, but that which subsists in the nature is an hypostasis.

But to call a human nature a substance and particular is not to use the meaning in which one calls an hypostasis a particular substance. "Substance" we speak of with the Philosopher in two ways: for the supposit, namely, in the genus of substance which is called hypostasis; and for the *what-it-is* which is "the nature of a thing." But the parts of a substance are not thus called particular substances—subsisting, so to say, in themselves; they subsist in the whole. Hence, neither can one call them hypostases, for none of them is a complete substance. Otherwise, it would follow that in one man there are as many hypostases as there are parts.

Now, to the eleventh argument in opposition. The solution is that equivocation is introduced by a diversity of the form signified by a name, but not by diversity of supposition. For this name "man" is not taken as equivocal because sometimes it supposes Plato, sometimes Socrates. Therefore, this name "man" said of Christ and of other men always signifies the same form; namely, human nature. This is why it is predicated of them univocally; but it is only the supposition which is changed, and, to be sure, in this: when it is taken for Christ it supposes an uncreated hypostasis, but when it is taken for others it supposes a created hypostasis.

Nor, again, is the hypostasis of the Word said to be the supposit of the human nature, as though subjected to the latter as to a more formal principle, as the twelfth argument proposed. This would, of course, be necessary if it were the human nature which establishes the hypostasis of the Word in being simply. This is obviously false: for the hypostasis of the Word is the subject of the human nature so far as He draws this latter unto His own subsistence, just as something drawn to a second and nobler thing to which it is united.

For all that, it does not follow that the human nature accrues to the Word accidentally, because the Word pre-exists from eternity, as the final argument was trying to conclude. For the Word assumed human nature so as to be truly man. But to be man is to be in the genus of a substance. Therefore, since by union with human nature the hypostasis of the Word has the being of man, this does not accrue to the Word accidentally. For accidents do not bestow substantial being.

John Duns Scotus

1266-1308

John was a Scot from Duns who joined the English Province of the Friars Minor and was ordained a priest in 1291. He spent 13 years at Oxford, leaving in 1301 for Paris. His inception as master at the University of Paris took place in 1305, the beginning of his most productive literary period. He went to Cologne in 1307 and died prematurely the following year.

"Duns Scotus was one of the most able and acute thinkers Britain has produced. Of a critical turn of mind and gifted with an ability to discover fine distinctions and shades of meaning, he possessed at the same time a power of constructive systematization" (Copleston). The Quodlibetal Questions were argued publicly by Scotus in Paris, probably in 1306. Such disputations were popular affairs at which anyone present could pose a question or raise an objection. All courses were suspended so that everyone could be present. At its best it was a virtuoso performance by a leading master. In this one we see Scotus rage over a wide field, deftly handling 21 different questions. The following selection consists of only one of these, question 19.

The discipline of the scholastic format is obvious. Scotus follows the customary three steps: 1) the question is introduced with short initial arguments pro and con; 2) then comes the body, or corpus; and 3) the replies to the initial counter-arguments conclude the treatment. The obvious strength of such a method is its precision; order is systematically introduced into chaos.

The overall subject of Scotus' disputation is "God and Creatures," but the question we have selected has to do with how the human nature of Christ was united to the Word or the second person of the Trinity. In his answer Scotus develops his theory of what it means to be a created person.

The subtlety of this kind of theology has often brought ridicule upon it, but one would have to be totally biased not to see something of its value. Even granting that it is not a style of thinking that appeals to many today, all must marvel at the intense concentration that characterizes it. If, as the proverb says, "the truth lies in distinction," it becomes clear why Scotus placed such value on them; they are but one mode of pursuing truth.

This is not the only work of Scotus dealing with Christology. On the contrary, it is just one question raised in a given context. In his Oxford work on Peter Lombard's Sentences *he stresses the primacy of Christ in God's creative design, denying that the Incarnation necessarily presupposes the sin of mankind. It was rather foreseen by God from eternity as the end, the goal of history. As he puts it elsewhere; "Christ in the flesh . . . was foreseen and predestined to grace and glory prior to the prevision of the passion of Christ, as medicine for the fall, just as the doctor wills the health of a man prior to prescribing medicine for his cure."*

The focus and concerns change as Christians contemplate the continuing significance of Jesus in and for human history. But one would have to search long and hard to find one who surpasses Duns Scotus in the energy, intensity, and acuity of thought which he brings to bear on the Gospel mystery.

GOD AND CREATURES:
THE QUODLIBETAL QUESTIONS

QUESTION NINETEEN

IS THE UNITY IN CHRIST OF THE HUMAN NATURE WITH THE WORD MERELY THE ASSUMED NATURE'S DEPENDENCE UPON THE WORD?

The next question has to do with the dependence of the assumed nature upon the Word. Is the unity of human nature with the Word in Christ merely the human nature's dependence upon the Word?

Arguments Pro and Con

It is argued it is not:

Here there is such unity as suffices for the nature to be truthfully predicated of the Person according to that dictum: "Such is that union that it made God man and man God" (*The Trinity*). Now dependence alone seems insufficient for this. What is dependent is not always predicated of that on which it depends. This seems to be the case here, for the assumed nature [also] depends upon the Father, yet the Father is not man. Therefore, in the case of Christ there is some other unity besides the dependence of the human nature upon the Word.

19.2 Against the preceding view it is argued that if you examine all the other kinds of unity, you seem to find no other unity present here.

Body of the Question

19.3 In this question three points need investigation: (1) What type of unity must be posited in this case; (2) How is such unity possible on the part of the Person assuming the nature; (3) How is it possible on the part of the assumed nature?

ARTICLE I
THE TYPE OF UNITY TO BE POSITED HERE

19.4 [Proof that it is a unity of order] As for the first point, it is an article of faith that human nature is personally united to the Word. "The Word was made flesh," (John 1) where "flesh" means man, according to Augustine. Also various Creeds of formulas of faith assert this truth expressly. From this the conclusion follows that the human nature in Christ is ordered to, or dependent upon, the Word.

19.5 Proof of the implication: Every union results either from a form informing a subject, or from aggregation, or from some order. Lest there be any altercation on the grounds that the essential perfections, notional properties, or other things are said to be united in God, let it be understood I am speaking about a unity of really distinct things.

In the case at hand, however, no union based on informing can be postulated since the Word is neither potential, informable, nor an act which informs the human nature.

Neither is there any union here resulting solely from aggregation, for the Word has this sort of union with my own nature, and the Father has such with the assumed nature [of Christ], and in general such a union obtains between any two things that are simply distinct. Furthermore, it is clear that such a union does not suffice to produce the unity characteristic of a person. All that remains therefore is the third type, namely, a union of order.

The order, however, is that of the posterior to the prior. The Word obviously is not posterior to [human] nature; hence it is the other way around. The nature is posterior with respect to the Word and thus dependent on him.

19.6 Another proof of the consequence: A union of a nature to the Word implies a real relation, not on the part of the Word but on the part of the assumed nature. Now every real relation that is neither mutual nor between equals is a kind of dependence, or at least requires in the *relatum* some dependence upon that to which it is related. Furthermore, we infer the nature has this sort of dependence upon the Word from this article of faith, namely, that only the Son became incarnate. From this it follows that the nature is not united to each person of the Trinity, but to the Son alone.

19.7 [Three Conclusions] From the above three conclusions follow.

First, this dependence is not properly one of caused to cause. According to Augustine: "In the relation to the creature, however, the Father, the Son, and the Holy Spirit are one principle."

19.8 Second, the formal ground or reason why the Word is that on which a human nature depends is not common to all three persons, for even prior to the actual dependence, there is always some ground in the subject for supporting such dependence and this ground is the term of the dependence. Therefore, if the ground for being that on which a human nature depends were common to all three persons, the Trinity as a whole would be the term of the dependence, which is false.

19.9 Here it is objected that even though something be common to the whole Trinity, it still exists in different ways in the different persons. Hence this could be the reason for grounding the dependence in one and not in another.

Answer: In what is common to all three persons, the only distinction would be that of origin. The first person, for instance, would not have the divine nature from anyone, whereas the second would have it from the first and the third from the other two. But this does not explain how one person and not another is that on which a [human] nature depends, for this distinction would be wholly the same whether no person had become incarnate or whether they all had or whether some other, for example, the Father, had become incarnate.

19.10 From this the third conclusion follows, namely, that the formal ground for supporting the dependence of [human] nature is the personal or hypostatic entity of the Word.

Proof of this: A real union requires some kind of real entity, be it that of the formal term itself or that of the ground for supporting [the dependency]. But every entity in the intellectual nature of which we are speaking is either one that is essential or pertains to the [divine] nature, or a hypostatic or personal entity. Now it has been proved [in 19.8f.] that the ground for supporting this dependency is not an entity pertaining to the essence or nature of God. Therefore, it will be hypostatic. In short, the dependence is not a relationship to something communicable but to something incommunicable or subsistent. This serves essentially as the supporting term or ground for the dependency of the dependent nature as communicable or communicated.

19.11 Objection: The same kind of union could exist with the person of the Father. Consequently, the union would have the same kind of formal term. But the hypostatic entities of the different persons are different. Therefore [it is not a union with any incommunicable subsistent entity].

Answer: One could reply in terms of what is common to the divine persons. For if one posits some other real feature they have in common, then one could grant that each of the three has this same common, not proper, ground for supporting such a relationship to himself.

Thus the first point [in 19.4ff.] appears clear, viz., that the union of the [human] nature with the Word is a certain kind of dependence and consists in the sort of dependence a communicable nature has upon something incommunicable and subsistent.

ARTICLE II
THE POSSIBILITY OF SUCH A UNION ON THE PART
OF THE ASSUMING PERSON

1. First Proof

19.12 [Statement of the Proof] As for the second main point [of 19.3] we must see how such a union is possible on the part of the term, i.e., how this incommunicable subsistent [person] is able to be the term on which something depends. This can be explained somehow as follows: If there were any impossibility involved, it would stem from the fact that [what the human nature depends upon is] either (a) a person or subsistent subject; (b) or a divine person; (c) or this particular person, who alone is said to be the term of this dependence.

19.13 But on none of these three counts is such a union incompatible with this person. There are two proofs for this;

First, there is nothing contradictory about something independent being that upon which something else depends. Although it has an independence of its own, there is nothing repugnant about something depending upon it. Entitatively the Word is independent, even so far as his personal entity is concerned, and this independence is something proper to that entity. Therefore, in none of these three ways is there anything contradictory or incompatible about [the Word] being that on which a human nature depends.

19.14 Proof of the minor: Whatever formally excludes imperfection also formally rules out any kind of dependence. The formal ground for excluding one will also be grounds for forbidding the other. This is evident since dependence is either formally imperfection or has imperfection as a necessary adjunct. Now the hypostatic property of the Son formally precludes any imperfection and is for him the formal ground why it cannot be present. For there is no feature of the divine reality that is compatible with imperfection. Otherwise it would be possible for some imperfection to characterize that particular feature. And assuming it did, it could still remain imperfection and if it remained intrinsic to God, then some imperfection could be intrinsic to God, which is impossible.

19.15 [Objections] Against this argument objections are raised. The first is to the major. If independence implies the possibility of being the term upon which something depends, then any independence of this sort could support any dependence of the same sort. But the consequent is false, as is evident from the following cases.

Take substance and accident, for instance. Every substance is independent; it lacks the sort of dependence an accident has on its subject. Yet not every substance can support any sort of dependence an accident might have upon a subject. A stone, for example, cannot sustain wisdom.

19.16 It is clearly the same as regards the dependence of the whole upon its parts. There are many things whose nature simply precludes being dependent in this way, and yet they cannot be that on which something else depends in this way. Every simple being which is neither a whole nor a part is such.

19.17 The dependence of caused upon cause illustrates the same point. An angel is independent of every created cause and yet it cannot be that upon which everything caused depends.

19.18 It is also clear in general of the property we are dealing with here. Since the personal property is absolutely independent, it could support any form of causal dependence a creature has upon God, which is manifestly false. For the formal basis of causation is not a personal property but something common to all three divine persons, as was said above [in 19.7] in the quotation from Augustine.

19.19 Therefore, this counter-reply is made to the major. Although it is not inconsistent that something independent, in virtue of its independence, should be that upon which something else depends, its independence alone does not suffice to make the other depend upon it. It must have in addition an essential priority or primacy as regards that dependent, since dependence relates what is essentially posterior to what is essentially prior. It is also necessary that the prior have some perfection lacking in the dependent.

As for the case at hand, the personal or hypostatic entity has no essential priority in respect to creatures, for an essential order obtains *per se* only between essences (in contrast to hypostatic entities), since it is "forms (i.e., essences) that are like numbers." Besides, the hypostatic entity is not, simply speaking, perfect and is not a pure perfection, as was said [in 5.16ff.] in the question on this topic.

19.20 The minor would be denied for the same reason, for if some entity were the reason why every imperfection is excluded, it would be a pure perfection. If the hypostatic entity then is not a pure perfection, it follows that the hypostatic entity is not the formal reason why all imperfection is excluded and consequently a divine person does not derive his independence formally from this entity.

19.21 [Solution of the objections] To the first [in 19.15]: Dependence can be distinguished in two ways: (1) formally, or specifically, as it were, on the basis of the distinct formal reasons for the dependence; or (2) materially, as it were, on the basis of the distinction among the things that are dependent, whether these belong (a) to the same order, or (b) to different orders.

To support several dependencies distinct in the first way demands in the supporting term formally different grounds or if there is but one ground, this must be as it were unlimited, containing virtually or eminently such formally distinct grounds as are required. But where the several dependencies are distinct in the second way all that is required is that the dependent entities be distinct. Sometimes these will be of the same order, namely, when they depend with equal mediacy or immediacy upon the same thing. At other times their order will be different, namely, one will depend mediately whereas the other will depend immediately.

Although these two propositions are false, "Something independent in a specific respect can support any kind of dependency whatsoever" and "Something independent in a specific respect can support the dependency of any dependent whatsoever," still this proposition seems probable, "Something independent in a particular respect can support something dependent in this same respect or in some prior respect, and it can support such either immediately or at least mediately." And this seems even more probable, "Something independent in every respect can support any dependent whatsoever, or at least can do so with regard to some dependent and with respect to some form of dependence."

The truth of these two propositions would be more apparent if we knew that every entity is prior or posterior *per se* to any other entity. And it seems we can know this from the interconnection and unity of things or from the unity of the universe which is a unity of order according to the Philosopher, for any entity which lacked any *per se* order of priority or posteriority would appear to have no connection with other things.

19.22 When it is argued that "If independence implies the possibility of being the term upon which something depends, then independence in a given respect could support dependence in this same respect," one way of replying would be to deny the entailment, for if something independent in a given respect could not support dependency of this same sort, this would be because of its limited independence which could have some imperfection conjoined with it. But this would not hold good of what is independent in a unqualified sense, because in something of this sort there would at least be no imperfection.

The entailment fails on another count, for it does not hold unless one understands in the antecedent that independence in an absolute and unqualified sense entails the possibility of supporting any kind of dependence. But this is not what we claim. We only say that what is absolutely independent could support some sort of dependence. This suffices for our purpose, since by the way of elimination, it follows that the sort of independent of which we are speaking, namely, the person or personal entity, if it cannot be that on which something depends causally, or as measured, or in some similar fashion, then it can be that upon which a nature depends insofar as a nature is communicable to something that exists incommunicably [i.e., as a person].

19.23 Another answer would be to concede the consequent independent in such and such a respect can support something that depends in this same respect or in some prior respect.

19.24 With this, the answer to the objections made above becomes clear.

As for the first [in 19.15], substance can support the dependence of some accident, namely, that which by nature can inhere in it. And even though there be some substance like the divine nature which is not susceptive of any accident, nevertheless it can support some prior dependency, for instance, that of something caused upon which the accident depends and by sustaining such the divine nature can support the accident.

19.25 The same solution can be given to the whole-part problem [in 19.16]. For while something simple that is neither a whole nor a part cannot sustain a whole in the way its parts do, it can support some dependency prior to that of the whole upon its parts.

If you ask how this applies to fire, which depends upon its parts, and the angel, who is simple, I reply: The dependence in this case is that of the less noble upon the more noble in the essential order of nature.

19.26 The answer to the third [in 19.17] is similar. An angel either mediately or immediately supports the dependency of any less perfect nature, a dependency that obtains because of the essential order among quiddities and is somehow prior or more basic than the dependence of an effect on its efficient cause. Indeed, this form of dependency [i.e., of the less noble upon the more noble] seems to be absolutely first. It can be commonly said to be found in the case of any independent thing as regards that with reference to which it is said to be independent.

19.27 As for the fourth [in 19.18], it is perfectly clear that what is absolutely independent must be able to support some form of dependence because otherwise it appears to have no connection with other beings. It is not necessary, however, that it can support every form of dependence, for if it is not simply perfect, it will not sustain a dependence that requires pure perfection in its term, such as the dependence of the caused upon a cause. But if imperfection is incompatible with it, even if no pure perfection pertain to it, it can still be independent. Now the hypostatic entity as such is not a pure perfection, but neither is it imperfect.

19.28 This refutes the reply given to the major [in 19.19], for to support any dependence in general cannot be repugnant to something completely independent either by reason of its independence or by virtue of something conjoined with it.

19.29 As for what is added there, viz., some essential priority is required to support such dependency, one could say that the priority of all three persons is one and the same, if we are speaking properly of essential priority as distinct from the priority of a hypostatic entity. However, if we broaden the notion of essential priority to *per se* priority as regards any entity be it essential or hypostatic, then the personal entity can be said to be essentially prior or, more properly, prior *per se* to everything caused. If we take priority in the second sense, then it is necessary that everything which supports or sustains some dependency be prior to the entity which depends upon it. It is not necessary, however, if we take priority in the first sense, unless the dependency be that of caused upon its cause or something similar such as the dependency of a later effect upon a prior one, or of one caused upon another cause, or of the measured upon the measure.

19.30 As for the claim [in 19.19] that only forms (i.e., essences) and not hypostatic entities are related to each other like numbers, in the sense that an essential order prevails only among them, we can distinguish two kinds of essential dependence. One is simply essential, where the notion of essence figures in both extremes, viz., the dependent term depends by reason of its essence and the supporting term supports by reason of its essence. The essential dependence of the creature, as caused, upon God, as cause, is of this type. But the dependence can be called essential in another sense, viz., when the supported term does depend by reason of its essence, but that on which it depends is not an essence but an entity distinct from the essence, for instance, a personal or hypostatic entity.

19.31 As for the added remark that the term on which something depends must be perfect, one could argue that perfection, like entity, pertains equivocally to both an essential and a hypostatic entity. Nevertheless, properly speaking, perfection seems to belong only to quidditative entity, for the hypostatic entity is not that by which something is formally perfected but that according to which [a person] receives perfection or at least ends up with the perfection received. And in this sense, one would have to deny this statement "It is necessary that the term supporting the dependence be perfect," for it suffices that the imperfection that marks the dependent be incompatible with it.

19.32 From this the answer to the objection to the minor [in 19.20] appears clear. If "perfection" be taken in its proper and unextended sense, this proposition must be denied "If some entity were the reason why every imperfection is excluded, it would be perfect or a pure perfection," for whatever can be really identical with something that is simply perfect cannot be in any way imperfect and still it is not necessary that it be simply perfect if we consider it precisely in its formal meaning.

2. Second Proof

19.33 [Statement of the Proof] Second, our proposed thesis can be shown as follows. In beings there is some dependence of the communicable nature *qua* communicable upon the suppositum or hypostasis to whom it is communicated; therefore, what ultimately supports this dependence is the incommunicable.

19.34 Explanation of the antecedent. Some natures like the substantial have their own *per se* suppositum, and here there is an identity of nature and suppositum; neither does the nature depend upon something extrinsic to itself as its suppositum. Other natures because of their imperfection do not have their own intrinsic or *per se* suppositum but require an extrinsic one. Thus the nature of an accident requires the suppositum of the substance, and there its dependency ends with a *per accidens* suppositum, since it can have none that is *per se*. But here the nature is not identical *per se* with such a suppositum *per accidens* because they pertain to different categories. But in this case there is a union that takes the place of this identity insofar as possible, namely, an actual dependence on the part of the nature and the actual sustaining of that nature and its dependency on the part of the suppositum. What it means for that nature to be actually dependent upon a suppositum then is simply that it be communicated to this as its suppositum, namely in the way this nature is able to have such, for unlike substance, it cannot have such *per se* but only *per accidens*.

19.35 The principal entailment is manifest. Since the suppositum is *per se* incommunicable, the nature's dependence as communicable will be to a suppositum that is *per se* incommunicable. And because a divine person is in the truest sense incommunicable, indeed the only thing incommunicable by a positive entity, as we shall point out in [19.69 of] the third article, there is no incompatibility on its part in supporting the dependence of a nature as communicable, thus playing the role not of its intrinsic or *per se* suppositum, but only of one that is extrinsic and of a different nature.

19.36 [Objection] It might be objected that no nature could depend upon a divine person as its extrinsic suppositum because the person cannot be informed *per accidens* by any nature in the way the suppositum of the substance is informed by an accident and becomes the *per accidens* suppositum of the accident's nature.

19.37 Furthermore, the accident's dependence is *per se* upon the singular or individual substance and not upon the suppositum *qua* suppositum, namely, on what being a hypostasis or suppositum adds to being an individual, for that is only a negation, it seems, and a negation is not adequate ground for supporting any dependency.

19.38 Confirmation: The individual nature assumed by the Word supports the dependence of the accident in the same way it would if it were not assumed. But as assumed it is no longer a hypostasis or suppositum of itself; therefore, when it is not assumed, its being a hypostasis or suppositum would not be the *per se* reason for supporting the accident's dependency.

You cannot say that when the nature is assumed, the dependence of the accident which inheres in it is now supported by the person who assumed the nature, for the dependence of the accident consists in its inhering. But an accident of the assumed nature does not inhere in the person assuming the nature.

19.39 [Solution of the objections] To the first [in 19.36]. For the incommunicable to support the dependency of some nature distinct from its own, it is enough that to do so is not something incompatible with it. Whether some nature other than that possessed by the incommunicable can actually depend upon it will be treated in [19.73ff. of] the following article.

19.40 What of the claim that the incommunicable, to be the suppositum of an extrinsic nature, must be informable by it (as substance is informable by accident)? I reply: There are two relations involved in an accident's inherence in a substance. One is that of form to the informable; here substance is the recipient and the potential term (potential, at least, in a qualified sense). The other is the accident's dependence upon the substance; here substance is essentially prior and the accident naturally posterior.

No nature can be related to the Word in the first way, for this would imply potentiality and therefore imperfection in the Word. The second sort of relationship, however, is possible, for all it requires in the Word is *per se* priority, and it is not incompatible that the Word have such a priority over every created nature. Here the dictum "God is that with reference to which every created substance is a quasi-accident" applies. For even though the accident-to-substance relationship of a qualified form to an informable subject is inapplicable, the relationship that a nature, posterior and extrinsically communicable, can have to a divine person is the sort of relationship the accidental nature bears to the suppositum of a substance.

19.41 To the second objection [in 19.37] one could say that an individual substance is incommunicable insofar as "incommunicable" is opposed to universal, which is communicable to many, but not insofar as all communicability is ruled out including that of form, be it the partial form (said to be communicated to informed matter) or the total form, i.e., the quiddity or nature (said to be communicated to the person or suppositum that shares it). Incommunicable in this second sense is not the mark of every individual substance, but only of that which is not a partial or total form. Such is what ultimately has the form or the informed being and what in turn is not the form of *principium quo* of being. This is a hypostasis or suppositum. Consequently, while the dependence of the accident is somehow upon the singular substance it only ends ultimately with the singular as incommunicable. For if it depends on the singular substance as communicable, since this substance is the being of that to which it is communicated, the dependence only ends with the latter.

19.42 I do not mean by this that the communicable substance in turn depends upon something incommunicable, and this is the reason why the accident depends ultimately not upon the communicable but upon this other. For the singular communicable substance does not depend upon the suppositum of the substance, since the substance and the suppositum in this case are identical. I mean rather that what depends ultimately upon a communicable singular substance actually does depend upon something incommunicable, since the communicable is the being or the nature of something incommunicable, and whatever depends upon the being of something or someone ultimately depends on the individual to which or to whom that being belongs. The incommunicable, however, never functions as anyone's being or nature; hence what depends upon the incommunicable requires no further dependence on some subject having the incommunicable as its being or nature.

19.43 As for the argument [in 19.37] that all that the notion of suppositum adds to the notion of singular substance is a negation, I reply: Even if this be so, at least this [ontological] priority obtains, viz., it must have such a negation before it can function as the ultimate subject on which the accident depends. Neither is it incongruous that the negation of some imperfection in a subject be prior to the fact that something posterior depend upon it. "Not to be irrational" pertains to man before "to be white" does. Such a negation is an immediate

427

consequence of what the definition of man affirms, and this would be so even if "to be white" never did or never could pertain to him.

19.44 As for the claim that negation is no adequate ground for supporting any dependency, I reply: To say "it depends ultimately" asserts two things: (a) dependence upon some term, and (b) there is nothing further on which it depends. To be the term upon which something depends is a positive notion, whereas the idea of its being ultimate is not, since this denies the term is communicable, for otherwise the dependency would not end here. For example, if one accident depended on another as some say color depends on a surface, the color would not depend ultimately upon the surface but upon what has this surface [i.e., the bodily substance]. And even if color did not depend upon the substance but was just a mode of being it had, the ultimate dependence would still end only with the substance.

19.45 To the confirmation [in 19.38] it would be said that the accident of the assumed nature [depends on the Word insofar as the accident depends on the substance assumed by the Word].

3. Proofs Proposed by Others

19.46 [Statement of the Proofs] Some defend the thesis proposed on these grounds: The divine person contains the perfection of any created person or suppositum eminently; therefore he could supply for the role any such suppositum would play in sustaining that nature.

19.47 Besides, every created nature is in obediential potency as regards a divine person; therefore a divine person could sustain any such nature.

19.48 [These reasons are defective] The first reason [in 19.46] seems inadequate on this ground: While a divine person does contain virtually every created being by reason of his essence, he does not seem to contain even one by reason of his personal property. If he did, by the same token he would virtually contain every single created entity and thus his personal property would itself be formally infinite. In Question Five, which dealt with this subject, we showed this was not so.

19.49 Besides, if the personal property did contain all created entity virtually, it could be, it seems the formal basis of creating, a claim denied earlier [in Question Eight].

19.50 The second argument [in 19.47] also seems defective. The obediential potency of a creature has reference to the omnipotence of the creator and is common to all three persons. Therefore the way the Son supports his created nature in virtue of omnipotence is common to all three. But the support by the person united to the nature is proper to the Son. The fact that the nature is in obediential potency as regards the person, therefore, does not entail that this person can sustain it hypostatically but only causally, namely as efficient cause.

4. Objection to the Conclusion of this Article

19.51 Against the conclusion of this article, it is objected in the first place that if the union itself is real, then it must have a real term. But the [personal] property and the essence are one and the same thing in reality, and what is identical in reality is also identical in the role played as the term of this union.

19.52 Besides, only its correlative depends upon the relative as relative. Therefore, the human nature does not depend upon the Word as Word, for only the Father is the correlative of the Word.

19.53 Reply to the first [in 19.51]: The formal distinction between a relation and the essence provides sufficient ground for saying that the property and not the essence is the formal term of the real union. The objection does seem to be effective, however, against those who claim the essence and the constitutive property of the person are both really and formally identical.

19.54 As for the second [in 19.52], one can reply by denying the antecedent. For it is one thing to depend on something relative as its correlative and quite another to depend on the Word, who is relative. For though the human nature assumed by the Word does depend upon him as Word, it does not depend upon him as its correlative.

ARTICLE III
THE POSSIBILITY OF SUCH A UNION ON THE PART OF THE ASSUMED NATURE

19.55 [Two points to be investigated] As for the third article, it is certain, according to Damascene, that the Word assumed an individual nature, yet one which lacked its own personality since this could not be reconciled with the assumption of a nature in the unity of the Person of the Word. But if the nature's own individuality were formally its own personality, its individuality could not exist without its personality.

For this reason, we must see (1) by what factor a created nature is formally and completely personalized in itself in order to see (2) whether it can lack its own personality and still be personalized by an extrinsic personality.

1. What Constitutes Created Personality?

19.56 [The view of others: human nature is constituted a person by something positive] There is some doubt as to whether personality proper is constituted formally by something positive. It seems so for the following reasons:

What is primarily incommunicable is not negation as such, for negation can pertain to anything. Therefore, if a negation is incommunicable it is only because it presupposes the incommunicability of something positive, and so what is primarily incommunicable is something positive. Now it is the personal property that is primarily incommunicable, for this is what formally constitutes the incommunicable, viz., the person.

19.57 Besides, negation is never primarily proper to anything; it is proper only because it is the consequence of some proper affirmation. But the personal property is primarily proper. Therefore, [it is not a negation].

19.58 What is more, imperfection is excluded by something perfect or at least positive. But to depend on an extrinsic person is an imperfection. Therefore, proper personality which excludes formally such dependence must be something positive.

19.59 Confirmation: Individuality in a nature comes from something positive, for singularity excludes the imperfection of internal division; hence the singular is called an "indi-

John Duns Scotus

vidual," i.e., something indivisible into more than one. In an analogous way, to be a person in oneself excludes dependence upon an extrinsic person.

19.60 [This view is untenable] But against this view are the words of Damascene: "God, the Word, lacked none of those things he implanted in our nature when he formed us in the beginning; he assumed them all . . . for he was wholly united to me, so that he might bestow the grace of salvation upon the whole; for what has not been assumed, cannot be healed." He wants to say then that every positive entity our nature contains is united to the Word.

19.61 That this is possible for any nature is proved by reason. Any nature whatsoever is simply in obediential potency to depend upon a divine person. Therefore, if there were some positive entity which made the nature a person in its own right, then this entity would have been assumed by the Word and thus Christ's human nature would be invested with a dual personality, which is impossible. For if it were personalized by something created, this would render it formally incommunicable to another person. Hence it could not be taken up by the person of the Word, and thus be personalized in him.

19.62 Besides, if human nature formally became a person by reason of some positive entity, the Word could not put off the nature he had assumed without either letting it remain depersonalized (which seems incongruous) or else giving it some new entity by which it would have created personality. But this too is impossible. This could be no accidental entity, since an accident is not the formal reason why a substance is a person. Neither could this entity be substantial, be it matter, form, or a composite substance; for then it would no longer have the nature it had before, but it would have another matter, form or composite substance.

19.63 [Scotus' own opinion] Therefore, we can say that the formal reason our nature is invested with a created personality is not something positive; for in addition to singularity we find no positive entity that renders the singular nature incommunicable. All that is added to singularity is the negation of dependence or incommunicability, the denial that it is given over to someone.

431

19.64 Negation of communicability or dependence can be understood in three ways. As we can conceive of dependence as actual, potential, or dispositional, so too with its negation.

The negation of actual dependence is the simple or bare denial of dependence. The denial of its possibility adds the note of impossibility. The third implies a contrary inclination or disposition. For example, a colorless or transparent surface is not white in the first way, since whiteness is only denied of it; an angel is not white in the second way, since it would be impossible for it to be white; a stone not up in the air illustrates the third way; not only does it lack any disposition to remain up; it has the opposite inclination to remain down.

19.65 To the case at hand: speaking of dependence upon an extrinsic hypostasis, especially a divine person, we can say that the simple negation of such actual dependence does not suffice to make one a person in his own right, for the soul of Peter is not dependent in this way and yet it is not a person.

19.66 The second negation is not found to be true of any created nature able to be a person, for nothing in it excludes the possibility of depending upon a divine person. Quite the contrary, every positive entity in such a nature is in obediential potency to depend upon such a person, and consequently this sort of negation does not constitute a created person.

19.67 Neither does the third type of negation alone suffice, since the nature even as assumed is characterized by such a negation. Being of the same type as my own nature, [Christ's] assumed nature has the same kind of dispositions and natural inclinations as mine, and thus has a natural aptitude to subsist in itself with no inclination by nature to depend upon an extrinsic person. Neither is it incongruous that the possibility be present without a corresponding disposition, since the same situation holds good for supernatural forms. And if there is any potency in the recipient to have such forms, there is still no natural inclination for them, since such an inclination properly speaking only exists in regard to a form which perfects naturally.

19.68 Therefore, a double negation is required to have a created personality, namely, the conjunction of the first and the third type. The third is habitual, as it were, and is found in the created nature necessarily whether this nature be a person in its own right or is personalized through an extrinsic person. But the absence of any actual dependence together with the absence of any natural inclination to so depend make for a complete personality of one's own.

19.69 [Reply to the arguments for the first opinion] One answer suffices for all the argument [in 19.56-59] claiming that one's own created personality is formally constituted by something positive. "To be communicable" or "to depend in this way" would admittedly be simply inconsistent with my being if, and only if, this being did possess some positive entity of its own which rendered it incommunicable or unable to be dependent. However, "to be communicated" or "to depend" can be repugnant in a qualified sense to something in virtue of a negation alone, for as long as the negation holds true, its opposite affirmation cannot be true. But this does not mean the affirmative situation is simply impossible unless the subject is such that it necessarily entails such a negation, and in this case the negation would be simply proper to it; otherwise the negation would be proper to the subject only in a qualified sense. For a negation is proper to something in the same way that its opposite affirmation is impossible. Now only a divine person has incommunicability in the first way, because he has some intrinsic entity all his own which excludes any possibility of such communication. A created nature, on the contrary, though it may subsist in itself, still does not have anything intrinsic that would make dependence [upon a divine person] impossible. Hence only a divine person has his own personality completely; a created nature personalized in itself, however, does not have such personality completely, since it does not exclude the possibility, but only the actuality, of such dependence, and it excludes this only in a qualified sense, namely, so long as the negation of actual dependence remains true.

19.70 As for the form of the argument [in 19.56] based on the notion of person, I say that simple or unqualified incommunicability, viz., that which excludes the possibility of dependence, does not pertain primarily to a negation or to any subject in virtue of a negation. Nor is such incommunicability found in a creature, even one who is a person. At best there is only a qualified incommunicability, viz., exclusion of actual communication to another person, and this only as long as the actual dependence is not there. Now such qualified incommunicability does not require a positive entity that is simply incommunicable, but only a positive entity as the subject of whom actual dependence is denied. On the other hand, if simple incommunicability did pertain to any negation it would only be because the negation is a consequence of some simply incommunicable positive entity.

19.71 I use the same argument against the other major premise based on dependence [in 19.58]. I grant that if the possibility of dependence is imcompatible with something, this is due to some perfection or positive reason; but such is not the case with any creature. All we find there is the absence of actual dependence. For example, if an accident is given existence apart from a substance, actual or possible inherence in a substance is not incompatible with it purely and simply but only in a qualified sense, namely, it cannot be present as long as the accident continues to exist apart.

19.72 In much the same way I answer the argument [in 19.57] that a negation is not what is primarily proper to anything. Unqualified incommunicability is simply proper only to what has this sort of incommunicability; but incommunicability in a qualifed sense is not simply proper to its subject; it is "proper" only in the sense that it belongs to this subject alone.

2. Can a Human Nature Depend upon an Extrinsic Person?

19.73 As for the second problem [in 19.55] of the third main article, some argue that to depend for one's personality on an extrinsic person is incompatible with human nature: first, because it is a substantial nature; second, because it cannot have something intrinsic that would be grounds for such dependence; third, because a human nature possesses an intrinsic reason why it cannot depend in this fashion.

19.74 First argument: What substantial nature is meant to give to the suppositum is being in an unqualified sense; hence it does not presuppose such being. But a nature which depends upon an extrinsic suppositum does presuppose such being in the latter since it presupposes the being of the suppositum's own nature, a nature which belongs to it even before the dependent nature does.

Proof of the antecedent: As an accident is entity in a qualified sense, so a substantial nature is entity purely and simply. Now the sort of entity a thing is formally is the sort of entity it gives. Thus an accident gives only qualified entity and presupposes a being that is simply such; a substantial nature on the contrary gives being in an unqualified sense and does not presuppose such being.

19.75 Second argument [of 19.73]: Everything dependent possesses an intrinsic ground for its dependence. But human nature does not and cannot have some intrinsic ground for depending in this way. Therefore, [it is not dependent in this fashion].

19.76 The major appears clear inductively if you consider one by one the various types of causal dependence.

Reason also proves the same. If one thing does not have some reason for dependence which another lacks, then the first would be no more dependent than the second. Now my nature does not depend upon the Word with this sort of dependence; therefore, neither does the assumed nature [of Christ] if it has no intrinsic reason for doing so.

Proof of the major: The independent does not become dependent, or vice versa, without some change or mutation. Now only an absolute form is the *per se* term of mutation; therefore, if a nature becomes dependent it is only because it acquired some absolute form as the ground for such dependence, a form which it loses when it regains its independence.

19.77 Proof of the minor: The Word could put off his human nature without anything absolute in it being destroyed. But if the reason why it depended on the Word were something absolute, then it would be necessary to destroy this absolute entity to make the nature independent [or a person in its own right].

Two natures of the same kind should have the same reason or ground for depending hypostatically on the same person or suppositum. Now Christ's nature is the same in kind as my own, and my nature does not have any reason or ground why it should depend hypostatically upon the Word; otherwise, for me to subsist as a human person would be doing violence to my nature.

19.78 Third argument [of 19.73] : The human personality that can pertain to this nature is really identical with this nature; therefore, as long as it continues to exist, this human nature has this personality. But a personality of its own is adequate ground for excluding dependence upon an extrinsic person. Hence [it cannot depend in this way].

Proof of the antecedent: It is certain that this human nature can have a personality of its own. Now this personality cannot be something other than this nature. It cannot be an accident, because an accident cannot be the reason why a substance is a person. Neither can it be some substance other than this nature; if it were, then this other would either be a composite substance or a substantial part. Now one composite substance is never the formal reason why another composite substance is a person. If the personality were a substantial part, then unless both substantial parts remained, the nature would not be the same.

19.79 [Scotus' own opinion] We should never assume two things are formally incompatible unless this is manifest from their definitions or it can be proved that they include such incompatibility or that such incompatibility is a consequence of what they are. But in none of these ways is human nature incompatible with dependence upon another person. Hence we should not assume such dependence is simply impossible so far as the nature is concerned.

The major is proved because everything should be assumed to be possible if there is no evidence of impossibility.

19.80 The first part of the minor is shown from the very notions of what we are discussing. It is more evident in the case of human nature, but the notion of the sort of dependence involved can be described as follows: "It is the dependence of a nature as communicable upon a person proper to another nature in such a way that this person is that upon which the nature depends."

19.81 This description is explained as follows: First, the expression "as communicable." Something can be communicated in such a way that the recipient becomes that which is communicated, for instance, the way the universal is communicated to an individual. In another way something is communicated as a formal principle of being and this can happen in two ways, one as a partial form which is communicated to informed matter and thereby to the composite constituted through the form; the other as a total form or quiddity is communicated to the suppositum, for example, humanity to Socrates.

In our case "as communicable" is understood in this third way, viz., the total form is communicated in such a way that the one having it can be said to be formally this sort of thing. Now when the nature is a suppositum in its own right, the suppositum is said to be this sort of nature, not because the nature depends upon it, but because there is a *per se* identity. But when the suppositum is not proper to the nature there can be no *per se* identity. What can be there in its place, however, is perfect dependence of the nature and on the part of the suppositum a perfect sustaining or supporting of this dependence. Such a suppositum, since it is *per se* the suppositum of another nature, is not the *per se* suppositum of the dependent nature. Since what is *per se* is prior to what is not, it follows that the suppositum or person has his own nature prior to having this dependent one, which is a kind of adventitious or second nature.

19.82 That dependence of this sort is not repugnant to human nature can be shown somehow by a proof similar to that given in the second article [in 19.12-14].

A divine person on his own can be the supporting term for some kind of dependence, not that of causation or, in short, of that requiring formal perfection in the term, but only that sort of dependence that a communicable nature has upon the incommunicable which sustains it. Therefore, it must be possible for some nature to depend in this way, for it would not be possible to support such dependence if some nature did not have a corresponding possibility of depending. But to depend in this way is not more repugnant to human nature than to any other nature.

19.83 We show this secondly in this way: An accident has this sort of dependence upon the suppositum of the substance in which it inheres. Although in this case the dependence is conjoined with inherence, the reason for dependence seems prior to the ground for inherence even as the essential priority by reason of which the term supports such dependence seems prior to its ability to be informed by or to receive accidents, which is the reason why they can inhere in it. There seems to be no contradiction, then, in thinking that some nature may be able to depend as communicable without inhering in that on which it depends, and this is precisely the kind of dependence we are assuming in the present case.

Confirmation: According to the Philsosopher in the *Metaphysics* one meaning of "quality" is the substantial difference; consequently, it is not repugnant to a substance to have a mode of existence like that of a quality.

19.84 We show this thirdly as follows: An accident can have the mode of substance [i.e., it can exist without inhering in a substance], although not perfectly in the sense that it would be repugnant for it to depend on a subject, but in some analogous way, viz., insofar as it does not actually depend; this is seen in the case of a separated accident. By the same token, it seems that a substance can have the mode of an accident, although not perfectly in the sense that it would depend or inhere in a subject, but in an analogous fashion, viz., in the sense of actually depending upon an extrinsic suppositum.

19.85 [Reply to the arguments for the opposing view] To the arguments in favor of the contrary opinion:

To the first [in 19.74]: I admit that the substantial nature gives substantial being, but it is only when the suppositum is *per se* that the substantial nature gives the suppositum its first being. But when its suppositum is not *per se* but belongs to another nature, it is this other nature that gives the suppositum its first being.

19.86 To the claim that what gives unqualified being to some subject does not presuppose such being in the subject, I answer: Some being may indeed be unqualified being in itself and yet, if its suppositum is not something it has in its own right, then it does not give that suppositum unqualified being in every sense.

19.87 To the second argument [in 19.75]: Something can be a ground for dependence in one of two ways. One would be if actual dependence necessarily accompanies or follows it. Another way would be if what necessarily accompanies it is not actual dependence but the aptitude to depend, and when actual dependence is present, the reason or ground is the proximate foundation for such.

Dependence of a creature on God is of the first type, because here the foundation of the dependence necessarily involves actual dependence at all times. The dependence of an effect upon a secondary cause is of the second type, since the effect could always be produced immediately by the first cause, and thus not be actually dependent upon the secondary cause even though the aptitude to depend is always there. The major is true then not of "a ground for dependence" understood in the first way, but only if we understand it indiscriminately of the first or the second way.

19.88 The first proof of the major [in 19.76] from an inductive consideration of the types of causal dependence proves nothing more.

19.89 To the second proof of the major which claims the dependent has some reason for dependence lacking in what is not dependent, I say this: It is necessary to have such if "reason for dependence" means the *formal* reason, which is the dependence itself, since without actual dependence nothing can depend. But if "reason for dependence" refers to some foundation of the dependence in the way that whiteness is the foundation for similarity, I deny that there is any more need for such in something dependent than there is in what is not actually dependent but has an aptitude to depend. For example, an accident when it is in a subject has no more grounds for depending than when it exists apart, for its own nature is the proximate ground for depending in this way. Nothing more needs to be added except the "formal reason" or actual dependence itself. Something analogous holds for the nature that is assumed and the nature that is not.

19.90 The third proof [in 19.76] seems to establish more, viz., that what is actually dependent always has some absolute entity as the fundamental reason for its depending. And we must simply deny the proposition on which the proof is based, viz., "Only an absolute form is the *per se* term of mutation."

439

There is movement from place to place, and yet place is not an absolute form. That this is not contrary to what the Philosopher says in the *Physics* was proved earlier in the [Eleventh] question on bodies and place.

19.91 Now the minor [of the second argument, viz., that human nature does not and cannot have some intrinsic ground for depending hypostatically] is not true in the sense that the major is true, namely where "ground" or "reason" may mean indiscriminately either a formal reason for depending or a fundamental reason which necessarily entails either actual or at least aptitudinal dependence. For the assumed nature has a formal reason, viz., the dependence itself, and it also has a fundamental reason. Indeed, the nature itself is the proximate fundamental ground of the dependence although what is a necessary consequence of the nature is not actual but aptitudinal dependence. Neither does the first proof of the minor establish anything more, for if the Word put off his human nature, nothing absolute in it would perish. Hence it never had anything absolute which was the necessary reason for its actually depending on the Word. But something absolute was the proximate subject of such dependence and it can remain without such dependence in the way that the foundation can exist without the relation if the latter is not a necessary consequence of the foundation.

19.92 As for the other proof [of the minor in 19.77] I say: While it is true that two natures of the same kind have the same aptitude to depend upon the Word, it does not follow that if one actually does depend, the other must also. The case of an accident separated from its subject and one conjoined with its subject makes this clear. Now although my nature does not actually depend upon the Word hypostatically, nevertheless it does have the same aptitude to depend as the nature he assumed.

Reply to the Initial Argument

19.93 To the argument at the beginning [in 19.1] I say that while not every form of dependence justifies predicating what depends of the subject on which it depends, nevertheless the dependence of a nature as communicable upon a suppositum that sustains it hypostatically is sufficient for predicating the dependent nature of the person or suppositum on which it depends. This is clear from the case of the accident that depends in this way upon the suppositum of the substance of which it is also predicated. And just as the predication of the accident of the subject, though true, is not *per se,* as would be the case if the nature were predicated of its own suppositum, so also the predication of human nature of the Word is not *per se.*